The Mirror of MONTE CAVALLARA

An Eighth Army Story

by

Ray Ward

Edited by Robin Ward

BIRLINN

First published in 2006 by Birlinn, West Newington House, 10 Newington Road
Edinburgh EH9 1QS www.birlinn.co.uk

ISBN10: 1 84341 031 1

ISBN13: 978 1 84341 031 7

British Library Cataloguing-in-Publication Data

A catalogue record for this book is available from the British Library

Typeset in Adobe Garamond, Gill Sans, and Johnston Underground by Robin Ward

Book design by Robin Ward

Printed and bound in the UK by Antony Rowe Ltd., Chippenham

'Ne obliviscaris'

'Do not forget'—motto of the 91st Regiment of Foot, the Argyllshire Highlanders.
◁ The motto and the Duke of Argyll's boar's head symbol on the Argylls' lapel
badge; also shown is the Duke of Sutherland's wildcat and the motto, 'Sans Peur'
('Fearless'), of the 93rd Regiment of Foot, the Sutherland Highlanders.

DEDICATED TO MY SONS ROBIN AND BRIAN, AND
TO THE MEMORY OF THOSE OF MY FELLOW ARGYLLS
WHO WERE KILLED OR WOUNDED DURING THE
SECOND WORLD WAR, OR WHO HAVE SINCE DIED.

R.I.P.

CONTENTS

Second Lieutenant Ray Ward, 1940

PROLOGUE

But it is exciting and amazing to see thousands of men, very few of whom have much idea why they are fighting, all enduring hardships, living in an unnatural, dangerous, but not wholly terrible world, having to kill or be killed, and yet at intervals moved by a feeling of comradeship with the men who kill them and whom they kill, because they are enduring and experiencing the same things. It is tremendously illogical—to read about it cannot convey the impression of having walked through the looking-glass which touches a man entering battle.

Keith Douglas. *Alamein to Zem Zem,* 1943

EDINBURGH, NOVEMBER 2005

My father, Thomas Raymond Ward, received his call-up for the Second World War in Glasgow in April 1940. Young, optimistic and feeling immortal, he joined The Argyll and Sutherland Highlanders at Stirling Castle. In December that year, he was posted to the regiment's 1st Battalion. He was an infantry officer for five and a half years, four and a half of them overseas: in Egypt, Sudan, Palestine, Eritrea, Abyssinia, the Western Desert, Sicily and Italy. He was in General Montgomery's Eighth Army, the crusading army of the Battle of El Alamein and other honours, a source of pride and inner strength that helped him cope with civilian life after the war.

After he was demobbed in 1946, he thought of emigrating. I remember finding a brochure he'd sent for in the 1950s, showing the Canadian Pacific Railway in the Rocky Mountains (an image that later inspired my gap year, as a fur trader with the Hudson's Bay Company). I asked why he didn't go. He said he'd had enough adventure for one life, during the war. He became a teacher and rose through the ranks of Glasgow Corporation Education Department, becoming a headmaster. His pupils and staff were certainly subject to his discipline, but teaching was also an idealistic choice. He told me once that every time a former pupil from one of his schools in Govan or Easterhouse came back to thank him for having been given an education and opportunity, he felt that his post-war years had not been wasted. He never surrendered his belief that wars are caused by prejudice, fear, greed, ignorance and stupidity. He also wrestled with the conundrum that war can bring out the best in women and men. When he came home in 1945, his church gave him a Bible, evidently a presentation edition. I have it still. The half-title page has King George VI's monogram and the words:

TO COMMEMORATE THE GREAT BATTLE FOR CIVILISATION 1939-1945

That was how he saw the war then. It is how the victors still it see today. He never doubted it had to be fought.

He died in Glasgow aged eighty-two on 1 November 1999, by curious symmetry my birthday (the date he joined the Argylls at Stirling is my brother's). His life was marked by the war, and my brother Brian and I have been too by his experience of it. We grew up in the 1950s and 1960s. At our school, Jordanhill, the cadet corps was run by a major straight out of *Dad's Army*. At the school show, he would let us aim (but not fire) the corps' Bren gun and Lee Enfield rifles. My fellow centre in the school rugby team was the son of Willie Rankine, one of my father's pre-war cricketing pals, also a soldier in Italy. My school bag was an army surplus haversack. Brian and I played on local bomb sites. The comics we read and the films our father took us to see were about the war. Without irony, they reiterated the moral certainties of his generation: the virtues of self-restraint, compassion, courage and honour.

Military-style discipline and eccentricities were not unknown in our house. Every day when he came home he would call out: 'Any news, mail, phone calls', as if still barking out questions to his lieutenants. For many years, he kept a pair of desert boots that were re-soled and re-heeled until the suede perished. When he put them on he would first shake them upside down, a desert army habit to expel scorpions. His glengarry and sporran hung in the hall. He was obsessed by the weather, another soldiering trait; when he went out he'd tap the barometer that hung by the front door. In the garden, he built dry-stone retaining walls, a skill he learned making sangars on the North African battlefields. If we criticised his driving, he'd say: 'What do you expect? I learned in the desert.'

He didn't talk much about the war, not even to our mother, Chris Mackay, who was in the Auxilliary Territorial Service (at Dundonald camp in Ayrshire where, as she used to tell us, she 'typed out plans for D-Day'). His post-war association with the regiment—attending the Balaclava centenary, and an 'old comrades' garden party', and research for an article he wrote for a 'Save the Argylls' campaign—was always welcomed by Lieutenant-Colonel F. C. C. 'Freddie' Graham DSO, his wartime commanding officer. But contact was fitful and fleeting, motivated by bouts of nostalgia. The nostalgia became more evident after he retired. So too his long-supressed memories, which surfaced like the shrapnel that had to be removed from his leg at Erskine Hospital ten years after the war. But the enigma that he survived when so many of his comrades fell was never exorcised. For over fifty years, he was plagued by flashbacks—what is now called post-traumatic stress disorder. He scoffed at 'the smothering care of compassionate counsellors and support groups'. We were often woken by his nightmares.

When he died, my wife Porta and I were moving from Vancouver, where we had lived for eleven years, to Italy. My brother called me with the news. We drove back from Tuscany to Scotland for the funeral and stayed on to help my mother clear and sell the family house. I spent some time going through my father's papers and possessions, turning over the layers of his life, deciding with difficulty what to keep and what to dispose. I found faded

photographs of his cricket team in the 1930s; of paddle steamers and row-
ing boats on the Clyde coast that I recognised from holidays in the 1950s.
There were opera programmes from the Glasgow Orpheus Club in which
he sang, and the piano music he and my mother played; press clippings of
freelance articles he wrote, and notes of books he read.

His retirement was spent mostly at home watching televised test
matches, listening to classical music, reading, and visiting the public libraries
of his boyhood. My mother told me that for several years he'd been a noisy
recluse, clattering away on a old typewriter in my old bedroom, writing a
memoir of his experiences during the war. Brian and I had pestered him to
do this, with little success, we thought. The memoir was left to me in his
will. It surfaced when I opened a wooden German ammunition box stored
in the cellar.

The box looked like it had just been excavated from the Western
Desert, where he found it in 1942 after the Battle of El Alamein. It was full
of military memorabilia: his Middle East Forces identification card, his army
number (156058), papers, photographs, books; his *sgian dubh* and sporran,
badges and medals. The medals included his Military Cross and Eighth
Army Africa and Italy stars; the books charted his war: *The Abyssinian
Campaign, Alamein and the Desert War, Soldier's Guide to Sicily, The
Campaign in Italy*, and his army Field Service Pocket Book. Clipped from
The Herald was a poem, 'The Permanence of the Young Men', by William
Soutar, written in 1940:

> *No man outlives the grief of war*
> *Though he outlive its wreck:*
> *Upon the memory a scar*
> *Through all his years will ache.*
>
> *Hopes will revive when horrors cease;*
> *And dreaming dread be stilled;*

But there shall dwell within his peace
A sadness unannulled.

Upon his world shall hang a sign
Which summer cannot hide:
The permanence of the young men
Who are not by his side.

And then there was the memoir. Tied to the manuscript was the following letter, clearly intended as an introduction to his story . . .

I KNOW THAT BOTH OF YOU, ROBIN AND BRIAN, have been urging me to set down on paper memories and impressions of my wartime service with the Argylls. This is an attempt to do just that. You were both astonished when you learned that during the 1940s, when I was in my twenties, I served for over five years in the army, most of them overseas. It was a big slice out of my life. But that's what happened to a whole generation of young people then. Generally biddable, we were not given to questioning authority, the established social order, or the imperial certainties of the time. We were patriotic. Military service offered an escape from humdrum lives at work or home. I was physically fit and romantically inclined. I looked forward to what seemed an exciting adventure—to being a soldier, performing heroic deeds, winning military glory and all that.

The War was the most momentous experience in my life, and in the lives of my comrades in arms. It had an enduring influence far beyond our muddled and immature appreciation of it at the time. It was only later we came to realise the effect our war service had on our subsequent lives and careers. Those who survived, that is.

I was one of the generation that grew up in the 1920s and 1930s, and fell heir to memories of the First World War—The Great War, as it was generally called then. Those memories lay deep in the national consciousness. The now fashionable view that the mass slaughter of the First World War was a futile folly would have been thought disrespectful to the victors and the dead. Almost every adult and child was related to or knew someone who had served in the Forces, and ended up in a sanatorium or a grave. Limbless ex-servicemen were seen everywhere. My father-in-law, Archibald Mackay, was gassed in the trenches in France and never fully recovered his health; his brother Hugh died in a Glasgow hospital, from tuberculosis contracted on service with the Black Watch. My father, Alexander Ward, a music teacher, composer, and bandmaster on the Cadet Training Ship *Empress* on the Clyde, was born in 1874 and thus too old for the frontline but did his bit for morale, conducting concerts in Glasgow parks.

The world then was constrained by class and codes of conduct, and secured by ties of family life, parental authority and the teachings of school and kirk. There was radio (the BBC) at home and there were films (every neighbourhood had a picture house), but no television. Society was not saturated with 24-hour news or advertising. I went to Sunday school; I joined the Boys' Brigade. I left school at sixteen. Few of us had the opportunity to go to university, or to travel abroad, unless you went to sea, or joined the colonial or armed services. Thanks to the army, Africa, Egypt, Palestine, the Red Sea, Abyssinia, the Sudan, the Nile, the Western Desert—even Sicily and Italy—became more than merely names in my school atlas. Even today, hearing or reading of such places evokes memories of times spent in foreign lands among strange peoples (we of course were the foreigners and must have appeared as outlandish to the natives as they did to us—never more so than when we marched through Cairo, Khartoum, or Ferrara wearing our kilts, with pipes playing and drums beating). All those factors were inescapable influences, affecting attitudes and behaviour in ways that young people now would find intolerable. Equally intolerable now would be my uncritical view of the British empire, which was seen—by its rulers—as an entirely benign phenomenon.

On 3 September 1939, when Nazi Germany invaded Poland, I was a 22-year-old clerk in the office of a Glasgow construction firm, John Train and Company, opposite the City Chambers in George Square. At a time when many were out of work (as my father had been periodically) and there was much poverty I was fortunate to have a white-collar job, with a company that built prestigious, American-style office blocks in the city centre. I lived with my parents and three brothers in Knightswood, which was then a new, garden city-style council estate. We moved there in 1928 from a flat in Apsley Street, Partick, where I was born. I played cricket for a local team in the Glasgow Parks league, and against Western Union second elevens and school former pupil sides. And I was beginning to make a name for myself as a singer, in church choirs, the Choral Union and the Orpheus Club (where I played my first part, Giuseppe in *The Gondoliers*, in 1939). Mum was a member of the club, but I met her first at Jordanhill Church, where I was leading bass in the choir. I used to get engagements at St Margaret's Knightswood, Drumchapel Parish and other churches, at Burns Suppers, and dinners at the likes of the Grosvenor, or the Central Hotel. Good extra income in those days, a guinea or two a time, often a fiver. I had little to complain about in my life, yet I looked forward to when my call-up would come.

An abiding memory of the office is of watching the Armistice Day services in the 1930s, when all the staff would gather at the windows overlooking the square and the Cenotaph, its white stone gleaming against the soot-black background of the City Chambers. We looked down in awe at the huge crowds, bare-headed and motionless during the two-minute silence. Then a bugler would sound the 'Last Post'—you know how moving that can be—followed by beating drums, the skirl of the pipes and the swagger of kilted soldiers in the March Past which followed the 11 o'clock ceremony. At that hour on that day, every year between the wars, everything came to a standstill. It was the same all across the nation, and overseas in the Dominions. The remembrance services today can never be the same as they were then, so much has changed since the two world wars. The Cenotaph was unveiled in 1924 by Field Marshal Earl Haig, who is now vilified, with hindsight, like Bomber Harris. But in the 1920s, almost every community unveiled a memorial to the memory of the fallen [there are 37,000 across the UK listing 750,000 dead]. You both know my favourite: the one to the Cameronians, in Kelvingrove Park, with the striking tableau of a machine-gunner, his fallen officer and a sergeant leaping forward.

There were two old soldiers in the office. One was the senior clerk whose clearest memory of the Salonika campaign was of a troop train full of bayonet-brandishing soldiers, inflamed by alcohol, fighting among themselves. He would regale the office juniors with a blow-by-blow account of the brawl, which he told as a warning against the evils of strong drink bringing out the violent streak in men. We were suitably impressed since we knew nothing of strong drink, and the only violence any of us had ever seen was in the school playground. The other veteran was the foreman joiner whose enormous, calloused left hand was minus two fingers. With grim relish he would tell how that very hand, after having been mauled by a piece of shrapnel from a German artillery shell one day in Flanders, had been thrust into a bucket of boiling tar to cauterise the wound.

Boys and young men in those days had their imagination stirred by stories of wartime heroism in books and films, and by middle-aged veterans with tales to tell. I only read Sassoon *et al* after my own war. In 1939, there was a willing acceptance of our duty to serve our country, and do our bit as the men of the previous generation had done. But there was no jingoistic rush to the recruiting offices at the start of the Second World War as there had been in 1914; more a phlegmatic acceptance of the inevitable, especially after the Munich crisis. I was certainly conditioned to respond without question when I was called up in 1940.

I was one of four brothers in the Forces during the war: Cecil joined the marines, was commissioned, and went out to the Far East with 42 Royal Marine Commando; Harold was called up and found himself in the Royal Air Force meteorological branch, in North-west Europe after the Normandy landings; Alex, the eldest, who worked in the Savings Bank, was in the Royal Navy, on the aircraft carrier HMS *Implacable*, with the Pacific fleet towards the end of the war (the authorities, showing unusual good sense, put him in the paymaster's office). Being the youngest, I was the first to go. I joined the army, went through infantry training, an officer cadet course, and gained a commission. I then served in 'A' Company, 1st Battalion, The Argyll and Sutherland Highlanders: first as a platoon commander, then second-in-command, and finally company commander.

Those who served as infantrymen, particularly in Highland regiments like the Argylls, belonged to a unique, almost tribal fellowship. All of us were ordinary men, of all types, cast in extraordinary roles, having to exist in the extraordinary conditions of the 'poor bloody infantry' at the 'sharp end of war'. These may have brought out the worst in the few, but they brought out the best in the many. Not all were heroes or paragons of military virtue. We were human enough to prefer comfort and safety to discomfort and danger. We had a natural instinct for self-preservation. Most units—and mine was no exception—had their fair share of misfits, scoundrels and shirkers. Some men would refuse to carry on and 'take a powder', as the act of desertion was euphemistically called. But many more showed considerable, often unexpected powers of physical endurance and mental fortitude as we soldiered on, sometimes bewildered, sometimes resentful at being often on the move. We lived up to our nickname, 'The Agile and Suffering Highlanders'.

Official histories, written by senior commanders who may have had a troubled conscience about some incidents, and encounters so disturbing that they were sanitised, or overlaid by a false or mistaken interpretation more acceptable to self-esteem, rarely tell the full story. What strikes me is their frequency of bald references: 'In the first salvo from the German gunners, D Company lost its headquarters; casualties were heavy.' No mention of the fear and panic, the pain and suffering, the blood and guts—realities that tend to be taboo in such accounts, as they are in the officers' mess, and at the Cenotaph on Remembrance Day. Only those who were on the spot—junior officers, non-commissioned officers and ordinary soldiers—know the full horror between the lines of such laconic, evasive statements: the horror that haunts every infantryman who survived it.

Now, fifty years on, after a sequence of wartime anniversaries, and on your urgings, Robin and Brian—and the need to lay some ghosts to rest—I am writing this wartime story. It may differ little from others that tell of similar experiences—except that it is my own.

T. R. Ward
Glasgow, October 1995

I read my father's memoir firstly as his son and later as an editor. His typescript was closely-spaced and frequently faint, as if to challenge me to read between the lines. I was not sure I ever really knew him or what I would find. He was an authoritarian figure, always rather remote, with his emotions well camouflaged. But in the memoir, he is an occasionally reckless, vulnerable and sensitive young man. That is how I see and begin to know him now.

If he joined the army for adventure, he was not disappointed. The deployment of the 1st Battalion followed no grand strategy: the Agile and Suffering Highlanders were sent where and when they were needed, each time in a different role. I was fascinated to read the diary my father wrote in a couple of army field message notepads, when he commanded General Montgomery's infantry bodyguard at El Alamein (against army regulations; keeping a diary was forbidden when in close contact with the enemy). The diary, and his narratives of the war in the Western Desert, in East Africa, of the invasion of Sicily and the Italian campaign describe events of over sixty years ago. But some passages read almost as if they happened yesterday. His account of the Battle of Monte Cavallara, when his leadership and courage were tested—what the Second World War soldier and poet Keith Douglas, who was killed in Normandy in 1944, called 'the looking-glass which touches a man entering battle'—is crystal clear.

Evidently, he wrote the memoir with few notes. He didn't need them: he was a well-informed reader of military history, and he witnessed the war he describes. But it is obvious that his focus was A Company and its platoons. Like all officers and men on the front line, he frequently had no knowledge of events over the next ridge, never mind of high command's strategy. I was frustrated by questions that cannot be answered, now that he's gone. I found gaps, repetitions and mistakes in the manuscript, which he seemed to have written in fits and starts. It needed editing, research and fact checking. He forgot, or chose not, to include some incidents he told me about; others, he passed over because they were accounted for in two battalion histories, books that are long out of print. Where I felt a need for clarity—strategy and technical detail, for example—I have added such information to his text, as I am sure he would have done had he revised the manuscript.

His desert diary runs from 3 July 1942 to 1 January 1943. The entries selected here reveal the most about his experiences and the workings of Montgomery's Tac HQ. I have edited them lightly for style and narrative. His words are unchanged. Also for clarity, his prose and diary are typeset in Garamond; my pilgrimage from Stirling to Siena and the Po valley is set in Gill Sans, as are army orders, prose and poetry extracts, picture captions, a glossary and bibliography (mostly books from his collection).

My father's papers, photographs and books were an invaluable resource. Among the latter was the *History of the Argyll and Sutherland Highlanders, 1st Battalion 1939-45* by Lieutenant-Colonel Graham, published in 1948. My father was sceptical of official histories, but he acknowledged a debt to Graham's book, which is sincere and unstuffy. It was his *aide-mémoire*, and it became mine. My primary sources of reference (apart from his papers and photographs) were the 1st Battalion War Diary, held at The National Archives, Kew, and the battalion's wartime album at the Regimental Museum at Stirling Castle.

Robin Ward
Edinburgh, June 2006

•

Part One

1 THE CASTLE

'Let's go; we share one purpose, that's clear:
  you are my guide, my lord, and my attorney.'
  So I spoke to him; and off he steered,

I undertook that deep, outlandish journey.

Dante. *The Inferno,* Canto II, 139

I didn't get round to reading my father's memoir until some time after he
died. My wife and I had to find somewhere to stay when the family house
was sold, and my mother needed help moving to a flat in Glasgow. After
living in Canada for so long, I hadn't expected to be back in Scotland.
Editing the manuscript helped me make the adjustment. My first stop when
I began to trace his wartime wanderings was Stirling Castle, where he
joined the Argylls. Regimental Secretary, Major C. A. Campbell, had printed
my father's obituary in the regimental magazine, *The Thin Red Line.* He suggested I visit the museum to start my research.

Approaching the outskirts of Stirling, I leave the M9 motorway to visit
the field of Bannockburn, which my father knew from his time at Stirling
but which I have never seen. An equestrian bronze of King Robert the
Bruce dominates the historic site, a treeless, wind-brushed plateau. The
statue marks the spot where Bruce planted his standard and deployed his
troops to defeat an English army in 1314, during the Wars of Independence.
Bruce, wielding a battle-axe, felled an English knight in single combat. Every
Scottish schoolboy in the 1950s was told the story of the victory at the

Battle of Bannockburn (and of William Wallace outwitting the English and beating them at the Battle of Stirling Bridge in 1297). The curriculum celebrated the Scots as a warrior race. It was unchanged for decades and would have been familiar to my father. He didn't dwell on the Highland Clearances or the Battle of Culloden. His preference was for Scottish victories, the romance and the legends.

Stirling Castle, sited on the crest of an extinct volcanic crag on the southern edge of the Highlands, dominates the Royal Burgh of Stirling and the landscape around it. The castle is visible from miles away, as daunting a prospect for army recruits as it was for English invaders. Above the old town, I park my Jeep on the Esplanade, the castle's parade ground, a blustery outlook the size of a football pitch. One of my earliest memories is of being here, on 9 October 1954. My father and mother were among the guests at the centenary of the Battle of Balaclava in the Crimean War, when the Argylls won a famous victory against Russian cavalry. I was hoisted on my father's shoulders to watch the parade, and deafened by the pipes and drums. When the ceremony ended, a kilted bear of a man strode towards us. This giant was Drum Major Bloomfield, my father's temperamental platoon sergeant during the war. He bent down, brushing me with his waxed moustache, and asked softly, 'Does your daddy take you and your mammy to the back court for Stand-to every morning?' I was barely four years old and seemed to have been enrolled into the ranks of the regiment.

The battlements seem unchanged from that day in 1954, except for the absense of sentries. On the Esplanade, another statue of Robert the Bruce and a Boer War memorial's kilted soldier are the only spectators. The last garrison of Argylls departed in December 1963, marching out over the drawbridge and across the parade ground that is now bare, except in summer when cars and coaches are parked there. Regimental Headquarters and the Regimental Museum still occupy the King's Old Buildings, once the officers' lodgings at the top of the crag. The museum is free but Historic

Scotland, the government agency that controls the castle, charges admission at the main gate. Stirling Castle is a tourist attraction.

I was last here in 1987, when I drove my father from Glasgow to attend a memorial service for Lieutenant-Colonel Graham in the Chapel Royal. Now, the castle's weathered stone buildings, which are grouped around a lower and an upper courtyard, are in various stages of repair. I am astonished to see the Great Hall, the Argylls' old barrack block, plastered in brand-new yellow harling. The interior, which is hired out for corporate and cultural events, looks like a movie set. Historic Scotland is 'restoring' the site to the style of the sixteenth century, when the castle was the palace of the Stewart kings James IV and V, and Mary Queen of Scots. For the moment, the King's Old Buildings stand aloof from this intervention.

I meet Rod Mackenzie, curator at the Regimental Museum. He has a 1st Battalion album to show me, which was found in a London bank vault and given to the museum some years ago. I spend an afternoon with the heavy, screw-bound folio, sitting at a dining table in a room whose fireplace, cabinets of regimental silverware, and portraits of kilted soldiers evoke a Highland officers' mess. I sense how my father, as a subaltern, would have been unable to resist the romantic allure of history here, in the castle's evocative architecture and the Argylls' fame and battle honours.

The album looks and feels well travelled—pages of photographs and documents record the 1st Battalion's war. Its provenance in unknown but, from my father's papers, I know that, in addition to the official War Diary, a battalion 'scrap-book' was kept. Freddie Graham would have had it when he was writing the battalion history in the late-1940s (when he was a staff officer in the Home Counties). The album begins in Palestine in 1939 and ends in the Po valley in 1945, dates that match Graham's periods of service. A letter to him from General Auchinleck in 1945, and the inclusion of his final address to the battalion give the album a personal flavour. I am completely absorbed in its pages. I feel a wave of pride to find my father here: with his platoon astride an Italian monument to the conquest of

Abyssinia; with General Montgomery in the North African desert; leading A Company across a canal at Ferrara in 1945, in pursuit of the Germans at the end of the Italian campaign.

Back in the museum, among the tattered colours from Balaclava, relics from the relief of Lucknow, regimental silver, muskets and medals, I recognise *The Thin Red Line*, the Victorian painting by Robert Gibb showing the 93rd Sutherland Highlanders beating off the Russian cavalry charge at Balaclava. For years, a framed print of this picture hung in our sitting room in Glasgow, alongside a bust of Monty.

I realise that the Argylls have been fighting Britain's wars—and been based at Stirling Castle—for over two centuries, but the Museum and Regimental HQ are all that's left. Every other trace of the Argylls' past at the castle is being erased by Historic Scotland's restoration of the Stewarts, and theme park tourism and corporate hospitality. (As for the regiment, on 28 March 2006, the Ministry of Defence, to the ire of traditionalists, amalgamated the Argylls with Scotland's other remaining regiments into a new formation, The Royal Regiment of Scotland, headquartered at Edinburgh Castle.)

My father would acknowledge the irony that liberty to interpret the past, as Historic Scotland is exercising, is part of the freedom he fought for. (He might even concede the MoD's case for efficiency in restructuring the regiments, but I doubt it.) I put a donation in the Museum collection box and leave, slightly depressed. Stirling is a market and university town but no longer an army one. Its post-war suburban sprawl extends to the field of Bannockburn where, as at the castle, tourists outnumber soldiers. It was a different place in 1940.

I WAS ON STAGE AT THE THEATRE ROYAL, GLASGOW, playing Captain Corcoran in Gilbert and Sullivan's *HMS Pinafore* when my call up papers arrived in mid-March 1940. Acting and singing on stage was not exactly a reserved occupation that would prevent me being drafted but, thanks to Tommy Torrance, President of the Orpheus Club, my papers were deferred because the show was for the benefit of the Red Cross and Forces Charities. A month later I reported to Whiteinch recruiting office, a wooden hut on Dumbarton Road, for an interview and army medical. The interview was with a whiskery First World War veteran who confirmed my date of birth 18 November 1916, passed me as fit and asked which branch of the services I wanted to join. He almost had me down for the navy, because my father had been band-master on CTS *Empress*. The process was all rather casual, like the Phoney War of the time.

I chose the army—the infantry—with a preference for the Argylls. My father had military connections and he came from Helensburgh, which lies in the shadow of the Argyllshire hills. And I had met Archibald Mackay, who later became my father-in-law. He hailed from Jura and had served as a quartermaster sergeant in the Argylls in the First World War. The fact that he was gassed in the trenches and never fully recovered his health, and that one of his brothers, Hugh, had died of TB in a Glasgow hospital after serving in the Black Watch, did not dispell the romantic notion I had of the Scottish soldier. The Argylls were based at Stirling Castle, near the battlefields of Wallace, Bruce and Bonnie Prince Charlie, whose exploits I had been taught at school and had read about in the novels of Buchan, Stevenson and Scott. I rather fancied the uniform too, with its wildcat and boar's head badge, its chequered glengarry, and tartan kilt bristling with a six-tasselled, badger-head, ceremonial sporran.

I was seen off on the Stirling bus by my elder brother Harold on that memorable day, 18 April 1940. I travelled with a group of young conscripts from Oban, Tarbert, Campbeltown and Glasgow. All were apprehensive about the prospect of six months' infantry training, except for one, the brother of a fellow in Train's office. He had been in the Territorial Army before the war and was very much the old soldier, master of all military lore it seemed and familiar with the strange rites through which I was about to be initiated. He passed on some readily forgotten, useless information and enlivened my journey by painting a vivid picture of the horrors and hardships of recruit training. I was glad to get out into the fresh air when the bus reached the town. Stirling was full of soldiers: squads of men marching here and there; individual off-duty officers and men walking about, saluting each other right and left; military vehicles all over the place. It was a garrison town, of course. And this was wartime.

The walk up the cobbled streets to the top of the town and the castle is a long one, and uphill all the way. We set out, clutching wee suitcases, duffle bags and even cardboard boxes, to put our civvy clothes in to take home on our first leave for our mothers to wash. We were a ragged outfit of all shapes and sizes and all manner of dress. The only thing we had in common was our youth and trepidation. Locals watched our progress knowingly as we climbed the cobbled streets. We separated into self-conscious groups of two or three or, as I did, walked alone. There was some diversionary banter but most of us were lost in thoughts, the heaviest burden on that initial ascent.

We emerged from the town onto the Esplanade, the parade ground we would come to know well. The castle's ramparts, turrets and crow-step gables rose before us. A wooden drawbridge was flanked by two sentry boxes. Neither sentry deigned to give us even a glance. We crossed the bridge and followed a vaulted passage, to find ourselves suddenly confronted by the castle's intimidating sixteenth-century gateway. Beyond it, at the Gatehouse, we got a foretaste of what was in store. We were stopped in our tracks by our first army command and challenge:

'Halt! Where do you miserable lot think you're going?'

The roar of sergeant-majors, the parade ground stamp of drilling troops, the rattle of musketry, the skirl of the pipes and the bugle calls that divide a soldier's day have echoed over Stirling's rooftops for over 200 years. The upper town retains façades of royal patronage, behind which army officers were entertained; the lower town, with its tenements, pubs and vennels, was the haunt of off-duty squaddies. Officers and men of the Argylls thus had a close relationship with the people of Stirling, from aristocratic families to pub landlords.

The regiment was formed for service in the Napoleonic Wars. In 1794, the Duke of Argyll raised the 91st Argyllshire Highlanders, recruiting men mainly from Glasgow and the west of Scotland; the 93rd Sutherland Highlanders was raised in 1799, from the Countess of Sutherland's militia and crofters. In 1881, the 91st and 93rd merged as, respectively, the 1st and 2nd battalions, The Argyll and Sutherland Highlanders. The 91st's base at the castle became the Regimental Depot. In 1940, it was the Infantry Training Centre where I was plunged into army life.

When the 93rd was raised, each man was invited to step forward for a customary dram with Major General Wemyss, cousin of the countess—the only formality required. But there was no whisky with the castle's commanding officer for us. Instead, we immediately lost our civilian identity in an army number and then our hair in a brutal cut. Next we got our kit: boots, battledress, balmoral and fatigues; mess tin, enamel mug, cutlery, sewing and shaving kit and, of course, brushes and polish for those boots. Later, we were issued with the other accessories needed by an infantry soldier: service rifle, ammunition clips, bayonet, steel helmet, gas mask and an anti-mustard gas oilskin cape. The weight of this gear was about fifty pounds. None of the items had changed much since the First World War. The gas masks provoked derision and hilarity.

The sergeant at the Gatehouse had directed us across the cobbles to our quarters in the Top Square, the upper courtyard. Most recruits at the castle were housed in the sixteenth-century Great Hall, once the Stewarts' ceremonial and banqueting chamber. This sounded rather grand, until you went inside. After the 1745 rising, the vast space was filled with three floors of spartan accommodation to billet soldiers sent north to subdue and punish the Jacobites. Our barrack was in the adjacent Chapel Royal, another venerable building which had also been crudely adapted by the army. In place of royal prayers, its walls absorbed the barrack-room ballyhoo of NCOs shouting commands and squaddies swearing. Some of the recruits were from Stirling and its hinterland. Others, like those in my group, were from Glasgow and Clydeside, west-coast towns and the crofts of Argyll. But we all soon identified with different places when we were split up into squads named after battle honours: Corunna, Lucknow, Paardeberg, Mons. I was pleased to find myself in Balaclava Squad as I had thrilled as a boy to the story of the Thin Red Line. A good omen, I hoped.

I'll never forget that first night. Some of my fellow conscripts were hardy country lads. Most were wee city fellas in poor physical shape—apprentices, labourers, the unemployed. This was the first night away from home for many of them. Some joked; others, thrust among strangers, were already homesick. I remember lying on my camp bed before Lights Out, reading *The Open Road,* a poetry anthology my father had given me. That set me apart from the start. And I was a few years older than most of them and taller, spoke differently, appeared to be educated and not too much put out by things. Some of them crept up to me for advice and encouragement. They told me their life stories. Most were pretty grim. Social conditions of the time—unemployment, poverty and ignorance—had made those fellows what they were: the poor bloody infantry, cannon fodder through the ages. Yet after six months of physical exercise, a healthy outdoor life, regular meals and a disciplined routine most of them were changed men: smart, fit, confident and proud to be Argylls.

Our day began with Reveille at 0600 hours, to shouts of 'Shake a leg!' from our tireless NCOs. We stumbled out of our beds into sandshoes, singlet and shorts. Then we were turfed outside for 45 minutes of physical training in the chilly dawn air. We shaved, washed and dressed for breakfast, which was taken in the Renaissance-style Palace Block, the old royal apartments. Our mess hall and kitchen were on the lowest floor, formerly James V's pantry and wine cellar. What wine there was now was out of bounds in the Officers' Mess, located in the former royal courtiers' and castle governors' chambers above us. That was a source of sardonic interest. So was the food, although some recruits thought it was better than they got at home. For the rest of us, mealtimes were when we missed our mothers most. The orderly officer reminded us that since civilians had to queue in the shops for rations, we should be grateful for what we got. Breakfast was basic: 'burgoo' (porridge), greasy bacon and eggs, swilled down with hot sweet tea. Complaints invited a glower and growl: 'This is the army, laddie, not the Café Royal.'

Our instructors were feared and respected, demanding instant obedience at all times. Drill was deafening. The words came rattling out through the drill sergeant's teeth like machine-gun fire: 'Eyes to the front. From the right, quick march. Left, right, left, right. Swing those arms. Squad, halt!' Right turn, left turn, about-turn . . . we birled around in our new army boots, trying not to slip on the cobbles or bump into each other. Anyone larking around was made to quick march around the square while the rest of us watched.

There was one conscript, the 'awkward' soldier that you find in every squad, a gallus local lad with two left feet—shambling, untidy, with no notion of how to carry himself, hold a rifle, or wear a balmoral in the required style. He drove the drill sergeant mad. One of the first things we were taught was how to stand properly to attention: head up, chin in, eyes to the front, stomach in, shoulders back, arms straight by the sides, thumbs to the trouser seams, and feet at an angle of forty-five degrees. 'Whit the hell's an angle o' forty-five degrees?' he muttered once. He was immdiately bawled out: 'Stand still. No talking in the ranks.' The poor chap was sometimes brought out in front and drilled individually, made a fool of in front of the rest of the squad. He wasn't cut out to be a soIdier, and he didn't last long with us. It must have been a blessed release for him when he was transferred to the Pioneer Corps—the army's labour battalions, and dumping ground for misfits.

I was the tallest man in the squad and in good physical shape. I learned how to wear my balmoral in the most acceptable manner, how to get a good shine on my boots and polish in my cap badge. I must have stood out among my fellows, for one morning, after having my ego inflated by being presented as 'the only man in this bloody squad who knows how to wear an 'effing balmoral', I was appointed 'right marker'. This meant I was expected to be first to take up position in the Top Square outside the Chapel Royal whenever the squad paraded, and on whom the front rank formed up and took its dressing.

'Left right, left right. Eyes to the front. Swing those arms . . .' We were marched under the Gatehouse archway and across the drawbridge to the parade ground, and beyond, many times as the months passed—on our way to and from athletics, battle training, church parades, lectures, route marches—sometimes for no apparent reason we could make out, just for the hell of it, as we thought bitterly, or by mistake. And all the time badgered and barked at by our NCOs, who I am sure heard our curses muttered *sotto voce*.

We drilled for battlefield formations which would have been familiar to the Duke of Wellington. I didn't think the Nazi *blitzkrieg* on Poland had been achieved that way. But drill had the intended psychological effect: replacing the individuality of civvy street with the unity of the regiment. Our appearance was quickly transformed from that of our undistinguished arrival, into tight, well-drilled and tolerably smart columns. I enjoyed the status of being right marker and being part of a cohesive group responding smartly to words of command. None of us had ever led such active and strenuous lives, hard at it from dawn PT to the last drill or training session of the day. I relished the physical well-being felt after sustained effort and the simple pleasures of a slap-up evening meal and comradely banter.

After breakfast I often slipped off with my mug of tea to enjoy a first cigarette of the day. While exploring the battlements I had discovered, above the south ramparts, a quiet spot with a panoramic view. To the south, the Church of the Holy Rude and Stirling's pantiled rooftops; to the west, open country and the distant mountains of Argyll. The cigarette break was my only chance in the day for a moment's solitude. Time up, I would toss the tea leaves down the side of the escarpment and send the fag end spinning through the air before dashing over the cobbles of the Top Square to prepare for the 0800 parade and the sergeant's shout: 'Right marker'.

We each took a turn as barrack-room orderly, floor scrubbing, tidying up and keeping an eye on the place while the squad was being harried about elsewhere. This also gave time for clothing and kit repairs, button and boot polishing, rifle cleaning, letter writing and reading. Time passed all too quickly and peace was soon shattered by the squad's returning clatter and chorus: 'How's the idle dodger?' followed by abuse if things were found not quite as they should have been. Each week, at the squad sergeant's command, 'Stand by your beds', every item of our bedding, clothing and equipment was displayed: uniforms precisely folded, mess tins spotless, rifles well oiled and polished, boots and belts buffed and badges and buttons sparkling. Any flaw exposed by this fetish for scrutiny and cleanliness usually provoked a verbal assault and a charge, which meant three days confined to barracks and menial tasks.

I was lucky to get occasional afternoon and evening breaks from barracks, thanks to Jean Bruce, the publisher and owner of the *Stirling Observer*. I had sung with her in the Orpheus Club, most recently in *HMS Pinafore*. She knew I was a recruit at the castle and managed to rope me in (with permission from my superiors) for various concerts. Otherwise, time off was spent in a canteen/recreation room run by the padre, where you could forget you were a soldier in training for a while. The padre, who was liked and respected by the recruits, was ever ready with advice and encouragement, and of much practical help in solving personal problems. There were many jokes about wishy-washy clergymen, save-your-soul types, bossy women of the Women's Royal Voluntary Service and canteen lassies with their chat and char. Yet they all in their own way brought great comfort to the troops and provided relaxation and recreation in barracks and army stations all over the country in those days, and overseas too.

We had little time to grumble about having our lives disrupted by the restrictions on our freedom and the demand for unquestioning obedience; by being shouted at all day; by the lack of home comforts and privacy; by the loss of personal identity in the military machine. When we were not being drilled, we attended lectures on military history, infantry tactics, aircraft spotting, trench and latrine digging, hygiene, or sessions on care of kit, clothing and weapons. Of course, what we really wanted to do was make Molotov cocktails and throw them at German tanks. The attraction of the army for young men was its potential to satisfy boyish delight in mischief and mayhem. Standing around on guard duty, I wondered if I would ever get the chance.

On the first day of the war, air-raid sirens had been sounded across the nation. Children were evacuated from cities. Identification cards and ration books were issued. Men in their early twenties began to be called up. The British Expeditionary Force landed in France; the RAF dropped propaganda leaflets over Germany; Winston Churchill was recalled as First Lord of the Admiralty. Action was isolated and main-ly at sea. I remember the newspaper headlines about the Battle of the River Plate, when the German pocket battleship *Admiral Graf Spee* was scuttled after a sea chase that read like a story from *Boy's Own Paper*. But in the six months since September 1939 there hadn't been much fighting in France, and there had been no major air raids. Most of the children who were evacuated went home.

On 9 May 1940, less than a month into our training, the unreality of the Phoney War was shattered when Hitler attacked Denmark, Norway, the Netherlands, Luxembourg, Belgium and France. Churchill became Prime Minister. A brief foray to save Norway resulted in an embarrassing defeat. Even worse, the *blitzkrieg* in France trapped the BEF at Dunkirk. The Argylls' 7th and 8th battalions were in France with the 51st Highland Division, but it was some time before we learned of their fate. Most of the 51st was isolated near Dieppe by a German panzer division and surrendered; 8,000 men became prisoners of war. Remnants of the two Argyll battalions escaped by sea from Le Harve. Oddly, Dunkirk was brought home to me with more intensity when I heard that the Clyde paddle steamer *Waverley,* which my father had taken me on as a boy, had been bombed and sunk.

The BEF's transport, tanks and artillery were destroyed or aban-doned, the RAF lost hundreds of aircraft in France, and the navy several destroyers during the evacuation. But propaganda turned the Dunkirk evacuation into a victory of sorts. The reality of a poorly prepared and equipped army, and a dysfunctional relationship with the French, was not publicised as it would be today. Newsreels, inflated by jaunty music and plucky voice-overs, featured uplifting items about how Britannia still ruled the waves and how the Dominions were rallying to our aid, as indeed they were. But the prospects seemed hopeless. The newsreels couldn't conceal from us the calamity of defeat in France and the fate of the Highland Division.

What did emerge from the debacle of spring 1940 and the fall of France was the feeling that we were better off alone. Our champion was Churchill. He had not been universally popular, but his pre-war warnings about Hitler and the Nazis were proven, and his wartime speeches and broadcasts were inspiring. His command of the English language and thunderous rhetoric expressed what we wanted to believe of ourselves. There may have been a few fainthearts among people who should have known better, but the feeling generally throughout the country was that we must all buckle to and win the war, whatever the cost.

A German invasion seemed imminent. The government set up the Home Guard. Church bells were banned, except as an invasion alarm. Concrete tank traps appeared on roads and beaches, trenches were dug in parks, pillboxes were built at tactical points and road signs removed or turned the wrong way to confuse the enemy. To remind civilians that the nation was in peril, the government asked housewives for pots and pans which, it claimed, would be melted down to make Spitfires. Victorian cast-iron gates and railings disappeared from city streets, supposedly to be recast as tanks. Even today, you can see the stumps where railings were cut from garden and park walls. But the kitchenware and cast iron cull summed up where we were: improvising and muddling our way through the crisis.

Our weapons training took on a sense of urgency and purpose. A soldier's best friend is his service rifle and we were thoroughly drilled in its proper care, use and purpose. 'She's your wife,' the instructors said, adding lewdly, 'Be nice to her and she'll give you full satisfaction.' Ours were Lee Enfield bolt-action rifles, single shot, with five-round ammo clips (later ten). We were also introduced to the Bren gun, a modern, Czech-designed, light machine-gun with a 30-round magazine. These were the standard British infantry small arms of the day, along with the officer-issue .38-inch calibre Webley service revolver. Because of a shortage of .303 ammunition for the Enfields and the Brens, visits to the rifle range were rare. We spent more time oiling and cleaning our guns than firing them.

At first we scoffed at the Lee Enfield, a rifle that had been introduced during the Boer War, until an instructor told us how British troops halted mass German attacks at Mons in 1914 with disciplined fire so rapid and accurate that the Germans thought they were facing machine-gunners. This seemed improbable until you learned how to fire it. I was astonished by the kick from the recoil if it was inexpertly held, but once you got the hang of its smooth and fast bolt action, the Lee Enfield was a joy to handle. It was reliable, and accurate up to half a mile, twice that if fired by a marksman. I became quite a good shot. I still remember how to get down to a prone firing position: toss the rifle into the left hand, catching it at the point of balance, drop spread-eagled, legs apart on the ground, breaking your fall with the right hand; push a five-round clip into the magazine, open and close the bolt to get one up the spout; rest elbows on the ground, raise the rifle to the right shoulder, adjust your sights; wait for the command; then hold your breath and squeeze gently on the trigger. Fire! Satisfaction at an Inner, joy at a Bull.

The Bren gun could be fired from the hip, but the prone position, with the gunner's mate lying alongside to change mags, was prefered. Being automatic and firing up to 450 rounds per minute it often seized up when it got hot. We were taught to loose off effective short bursts rather than just blaze away, and to change mags quickly, and clear the mechanism when it jammed. I think I could still strip and reassemble a Bren today, repeating aloud the shouted commands: 'Mag off. Press. Cock. Release. Fire. Mag on. Safety catch on.' We were also shown how use the Mills bomb, a cast-iron hand grenade. You threw it cricket-style, no problem for me. Again, there were shouted commands: 'Lever down. Safety pin out. Aim. Throw!' The lever sprang up, its plunger hit an explosive cap which ignited the fuse that detonatated the grenade. As in Hollywood movies, you only had four seconds to take cover; unlike them, the pin was too strong to be pulled out by the teeth.

And then there was bayonet training. Shooting practice was obviously necessary but I thought bayonet drill was daft. Despite frontline service throughout the war, I never met a single soldier who had ever used his bayonet in earnest. We had the usual barrage of commands: 'Squad attenshun. Fix bayonets. Slope arms. Quick march. Charge!' We were shown the straight jab to the belly and the rifle-butt stroke to the face. We practised them repeatedly in lieu of target practice because we had so little ammo. But I think the army's real interest in cold steel was ritualistic—an exercise designed to get the adrenaline flowing, stir the blood and arouse the killer instinct. This was further stimulated by shouts and curses from our instructors as we charged and lunged at canvas and straw dummies, maniacally roaring our heads off all the while. Bayonet exercises were an excuse to let off steam. We imagined the dummies were the instructors and dealt with them with relish.

Our pernickety, hectoring NCOs were a mixed bunch, some evidently of limited intelligence and vocabulary, other than the profane. All were anxious to appear hard as nails and as belligerent as legally possible. In Balaclava Squad we had one corporal instructor, an old China and North-west Frontier hand for whom travel had not broadened the mind. He was foul-mouthed and brutal, fortunately an exception. Others fell in our esteem when we saw the cringing deference they showed towards the officers. But most were good types: older regular army men of outstanding reliability and rectitude who had memorised, and behaved according to, a strict code of conduct learned from years of service. Their brightly polished boots and brasses, their immaculate turnout, their brisk commands and air of authority impressed and chastened us all. But they lacked our youth, initiative and resourcefulness, and some perhaps knew this. Off duty they were often approachable, even sensitive, and helped us with problems and grievances. They taught us tricks of the trade: how to keep out of trou-

ble and flannel a way out if landed in it; how to beat the system without over-stepping the mark; how to shortcut army bullshit, and military
bureaucracy that plodded on at peacetime pace.

They knocked us into such good shape that Balaclava Squad was
named the best-drilled in the class. Eventually we paraded in platoons
of thirty or companies of one humdred men. With the prospect of active
service, few of us wished to return to civvy street's office politics, assembly lines, or the dole. Army camaraderie changed us all. We learned how
to look after ourselves and each other, having discovered qualities of tolerance, decency and kindness we shared, especially with those whose
backgrounds and upbringing had done little to foster such character
traits. But if the army's intention was to dehumanise and brutalise us
to fight the Nazis, it was unsuccessful. We were free-thinking, egali-
tarian men at arms—members of a citizen army, not professional killers.

Because I'd been a clerk and could read and write, I was sent to
Dundonald camp at Troon to help with the documentation of a new
intake of conscripts. I was promoted lance corporal (acting unpaid) and
given my first stripe. At the camp, I sat at a trestle table, pen in hand
and papers in front of me, my lance corporal's stripe lending me brief
authority—and behaved as obnoxiously as the Territorial on the Stirling
bus. I felt smugly superior to the nervous, suitcase-carrying civilians
who shuffled forth. I'd forgotten that I had been in the same position
myself a few months before. I must have had a sneaking sense of the
dangerous, corrupting influence of power and authority, and the importance and significance of rank in the army, and began to understand
better the attitude of the few officers I had been in contact with. Of
course, I was brought back down to earth by my fellow squaddies:
'Chancer, scrounger, pee-hee-er, sergeant's pet,' were some of the more
polite comments when I got back to barracks.

I managed a few days leave after Dundonald. My parents and two
elder brothers, Cecil and Harold, had just returned from St Anne's-on-

Sea, where my eldest brother Alex had just got married (Harold also married during the war). Cecil and I had a game of cricket at our club, where he had scored 75 and I took 6 wickets for 10 runs in a thrilling match before the war. We recalled those days fondly. But I was happier not in cricket whites but in my army uniform with its lance corporal's stripe. I strutted around welcoming the approach of any passing officers on whom I could practise my well-learned salute: 'Longest way up, shortest way down.' I wore that stripe with as much pride as a brigadier with his brass badges. It was the first step on the military ladder I was determined to climb.

I blotted my copybook only once during initial training. Weekend passes were issued infrequently. I had one and was hurrying down from the Top Square. On the Bottom Square, which I had to cross, a squad had formed for a guard-mounting parade. Unseen by me, around a corner of the Great Hall, stood the duty officer and his sergeant, about to march forward to inspect the guard. Impatient to be off, I took a risk and stepped out across the square, arms swinging and giving the officer, when I saw him, my best salute. I was stopped by a furious roar from the sergeant: 'You there. That man. Where the bloody hell d'you think you're going?' I was still ignorant of military etiquette and had interrupted hallowed routine. I was made to stand there, mortified and resentful, until the whole thing was over. The officer was too aloof to speak to me, but by Jove the sergeant did. I've never had such a telling-off. My pass was cancelled and I was confined to barracks, where I had time to reflect on life's injustices and the infernal cussedness of things. It was a valuable lesson, which produced in me a healthy respect for army authority and a desire to create a good impression.

That incident made me decide to apply for a commission, as soon as I could win myself into favour again. I must have succeeded because Corporal Stewart, the bullying China and North-west Frontier veteran, surprised me by saying I was 'officer material', and suggested I apply for one. Not long afterwards I was summoned to a Selection Board, where I was faced with a couple of elderly majors and an imposing Kiplingesque colonel. I had never seen such a high-ranking officer before and was struck and initially daunted by the impressive staff officer's red tabs he wore. He sat in the middle. All three, with my papers in front of them, had fountain pens at the ready.

The colonel invited me to sit, which I did as if I'd been bolted to the chair. He asked why I wanted to become an officer. I said I needed a challenge, something to aim for. They seemed satisfied by that clichéd response. What I really wanted to say was that I liked the uniform and dreamed of martial glory; that now I was in the army I wanted to get on and make the most of it; that I was attracted by the privileges of rank, its better living conditions and pay; that I was fed up being bossed about by ignorant NCOs and that I looked forward to doing some ordering about myself; that I would make as good an officer as some I had met.

There were the usual questions about family background, schooling (Hyndland Secondary, which I doubt had any significance for them), civilian occupation, sporting activities and hobbies. It must have been on my record that I was a singer because I was asked about that as well. That was something that set me apart from my fellows, and that I had helped to raise funds for Forces Charities. Without stretching the truth too far I presented myself in as good a light as possible. I felt I was playing a game where they had made the rules; felt justified in bending them in my own advantage.

I told them my father had been a naval officer, hoping they'd think he'd been a destroyer captain, not merely bandmaster on the *Empress,* a pensioned-off sailing ship where orphans and the miscreant youth of Glasgow were given a second chance, as cadets. I told them, with some truth, that my favourite authors were Buchan and Kipling. That went down very well. On the strength of frequent visits to Whiteinch baths, rambles on the Campsie Fells as a boy, and youth hostelling in the Trossachs where I'd once climbed Ben Venue, I made myself out to be a champion swimmer and skilled mountaineer. When I mentioned cricket, the colonel's eyes lit up.

'Cricket, eh!' he barked. 'Who did you play for?'

I'd anticipated that one. My local Baldwin Cricket Club would have meant nothing to him.

'West of Scotland, sir.'

I didn't blink, or mention that I'd only played at their ground, and against their second eleven.

'Batsman, eh?' the colonel went on.

'No, sir. Fast bowler.'

I couldn't have done better. The three officers exchanged knowing smiles and made marks with their pens. I was obviously the spirited, fiery, aggressive type they wanted. I could tell I had made it when the colonel smiled and said: 'Good man.'

2 CODEWORD CROMWELL

AT THE END OF AUGUST 1940, I was posted to 165 Officer Cadet Training Unit at Dunbar, the North Sea fishing town and holiday resort. I remember boarding a train at Stirling station, elated with a sense of adventure, and casually chucking my kit bag up onto the luggage rack. Trains were packed in those days and I was lucky to get a seat. After stopping briefly at Waverley station in Edinburgh, the train steamed across the fields of East Lothian. The landscape was ablaze with crops ripening in the glorious weather of that fateful summer of 1940. Passing near the RAF airfield at Drem, I saw a Spitfire buzz overhead about to land.

Dunbar, like Stirling, has historic military connections. It became a garrison town during the Napoleonic Wars, with artillery batteries sited on the cliffs near the ruined castle by the harbour. Outside the parish church, an obelisk commemorates men of the Lothians and Berwickshire Imperial Yeomanry killed in the Boer War. The yeomanry's barrack and HQ was at Lauderdale House, an Adamesque mansion at the harbour end of the High Street. We paraded regularly on Barrack Square, originally the mansion's clifftop garden.

Scores of cadets from practically every infantry regiment in the army were being trained at Dunbar. The OCTU was organised like a battalion, with four companies, A, B, C and D. Each was billeted in a different hotel. I was in A Company, the recruit company (the other companies' cadets were already serving soldiers). My billet was the Roxburghe Marine Hotel. Like others in the town it had been requisitioned to accommodate the training unit's staff, the cadets and other military personnel based in the area. About 100 cadets were quartered in the Roxburghe, mostly four to a room. I shared digs with three other cadets: Jim Henderson, a Glaswegian of my own age, who was later commissioned in the Highland Light Infantry; Dai Davis, a high-spirited wee Welshman from the South Wales Borderers, and Hank Richards, a big country lad from a Border regiment. The hotel, which had a panoramic setting overlooking the beach and the sea, had been built for Edwardian holidaymakers, who once relaxed in its saltwater therapeutic baths. Little remained of that period or its style. The interior, stripped of its normal furnishings, was reduced to wartime austerity.

Men in uniform were looked upon as courageous defenders of the British Isles and our status as cadets raised us above the common soldiery. People invited us to their homes, clubs and churches. I had no shortage of invitations, especially after one girl I met discovered that not only was I an officer-in-training but also a singer with a repertoire of romantic ballads and patriotic songs. Such hospitality was touching, but we cadets were desperately keen to get on with our training, secure postings to the regiments of our choice and play our part in the war. Dunbar seemed far away from any action. There had been sporadic air raids on the east coast in 1939. The Luftwaffe bombed Rosyth navy base but missed the Forth Bridge which was promptly protected by barrage balloons. Spitfire pilots flying from Lothian aerodromes made headlines after they shot down some of the German bombers, the first enemy planes destroyed over the UK. Passengers on a train crossing the bridge saw the bombs bursting in the water, while in Edinburgh, because air raid sirens were not sounded, people who saw the planes didn't realise what was happening.

In mid-August 1940, the real thing began over the skies of Southeast England when the Luftwaffe began bombing RAF airfields and radar stations. I recall sitting with other chaps in the Roxburghe's lounge listening to nightly BBC radio reports that listed, like cricket scores in our favour, the numbers of RAF and Luftwaffe planes shot down. These attacks were the prelude to an expected invasion, the threat of which was not confined to southern England. The sandy beaches on the east coast of Scotland, from the Border all the way up to the Moray Firth, were potential landing sites for the Germans. The coast was a restricted area. Fife and Angus were defended by Polish troops—who had escaped to the South of France via the Balkans, were evacuated from Dunkirk and Brittany and re-formed in Scotland as the 1st Polish Corps. East Lothian's beaches were fortified with concrete tank traps, artillery, searchlights and ack-ack batteries. Navy ships patrolled the Firth of Forth. Minefields were laid at sea. The Royal Observer Corps had observation posts along the coast, including one at Dunbar. Trenches were dug and landmines laid on the East Links next to our hotel.

On paper these deployments seemed impressive but the reality was not encouraging. Boy scouts were recruited to fill sandbags and act as coast watchers. Road blocks were manned by enthusiastic but ill-equipped Home Guard volunteers. Their big idea was to spray petrol in the path of Nazi tanks and then lob Molotov cocktails at them, provided the panzer commanders would be sporting and keep to the roads. At Dunbar harbour, there was a plan to set the sea ablaze in similar fashion to engulf enemy landing craft. There was even an armoured train that puffed up East Lothian's railway lines, perhaps in hope that the Germans would obligingly not blow up the tracks. During my time at Dunbar I never saw any tanks, field guns or mobile reserve troops, apart from an officer cadet bicycle platoon that was expected to foil parachute attacks. In fact, I didn't see a tank until I arrived in the Western Desert.

On 7 September, I got my first taste of action when the 'Cromwell' balloon went up. Cromwell was the government's codeword for an imminent invasion alert. It was a Saturday, so duty officers and military police had to round us up from the cinemas, hotels and bars. Mustered in the gloaming amid scenes of excitement and confusion, some of us in various stages of inebriation, we were hastily organised into our platoons and issued with rifles and five rounds of .303 ammo apiece. Then we were marched off or shoved into trucks and driven to improvised positions up and down the coast. At first we thought this might be an exercise to test our emergency readiness—or had the enemy already landed? Rumours of spies, landings from the sea and paratroop assaults had circulated for weeks. My platoon was deposited on the sand dunes of Tyninghame, a bay west of the town. The dark sea was swept occasionally by searchlight beams. I thought of Churchill's 'We shall fight on the beaches' speech, and wondered what use my five bullets would be. I wrote home the next day describing the experience:

Dunbar
Sunday 8 September 1940

Dear folks,
The most important news to date is that last night we got the biggest scare of our lives and spent the most uncomfortable night since joining the army.

At 2215 hours, notices were projected onto the screens of the cinemas calling all soldiers and cadets back to their billets. Amid excited talk of 'invasion' and the 'real thing' we all got our equipment together, dressed ourselves up in our battle array and marched off to take up our position on the coast three miles away. I was a bit late and fortunately so, as I got a lift down in a truck. There was tremendous excitement as we thought an invasion was being attempted—in any case we knew it wasn't a practice alarm.

Our platoon was to keep a sharp lookout and defend a certain part of the coast. Weapons pits and trenches had been dug all over the place. A weapons pit is not exactly the most delightful place to spend a night; it measures only three feet deep by two feet wide and five foot long. We were shoved into these holes and had to spend the whole beastly night in them, two men in each.

It was impossible to sleep as, apart from the bitterly cold wind that blew, there wasn't enough room. For the first few hours, we were expecting any moment to see the sea black with ships and the sky black with planes, but nothing happened. We spent the night in a curious state of semi-conciousness, alternately cursing and laughing, and shivering all the time. A state of absolute misery was reached when our cigarettes and chocolate ran out. I was never so pleased to see the sun rise.

We heard from our officers that London had experienced a fearful succession of air raids; I suppose the authorities considered them to be a curtain raiser to something even bigger and called out troops all over the country as a precautionary measure. We were also told that we would likely be kept in our positions for three or four days.

After breakfast, we had just resigned ourselves to more nights of misery when a dispatch rider drove up with a message that the scheme had been cancelled. Elated, we bundled ourselves into trucks and were driven home to our hotels to enjoy a wash and shave, change of clothes and a good sleep. It was an exciting adventure . . .

Love,

Ray

That was the night of the Luftwaffe's first big air raid on London, the start of the Blitz. On 15 September, the RAF won a decisive battle over Kent. Without air and naval superiority the German armada was unlikely to sail. The invasion threat was thwarted. Our night watch on Tyninghame Sands was my part in that great turning point of the war.

We were kept at readiness for a week after the Cromwell scare, manning checkpoints and patrolling the coast and countryside. Then our training resumed. Days began with Reveille at 0600 followed by PT.

We were used to that but not to swimming exercises at that hour in Dunbar's unheated saltwater pool. After breakfast we were drilled by a formidable team of Scots Guards sergeants of immense dignity and authority, armed with pace sticks, powerful voices and a rich vocabulary. Afternoons were spent on exercises. In the evenings, we attended lectures on military history, army routine, leadership and tactics. Lights Out was at 2215. At weekends we were allowed to stay out until midnight.

Our more affable NCOs turned a blind eye to our occasional high-spirited misdemeanours in training, in the bars in the town, or at the Friday night dances at North Berwick Pavilion. We had a platoon comic, a cadet called Sellars, of boundless good nature and happy disposition. And of some nerve too, always laughing and, to the envy of the rest of us, able to take everything in his stride. He was indulged like a court jester and would talk back, politely of course, to our drill sergeant and exchange pleasantries with him. Somehow, by native wit and inoffensive audacity, he managed to get away with it. Theirs was a curious relationship based on mutual tolerance, the good effects of which were felt by all of us in what became a very happy platoon.

We studied training manuals and technical papers, and were lectured on the tactical use of artillery, machine-guns and mortars. We learned about intelligence gathering, artillery observation, sappers, and signals. We practised with Bren guns, grenades and mortars; were instructed in map and compass reading; became experts in the art of constructing fieldworks and in the use of entrenching tools and rolls of Dannert wire. We were taught how to make out reports, note the military significance of topography in sketches and appreciations, how to handle sections and platoons in mock battles, care for men and equipment and the hundred and one other skills an infantry subaltern needed to know. We were trained to give orders and to obey them.

High standards were expected of us, not least of which were those of 'gentlemen'. The army in 1940 was still stratified according to class. While lairds could no longer raise and command their own regiments, or would-be officers from the landed gentry buy commissions, most army officers still came from privileged social backgrounds. Many were were university-educated, often aristocratic. Ordinary soldiers rarely rose higher than NCO or warrant officer and few sought, or were encouraged to seek, further promotion. In 1939, the War Office decreed that all recruits, whatever their social status, had to start in the ranks. But the way candidates were selected for officer training—recommendation by the CO and a 15-minute interview—maintained a public school and, as I had found to my advantage, sporting bias. The sons of army brass, Argyllshire lairds and Perthshire landed gentry set the tone in the officers' mess as they had done before the war. The atmosphere at the OCTU was as I imagined boarding school to be, an effect heightened by Lauderdale House's Georgian architecture.

Our instructors called us 'Sir', as in 'Hold that rifle properly, sir'. This courtesy was often tinged with sarcasm when they supervised assault and obstacle courses to measure our courage, route marches our stamina, weapons training our marksmanship and written tests our intelligence. Officer cadets we may have been, but we were not spared the fastidious formalities of kit and room inspections. I am certain that the floor of my room in the Roxburghe Hotel remained deeply stained where I spilled some rifle oil. It defied all scrubbing but escaped detection while I was there. When the inspecting officers appeared I would come to attention firmly planting my feet on the offending stain. The memory of being bawled out at Stirling was still fresh and I didn't want to put another foot wrong. Those who passed the course would be commissioned as second-lieutenants, posted to a battalion and given the most junior command, a platoon.

Each cadet was required to study the officers' and sergeants' bible: the army's Field Service Pocket Book, a sort of boy scout guide for the infantry. It began with a GLOSSARY OF MILITARY TERMS AND ORGANIZATION IN THE FIELD followed by a series of bound pamphlets with the instruction NOT TO BE TAKEN INTO FRONTLINE TRENCHES where, of course, it would have been most useful. I still have mine. Among its tips were: what to do with prisoners and captured documents; how to lead a patrol and what to look out for; how to interpret aerial reconnaissance photographs, camouflage your position, block roads with felled trees, defend a building, lay demolition charges; how to purify water, cook with mess tins and camp kettles (recipies for stews included), camp in 'uncivilsed countries' . . .

We learned the army's operational structure:

SECTION: ten men; three sections, a PLATOON: three platoons, a COMPANY: four companies, plus an HQ company, a BATTALION (at full strength, around thirty-five officers and 750 men): three battalions a BRIGADE: three brigades, a DIVISION: three divisions, a CORPS: three corps, an ARMY.

Infantry companies (normally nine officers and 120 men) were identified A, B, C and D. In the field, three would be active and one in reserve with the HQ company. Infantry companies had machine-gun, mortar, anti-tank and Bren gun carrier platoons or sections; two supporting echelons (A and B) handled logistics. Artillery and armoured support was expected from attached units. We learned the system of command, and noted the difference between standing orders and operational orders: the first regulated daily routine in the field; the second tactical manoeuvres and assaults. There was a mantra to memorise:

INFORMATION—about the enemy's positions, units and strengths, and our own. INTENTION—the objectives of operational orders. METHOD—the tasks to be carried out to achieve the objectives; the sequence of who, how, where and when; infantry weapons to be used; air, armoured, artillery support expected. ADMINISTRATION—fuel, food, water, ammunition, medical supplies, transport. INTERCOM-MUNICATION—location of command posts, company and battalion headquarters, radio frequencies, recognition lights, passwords . . .

This battle-order formula was, as I found on active service, followed scrupulously at every operational briefing and was rarely deviated from. Some discretion was permitted to the junior officer in battle but generally everything was done by the book. Every command was passed down the line in written or spoken form in a unambiguous manner and acknowledged—at least that was the idea. If the command was verbal there would invariably be a final, 'Any questions?' Those were rare: ours was not to reason why.

Two operational case studies lay on our doorstep: the battles of Dunbar and Prestonpans. The Battle of Dunbar took place outside the town in September 1650. Oliver Comwell commanding parliamentarian troops was opposed by a royalist and covenanting army led by General Leslie. Cromwell had followed the flat coastal route north, made two unsuccessful forays to Edinburgh and retreated to Dunbar where he could receive supplies by sea. Leslie occupied Doon Hill, two miles south-west of the town. Cromwell's position had been on the links next to our hotel. He declined to give battle. His army had been struck by sickness, was demoralised and faced a Dunkirk situation. But Leslie's Information, Intention and Method were flawed. Provoked by impatient advisers he came down from the hill to attack. Cromwell executed a tactical overnight deployment and scattered Leslie's extended right flank at dawn. Leslie lost a battle he should have won.

In September 1745, during the Jacobite rising, General Sir John Cope landed a Hanovarian force at Dunbar. His dragoons found Bonnie Prince Charlie's troops at Prestonpans. Cope failed to guard a marsh to the east of his defences. The Prince had a reliable source of information—local knowledge that there was a path through the mire. During the night of 21 September the Jacobites crept along the track for a dawn attack. Cope reformed his line but in the hullabaloo of the Jacobites' Highland charge his artillery was overrun, his infantry and cavalry fled and his baggage train was captured. Cope managed to escape to Berwick with a couple of hundred men. It was a smaller battle than Dunbar, no more than a few thousand men on each side, but offered similar lessons in tactics, use of intelligence, topography, surprise and the effect of the Jacobites' *esprit de corps*. Adam Skirving, a local farmer and bard, lampooned the hapless Hanovarians in the verse 'Hey, Johnnie Cope', one of our favourite marching songs.

The only fighting I experienced at Dunbar was in a boxing ring. Each cadet was set against another of similar height and weight and forced to fight a three-minute bout. One poor fellow, physically ill-equipped for such an encounter, was mauled by his opponent and the bell had to be rung early. Seeing this, some of us came to mutual understandings that we would contrive to hurt each other as little as possible—survival on the cadet course was for the fittest, or the smartest. Not my opponent though. He was a strapping cadet from a Border regiment and looked like a rugby forward. As soon as I saw the glint in his eye I knew he meant business. The ritual handshake over, I received a sharp jab and a bloody nose. The other cadets roared with glee. I counter-attacked, arms flailing wildly, and survived the round without humiliation. I still think those boxing matches were a show put on to satisfy the PT instructors' taste for gratuitous brutality.

Towards the end of our course we got some idea of what real soldiering might be like. We were mustered on Barrack Square and briefed for a three-day, 60-mile training exercise over the Lammermuir hills, where we would sleep rough, undertake long forced marches over difficult ground, and simulate attacks on dummy positions.

We set off in Field Service Marching Order, each of us with fifty pounds of kit, rations, steel helmet, rifle and ammo. We sang the Jacobite song as we marched in a three-abreast column following Cope's route along the northern edge of the Lammermuirs. We negotiated checkpoints manned by the Home Guard, whistled at Land Army girls stacking hay in the fields and joked and smoked on hourly, 10-minute halts. On the Lammermuir plateau I checked my map, finding names that sounded like scenes from the stories of Stevenson and Scott: Bleak Law, Black Wood, White Castle, Whittingehame, Friars Nose. I marvelled at the panorama to the north: the golden Lothian farmlands, the warships on the Firth of Forth, Polish-defended Fife on the horizon and the occasional Spitfire sighted in the sky. I am sure most of us sensed history in the making and that we might play a part.

Our instructors were waiting at the battle-training area, smoking by their trucks and Bren carriers on a heather-covered moor. Officers with maps and clipboards sat in open-top staff cars. Tactics were discussed: Information. Intention. Method. 'Any Questions?' None.

We formed platoon and company battle formations and were directed to capture a ridge. Bayonets were fixed and we charged forward, wind in our faces and the sun overhead, whooping and yelling our heads off like the Highlanders who had scattered Cope's dragoons. The mock battles in the heather were made more realistic by harmless but frightening explosive charges and bursts of live rifle and machine-gun fire aimed over our heads by our gung ho instructors.

For two nights, we kipped down in the heather, under a starry sky. On the third day we followed Whiteadder Water towards the sea, sleeping in a barn at Abbey St Bathans that night. We were in a jolly mood on the march back. There were brambles to be picked from roadside hedges, apples from orchards we passed and the welcome puff at a cigarette at our halts. On the coast road from Cockburnspath to Dunbar we stepped and sang 'Pack up your troubles' and popular songs of the time, with ribald variations accompanied by laughter provoked by the irrepressible Sellars—a display of careless abandon and high spirits that we were seldom to feel again. We were young and fighting fit, and the weather in that late summer was glorious. We entered Dunbar at sunset, our heads held high and rifles at the slope, feeling we could take on the whole German army.

That toughening-up exercise was the final stage of the course which would end with our being judged fit to hold His Majesty's commission. I think we knew already who would pass and who would fail. Some cadets had instinctive leadership qualities; some learned the art of command during the course, aided by the army's hierarchy and respect for rank. In both cases, orders would be obeyed without question. Those who failed—and we had a few duds and misfits among us—couldn't control other cadets or lead them without provoking dissent. They were RTU'd and to the ranks. I escaped that fate.

We had to be dressed in our regimental colours for the Passing Out Parade. I remember marching along George Street in Edinburgh to Anderson's Regimental and Highland Tailors, dressed as a cadet with a white-banded forage cap. I left as a second lieutenant in the Argylls with the glengarry I had dreamed of wearing, and black brogues, tartan trews, a Sam Browne belt and service dress tunic with my first pip on the shoulder tabs. I stole glances at myself in shop windows, in between being saluted by every squaddie who stepped by. I felt suitably dressed for the Café Royal, where I stopped on the way back to the station. The parade was held on Barrack Square. We slow-marched with the precision of guardsmen to a haunting pipe tune then took 'Cock o' the North' and 'Hieland Laddie' in quick time, watched by visiting brass hats. Our instructors wished us good luck. Then a few drinks in a bar, a round of farewells and home on a brief leave before reporting to our various regimental depots. I can still picture those happy fellows, but most of us never met again.

On the train I took out my Field Service Pocket Book and signed it with my new rank: 2/LT. T. R. WARD, A & S H. I carried that book with me until the end of the war, along with my service revolver. I arrived at Queen Street station on a foggy Glasgow evening. I could barely find my way. I had forgotten the blackout. From dusk until dawn, street lights were extinguished and all windows blocked out with blinds, curtains or cardboard. ARP wardens who, like the Home Guard, were volunteers promoted to sudden authority, patrolled the streets shouting: 'Put that light out. Don't you you know there's a war on?' Vehicle headlights were masked, with horizontal slits cut out to avoid collisions. The blackout caused so many accidents that pedestrians were allowed to use torches. The authorities allowed some lights in shops, cinemas and other public buildings, but these were switched off when air-raid sirens were sounded.

I don't think I ever saw Glasgow appear so forbidding as on that wartime evening. Virtually all the architecture was Victorian and none of it had been stone-cleaned, as it is now. Decades of coal smoke and industrial pollution had turned every façade of the 'second city of the empire' soot black. I stumbled across the previously familiar George Square, the Cenotaph and statuary looming out of the gloom. Torches flickered as crowds of people passed by. Trams squeaked and rumbled and appeared out of the foggy darkness, trolley poles sparking.

Many buildings were sandbagged, and windows cross-taped to minimise flying glass from bomb blasts. The Glasgow area offered plentiful targets for the Luftwaffe. Near my home there was Barr and Stroud's factory where rangefinders, periscopes, binoculars and gunsights were made. There were dozens of shipyards, docks, and ships on the Clyde. There was a Rolls-Royce aero-engine plant that made Merlin engines for Spitfires, a Royal Ordnance explosives and munitions factory, artillery and tank manufacturers, locomotive works, railways, steel mills, power stations—and over a million people, most living in densely-packed tenements. Scores of barrage balloons had been hoisted above the shipyards and docks west of the city centre. The city had been bombed for the first time in July, although not seriously. During a bigger air raid in September, a bomb exploded near my old office in George Square. The subway station near the street where I was born was hit. In Yorkhill dock nearby, the cruiser *Sussex* was set on fire. A mile of river bank was evacuated for fear that the warship's ammunition might explode.

Glasgow escaped the worst raids of 1940 (there was nothing like the destruction of Coventry in November or the City of London firestorm at the end of the year, the raid that produced the memorable image of the dome of St Paul's standing amidst the smoke and flames). To prepare for serious attacks (which were to come soon), schools, churches and municipal halls were commandeered as bases or billets for Royal Artillery ack-ack gunners, ARP, Home Guard, bicycle message boys, nurses and tea ladies. My friend Chris Mackay helped out at a canteen at Jordanhill Church. Her First World War-veteran father, a director at Highland Distillers, was in the Home Guard (her brother Tom's poor eyesight placed him in reserve; her other brother, Angus, was called up and served with the Royal Artillery in India). Her father had enough petrol to continue to use his black Wolseley, and Chris would drive him from their home at 87 Munro Road to and from his base at Hyndland school. Bankhead school, near my home in Knightswood, had become an Auxiliary Fire Service depot, ARP centre and first-aid station. There was an ack-ack and searchlight battery not far away. My parents had an Anderson shelter in the garden. My mother, ever the optimist, never thought it would be used.

I cut quite a dash in my new uniform when I turned up out of the blackout and the fog. I caught up on local and family news, feigning interest but feeling detachment. My mother moved quietly around the house, fiddling with the blackout blinds. My father, as usual, chatted about music and books. My brothers, Cecil and Harold, who were antic-ipating being called up, wanted to know what the army was like. I was a novelty for local children and girls I knew. On the tram to the station to catch a train back to Stirling, I remember passing Botanic Gardens and the ice cream shop where my mother had taken me as a child. These places now seemed an irrecoverable part of the past. The ice cream shop had closed. It was owned by an Italian family which, like most in Scotland, had immigrated years before. When Mussolini declared war, Italians in the UK were branded enemy aliens. Rumours circulated that their shops were fronts for spies and they were attacked by mobs. The Italians were sent to camps or deported after Churchill ordered the police to 'collar the lot'. The Scottish-Italians seemed the most unlike-ly fifth columnists to me, but the public mood was changed by the war.

I had arranged to meet five fellow subalterns in the lounge at the Central Hotel: Ken 'Tattie' Shaw, a wee chap from Lancashire who had been a law student and had a great sense of fun, whom I had met at Dunbar; Alex 'Sandy' Graham, formerly a student at the Glasgow School of Art, whom I knew from Stirling, who was returning from Bulford OCTU, Wiltshire; Gilbert MacDougall, a medical student at Glasgow University who gave up his studies to volunteer for the Argylls, also a Bulford graduate; and two other newly-commissioned second lieutenants, MacDonald and McGill. We ordered drinks and sat around smoking and comparing notes. Almost everybody smoked in those days, especially soldiers. Tobacco was the universal comforter. We puffed away, agreeing that although we had been on leave and seen our families we wanted no other life but the army, especially as we were officers now. Shaw, Mac and I became inseparable friends.

We arrived at the castle in high spirits and in style—none of the foot-slogging up the cobbled streets that had marked my first arrival. We bundled ourselves and our kit into two taxis and motored up the hill to the Esplanade where I had square bashed not so long before, crossed the drawbridge, scraped through the Gatehouse arch and pulled up to the Top Square. We gathered our kit and ourselves together at the steps of the Officers' Mess and stood around suddenly nervous. We realised sheepishly that we didn't know what to do or where to go and argued about who should lead the way. So much for our cadet course in quick thinking, initiative and taking command. Eventually we sorted ourselves out and reported to the CO, a kindly First World War veteran who directed us through the formalities and showed us to our quarters in the King's Old Building. Then we began tentatively to explore our new surroundings.

The Palace Block's inner courtyard, where the Stewart kings were reputed to have kept their pets, was known as the Lion's Den. We felt we were going to be thrown into one, painfully aware we were at the bottom of a rigid pecking order. So it was a relief to be treated with hospitality typical of a Highland regiment. Dinner at our inaugural Mess Night was accompanied by ritual and etiquette: the formal dress, the fire blazing in a baronial hearth, the polished mahogany table, the regimental silver, and passing the port while toasts to battle honours and the king were fired across table-top candelabra. This was our first experience of the privilege, not to say luxury of rank, and I liked it.

The room was decorated with relics: a picture of The Thin Red Line; the battle-tattered Balaclava colours with the crown and thistle emblem that the Highlanders saw as they held the line when the Russian cavalry charged; the Lucknow Pipes, played during the Indian Mutiny when the regiment raised the siege of the British Residency, winning six Victoria Crosses; weapons from the Peninsular War when the Argylls fought Napoleon's forces during the retreat to Corunna. This was intoxicating stuff on top of the whisky we had drunk. Sitting beneath the regimental colours and flags of the past, which swayed in and out of focus before my eyes, I felt had joined an élite whose valorous tradition I was destined to uphold.

The pipe major, a man of special standing in a Highland regiment, initiated us into an unexpected regimental tradition—when he took us outside to start early morning lessons in Highland dancing. The squaddies found this highly amusing and we didn't take it seriously, until the pipe major told us about the winter Regimental Ball and the bonnie lassies from Stirlingshire's aristocracy who would be just itching to dance with handsome and accomplished young officers.

I shared a room with Sandy Graham. We were both adjusting to army life and wartime uncertainties and had experiences of civvy street and interests in common. An artist and a bit of a rebel, he was not all that interested in being a soldier. I enjoyed walking round with him as he sketched the gargoyles on the Palace Block's façades. He was a fan of the cartoonist David Low, whose most famous creation was Colonel Blimp. I met a few Colonel Blimps during the war, but not in the Argylls. Graham and I enjoyed for the first time the privilege of being wakened at Reveille by a batman bringing us our 'gunfire' (mugs of hot sweet tea). We also felt rather smug being saluted right, left and centre by our former NCO taskmasters. That punctiliousness didn't last. They knew that the makings of a good officer meant more than a fancy uniform, a pip on the shoulder and a swagger stick. They told us so and put us in our places. Second lieutenants were two a penny, now that OCTUs were churning out junior officers by the hundreds for the expanding army and, rather ominously, to replace casualties.

At the beginning of December, Shaw, MacDougall, MacDonald, McGill and I were posted to the 1st Battalion in the Middle East. Some of us would have preferred the 2nd Battalion, the 93rd of Balaclava, then in the Far East. I was later to be grateful for the luck of the draw and the mysterious workings of Providence that sent us to Egypt and not to Malaya.

I looked forward with the eagerness of youth to my first taste of travel, adventure and military glory, facing whatever challenges awaited me as a test of my manhood, ignorant though I was of all that they would involve. The others felt the same. We knew nothing of war then, or what it could do to a man. We had noted but didn't speak much of the odd and disturbing behaviour of one officer. He was a survivor of Dunkirk, generally thought to be 'off his chump' and was humoured gently in the Officers' Mess. I wondered what terrifying experiences he must have gone through that made him cry out in the night. By day he would talk and shout commands to his dog, which had been left in France. Later in the war, I understood his malaise: once I'd seen more cases of 'battle fatigue', its causes, and felt it myself.

3 CROSSING THE LINE

I was the youngest son in my family, the first to be called up, and the first to be posted overseas. Only a few days' embarkation leave were allowed and my memory of these is of awkward farewells. My departure meant the prospect of a long separation and who knew how many years of uncertainty for my parents? The Argylls' 1st Battalion was in Egypt, but it might be deployed anywhere. Soldiers' families faced months or years of anxiety before prayed-for good news and safe returns. All feared the War Office telegram with its blunt summary of wounds or worse. My brothers made light of such forebodings. My mother tried to be cheerful and optimistic as she fussed over the food, explaining that rationing had begun to bite. My father and I chatted aimlessly to mask feelings unexpressed. He gave me a new edition of Shakespeare's Sonnets; my mother gave me her *Pocket R.L.S.* It was a cold morning when I left. I wasn't to know then, but I would never see my father again.

I had orders to report to Worcester army depot, to join a draft of men of the Worcester Regiment and accompany them as reinforcements to their battalion in the Middle East. Shaw, MacDougall, MacDonald and McGill had the same instructions. It was with mixed feelings that we met at Central station's rendezvous, a First World War howitzer shell used as a charity box. Groups of soldiers and sailors stood around, some with sweethearts saying goodbye and crying. Our train was packed. We shamelessly flaunted our travel warrants and rank to secure a compartment and settled down as the train steamed and rumbled across the Clyde. We chatted for a while, joking about the regimental ball we'd miss. Crossing the border into England was hardly an adventure for me, or for Shaw who was from Oldham. The route was familiar from holiday trips to visit relations in Morecambe and St Anne's. I had also enjoyed a cricket tour to Yorkshire with Cecil before the war. My father was Scottish but my mother, Alice Mary Norris, came from Lancashire. Being an Argyll, I tended to play down my English side, although I was proud of it.

The three Macs didn't relish the prospect of being associated with men of a mere English county regiment. MacDougall, a dour, pure-blood clansman from Islay, felt affronted at having anything to do with the likes of the Worcesters. Our arrival caused a stir. Few folk in that part of rural England had ever seen a kilted Highlander, and MacDougall's evident contempt for all things English (Shaw exempted) caused some tension. I thought the Worcesters were fine men, evoking the England of yeomen and eccentrics we were defending against Nazi tyranny. We established mutual respect by comparing campaigns our regiments had in common. Some of the draft had been evacuated from Dunkirk; their 1st Battalion was in Egypt, their 2nd in India. Like the Argylls, the Worcesters had fought in the Peninsular War, the Indian Mutiny and the Boer War. They had also been at Culloden, which didn't please MacDougall at all.

We saw little of Worcester, as after reporting to the depot the five of us, together with two Worcester subalterns, Mellors and Williams, were billeted at Priors Court, a rambling Tudor-style manor house near the village of Callow End. This was Elgar country which I would otherwise have enjoyed. But that winter of 1940/41 was the coldest in years, with frost and snow all around. Priors Court, its eaves festooned with icicles, the interior primitively furnished from army stores, was a bleak billet, mercifully kept warm by log fires. There we lived a spartan existence for a few weeks, on duty at the depot each day. We got to know the men of the draft, supervised kit issues and attended parades and inspections. We had little time for fraternising with the locals and there were few off-duty pleasures to be enjoyed. A dance, a concert, or film show, or a fleeting friendship with any girl we were lucky enough to meet was about the extent of our socialising, apart from a retired brigadier inviting us to his house for sherry. We expected the stereotype of a crusty old officer, a Colonel Blimp. He turned out to be quite different: a courteous, kindly, cultivated gentleman, well versed in local lore and military history. Worcester was associated in my mind with the battle in the Civil War and two of my other interests, music and cricket. I was agreeably surprised to find a kindred spirit who was both an Elgar enthusiast and a cricket follower.

He had served in the Middle East and knew Egypt and talked about Allenby's campaign with Lawrence of Arabia. I was fascinated by this having read *Seven Pillars of Wisdom*. He was inclined to go on a bit as he recollected his early service days and insisted on showing us his photograph albums. He reverted to type when we discussed modern military matters, the course of the war and the part we might play in it. As soon as politeness permitted, we rose to take our leave.

'Remember always keep your feet dry and your bowels moving,' was his parting shot.

'Silly old bugger,' MacDougall muttered rather uncharitably as soon as were out of earshot.

We spent a Dickensian Christmas in our icy billet, huddled around the hearth. Hogmanay passed with little celebration. But after New Year, a dispatch rider delivered our embarkation orders—SECRET: TROOP CONVOY, NO. WS5B, LIVERPOOL. At Pier Head station the next day, I was shocked to see the damage that aerial bombardment could do in a built-up area. The city and the docks had been bombed by the Luftwaffe since August. Two air raids just before Christmas caused the widespread wreckage we saw.

The river swam with warships, ocean liners, oil tankers, merchantmen and Mersey ferries, all belching smoke into the foggy air. The quays were crowded with soldiers, sailors and stevedores. Cranes swung to and fro hoisting cargoes. Because of the Blitz, Liverpool and Glasgow were handling most of the UK's seaborne trade. Convoys of ships arrived with food, fuel, raw materials and armaments from North America and other parts of the world, to keep wartime industries working, the Forces fighting and people fed. Outbound ships carried warplanes, ammunition, supplies, trucks, tanks and troops to defend the Empire. U-boats threatened the trade on which the war effort depended. Their spectre haunted every ship's crew that ventured into the North Atlantic.

Six liners were waiting to take troops aboard. Ours was HMT (formerly RMS) *Windsor Castle,* one of the finest ships of the Union Castle Line. It had been built in 1921 by John Brown, Clydebank, and modernised in 1937. Now it was a grey-painted troopship, having been requisitioned by the Admiralty at the start of the war. Its hull, patterned with portholes and riveted steel plates, towered above us like a cliff as we clutched our kit and clambered up the gangplank. It took a day for some 2,500 officers and men from various regiments to embark, and for their equipment and stores to be loaded on a ship that normally took 600 passengers, their baggage and 290 crew. We scrambled to find our accommodation, climbing up and down ladders and along passageways, bumping into RAF pilots, naval officers and ratings, and other army personnel.

We sailed on the afternoon of 7 January 1941, the *Windsor Castle*'s hooter booming and echoing off the façades of Liverpool's grandiose waterfont buildings. Hundreds of soldiers crowded the decks, leaning on the ship's rails, watching the shore as the light faded. We followed the convoy commodore's flagship, the *Athlone Castle*, a modern Union Castle ship; the Canadian Pacific liner *Empress of Australia* was directly astern of us. Both were transporting New Zealand and Australian troops who had been training in southern England. There must have been some delay in assembling the convoy because we anchored off North Wales. At night, we saw the searchlights and flashes of more raids over Liverpool. On the evening of the 10th, we sailed to Belfast Lough to await ships from the Bristol Channel and the Clyde. At 0500 on Sunday 12 January 1941, our armada of shadowy shapes slipped seawards towards the North Channel, where eleven liners from the Clyde joined the convoy. Our last sight of land was of the south coast of Islay. That was a special moment for MacDougall whose people came from Port Charlotte. We had no idea how long we would be at sea. All certainty seemed to vanish in the cold dawn haar.

The Worcesters had been issued with tropical kit, including solar topees. There was much speculation about where we were heading. In case we talked indiscretely before embarkation and were overheard by spies—there was paranoia about them at the time (posters in railway stations, warned: 'Loose lips sink ships' and 'Careless talk costs lives')—our destination was never officially confirmed. It was entirely possible that the Worcester draft would be sent to India, Hong Kong or Singapore. I'd heard that the Aussies and Kiwis had sailed for Egypt in 1940, but been sent to the UK because of the invasion scare. We did know that, to avoid Italian submarine and air attack, we would not be sailing to Egypt via the Mediterranean. The convoy steamed west, so far out that the seagulls left us.

I stood on the promenade deck and counted twenty-one passenger ships, the majority Union Castle, Canadian Pacific and Cunard White Star liners. Judging by the number of men on the *Windsor Castle*, there must have been over 40,000 troops in that convoy, at great risk to U-boat attack. There was a powerful escort. The unmistakable silhouette of a battleship [the First World War-era *Ramillies*], squatted on the horizon, along with three cruisers and twelve destroyers. The commodore [Vice Admiral Sir Richard Hill] manoeuvred the troopships into seven columns spread across three miles of ocean, each column with three ships in line ahead, all led by a cruiser [HMAS *Australia*]. Astern were two other cruisers [HMS *Naiad* and *Phoebe*] and our battleship. The destroyers formed an anti-submarine screen on both beams. U-boats would have to penetrate the screen to get among the ships. That they might was the danger. The destroyers, bristling with guns, sped about churning up white bow waves. One of the cruisers surged past, raising its big guns skywards, and loosed off a volley from its pom-poms in practice fire. Signallers flashed Morse code messages from Aldis lamps. Blenheim bombers and a Sunderland flying boat flew over on anti-submarine patrol; Hurricanes buzzed about in case of air attack. The *Windsor Castle* picked up speed as the convoy began to zig-zag, an anti-submarine measure.

Despite their speed, liners were easy targets. In October 1940, the Canadian Pacific ship *Empress of Britain*, en-route from Suez to Glasgow via the Cape, was attacked off the Irish coast by a German bomber. Two bombs struck the ship which was set on fire. Most of the 600 or so people aboard were rescued by the navy. While the smouldering hulk was being towed to the Clyde, it was sunk by a U-boat alerted by the bomber's crew. We were alarmed to be told that in November, our ship had also been attacked. A 500-lb bomb lodged in the first-class lounge but failed to explode. It was removed at Greenock the following day. The *Windsor Castle* had a double bottom hull and watertight compartments to keep the ship afloat in case of shipwreck or collision. I was not convinced these features would be much use against bombs and torpedoes. We exceeded the ship's peacetime passenger complement by a factor of four and I doubted that there were enough lifeboats to go round. We didn't complain when we were obliged to take turns on anti-submarine watch, and jumped to calls of 'Action Stations' and anti-aircraft drill.

U-boats and enemy bombers were not the only danger. The troopship convoy that preceded us had been attacked by a German cruiser. And we all knew about the exploits of the *Graf Spee* before it was scuppered. Its sister ship [*Admiral Scheer*] was rumoured to be at large in the

Atlantic. It might out-manoeuvre our battleship. Even get the better of the cruisers. It certainly would not be deterred by the 6-inch gun the navy had mounted on our stern to shoot at U-boats, which were known to surface and attack ships with gunfire to save torpedoes, or by the army's 40-mm Bofors ack-ack guns on deck. We took boat drill very seriously.

Notice-boards around the ship displayed 'friend or foe' aircraft silhouettes, safety notices and lifeboat drill times. Twice a day, sirens sounded 'Boat Stations'. At first, we didn't know what passage to take, ladder to climb or deck to be on as we scrambled outside. But the ship's officers knew the ropes, assigned us to muster stations and told us which lifeboats or life-rafts to use. Roll calls were taken, emergency rations and equipment inspected and life jackets checked. Every soldier jealously guarded his own. Woe betide any man who lost or mislaid his or tried to swipe someone else's. Nervous banter failed to conceal our real fear of ending up in the drink. At night, a blackout was enforced. Smoking was banned on deck. Ship's officers roamed around shouting: 'Put that fag out and get inside.' We could see nothing of the other ships, but heard distant depth charge explosions. For us landlubbers every unusual sound or abrupt change of course caused immediate anxiety. We slept fully clothed. Dreaming, I heard the cry: 'Abandon ship!' But in the morning when I scanned the convoy there were no losses. The *Windsor Castle* steamed majestically on.

I had never been so far out to sea and the experience was exciting and unnerving. The sight of the other ships, and our escorts tacking back and forth at speed, was a reassuring and fascinating daily choreography. I never tired of seeing the destroyers surge off to investigate suspected sonar contacts. Depth charges would be dropped, followed by muffled explosions. Then the destroyers would return, weaving in and out on our beam like sheepdogs. We were now beyond the range of fighter escort. Soon, even the long-range Sunderland left. To avoid U-boats, we sailed in the pale winter sun on a semi-circular cruise that seemed to be taking us first to Canada. The weather was freezing. Battledress and greatcoats barely kept us warm. 'Look out for icebergs,' Mac said. No one laughed. At the purser's office a map of the ship's pre-war route—Southampton to Cape Town, Port Elizabeth, East London and Durban—was still pinned up, along with notices for deck games, dances and shore excursions to Madeira. We never saw Madeira.

At least we travelled in style—the officers that is. The first-class dining room and other upper deck facilities on board the *Windsor Castle*, were still organised on a peacetime basis. We enjoyed four- or five-course meals, served by Union Castle Line stewards, and comfortable two- and four-berth 'Cabines-de-Luxe'. The ship was less of a holiday for the other ranks, living and messing together as they were compelled to do in cramped and squalid quarters below decks. They were squeezed into steerage cabins or slept on hammocks slung in the second- and third-class dining rooms, and endured basic army food accompanied by the noise of the *Windsor Castle*'s engines.

The squaddies groused about the conditions but generally bore their confinement with good humour. Since idleness was more likely to provoke the more mutinous among them and be damaging to morale, daily efforts were made to keep the men occupied. We paraded platoons of Worcesters around the promenade decks as if on route marches; kept them alert with the usual army routine of inspections. The injustice revealed by the contrast between the lifestyles of officers and other ranks almost made me turn Socialist. I like to think it made me a more tolerant officer. Experiences such as these no doubt influenced thousands of servicemen in casting their votes in the post-war general election, when Churchill lost to a Labour landslide.

We must have been half way to Newfoundland when six of the destroyers turned back, having escorted us through the most U-boat-infested waters. The convoy veered south. [*Naiad* and *Phoebe* and two liners departed for Gibraltar; *Ramillies* left west of the Azores; another cruiser, HMS *Emerald*, joined.] A week later, the seabirds returned, the weather warmed up, and we began to feel we were out of danger. We had seen no U-boats. We had encountered no winter storms. The ship's officers appeared in gleaming white tropical kit and scanned the eastern horizon with their binoculars. The sun now rose out of vast billowing cloudscapes ahead of us. After the pewter sheen of the North Atlantic, its glare on the sea and on the officers' whites was blinding. We discarded our winter gear for khaki shorts, shirts and our solar topees. Instead of salt we smelled land, vaguely aromatic: the coast of West Africa.

On 25 January, we sighted a peninsula of mangroves, palm trees and vivid green hills. The air was humid and the temperature rose. We began to sweat. This was Freetown, Sierra Leone, my first glimpse of the mysterious mountains of the Dark Continent. My knowledge of Africa had come from the adventure stories of Buchan, Henty, and Rider Haggard and the novels of Conrad. That knowledge was soon to be considerably enlarged.

Freetown was one of the few ports of call on the convoy routes to and from the Indian Ocean, and its anchorage was crowded. It was remembered by every landlubbing soldier who cast eyes upon it as a bay of disappointment. The *Windsor Castle* slowed as if smitten by the heat and anchored inside an anti-submarine boom. Flotillas of filthy bumboats and oil barges came alongside. We leaned over the rail watching them as they irreverently bumped against the *Windsor Castle*'s privileged hull. Army and air force chaps came aboard, with news and gossip. Others were ferried ashore, where Europeans wearing solar topees stood apart from natives swathed in coloured cottons. Beyond Freetown's tin roofs and wood and brick colonial buildings, and the barracks of the West African Regiment, a range of mountains, not particularly high but coated with steaming rainforest, disappeared into the interior—a world of district commissioners' bungalows, mud and straw huts, gold mines, witch doctors, deadly snakes and disease, or so I imagined. We were issued with anti-mosquito cream but not allowed ashore because of the risk of malaria, so we stayed cooped up on the *Windsor Castle,* like slaves.

Around this malarial and malodorous settlement the sea eddied into mudflats and mangrove swamps that would have been seen by the fifteenth-century Portuguese navigators who named the coast for its reclining lion-shaped hills. In the eighteenth century, the British Government had considered Sierra Leone for convicts but abandoned the idea for the more bearable climate of Botany Bay. Instead, it sponsored a settlement for freed slaves. In 1807, a Royal Navy squadron was based at Freetown to catch foreign slave ships. The place didn't look or feel like much had changed since then. A tattered square-rigger at anchor heightened this impression. Sierra Leone was not John Buchan territory but the darker world of Joseph Conrad.

Our only amusement was the antics of natives, who paddled out in long, slim dug-out canoes that the jacktars of the early nineteenth century would have recognised. We leaned over the side of the ship to see a score of canoes, loaded with wood carvings and fruit, bobbing in the swell. Trading with Africans was against army regulations but we lowered rope baskets with tins of bully beef and army blankets, and hauled up melons and bunches of the first bananas I'd seen since the start of the war. The younger natives, naked except for loincloths, dived for coins we threw. Their grinning black faces would surface with sixpenny pieces sparkling between their gleaming white teeth, to be greeted with laughter and howls of racist abuse from the squaddies.

We sweltered for four days in Freetown's fetid bay. Then, the ship's crew turned salt-water hoses on the canoes to drive them away as we raised anchor. We steamed out with an escort of two cruisers [*Australia* and *Emerald*] and five smaller warships. A few days out, we heard gunfire and saw the cruisers laying a smoke screen. When it cleared, there were no enemy ships in sight. A false alarm. We settled into our closed world, lulled by the whirr of cabin fans, the hum of the *Windsor Castle*'s turbines and the creaking of its double-bottomed hull. Now that we were in the tropics, the men were allowed to sleep in the fresh air out on deck. There they could breathe easily, take salt water showers, gaze on a sky lit by myriads of unfamiliar stars and dream of home, or watch the phosphorescence on the ocean and dolphins diving or flying fish darting in and out of the water. I marvelled at the southern sea's slow dawns and sudden, fluorescent dusks; at the seemingly limitless expanse we sailed on, under skies that were cloudless and sunny by day and moonlit at night. I'll never forget watching the ship's wake dissolve astern and the ocean covering our passage as if it had never happened.

Most of us sat on deck sunbathing and reading, played deck games and took part in tug-of-war competitions. An entertainment committee organised plays and concerts, in which I played a modest part. These were of a high quality for there were many accomplished and experienced performers on board. There was an element of 'dance and skylark' about these entertainments, especially the Crossing the Line ceremony. I joined King Neptune's Court—a dozen of us in home-made costumes on a makeshift stage on deck, watched by an audience of hundreds of the men. Proclamations were read to welcome the ship's 'Captain and Merry Band of Matelots' across the Equator. The men roared with delight at the spectacle of their officers being put through Neptune's initiation rites—by being dooked by me in the *Windsor Castle*'s outdoor swimming pool.

We kept up the regular routine of inspections—of the men, their quarters, weapons and kit, mess decks and galleys—and boat drill. Among the duties of young subalterns accompanying drafts of reinforcements was to give occasional talks and lectures to their men. Since none of us had any experience of warfare, had ever fired a shot in anger, or commanded troops in action this was a daunting task. We tried to flannel our way through by enlarging on some of the things we had been taught at OCTU or on tales told by men back from Dunkirk. But our pronouncements, hesitantly delivered on the tactics to be employed in the face of the enemy, must have seemed far from convincing. Fortunately our prestige had risen during the voyage. Before we left Liverpool, General Wavell's great offensive in the Western Desert had begun. News had come through of the significant part in that campaign played by the 1st Argylls at the Battle of Sidi Barrani, when the battalion, then with the 16th British Infantry Brigade, 4th Indian Division, charged through sandstorms and machine-gun fire to take Italian positions. We held our heads a bit higher in the reflected glory of the battalion we hoped to join and wore our glengarries and tartan trews whenever opportunity came aboard ship. We must have seemed insufferably arrogant to the men of the Worcesters and to other officers.

After a month at sea, we saw the mist on the mountains of the Cape of Good Hope. The next morning we awoke to find that half the convoy had veered off to Cape Town during the night. Three days later, we steamed into Durban Bay and saw the city gleaming in the sunlight. This was the view that Churchill saw as a 25-year-old cavalryman and war correspondent after his escape from a Boer PoW camp in December 1899. I had read his account of his escape and made it one of my talks. Churchill was fêted in Durban and so were we. His reception could have been our own:

> . . . we approached our port, and saw the bold headland that shields it rising above the horizon . . . An hour's steaming brought us to the roads. More than twenty great transports and supply vessels lay at anchor, while three others, crowded from end to end with soldiery, circled impatiently as they waited for pilots to take them into the harbour . . . I perceived that a very considerable crowd had gathered to receive us . . . their enthusiasm was another sincere demonstration of

their devotion to the Imperial cause, and their resolve to carry the war to an indisputable conclusion.

The people of Natal were patriotic and we too received enthusiastic cheers from a crowd on the quay. Despite the pro-German attitude of many Afrikaners, South Africans were fighting with Wavell's forces against the Italians in East Africa and in the Western Desert. Durban families came to the docks to invite us to their homes for lunch or tea. We were welcomed everywhere we went. Every troopship that docked at Durban received the same attention. Many men remember the 'Lady in White' who stood on the quay—a soprano in a white dress and hat who sang 'Land of Hope and Glory' and other patriotic songs through a megaphone as the troopships docked and departed.

Churchill had been placed in a rickshaw and was peddled along the streets to the steps of the old City Hall. We paraded past the new one, an Edwardian baroque fantasy, festooned with Union Jacks. We were cheered by Anglo-South Africans who showered us with gifts of cigarettes and fresh fruit, the festivities watched by impassive, dignified Zulu rickshaw men, and East Indian traders standing outside their open-fronted shops. The ships' crews enjoyed club-like facilities at the Seamen's Institute and the soldiers made the most of unrationed food in the city's service clubs and restaurants. We five Argylls strolled along Victoria Embankment, a palm-fringed promenade with views of the bay. After blacked-out Britain it was amazing to be in a city illuminated at night. However, a blackout had to be introduced after Japan entered the war.

Durban city centre was solidly British colonial, with institutions, architecture and names to match. A statue of Queen Victoria, a Boer War memorial and First World War cenotaph stood among palm trees outside City Hall; the Durban Club on Victoria Embankment was an offspring of the gentlemen's clubs of St James; leafy suburbs named

Morningside and Windermere had a comforting ring. My brother Alec, who sailed around the world in the navy, thought it could have been Sydney or Vancouver—the imperial reach left the same names everywhere—a city of hillside villas, botanical gardens, sea views, cricket and colonial comfort, but with a frisson of Zululand on its edges.

Shaw had found a Union Castle brochure advertising Durban's beaches, sightseeing at Victoria Falls and safaris to big-game reserves. The closest we came to the bushveld were the trophies on the walls and animal skin rugs on the wooded floors of a country club where we were invited to lunch. We enjoyed excellent food—steak, vegetables, exotic fruit, and wine—served by Zulu servants in an atmosphere that would have made Rudyard Kipling and Rider Haggard feel at home. Looking towards the Drakensberg Mountains, I rather fancied I saw Allan Quatermain, Haggard's big-game hunter hero in *King Solomon's Mines,* lounging on the club's verandah: '. . . laid up here at Durban since that confounded lion got hold of me . . .'

Among the antelope heads on the walls was a portrait of the region's most celebrated, now notorious empire builder, Cape-to-Cairo railway dreamer Cecil Rhodes. I was never really a Rhodes fan but I didn't contradict our hosts' opinion that, thanks to him, Africa had been civilised. We all agreed in jolly harmony what a wonderful fact it was that, while Rhodes' railway was never completed, one could travel from Cape Town to Cairo without leaving British-ruled territory. I didn't care much for the smug bearers of the White Man's burden at the country club, but we didn't decline their hospitality. Our small talk was confined to safe territory: the Empire, cricket and the war. I don't know if the word 'apartheid' was used then but its existence was apparent everywhere. In Durban a darker past trotted by.

Haggard and Kipling would have been saddened and astonished, as I was, at the sight of the Zulu rickshaw men, members of a noble warrior race now tamed. They were magnificent, tall, muscular fellows,

clad in leopard skins and feather head-dresses. They moved as effort-
lessly as their forebears, the assegai-wielding hordes of King Cetewayo
who defied the British in the nineteenth century. As a boy I had read
about Rorke's Drift where, in 1879, a company of mainly Welsh soldiers
held out against 4,000 Zulu warriors—the very essence of imperial
adventure. Less well known was the fact that shortly before the siege of
Rorke's Drift, 20,000 Zulus ambushed a 1,200-man British force at
Isandhlwana and killed all but fifty-five. The British commander, Lord
Chelmsford, was exonerated, thanks to his establishment and royal connections. The Zulus were defeated after a swift British campaign in
which the 91st Argylls took part.

We changed ship at Durban—to which one I don't recall, except that
it was overcrowded—and sailed after five days. The Cape Town ships
rejoined us at sea. Four liners, including the *Windsor Castle,* steamed
away for Bombay. After another week or so, we passed the Horn of
Africa and saw the mountains of Arabia. We knew we were destined for
Egypt when we passed Aden and entered the narrows into the Red
Sea—and were at action stations again.

When the Italians entered the war they captured a few frontier outposts in the Sudan, annexed British Somaliland, bombed Aden and
attacked British shipping in the Red Sea. Enemy destroyers and submarines were based at Massawa in Eritrea, the Italian colony from where
Mussolini had invaded Abyssinia in 1935. The Italians in East Africa
were a threat to the security of Egypt and the supply route to the Suez
Canal. Wavell had launched a campaign against them and Eritrea was
under siege. Most of the Italian warships had been sunk by the navy
and RAF, but some remained a threat. Italian mines drifting in the shipping lane were also a hazard. To our nervous eyes, bobbing turtles looked
like them, so we had frequent false alarms. We expected E-boats or
destroyers to be lurking among the islands we passed. Our escort had
diminished to one cruiser [HMS *Hawkins*, which had joined the con-

voy north of Durban]. But all we sighted were dolphins and flotillas of white-sailed Arab dhows, which parted in our path.

Suez was felt before we saw it. A wave of heat enveloped the ship. To port and starboard, red hills shimmered in the haze. A mirage, a phenomenon I would soon get used to, animated the coast. Strange shapes materialising as mosques, oil tanks and barrage balloons; smudges on the water solidified into a score of ships at anchor. We disembarked at Port Tewfiq, a man-made spit of land at the southern entrance to the Suez Canal. It had been built with fill from the canal diggings, and it was where we were unceremoniously dumped into the sights, sounds and smells of Egypt.

It was a hectic scene at the quayside with ships being unloaded, troops disembarking, military vehicles coming and going, railway engines steaming and everyone shouting—all in the glare of scorching sunlight. Across a causeway, the streets of Suez were even busier and noisier, with white-robed figures wearing turbans and tarbooshes, representative it seemed of every race and tribe in Africa. A sea of eager eyes, white teeth and black and brown faces washed up against our train. Hawkers tried to jump aboard, screaming at us to buy their cheap cigarettes, soft drinks and dirty postcards. I was completely disorientated by that baffling landfall. It was 8 March 1941. We had been at sea for two months and sailed 15,000 miles.

4 CAIRO

THE TRAIN STEAMED NORTH along a dismal desert corridor. The canal, on a parallel course on our right drifted in and out of view, making the occasional ships we saw, whose masts, funnels and upper decks could still be seen, appear like wrecks marooned in the sands. Those of us who had imagined an ancient land of palm-fringed oases, Arab sheiks on white stallions, or Shelley's 'Ozymandias' were initially disappointed as we passed army camps, ack-ack guns, and mud-brick villages barely distinguishable from the desert. There was no relief from the stink of coal smoke, from the hard wooden seats, the heat and the hawkers at every stop.

That inauspicious first impression coloured our subsequent dealings with the Egyptians, few of whom we trusted and most of whom, I suspect, despised us in return. The Egyptians had no love for the British empire. In the 1860s while the Suez Canal was being dug, Egypt's French-educated ruler, Khedive Ismail, began to modernise the country and bankrupted the state. The British invaded Egypt in 1882, primarily to secure the canal. In 1914, the Turkish-appointed khedive was deposed ending four centuries of Ottoman rule. None of those events, or the influx of soldiers from Britain, India, Australia, New Zealand and South Africa, had much impact on Egypt's essential character: its antiquity, Islamic courtesies, heat, dust and squalor.

I remember the unexpected chill in the desert air after dusk when we arrived at the township of Geneifa, south of Ismailiya, 100 kilometres east of Cairo. We tumbled off the train and, bombarded by commands, formed up to march to the Infantry Base Depot. In the dark it looked like a set from one of those post-war PoW escape films. The next day we found that we were living like ants, in a small part of a vast camp where soldiers new to Egypt were sent for acclimatisation, desert training and postings to their regiments. We were quickly relieved of our responsibility for the Worcesters, who were posted to their 1st Battalion, then in Eritrea, and whatever fate awaited them.

Parade-ground rows of tents and wooden huts—bivouacs, barracks, bath-houses, messrooms, cookhouses and offices—stretched away into the desert. There were hundreds of men of all types and nationalities, a cross section of Wavell's desert army. At first, I felt lost among them all. Most were drafts of reinforcements but we also saw suntanned and sharp- or glazed-eyed desert hands hurrying purposefully to and fro in transit, returning from courses, or recovering from sickness or battle wounds. We regarded these veterans with awe. They returned our interest with a mixture of sympathy and superiority, and called us 'pinkies', until we aquired their desert tans. Anyone with a few weeks in Egypt proclaimed expert status. Some had been in the desert too long. I remember the odd behaviour of one older officer who attracted attention to himself by wandering about wearing a monocle. He would turn and glare whenever he felt someone was staring at him, detach the monocle and tap his glass eye with it, then about-turn and march off. Other officers had wangled cushy jobs at the base depot. Far from being old desert hands, they had no intention of straying further than the services' clubs and fleshpots of Cairo.

No newcomer to Egypt was exempt from gyppo tummy or the flies. I must have swatted my first million or so at that inhospitable camp. The parting words of the brigadier at Worcester had little relevance for us in our sorry state as we trotted or staggered to and from the latrines during the first few weeks. Other horrors were in store. Few of us escaped itching groins caused by lice, sweat rashes provoked by prickly heat, dysentery and typhus carried by water, flies and lice, or scabies and crab lice picked up from infected blankets and laundry. Not that conditions were insanitary or unhygienic. The army could be faulted on many aspects of its administration but as far as the health of the troops in the desert was concerned the authorities were fully alert to the many dangers. A regular stream of orders and instructions descended on unit commanders stressing the need for vigilance in such matters. But human nature being what it is they were not always followed strictly to the letter, especially among large bodies of troops where the risk of infection was highest. Even those most dedicated to the cause of health and hygiene fought a losing battle against the constant menace of millions of flies, bugs and parasites. I still mourn the death from typhus of a boyhood friend, Davie Rankine, shortly after his arrival in the Middle East early in 1943.

Occasionally we escaped from the camp, to the Bitter Lakes where we swam in clear and buoyant water. Within weeks, I was as bronzed as any desert warrior. On some evenings we were entertained under the stars at the camp's outdoor cinema (bench seats for the men and wicker chairs for officers), where films were projected onto a canvas screen through a haze of dust, cigarette smoke, flying bugs and moths.

It was after one of those film shows that one of our gang got himself arrested. He was the son of my brother Harold's boss at Scottish Legal Assurance, had been a friend of MacDougall's at university and was now a second lieutenant in the HLI. To relieve the monotony of our existence we would go into Ismailiya for a drink and a meal at the Officers' Club and a wander round the town. One evening, this bold lad drank too much and fancying perhaps that he was in the Western we had just seen went on the rampage, recklessly taking pot shots at street lamps with his revolver. The few Egyptians who were about fled for cover as we tried to restrain him. Soon, the sheriff arrived in the shape of a lieutenant and two other members of the Military Police. The luckless subaltern was disarmed and placed under close arrest. A court martial followed and he was cashiered and sent back to the UK. It was to his credit that he overcame that disastrous setback to his military career and made good by regaining his commission and serving in another regiment.

Word of the 'Shoot-out at the Bitter Lake' got around, so we were lucky to be allowed day passes to Cairo. Most of the way the road ran alongside the Sweetwater Canal, a misnamed ditch linking the Suez Canal with the Nile. At the drop-off point at Ramses railway station, hordes of street touts and crippled, diseased beggars even more numerous than those at Suez held forth hands for baksheesh and yelled abuse when ignored. Negotiating these obstacles, I felt that MacDougall's contempt for the local riff-raff—'bloody wogs'—was amply justified. If the Italians and Germans had taken Cairo, they too would have been greeted with the hawkers' obsequious truculence and cheated at every transaction.

Every mode of transport invented seemed to be on the streets of Cairo: squeaking carts and gharries, donkeys loaded with bales of cotton, clanking single-deck trams, army trucks and big American cars. Pavements were packed with shoe-shine boys, street-stall sellers, taxi touts and groups of off-duty soldiers keeping together. Cairo may have been the HQ of Middle East Forces with General Headquarters based in a villa by the Nile but, apart from the soldiers, you wouldn't have known there was a war on. There seemed no shortage of goods in the department stores. There was no rationing and there was no blackout. Shops and cafés were lit, except when air-raid sirens sounded. The city was not bombed because the Italians and Germans hoped the Egyptians would welcome them, and Churchill had let it be known that if Mussolini raided Cairo the RAF would bomb Rome.

No city can have been less affected by the proximity of war. British civil servants and base wallahs seemed to put in a few hours' work in the mornings and spent afternoons at Groppi's Parisian-style café, Shepheard's Hotel or the Gezira Club. The club, located on an island on the Nile, boasted tropical gardens, sports fields and a lido. I recall watching a cricket match there and found myself standing next to an RAF officer at the bar, no less than Walter Hammond, one of England's finest players. It didn't matter that he only held a sinecure in the air force recreation unit. He was a boyhood hero of mine and I was too overawed to dare speak to him. I went to a concert at the Société de Musique d'Egypte, bought sheet music at J. Calderon (Pianos, Musique, Phonos and Radios) and books at Librairie La Renaissance d'Egypt. I saw *Merrie England* at Cairo Opera House, an Italian-designed building opened in 1869 to celebrate the completion of the Suez Canal. I enjoyed the irony of its auditorium resounding to the robust strains of 'The Yeomen of England', when the Italians were still smarting from their crushing defeat in the Western Desert.

Cairo's press was censored except, it seemed, for the society columns, the authorities being obsessed with keeping the Egyptians in awe of British pomp and power. The effect of this was a base wallah culture of complacency. At Shepheard's Long Bar, notorious for gossip and rumoured battle orders, off-duty officers were served by silent *sufragis*. In the Moorish-style lobby there were two Nubian caryatids whose voluptuous breasts were well-polished, having been fondled by three generations of British officers. The ghosts of Churchill, in Cairo after the Battle of Omdurman, and Lawrence of Arabia, after taking Aqaba from the Turks, roamed the corridors. Cocooned in the imperial past at Shepheard's you felt no enemy threat. Soldiers who knew the reality of retreat after Rommel's Afrika Korps arrived in Tripoli in February 1941 detested the place and scoffed at the newspapers' 'jolly good show' journalese.

A remembered highlight of the unreality of wartime Cairo was a visit to the Sphinx, whose battered features might have inspired the colossal wreck of 'Ozymandias' half buried in the desert sands. I also made a stiff climb to the top of the great Pyramid of Giza accompanied by an Egyptian guide and a Scots Guards officer, Lieutenant Raymond Willis, whom I met at the base depot. The sun was dipping into the desert as we pulled ourselves up the monument's stone blocks. From its 140-metre summit, its lengthening shadow spread towards Cairo, where the domes and minarets of the old city glinted in the dusk. I remember running my hand over some graffiti. The most eroded marks were French: Napoleon's soldiers, now forgotten.

Old Cairo's mosques and souks remained a mystery to most of us as we rarely strayed from the European quarter's French boulevards. It was possible for the tens of thousands of soldiers stationed in and around Cairo to avoid mixing with Egyptians other than the hired help. The army's guide to Cairo listed approved hostels and clubs. These offered beds (soap, towel, bath, or hot or cold showers provided), games rooms, reading rooms, dining rooms and bars for officers, and canteens for other ranks. The Services Club at Ezbekieh Gardens put on dances and concerts to which members of HM Forces were 'invited to bring their lady friends'. The guide did not mention the Berka red light district, for many soldiers the city's main attraction.

We had been without mail for over two months while we were at sea and it took some time for it catch up with us. When it did we were able to read first-hand accounts of the air raids at home. On two consecutive nights in mid-March, hundreds of German bombers attacked Clydeside. Clydebank's shipyards and factories escaped serious damage, but the town was devastated. The red sky from the fires was seen from Edinburgh, fifty miles away. In Glasgow, bombs hit Partick and other west end neighbourhoods I grew up in. The Art Galleries had a near miss. Suburban Knightswood was hit—the German pilots, it was thought, mistook the moonlit surface of nearby Great Western Road boulevard for the Clyde. Over a hundred people were killed or injured when the AFS depot and first-aid post at Bankhead school was hit. One huge parachute mine fell on our minister's house in Baldwin Avenue, barely 250 yards from our own home. My parents and brothers spent the terrifying nights listening to Heinkels and Dorniers droning over-head, and being shaken by bomb blasts as they huddled inside the Anderson shelter that my mother never expected to use. My father had a heart attack brought on by the bombing.

The fact that our families and homes were in danger and as much in the front line as any combatant gave us an added sense of purpose and a better grasp of why we were fighting. We were anxious to get on with it and impatient for our postings to come through. When they did they brought disappointment for me, because only four officers were required at that time. Their names were picked alphabetically. To my chagrin, the three Macs and Shaw were sent for. I was left behind feeling down-cast at being parted from my pals, forced to stay at the IBD and missing whatever action they might see.

The 1st Battalion was training at the Combined Operations Centre at Kabrit on the Great Bitter Lake, in preparation for an amphibious landing on Rhodes. That was cancelled after the Nazis invaded and occupied Greece. Many of the troops sent to help the Greeks were evac-uated to the island of Crete. In the Western Desert, the Afrika Korps had advanced to the Egyptian frontier and Tobruk was under siege. The Argylls were moved to desert, to dig defences at Mesra Matruh and to guard RAF airfields. I found myself spending more time in Cairo, on a course at the Middle East Tactical School.

I suppose I should have been grateful the luck of the draw served me so well then and did throughout the war, because the battalion was sent from the desert to disaster on Crete.

The newspapers of Cairo gave little away about the Battle of Crete. However, Shaw, MacDougall and McGill told me stories that made my hair stand on end. At Alexandria on the night of the 17/18 May, the battalion boarded HMT *Glengyle* and sailed for Crete, escorted by an anti-aircraft cruiser and two destroyers. The Argylls landed in darkness at Tymbaki, on the island's south coast, after a 24-hour voyage. On the 20th, the Germans launched a massive paratroop assault on the north coast. Half the battalion remained in the south: to defend the beach for reinforcements which never came; to foil parachute landings, which happened miles away; and to prepare an airstrip, which wasn't needed because the RAF lost or evacuated the few aircraft it had on the island. The CO, Lieutenant-Colonel R. C. B. Anderson, led the other half of the battalion through the island's mountainous spine to help the 14th Infantry Brigade at Heraklion on north coast. He found a hopeless situation.

Despite a furious initial defence of Crete by New Zealanders and armed locals, the Germans secured three bridgeheads. Their first assault battalion was wiped out by Kiwi sharpshooters as it landed, but the Luftwaffe established complete air superiority. Gliders and transport planes landed more German paras. The Allied force—a mixed bag of British, Australian, New Zealand and Greek units—retreated to the south coast in disarray. Lack of transport and petrol, and useless radios, added to the shambles. Communications were so bad that our troops listened to BBC news bulletins to find out how the battle was going in other sectors. Heraklion was almost surrounded. Anderson's men fought their way through amidst confused fighting. A platoon led by Shaw walked into the town unopposed; others ran a gauntlet of Stuka dive-bombers and massed paratroop drops. Second Lieutenant J. W. S. 'Jock' Hamilton of A Company told me how, armed with a rifle and fifty rounds, he had hidden in a ditch and helped break up an enemy dawn attack, shooting Germans until his ammo ran out. When the CO congratulated him, Jock had replied: 'The place was hoaching with Jerries. I couldn't miss, sir.' But individual acts of courage on Crete were not enough in the face of overwhelming odds.

On the night of 28/29 May, my friends, with their half of the battalion and the Heraklion garrison, were evacuated by the navy. At 2330, two cruisers and six destroyers appeared offshore. By 0300, more than 3,000 men had silently left their positions and embarked, the Argylls aboard the destroyers *Hotspur, Imperial* and *Kimberly,* and the cruiser *Orion.* The flotilla's commander [Rear Admiral H. B. Rawlings], knew he had to steam out of the Luftwaffe's range before dawn. But there was a delay: *Imperial*'s steering jammed, caused by a near miss the day before, and the crew and troops had to be transferred to *Hotspur,* which was then torpedoed and left to sink. When the first Stukas attacked at 0600, another destroyer, *Hereward,* was hit and turned back, was beached, and the soldiers and crew captured. *Hotspur, Kimberly* and the other ships were attacked repeatedly by Stukas on the way back to Alexandria. Bombs plunged through the decks of the cruisers *Dido* and *Orion,* causing hundreds of casualties, in scenes of unimaginable carnage. The attacks continued until 1500. By the time the survivors arrived at Alexandria, 800 of those who had embarked at Heraklion were dead, wounded or missing.

On the south coast of Crete, the remaining Argylls were stranded and taken prisoner. Out of a battalion 655 strong that had embarked just ten days earlier only 312 returned to Alexandria. That number was later increased when a score of men managed to escape and return by devious routes to Egypt to rejoin the battalion.

Despite what lies behind the grim statistics of Crete and all that I heard from those who survived the fighting and made a safe return to Egypt, and all that I have read about the campaign since, I have always regretted not taking part: to be able to declare with pride, 'I was in the Battle of Crete.' While the battalion was in action, I had finished the METS course and was stuck at the IBD suffering bouts of dysentery and infection from crabs and scabies—nothing to what my friends had been through I thought, when they asked how I had been.

'Sick,' I told the trio, then admitted not seriously enough to prevent me going to Cairo to break the tedium of an idle existence.

'Cricket at the Gezira Club,' MacDougall muttered.

'Swanning around Shepheard's,' smirked Shaw.

'And Groppi's,' added McGill.

Frontline soldiers despised the base wallahs who frequented these places, calling them contemptuously the 'Short Range Shepheard's Group', 'Groppi's Guards', or 'Zamalek Lancers'. I certainly didn't want to become one of those. I needed to prove myself in action.

On 10 June, I was one of seven officers and 350 new men who joined the battalion at Qassasin, another desert camp, about 20 kilometres west of Ismailiya. The new officers were Major D. C. Provan, lieutenants R. A. P. Caldwell and C. H. Roberts, second lieutenants G. J. Moncur, I. H. Scheurmier and J. C. Pyper. Also joining around that time were Second Lieutenant J. Hunter and Rev. W. C. B Smith, a new padre. It was to Qassasin that the survivors from Crete had been sent—and where stragglers turned up. Nine Jocks posted as 'missing' returned after escaping from the south coast with around sixty other Allied soldiers and nine officers. Their motor launch was stopped by an Italian submarine. The Italians took the officers for questioning but let the men sail on. Navigating with an army compass they reached Mersa Matruh, having sailed 300 miles.

I learned that one of those killed on Crete was Allan MacDonald, one of our group of five young subalterns who had sailed with the Worcester draft a few months before. He was a West Highlander from Oban of proud and fiery spirit and we, his four friends, felt his loss keenly. It was perhaps just as well that we didn't have time to dwell on the matter. On the 14th, the reinforced and reorganised battalion entrained at Qassasin for Sidi Gaber station, Alexandria. The journey was overnight. We arrived at 0600 and formed up to march to Mustapha barracks, where I was followed to my quarters by one of the new men.

He saluted, introduced himself as Private Walter Sanders, and reported for duty—as my new batman. I had forgotten I was due this privilege of minor rank. It seemed more in keeping with Sir Ralph Abercromby's army that had landed at Aboukir east of Alexandria in 1801 to beat the French than with Wavell's in 1941. Sanders was also a throwback to the past, like a couthy character from Walter Scott. He had been a janitor at the Bible Training, and Christian institutes in Glasgow where he lived in the attic of their gloomy gothic building. He was devout and abstemious. He must have been unique in the Argylls for I never once heard him utter a blasphemous word, or saw him smoke or take a drink. That fastidiousness was enough to set him apart from his fellows, most of whom drank whenever they got the chance, smoked like chimneys and swore like proverbial troopers.

He disapproved of my occasional lapses into insobriety but was tolerant otherwise, always reliable and blessed with a pawky sense of humour. He always gave me his beer and cigarette rations. 'Waste not, want not, sir', he'd say as he handed them over. That saying might have been engraved on his heart, such was the pride he took in thrift. He was a tiny island of order in the waste and extravagance of the war. He often spoke of himself in the third person. His favourite refrain to me, other than his biblical ones, was: 'I'm thinking it's the lucky man you are with Sanders to take proper care of your kit.' Each day, he woke me with a cry: 'Shake a leg, sir!' Then he'd rustle up his trademark breakfast of tea and pancakes. He cheerfully looked after me like a mother hen (when I got married after the war my wife declared that Sanders had thoroughly spoilt me). We got on famously together: the opera-singing fast bowler and the bible-quoting batman. He was a gem of a man and I treasure the memories I have of him.

I had just been given command of the thirty men in 9 Platoon, A Company. Most of those in the platoon had arrived with the new draft, so I was not the only rookie. But having missed the expedition to Crete,

I felt out of touch and not entirely confident. Fortunately, the company commander, Captain Ted Tidmarsh, made me feel part of his team. He was a splendid regular soldier, commissioned from the ranks early in the desert war and a veteran of Crete and Sidi Barrani, where he had been wounded and was Mentioned in Dispatches. His company sergeant-major, McCutcheon, was also an excellent fellow.

The hardened regulars in A Company had served in the desert and on Crete. Some were veterans of the North-west Frontier and Palestine before the war. I was lucky with my platoon sergeant, Alexander Bloomfield. He was a regular soldier who had joined the army in 1936 as an eighteen-year old Territorial. He had served with the 2nd Battalion in the Far East, joined the 1st in Palestine and had seen action at Sidi Barrani and Crete. He came from Greenock, the port on the Clyde, and he was better-groomed than any ship's captain. His impeccable dress and manly bearing set a standard that he expected of us all, particularly impetuous junior officers like me. He understood my evident lack of experience and became my constant guide with his advice, efficiency and loyalty. Kipling once wrote: 'The backbone of the army is the non-commissioned man.' Sergeant Bloomfield, until I found my feet, was mine.

The platoon was billeted for a while in an insalubrious quarter near the Western Harbour. Mustapha barracks wasn't much better. We were plagued by fleas and bedbugs. Shaw and I used blowlamps on our iron bedsteads to deal with the bugs, and shone torches down our bedsheets at night to catch the fleas on the hop. We were in 'Alex' for security duties: airfield and harbour defence; guarding PoW pens full of Italians, and policing, especially to control civil disturbances or looting during air raids. Once a week, a platoon was rotated to guard Nuzha aerodrome, where I had my first sight of the Desert Air Force in action. Suez and the Canal Zone were raided often (around the time I arrived in Egypt, the canal had closed while parachute mines were cleared) but

Alexandria took the brunt of the attacks. It was the navy's main base in the eastern Mediterranean, and a departure point for Malta convoys and supply runs to Tobruk. A cruiser [*Phoebe*] patrolled outside the harbour on anti-aircraft watch. The air raids, while frequent—sometimes nightly—were ineffective. The bombers flew high to avoid ack-ack and rarely pressed home their attacks. The main hazard during the raids was not enemy bombs but the rain of shell fragments from ack-ack put up by the navy's ships and by enthusiastic Egyptian gunners (nationalist agitators made the Egyptian army suspect and it was confined to home defence). The bombing didn't do much damage to the ships or the docks, but the workers' quarter where we were billeted for a time was hit.

I was just beginning to get to know the other officers and the men in A Company when Captain Tidmarsh sent me on a four-week junior officers' course at the Middle East Weapon Training School in Palestine. I felt that those who had recently been in action deserved a break from battalion duty, but my friends said that they didn't need weapon training after Crete.

I left Alex by train for El Qantara, where passengers for Palestine crossed the canal to the railhead of the Sinai railway. It had been built across the desert during the First World War to supply Allenby's offensive against the Turks, the campaign made famous by the exploits of Lawrence of Arabia. Since that time, British administrators and energetic Zionists had brought progress to Palestine's biblical byways. I found the Arabs courteous, if sullen. Despite having helped defeat the Turks they had been betrayed by the British and French at Versailles, and now felt dispossessed by Jewish immigration. Before the war, there had been an Arab revolt, which the Argylls helped suppress by searching villages for guerrilla fighters and weapons. In March 1940, the battalion had to quell Jewish protests in Tel Aviv. Peace-keeping was not a role the Jocks, some of whom were now in my platoon, had expected to play when they joined the army.

The MEWTS was at Bir Salem, on a low ridge by the Jaffa to Jerusalem road, near a Jewish colony, Rishon le Zion, and the Arab town of Ramla. The training area was centred around a commandeered Lutheran mission—the very place where Allenby set up his HQ after the capture of Jerusalem in 1918. I shared accommodation in the two-storey, stone schoolhouse, with young fellows from a variety of units in the British army and some Australians and New Zealanders. We were all greenhorns with no battle experience, but used to the PT, drill and bayonet training we got. More stimulating were lectures on tactics, with emphasis on desert fighting, and instruction on infantry weapons including the Thomson submachine-gun, the 'tommy gun' favoured by Chicago and Hollywood gangsters. It was all very exciting, the perfect summer camp for hot-blooded young men.

The climate was benign and the location, among cypress and eucalyptus groves and orchards, was delightful. We enjoyed an active, open-air life free from the infections of Egypt, and were well fed and looked after. Huge Jaffa oranges grew abundantly in the region and we relished their rich, juicy fruit. We enjoyed an open-air swimming pool and an occasional meal and drink at a nearby officers' club. An added interest was the presence of a military hospital not far away. Groups of nurses would join us at the pool or for a dinner and a dance at the officers' club. I had a fling with one of those girls, the daughter of a Highland laird. A year later, I met her in Alexandria, in hospital after a traffic accident. MacDougall and I had been out on the spree, when our gharry crashed into another and a shaft slashed my right leg. I had to restrain Mac from beating up the driver, then passed out. I remember coming to, wakened by a kiss on my forehead. I opened my eyes to see her smiling face. My convalescence was aided by her company around town. That brief renewal of our friendship came to an end some time later in Cairo. By then she was engaged to a Royal Army Medical Corps doctor, so that was the end my only wartime romance.

While in Palestine, I made day trips to Jerusalem and Bethlehem. The influence of my devout parents, a church-going background, scripture studies and a love of psalms and hymns had made me susceptible to biblical resonances. But in both places, I found the most sacred sites woefully commercialised. In 1917, Allenby and Lawrence had walked through Jerusalem's Jaffa Gate to be greeted by liberated citizens. I was surrounded by souvenir sellers. I escaped to the walls, and walked above the city's carpet of rooftop domes and sunless alleys. From the Mount of Olives, the view of the blue-tiled Dome of the Rock, and the Holy City, looked like a Renaissance painting. Amidst mosaics and flaking frescoes in the Church of the Holy Sepulchre, apparently the site of the Crucifixion, I touched crosses scratched in the stones by pilgrims since the Crusades. The Arabs and Jews felt Jerusalem was theirs. I too began to feel proprietorial, sensing the fervour of the Crusades and the conviction of the Christian soldier. It was not a coincidence that the symbol of the Eighth Army was a Crusader's shield and cross.

After the weapons course, we appeared to be confident young officers, keen to get back to our battalions and into action. That was what we said to each other on the train back to the canal. But I am sure the others shared my private doubts and fears: of being killed or maimed, or exposed as cowardly or incompetent.

When I got back to Alex at the end of July, I found that my tin trunk, which had been left behind, had been broken into by thieves and the contents rifled. One of the items stolen was my army greatcoat which no doubt kept some scoundrelly Egyptian warm at night for many years thereafter. Of more concern was the disappearance of the thirty-one officers and 631 men of the battalion. All gone. There were no orders or messages. Then I bumped into Shaw, who had stayed on to play a legal part in a court-martial. The battalion had left for Suez and Eritrea two weeks before.

The court-martial was delayed. Shaw persuaded me to stay and we hung around Alex for a few weeks—no duties, time on our hands, and money in our pockets, living the life of Riley, at Pastroudis Café, the beaches of Stanley Bay, the Sporting Club, the Union Club and the Cecil Hotel. Pastroudis, in the European quarter, an area of avenues, period architecture and rattling trams, still served a pre-war menu of ice cream, pâtisseries and Greek coffee. The Corniche, with its beaches, sea breezes and glorious vista of the Med, was unchanged by the war, apart from numerous off-duty Forces personnel who sunbathed and swam there and at the Sporting Club's pool. The Union Club's restaurant and the bar at the Cecil Hotel, a source of much uncensored information, had never been busier. The Moorish-style Cecil, on the Corniche, was *the* watering hole for desert army officers. It fairly brimmed with them, and a hotchpotch of navy and RAF types, Waafs, Wrens, Free French, Levantine merchants, Balkan riff-raff, war correspondents and possibly spies. The producers of *Casablanca* could have taken it as their model.

Our day of reckoning came at the end of August, when we were ordered back to Qassasin to join a draft of troops being sent to Eritrea. We reported to Suez, from where we sailed for Massawa. As we steamed out of Port Tewfiq, we passed a wrecked troopship, the *Georgic,* half-submerged, beached and rusting after being bombed. We were to see many more wrecked ships shortly.

5 ECHOES OF EMPIRES

WE SAILED ON THE 'WESTERNLAND', a wheezing, geriatric steamer built in 1917 that had been fitted out for the North Atlantic, not the tropics. The heat was breathtaking, even when we stood by the rail to catch the limp breeze the old steamer's progress aroused. The azure of the Red Sea, the white coral sand on the red desert shores, and the humidity were intense. The teak decks were scorching. Metal fittings burned fingers at the touch. Our cabins were oppressive. Prickly heat plagued us. The food, army tinned bully beef, spilled from its containers like steaming farmyard slops. The lavatories stank and so did we as we sweated on the week's voyage to Massawa.

To open the harbour for navigation after Allied troops captured Massawa from the Italians in April, minesweepers had swept the narrow approach channels that flowed between barren islands and coral reefs. We had plenty of time to observe these because, instead of docking, the *Westernland* shuddered to a halt and anchored offshore. Only one vessel at a time could enter the port and several ships were waiting. So we spent a further miserable night aboard our good ship before being ferried ashore in bumboats in the morning.

We could not have disembarked at a more dismal backwater. This was where the battalion had landed at the end of July. It is one of the hottest places on earth. James Bruce, the eighteenth-century Scottish adventurer, recorded its climate: 'I call it hot, when a man sweats at rest, and excessively on moderate motion. I call it very hot, when a man . . . sweats much, though at rest. I call it excessively hot . . . when all motion is painful . . .' Massawa was excessively hot.

The entrance channels and the harbour were blocked by a disabled Italian destroyer and rows of half-submerged merchant ships, methodically scuttled at anchor. Other ships were beached or waterlogged by the quays. Cranes had been blown up and had toppled into the harbour. Dry docks lay abandoned and warehouses were wrecked. The town, the gateway to the Italian East African empire, was built on two islands linked by a causeway. Before the war, it may have been picturesque, almost Venetian. Its most prominent building was a domed and arcaded nineteenth-century palazzo built for the Ottoman governor, from where the Italian commander, Admiral Bonetti, before surrendering, had ordered the port to be destroyed.

We hung around the docks panting like dogs, idly watching salvage teams sweating aboard the wrecked ships. Paint peeled from VIVE IL DUCE slogans on warehouse walls. Shaw and I wondered how in this climate there could be much enthusiasm for anything. Mussolini had ordered Bonetti to fight to the last man. But the Italians had already been defeated in the interior. Asmara, the colonial capital, capitulated on April Fool's Day, appropriately because plans of Massawa's defences were found there. The British commander's staff invited Bonetti to surrender. They telephoned him from Asmara (it was that sort of war), adding that their CO, Lieutenant-General Sir William Platt, would not be responsible for feeding the 50,000 or so Italians in the capital if the port was sabotaged. Bonetti blew it up anyway. He was captured at the palazzo, surveying the destruction he had wrought.

A column of 15-cwt trucks turned up and we were relieved to be told we were leaving immediately for Asmara, 100 kilometres away in the airy uplands of the interior. Thus we began a trek, following the path taken by Bruce in 1770, that would take me to Gondar in deepest Abyssinia, 400 kilometres as the crow flies. We were not crows. After crossing the causeway to the mainland, we passed a fort pockmarked by shellfire and captured when the HLI, Indian troops and Foreign Legionnaires had attacked in April. We sped on. The road was paved and ran across salt flats towards a seemingly impenetrable escarpment, which we had seen from the ship the day we arrived.

Our route paralleled the course of an earlier campaign. In 1868 General Sir Robert Napier led a punitive expedition from Bombay against an Abyssinian emperor, Tewodores, who was holding a group of Europeans hostage. Queen Victoria's diplomats failed to secure their release. Napier landed 50 kilometres south of Massawa with an Indo/British army of over 13,000 men, and thousands of animals, including forty-four elephants, to carry mountain guns and supplies. He also had 500,000 Maria Theresa silver dollars minted in Vienna, the only currency recognised by Abyssinians and Arab traders. Like us, each of Napier's men carried fifty pounds of gear. It took them two and a half months to penetrate the interior. Our perilous drive took six hours. At the Battle of Magdala, superior weapons and discipline routed the Abyssinians. The hostages were freed. Rather than be captured, Tewodores shot himself, with pistols sent earlier as a gift from Queen Victoria. The Argylls' arrival at Massawa was the first British foray from the Red Sea into the territory since that time.

Soon we were swallowed by lightly-forested glens. We emerged from these to face a succession of steep curves and hairpin bends clinging to fearsome rock- and cacti-strewn screes. A railway—the *serpente d'acciaio* (steel snake) as the Italian engineers and Eritrean navvies who built it at the turn of the century called it—swept elegantly through tunnels and across stone-built viaducts as it climbed from the coast. Like the road, the railway was a superb piece of Italian engineering, and I soon wished I was on it.

The mountainous scenery, when I dared open my eyes to see it, was as melodramatic as any Victorian painting of Glencoe. Each sharp turn offered a new prospect of disaster. Our drivers, mad Indian Army Service Corps men, charged up the tortuous road which in 50 kilometres climbed to 2,000 metres. Unwilling to lose momentum as the trucks laboured on the inclines, the drivers crashed through the gears and took each bend at full speed, hunched at their steering wheels and turning at the last moment to avoid flying into the abyss. There were no safety barriers. Below my truck's running board all I could see were dizzying drops. The sight of Coptic shrines, and a monastery perched on a peak, offered little reassurance. I had never felt closer to my Maker. My driver was elated when the road levelled out on the Eritrean plateau. I was dazed with relief. Except in dreams later, I never saw that road again.

We drove across an undulating savannah broken by rocky and terraced hillsides, clumps of eucalyptus woodland and bubbling streams. The air was fresh, under immense cloudless skies. To the south, jagged peaks floated on the horizon. Because of the recent monsoon we were halted periodically by road crews repairing washed-out culverts. At one such stop, smoking and chatting with Shaw, who was riding in another truck, I heard a rumbling to the south that echoed like artillery fire. A furious electrical storm was blasting the peaks, a distant deluge that accentuated the otherworldliness of the landscape and our expedition. The rains had produced a cornucopia of vegetation. After the steaming purgatory of the coast it seemed we had found a garden of Eden. My driver grinned as he pointed to a road sign: ASMARA, ALTITUDINE, M 2,350. Suddenly, we on the palm-lined avenues of an elegant colonial town.

Asmara enjoys a glorious climate and we reckoned it was one of the better stations we served in. Though the restrictions of a wartime occupation had altered the Italians' lifestyle, cafés were open and there were shops a-plenty. There was none of the dilapidation of Massawa and the destitution and beggary of Cairo and Alexandria. The Italians had been ruthless in their conquest and exploitation of this part of East Africa but they had evidently brought many benefits: the road and railway, and irrigation for crops and fruit trees. In the countryside, they built tidy townships in the image of home for settlers who came out from Italy. They lost it all because of Mussolini's war.

△ Stirling Castle seems unchanged since the war: the Palace Block (left), the Gatehouse, and the Great Hall's crow-stepped gable. ▷ Orpheus Club programme cover for *HMS Pinafore*, at the Theatre Royal, Glasgow, March 1940. ◁ *'Batsman, eh?' the colonel went on. 'No, sir. Fast bowler.'* The Baldwin Cricket Club eleven, Glasgow c.1938. Brothers Ray and Cecil Ward (right and left, back row).

PROGRAMME

THEATRE ROYAL
GLASGOW

△ ▷ 'We sat on deck, sunbathing and reading, played deck games and took part in tug-of-war competitions.' Troops on the *Windsor Castle* en route to Egypt, February 1941.

▷ Troopship convoy in the Atlantic: '. . . twenty-one passenger ships, the majority Union Castle, Canadian Pacific and Cunard White Star liners.' ◁ Left to right: MacDonald, Shaw, Ward, McGill and MacDougall (Argylls), and Williams (Worcesters).

△ The shadow of the Great Pyramid, April 1941. ▷ Ray Ward (left), at the Middle East Weapon Training School, Palestine, July 1941.

▽ Ray Ward's ID card photograph (his Argyll glengarry cut by the censor, in case of capture). △ The view from the top of Wolchefit Pass, and ◁ Gondar Castle, both in Abyssinia, November 1941. ▽ *'All the privileges of representatives of King and Empire.'* MacDougall and Shaw (left) at the Sudan Club, Khartoum, January 1942.

△ *'MacFie had brand-new 3-inch mortars. He was very keen to use them.'* Bombs bursting on Italian-held Venticinque, seen from the Argylls' position on Green Hill, Abyssinia, November 1941. ◁ Abyssinian guerrilla fighter, Gondar. ◁ Left to right: Second Lieutenant 'Jock' Hamilton, Lieutenant Oxborrow, and Captain Tidmarsh at Gondar. ▷ Italian officers captured by the Argylls, Ambazzo Hill, Abyssinia.

△ Jocks of 9 Platoon, 'A' Company, 1st Battalion, the Argylls on Green Hill, cleaning their Lee Enfield rifles before the fight at Venticinque; a 3-inch mortar stands in the foreground. ▽ Piper McCamley leads 9 Platoon on a route march, Eritrea, 1941.

△ 9 Platoon, 'A' Company at Gondar, astride the monument to the Italian conquest of Abyssinia. ▷ Ray Ward at a rest-stop on the Asmara to Khartoum trail. ▽ The Argylls and 15-cwt infantry trucks at Gondar (Ray Ward stands beside the motorcycle sidecar).

The battalion was based at Officio Genio barracks where I found my billet—and Sanders, who fixed me with a mock-reproachful gaze through his wire-frame spectacles.

'Mug of tea, sir?' he said, and then gave me his impish smile.

Bloomfield's greeting was cooler.

'Thought we'd never see you again, sir.'

I sensed some furtive gossip among the men. Bloomfield had seen it all before—the inexperienced platoon commander missing the boat. I had to win his confidence, because if I didn't, he and the men would be reluctant to follow me anywhere. My limited experience in the army told me that their trust and respect were conditional, rank notwithstanding. It didn't work the other way round.

As I dumped my kit, Sanders said the battalion had disembarked at Massawa and been bundled into diesel railcars—except for its sixty-eight tons of baggage, the CO's staff car and A Company, which went by road to Asmara. They had seen the bombing of the *Georgic* on the night they left Suez aboard the *Westernland,* and had sweltered for four days at Port Sudan while the old ship took on coal.

We were interrupted by Captain Tidmarsh. 'The CO wants to see you. At the double!'

Lieutenant-Colonel Anderson was a legendary figure, easily recognied by his habit of wearing a faded glengarry and white mackintosh. Those who knew him well called him 'Andy'. I never got that far. The rest of us nicknamed him 'Cockle-ankles' because of his hobbling walk, the result of bullet wounds in France during the First World War, when he had been a company commander and won an MC. Between the wars, he had been with the 2nd Battalion in China and Hong Kong. He served in Palestine with the 1st Battalion and led it at Sidi Barrani (winning a Distinguished Service Order) and at the Battle of Crete (Mentioned in Dispatches). So it was with some trepidation that I entered his office, stood to attention and saluted him smartly. He had a greying moustache and hair but his face was suntanned and he looked fighting fit. When he rose from behind an antique Italian desk he was obviously ready to give me a good kicking. He demanded an explanation for my late return from the weapons course in Palestine. I put up a spirited defence and made excuses, although I knew I had none.

'Where's your initiative, man?' he countered. 'You could have hitched with the navy or the air force. I've got men here who made it back from Crete quicker than you.' He waved a sheet of paper at me. 'I was about to have you struck off and returned to the IBD.'

I was lucky to escape severe military discipline. My future conduct would be watched. He let me off with an almighty rocket.

'Ward, you're lucky to keep your pip!'

Fortunately I was able to redeem myself in his eyes on one of the company training exercises. I had to take my platoon up an escarpment, re-group at the top, and lead a bayonet charge against an imaginary enemy position. Unknown to me, the CO and the battalion adjutant, Captain B. A. Pearson, were watching us through field glasses. Tidmarsh told me they thought it was great stuff and that I did well. But I don't think Cockle-ankles ever really forgave me for the earlier transgression.

The Argylls had taken over garrison duties in Asmara from the HLI and the Worcesters. The Italian military in East Africa had surrendered in May. But 20,000 Italian and native soldiers commanded by Lieutenant-General Nasi were holding out in northern Abyssinia, at the old imperial capital of Gondar. Their presence tied down British and Commonwealth forces needed for the defence of Egypt. The Argylls had been sent down the Red Sea to help mop them up. Weekly patrols were sent down the Gondar road to Debivar, to advertise to the Italians holding Wolchefit Pass that the British were in the area. The enemy made no attempt to take the offensive, apart from sending a Fiat CR42 fighter to scout over our lines most days.

The battalion's main task was to guard and administer a PoW camp at Fort Baldissera. Thousands of Italian and native prisoners had been processed through camps at Asmara since April and thousands remained. By a strange coincidence I came across an Italian called Toffolo who was related to a family whose company, a terrazzo tile manufacturer called Toffolo Jackson, I had dealt with in my job before the war. Soldato Toffolo PoW had been an unwilling conscript and like many Italians was far from being wholehearted in his support of Italy's entry into the war on the German side. He had lived in Glasgow for a time, liked it, and felt at home in our country. Like the other PoWs he was greatly impressed by the fine show of guard mounting we put on at the camp. He made a cigarette lighter for me in the camp workshop which I used for some years thereafter. He said he hoped to be shipped to Scotland but I suspect his fate was to be incarcerated in a camp in Kenya, where his army's commander, the Duke of Aosta, Viceroy of Abyssinia, died in 1942 after refusing repatriation, preferring to stay with his men.

Asmara boasted all the trappings of an Italian colony established in 1885. The governor lived in a palladian palazzo set in bougainvillea-draped parkland; the bishop celebrated Mass in a Romanesque-style, red-brick cathedral. There was a Piazza Roma complete with a baroque fountain and a Banca d'Italia. Verandahed villas were set in large gardens with fruit trees and tidy lawns. The European cemetery was cluttered with sobbing angels and florid family tombs. Indeed, there were more architectural surprises in that curious corner of Africa. The wide, tree-lined streets were graced by public buildings of unexpected modernity: a Fiat dealership, shops, offices, Neapolitan cafés, a Teatro Augustus and Cinema Imperio (now screening British newsreels). Mussolini had created a showpiece capital of pastel-coloured art deco buildings no more than five years old. Some still bore Il Duce's sinister motto: CREDERE, OBEDDIRE, COMBATTERE (believe, obey, conquer).

We enjoyed what opportunities Asmara offered for relaxation and entertainment. I remember its special sound: the muezzin in the mosque and the cathedral's bells at the start of each day. Each week we added the bagpipes to this duet, when our band paraded in its kilts along Viale Mussolini to impress the locals. I recall a memorable haircut I had there. Short back and sides was the limit of barber shops at home. The Italian barber in Asmara took one look at my army cut and gave me the works: shave and shampoo, haircut, ears, moustache, manicure. I was treated with the deference due a Roman conqueror. Electricity from the power station at Massawa had been restored, so we were able to go to the pictures and the occasional dance, where our attempts at fraternisation with Italian girls were thwarted by wary mothers and aunts. MacDougall, Shaw and I would squeeze into a brand-new, soft-top Fiat Topolino which McGill had acquired somehow and drive about the town on off-duty jaunts, until Cockle-ankles put a stop to such flamboyance and commandeered the car for Battalion HQ.

We had regular cigarette and beer rations—there was no shortage of the local Melotti beer, the brewery having been kept open as an essential military service (and drank a fair amount when we heard that Bloomfield had won a Distinguished Conduct Medal, Jock Hamilton an MC, and Corporal Jennings a Military Medal, all for bravery while serving with A Company on Crete). On Viale Mussolini, I was astonished to see Carabinieri on traffic duty and bureaucrats walking to the jobs that they had been allowed to keep. They were ingratiating and happy to work for us. In return we did not interrupt their siestas. This arrangement was convenient for the British administration. Even Mussolini's apartheid laws were still in place, with the Africans confined to shanties outside the European quarter.

Before the war, British from the Sudan and Kenya were familiar figures in Asmara and the Italians had good relations with them. The polo-playing, anglophile Duke of Aosta had been a regular guest of

British governors at Khartoum and Nairobi. My impression was that the war in East Africa had been a huge inconvenience for the colonial ruling class on both sides. When Aosta surrendered, the British agreed to his very Italian request for 'Honours of war': formally surrendering without being disarmed first. The duke's word ensured that the Italian weaponry was surrendered without sabotage, and he could maintain his dignity and the pretence that the war in East Africa was a gentlemanly affair. It wasn't. During Mussolini's invasion of Abyssinia, Aosta's predecessors, generals Badoglio and Graziani, had used aircraft to attack the natives with poison gas.

A and C companies left Asmara on 1 November, to join the 12th African Division on the road to Gondar. B Company had already gone, having been been ordered to Wadi Halfa on the Nile, where it was flown to the Libyan desert to garrison Kufra oasis, the HQ of the Long Range Desert Group. D Company stayed on at Fort Baldissera.

After crossing the Abyssinian frontier we bivouacked at Adwa. It was there, in 1896, that an invading Italian army was scattered by a native attack and 6,000 Italians and *askaris* were slaughtered. The memory of that humiliation provoked Mussolini's brutality when the Italians invaded again in 1935. Adwa was one of the first places to be bombed. Graziani imposed a ruthless Fascist régime. In 1937, he survived an assassination attempt and dealt out merciless reprisals, but failed to pacify the Abyssinians. We drove on an asphalt road that linked newly-built but now deserted settlements. We saw no Italians in the countryside. Guerrilla fighters and bandits roamed the land. In every valley, we passed clusters of conical, grass-roofed mud huts. Natives peered out of the shadows or stood by the road watching as their naked children shouted and scraggy dogs barked at us. The Italians had not been welcome and I'm not sure we were. At Aksum, once the Queen of Sheba's capital, we saw numerous obelisks. One of the largest had been dismantled and shipped to Rome for Mussolini's pleasure. But Il Duce's minions failed to find Aksum's other treasures. Ethiopian Christians will tell you that the Ark of the Covenant lies there and that the mountains hide King Solomon's mines.

The East African air on the high plateau was freezing at night, the sky crystal clear, glittering with a kaleidoscope of stars which enveloped our elevated camps. After Stand-to, we would snuggle down in our bivvies and lie there listening to jackals howling. Each morning, we woke to the hooting, honking and screeching of birds and the hissing chorus of cicadas. We would eat, strike camp, load the trucks and—leaving the place to its giant lobelia plants, acacia trees, and wildlife and wildfowl—set off at sunrise on the next stage of our safari. To traverse the Tekeze gorge we negotiated 12 kilometres of hairpin bends. Wolchefit Pass, which had been seized from the Italians a month before, was a similarly daunting obstacle. Far away to the south, through fantastic tangles of vegetation, the Simien mountains appeared in dreamy clarity, rising above canyons and islands of table-top hills to 4,500-metre cloudy peaks. Abyssinian emperors once retreated into this formidable splendour to escape enemies, or lure them to destruction.

The Addis Ababa newspaper, *The Ethiopia Star*, sent a reporter to the Gondar front. He noted '. . . hill after hill, each a potential fortress, facing bastion-like eastwards . . . the cheerful Africans, the sturdy Tommies, a famous Scottish regiment which was in the Battle of Crete, tanks, armoured cars, supply convoys and artillery—all are preparing for the final elimination of Mussolini's last stronghold in East Africa.' Bloomfield thought the landscape looked like the North-west Frontier—ideal for ambush. But, so far, there had been no sightings of Italian troops, or the CR42 [the Italian air force in East Africa had been destroyed by that time]. We camped at Dabat, a bleak moorland fuel dump and airstrip 50 kilometres from Gondar. Then the CO recce'd the road ahead and was shot at.

We were sent into action.

Our orders were to attack, capture and hold 'Venticinque', a 200-metre-high ridge overlooking the road 25 kilometres from Gondar. It was one of several points the Italians had fortified on the approaches to the town. These features were about to be assaulted by co-ordinated Allied units (troops in that curious campaign included Gurkhas, Indians, West Africans, South Africans, Rhodesians, Kenyans, French Foreign Legionnaires, Scottish Highlanders and English yeomen). We studied sketches and maps, drawn by intelligence officers and the division's Survey Section to plot the enemy positions. We took over from the 3/6th King's African Rifles on the night of 14/15 November, on a ridge identified in army lingo as Green Hill. As we climbed, we were passed by a single file of black soldiers descending, all smiles and white teeth gleaming in the dark as they whispered greetings of 'Jambo, bwana'. At dawn, as the mist rose, we saw Venticinque a kilometre or so west of our position, across a savannah-like valley. Beyond it lay Ambazzo Hill, another Italian redoubt, then the road descended to Gondar.

As we dug in, the battalion's mortar platoon led by Captain A. N. MacFie arrived. MacFie, who had attended the MEWTS earlier that year, had brand-new 3-inch mortars. He was very keen to use them. We watched the Italian positions through our field glasses and waited eagerly for MacFie's men to fire. Thirty bombs were duly lobbed at the enemy, raising puffs of smoke on the flanks of Venticinque and provoking some inaccurate return fire, which continued sporadically the following day.

On 17 November, the day of the attack, the brigade's 4.5-inch howitzers and 25-pounder field guns bombarded the Italian positions during the afternoon, an accompaniment to an early dinner which we ate on Green Hill at 1530. At 1645, several planes dive-bombed and strafed enemy artillery and mortar positions on Venticinque and neighbouring points. The air attack was followed by mortar fire registered on the same targets. Captain Tidmarsh had established a forward HQ at a captured sentry post in the valley, and two platoons, one from A Company (Second Lieutenant Moncur) and the other from C Company (Lieutenant J. M. Sceales), waited nearby.

At 1730, they leapt from their start lines and rushed forward. The KAR gave covering fire on the enemy's flanks; our machine-gunners on Green Hill fired directly across the valley; MacFie's mortars popped away, adding to the din. The Italians, who had kept their heads down during the initial bombardment, started shooting back. I watched the assault through my field glasses, seeing the tiny figures briefly obscured by a smokescreen from MacFie's mortars as they scrambled up the hill. I was shocked to see Moncur killed by a mortar bomb as he and his men reached the summit. Minutes later, a breathless runner from Battalion HQ, sent by Second Lieutenant Iain Scheurmeir, the IO, handed me a scrap of paper with Scheurmeir's urgent pencil scrawl. I have it still:

> *To Ward: you will proceed direct to Capt. Tidmarsh at HQ just below where the sentry box was and take over Moncur's platoon on hill.*

At the briefing that morning I had methodically written out the plan of attack in a field message pad, as I had been taught to do at Dunbar—INFORMATION, INTENTION, METHOD. All that was immediately chucked as I breenged forward to rescue the leaderless platoon. This was my first chance in action and the order was too exciting for me to feel scared. I sprinted across the valley and dashed up the hill, exhilarated even when bullets from an enemy outpost whistled past my ears as I ran. I imagined myself the hero of a John Buchan adventure story engaged in a daring military exploit. Bloomfield told me later that my platoon had watched, fascinated as I covered the ground in leaps and bounds like a gazelle. I was greeted with relief by Moncur's rather demoralised platoon. Daylight was fading. One of the men was shell-shocked. A breeze sprang up, chilling the sweat that I suddenly realised had broken out all over me.

I must have been oblivious to the risk. I could have approached the hill more prudently but I was keen as mustard to prove myself, and intoxicated with virility and by the violence. Later, I realised that I was lucky to have survived that first foray and not been a statistic like poor Moncur. Among the brutal certainties of the infantryman's war was that the casualty rate among inexperienced but eager young platoon commanders was high.

The moment Moncur was killed the Italians abandoned the hill, throwing a few of their ineffective flash grenades as they left. They lost a dozen men whose bodies lay crumpled over sandbags, water bottles, tinned sardines, ammo and weapons. In one gunpit, an Italian soldier was sprawled over the breech of a Breda machine-gun and two others lay dead beside him, all hit by shrapnel that seemed to have left them unmarked. I turned away from that weird tableau and shouted at the men to organise a defensive position on the hill, where we had orders to remain until 0430 the following morning—to little purpose, it turned out, as the Italians had no intention of retaking the position.

Sceales' platoon withdrew temporarily. African sappers blew up the fortifications, attracting some enemy machine-gun fire which ceased after a stonk. We spent an uneasy night, made more so for me by unwelcome orders from Battalion HQ to recce the ridge. I argued with the adjutant about that; said it was not necessary because I had seen the 'Eyeties' skedaddle. To no avail, so Sergeant Grant and I scoured the top of the hill. We found only more abandoned equipment and empty slit trenches. Later we all got the fright of our lives when some prowling animal jumped on Sanders' bald head as he lay asleep. His bloodcurdling scream set all our nerves a-jangling. Otherwise the night passed uneventfully and we returned to Green Hill the next day, which was my 25th birthday.

That evening there was a skirmish with an Italian patrol. Shots were exchanged, although neither side knew where the other was. There were no Argyll casualties. Lieutenant E. A. F. Oxborrow of A Company reported this activity. The CO decided to reoccupy the position. The ridge was secured at 0200 on the 19th by Sceales' platoon. Back on Green Hill we were woken by a single shot followed by angry shouts in the dark. An investigation into the cause of the rumpus made things clear. Shaw and six men had passed through our lines on a night patrol. On their return a trigger-happy sentry let off a shot that wounded Shaw in the arm. It was only a flesh wound but Shaw was mortified at becoming a casualty in such an ignominious manner. Confusion over the password or the time and place of the patrol's return was the likely cause.

At the end of the week we had a bash in the company commander's tent, my birthday being the excuse. The evening ended with our quartermaster sergeant on his back in front of our position singing and howling obscenities at the Italians. The next morning we struggled to our posts for Stand-to, and watched and listened for the enemy who, we were convinced, had heard every word of the drunken abuse and would be insulted enough to attack us. What we heard was unidentified initially. It became a whisper and a rustle, then a swish and a clatter. We exchanged bewildered looks and reached for our weapons. Seconds later a wave of jabbering clamour broke over our position. We ducked as a stream of dark shapes flashed past, leaping and swinging through the bushes and across our trenches, yelping and shrieking like devils . . . then a rustle and a whisper and they vanished as mysteriously as they had come: a colony of baboons on the march.

Staying on Green Hill was a soft introduction for me and the men new to active service: dug in and bivouacked on our airy hilltop commanding views of the peculiar landscape; an equable climate, good grub from our company cookhouse, cigarette and beer rations, not to mention a rum issue for the cold nights; little chance of encounters with the enemy. In no-man's-land, I was surprised to see peasants threshing corn, as if nothing had happened. The Italians, being attacked from other directions, were retreating to Gondar. They surrendered at the end of the month.

Two of our officers, Major J. H. Carmichael MC and Captain C. H. Roberts MC, involved in the negotiations, were injured when their truck struck a mine. Landmines were not the only hazard. Bloomfield warned me that a favourite Eyetie trick was to hold their hands up or wave white flags and, as we lowered our guns, chuck grenades. Fascist swine. Then they would have the cheek to defend points of honour. When Lieutenant Sceales invited the garrison commander on Ambazzo Hill, Colonel Polverini, to surrender, Polverini announced grandly that he had received no orders from Lieutenant-General Nasi to do so. After an exchange of artillery fire he changed his mind and walked into captivity a contented cavalier, honour satisfied. As far as we were concerned there were no honours of war at Ambazzo and Venticinque. At that moment I despised the Italians for killing Moncur, and for their vanity, their token resistance and their habit of throwing grenades and then running away.

We arrived at Gondar in time for the final Italian capitulation. Nasi surrendered unconditionally an army of 11,500 Italians and 12,000 *askaris*, along with 400 machine-guns and dozens of mortars and field guns, and ammunition and small arms. The defeat was the curtain call of Africa Orientale Italiana: the Italian East African empire.

We took part in a victory parade. Among the Allied units was a frightening band of Abyssinian irregulars: the Patriots. They wore Italian army boots and bandoliers, and carried machetes and Italian-issue Austro-Hungarian rifles, or weapons supplied by British secret agents. These 'fuzzy-wuzzies' evidently terrified the Italians who we rounded up, disarmed and put in PoW pens. Mussolini's conscripts were a dispirited bunch. His officers were a comfort-loving, haughty lot who smelled not of sweat but of *eau-de-cologne*. They were immaculately dressed in gold-braid, riding breeches and leather cavalry boots and coats. The élite Bersaglieri wore cockerel-feathered hats. Not since the most formal occasions at Stirling Castle had I seen such a display of elegant military plumage. They liked their home comforts too, with wines, brandy and toiletries among their personal effects. It was as if we had travelled back to the etiquette and pageantry of Napier's era: that we were the victors of a nineteenth-century colonial war.

Looting was endemic in the town despite dire warnings against such activity from higher command. It was small scale among the troops, including the Jocks, large scale by some senior officers, who were summarily court-martialled. My platoon was ordered to guard the Gondar branch of the Banca d'Italia, from where a cache of Maria Theresa dollars had been stolen. A few sacks of the coins were still there. I like to think these dated from Napier's expedition but they were new. [SOE had been smuggling in Maria Theresa dollars minted in Bombay to bribe tribal chiefs, and Mussolini had sent one million from Rome for the same purpose.] I didn't get any but other precious items fell into my lap. Bloomfield would sidle up: 'Would you like a camera, sir; a typewriter; a gramophone?' I got all three. The resourceful 'Bloomie' then produced a box of Italian opera records. Having fought at Sidi Barrani, he had no scruples about getting his own back. I played those records in tent, bivouac and barrackroom, and they were a great inspiration and consolation to me throughout the war.

We took photos of ourselves on the plinth of an obelisk that commemorated Mussolini's conquest of Abyssinia. The Italian tenure had been short-lived. We had the novelty of reading about our recent exploit on the front page of *The Ethiopia Star*:

GONDAR OPERATIONS
FROM OUR SPECIAL CORRESPONDENT

. . . British troops showed great dash and stamina in the attack on November 17 on Venticinque. One platoon scaled the precipitous slopes in the face of strong fire. They mopped up the summit with bayonets and tommy guns. Another platoon covered a demolition party, an East African field company. The African sappers remained very cool under fire from an enemy machine-gun post, which was eventually silenced by the accurate shooting of an EA field battery.

The paper ran stories on British advances in Libya, the Red Army's defence of Moscow and a piece about the 'Graziani Massacre'—when the Italians murdered around 3,000 Ethiopians after the assassination attempt on the viceroy. What struck me most were the advertisements. As in Asmara, the Eyeties in Addis were still in business:

CASA DEL DISCO, LITTORIO SQUARE—gramophones, symphonic records and complete operas.
RISTORANTE BARGELLO FIORENTINO, CORSO VITTORIO EMANUELE (lunch at fixed price, 30 lire. try it!)
BUY YOUR FURS ONLY AT PALAZZINI, VIA UMBERTO (beside the Bank of Rome)—we have the largest assortment of Ethiopian furs.

Baboons, perhaps.

Gondar's landmark was the picturesque and ruinous seventeenth-century Gondar Castle, set among eucalyptus and cedar groves above the town. Formerly the imperial court where James Bruce stayed in 1770-71, it was a source of wonder to him, as it was to me when I explored it with Tidmarsh and Oxborrow. I also went on a shooting trip with Ted and three other chaps to Lake T'ana, which Bruce had identified as the source of the Blue Nile. We had acquired Italian shotguns and a couple of native guides. We hoped to see hippos, leopards and lions but the guides advised us to beware of snakes and leeches in the elephant grass. Our only bag was a brace of pigeons. We spent most of the time lighting cigarettes, to burn the leeches off our legs.

The battalion was relieved on 5 December and returned to Asmara. There, we were amazed to find Lieutenant Malcolm Macalister Hall waiting for us. He had last been seen on Crete, where he had been captured. He held us agog in the Officers' Mess when he told of his escape from a PoW camp at Athens. He went over the wall with two Maoris and an English officer, a classical scholar. They baffled German sentries at checkpoints by babbling in Maori and ancient Greek (like three 8th Battalion Argylls who escaped across France in 1940 by speaking Gaelic when challenged). After the group split up, Macalister Hall reached Turkey by boat with some fugitive Greek army officers. The British consul at Smyrna gave him a fake Jewish identity card and a train ticket to Palestine. Three and a half months after escaping, he reached Egypt and was awarded an MC for his enterprise.

We stayed only a few days in Asmara before we were posted to Khartoum. I remember driving through the bomb-damaged town of Keren and then the road plunging abruptly into a gorge, eight-kilometres long, where the Italians had stubbornly held Platt's forces during the 53-day Siege of Keren, before they lost Asmara and Massawa. The fight at Venticinque seemed a sideshow when I saw that malevolent gorge, its shell craters, trenches and battlefield wreckage.

Our safari continued through the wild, mountainous country of western Eritrea to Kassala and across the flat deserts of the Sudan—a 1,000 kilometre drive on increasingly rutted tracks and a complete change in climate and topography. We camped for a night or two at Kassala in similar fashion, I imagined, to the old campaigners of Kitchener's army forty odd years before; rows of tents and bivouacs, burrowing into our bivvies, listening the wailing of wild animals outside and periodically venturing outside to inspect the guards. After striking camp, loading the trucks and leaving the place much as we had found it, we set off across the Nubian desert on the final stage of our trek to Khartoum. Asmara's art deco architecture and the spectacular mountain roads I had taken from Massawa to Gondar faded as quickly as a dream. As for Venticinque, that small battlefield in Abyssinia in 1941 . . . I see it now like the band of baboons sweeping across our camp: a passage that has left no trace. I doubt that any Ethiopian passing Venticinque now either knows of the Argylls or why we were there.

Second Lieutenant T. R. Ward. 1st A & S H, M E F
Tuesday 13 January 1942

Dear Harold,
One of the things we subalterns had to do yesterday was to write an essay on whether or not, in the light of our experience, we thought the training we received before being commissioned was suitable. When I was writing mine, analysing and pondering over the training I did receive, my mind kept wandering back to those days I spent at Stirling Castle and Dunbar, and all the troubles and trials, pleasures and excitements that the strange new life held for me. The four sides of foolscap stipulated as a maximum were inadequate for all I wished to say . . .

I had few criticisms to offer. My training has been of great value, especially the habit of self-discipline and self-control, which is so necessary to happiness in anyone's life, especially that of a soldier . . . I resigned myself to whatever the future held . . . tried to take everything as it came, good or bad, making the best of things, keeping cheerful and trying to keep in touch with old associations, interests and whatnot.

This sounds very highfaluting talk, but one is never full of such noble thoughts when one is enduring privations: getting up at five on a bleak, cold morning for Stand-to, being shelled, or other times when vitality is at its lowest ebb.

These thoughts are inspired at this time probably by the easy, well-fed and comfortable existence which we enjoy. It really is a good life we're leading these days, and we've every justification in enjoying it while we may, for one never knows what lies around the corner, or when the dogs of war will be loosed on us once again.

It's a strange and merciful peculiarity of the human mind how it so rapidly forgets physical and mental discomforts and unpleasant experiences, and how the memory has a fondness for keeping ever green and fresh those things in our lives which were most moving, beautiful or brought us most happiness—but locks the door on those impressions we get in times of physical and mental stress. Perhaps this is a gift from the Creator, or due to unconcious reasoning, because when I think of all that happened during last November, I find it difficult to remember the dangers and discomforts and can only think on how happy I was through it all!

The camaraderie we enjoyed, the exquisite feeling of freedom, the health and strength we revelled in, the tremendous appetites we had . . . All these things, together with the knowledge that we were doing something worthwhile—and were living, in fact as our ancestors lived, in sight of death and fear of God—made a impression greater than all the petty annoyances and fears I had. It did me a tremendous amount of good in every way, and I can look back with pleasure and thankfulness on that little campaign. I'll tell you all the details of it when I come home . . .

I ought really to be doing some work now. The company at the moment is outside on athletic training and it's time I joined it . . .

Assure Mum and Dad my continued good health and spirits and

give them both my love. It's about time I was hearing from you, old chap. Write often and tell me about your doings. How are you and Cecil placed now with regard to National Service?

Best wishes.

Ray

The letter above, to my brother Harold, was written at Khartoum, censorship preventing me telling him where I was. I must have sent hundreds of letters (and received as many) while overseas. Most were aerograms and 'airgraphs'—letter cards which were micro-photographed by the army and sent by air to the UK, where a print was made and forwarded to the recipient. None of mine was kept.

The battalion arrived at Khartoum towards the end of December 1941. There, we enjoyed three months of more or less peacetime soldiering in the style of a past age of imperial power. We were stationed in old-style, colonial army barracks dating from Kitchener's time—verandahed buildings and tents covering a vast area near the centre of the town. Occasional ceremonial parades, guard mounting, drill, desert training, and a strictly observed military routine punctuated at regular intervals by bugle calls were the order of the day. It was all very Kiplingesque. Mac, Shaw and I attended a Christmas service in the Anglican cathedral, where we sang 'In the Bleak Midwinter' and other carols, as we stood in our kilts under whirring ceiling fans. Whenever we mounted guard at the Governor's Palace, a building that oozed Raj-like self-importance, we passed a bronze statue of General Gordon seated on a camel, facing the Nile promenade.

Training exercises were mostly by platoon or company but one involved the whole battalion on the site of the Battle of Omdurman. Conditions there were excellent for desert warfare training—assault and obstacle courses, or footslogging aimlessly, as we thought, across the desert plain. I had acclimatised to subtropical heat by that time and took to it quite kindly, but the ferocious 100 degree blaze of the mid-day sun at Omdurman was no joke. Training took place in the mornings only. The mugs of tea we drank poured out of every pore of our bodies. I imagined the men of Kitchener's army suffering similar discomfort as they prepared to crush the Islamic uprising of 1898. I pictured rows of tents and bivouacs, the ranks of infantry, the impatient cavalrymen and the general's flashing heliographs before the battle, when a Sudanese army was destroyed. Churchill, then a trooper with the 21st Lancers, took part and wrote an account, *The River War,* a copy of which I found and read at the Sudan Club.

Visiting officers were admitted as temporary members to the Sudan Club and its colonial comforts. We dined there occasionally, swam in the club's Moorish-style pool, played cricket and enjoyed all the privileges of representatives of King and Empire. We would sit on wicker armchairs set out on the club's immaculate lawn and order lemonade, or afternoon tea, or whisky and soda in the cool of the evening, attended by a trio of white-robed *sufragis* who served us with courteous deference. We were invited to the club's garden party, where we were stunned by the spectacle of Khartoum society looking and talking as if wafted from the pages of P. G. Woodhouse.

We celebrated Hogmanay in traditional fashion and went to a Burns Supper at the Khartoum Caledonian Society. I got into a bit of a panic when I was ordered by the CO to run the battalion Highland Games when I could scarcely organise a sunday school picnic. Fortunately my company commander, Ted Tidmarsh and his friend Captain Jock Hunter, came to my rescue and organised things for me. I took part in some events myself with little distinction apart from coming second in the long jump. In the Officers' Mess some evenings, Mac, Shaw and I would entertain Cockle-ankles and Pearson as they drank whisky and soda, by singing in close harmony 'Swanee River', 'Danny Boy' and other songs (rather like the musical cameos in the John Ford US cavalry films I enjoyed after the war). Those evenings always ended with the appearance of the orderly officer of the day, a role at which I took my turn. In full uniform, I would tour the camp at Lights Out, inspect the guards and receive reports from the CSMs, then march back to the mess and report: 'All companies present and correct, arms and ammo secure, guards counted . . .' I would be dismissed by the adjutant with a courteous 'Thank you' before going off to bed.

I shared a room with Padre Smith, a jovial fellow who took a passionate interest in the welfare of the men and was as much concerned about their physical as well as their spiritual well-being. He got to know all the men in the battalion, and they had great respect for him. He also knew how to 'fight the good fight', for he had been a champion boxer in his student days. We relished our many arguments and discussions on every subject under the sun, light-hearted or lofty. One of his duties was to conduct the annual Divine Service to commemorate the Raising of the Regiment on 10 February 1794. The 148th anniversary service, with its unchanging programme of Kipling's 'Recessional' and the 91st Psalm, was held in Khartoum cathedral on Sunday morning, 8 February 1942. Some nights later, after a day of excessive heat, we were woken by tremendous thunderstorm, the rain hammering on the barrack roofs. All of us rushed outside, jumped over the verandah balustrade and stood in our underpants or stark naked, soaking up the blessed cool rain. Padre Smith was there too, in his birthday suit laughing at the absurdity of the scene.

For us the war seemed far away, especially the fighting in the Far East. We had heard of the Japanese attack on Pearl Harbor when we were in Abyssinia. Now we got the numbing news that Singapore had fallen. The Argylls' 2nd Battalion, to which I could well have been posted in 1940, was the last unit to cross the causeway from Malaya to Singapore before the surrender. We were back in Egypt by the time we learned of its exploits and fate.

Led by Brigadier Ian MacAlister Stewart—one of the few British senior officers in the Far East to show aptitude for the job in hand—the Argylls fought a tenacious, 53-day rearguard action down the length of the Malayan peninsula. The press headlines summed up the story: THIN RED LINE OF MALAYA. ARGYLLS' 400-MILE EPIC. Casualties were heavy but, according to Stewart, whose story was broadcast and printed, the Jocks accounted for eight times as many Japs. Those Argylls not killed in action became PoWs and suffered in camps and as forced labour on the 'death railway'—fictionalised after the war in *The Bridge on the River Kwai*. Because of his knowledge of jungle warfare, Stewart, with three other Argyll officers, was shipped out three days before the capitulation. Details of the 2nd Battalion's heroism were first obtained by our CO, from Stewart at GHQ, India, and circulated to all ranks. When Bloomfield heard the story, he told me he had arrived at Singapore from India with the 2nd Battalion in August 1939. Fortunately for him, his overseas tour ended before the attack on Malaya. He was posted to the UK, then to the 1st Battalion in Egypt.

Of more immediate concern to us, battles still raged to and fro across the Western Desert. We had a visit from a Major Roosevelt, a son of the President of the United States, sent on a fact-finding mission to British Middle East Forces. Our lifestyle no doubt confirmed him in his father's jaundiced views of the British empire. He was an amiable fellow who took in good part some ragging about America's part in the war. We hoped he'd report back home on our firm belief that it would all end in victory for John Bull and Uncle Sam.

Towards the end of our sojourn at Khartoum, second lieutenants Johnnie Scott-Barrett and George H. S. Rome joined with 153 ORs. McGill transferred to the Trans-Jordan Frontier Force. (When we returned to Egypt, another friend, Second Lieutenant Pyper, was posted to the Indian Army and Captain Pearson left for the Middle East Staff School, Haifa). Lieutenant-Colonel Anderson was promoted to lead the 29th East African Brigade. He was succeeded by Lieutenant-Colonel Ronnie McAlister, who took command on 10 April. Like almost every older officer I met, he had served in the First World War. He had been with the Argylls in Palestine in 1939 and had lectured at the METS in Cairo and at the East African Tactical School in Nairobi, where he had recently been Commandant and Chief Instructor.

On 4 May, we left Khartoum on a 1,500-kilometre journey to Cairo, by single-track railway, river steamer and another train. The Wadi Halfa to Khartoum railway had been completed in 1898 in record time, to bypass the Nile rapids and supply Kitchener's army. Our train was the heir to that enterprise. Before the war it was called the Nile Valley Express. Now it was hot, cramped and slow.

'Open the windows!' Shaw gasped, and let in a noxious brew of smoke, cinders and sand.

Pulling down the slatted shutters made the heat worse.

'Try the fans,' I shouted.

They worked. Mac produced a bottle of whisky.

'Courtesy of the Sudan Club,' he grinned.

At a desert halt we stretched our legs while the hissing locomotive took on water. I noticed its maker's brass plate: NORTH BRITISH LOCOMOTIVE COMPANY, GLASGOW, a guarantee, I hoped, of its stamina and reliability. We were about to cross the Nubian desert. The railway track ran dead straight for 370 kilometres. I fell into a stupor as the train rattled across a landscape whose only features were the line of telegraph poles beside the track and infrequent, numbered water halts. We were 15 hours on that infernal train before rejoining the river at Wadi Halfa, where a rusty paddle steamer waited to take us on. It listed to shore as we boarded. Most of us slept on deck because of the heat and to swim to safety if the overloaded ship sank. Flamingos took off at our approach. Feluccas steered clear like startled swans and vanished astern in the plume of black smoke the steamer trailed as it churned in midstream. For a further 15 hours, we saw nothing but the Nile and its desolate hinterland, punctuated by occasional mud villages with their clusters of palms and shadowy inhabitants. Thomas Cook's tourists, for whom the steamer had been built, would have had their money's-worth with the sunset and sunrise I saw on that passage. At Aswan we collected our kit, tumbled off the steamer and marched to the station for a night train to Cairo where we arrived completely knackered on 13 May.

The battalion was assigned internal security and ceremonial duties: parades for Empire Day, the King's Birthday and Bastille Day; mounting guard at the British Embassy. B Company, which had returned from Kufra, was based with D Company at the Citadel barracks. MacFie's mortar men were sent to help defend the Delta Barrage, a dam that controlled floodwaters on the Nile. Another platoon was flown on a brief adventure behind enemy lines, to guard a secret desert airstrip. A and C companies were ordered to Alex for security duty, patrolling the docks on the lookout for parachutists and saboteurs. These threats were taken seriously. Wags at the Cecil Hotel told me to keep my eyes peeled for frogmen. That was not a joke. A few months earlier, Italian divers on mini-submarines had fixed limpet mines to the battleships *Queen Elizabeth* and *Valiant*. The raiders were caught and held aboard one of the ships, both of which sank when the mines went off. Admiral Cunningham, in the best traditions of the navy, kept his flag flying. As the harbour was only three fathoms deep, the warships were refloated but spent two months in dry dock.

The present danger, however, was not frogmen. It came from the Western Desert, where Rommel's Afrika Korps was on the offensive.

6 THE PERFECT BATTLEFIELD

It has been quite an experience.

All against the desert, the greater enemy.

Captain van der Poel. *Ice Cold in Alex,* 1958

03-06 JULY 1942. Friday. Mustapha barracks, Alexandria. Prepare to move sometime tomorrow. Blankets rolled in section bundles. Picks and shovels, box of .45 ammo, Breda gun, ammo, hand grenades, all to be taken to Company HQ at breakfast. Platoon area, dugouts and pillboxes cleaned up directly after. Inspection at 1030 hours. March off in FSMO. Sidi Bishr barracks, Alexandria. One hour's notice to move from this morning. Equipment deficiencies: identity discs, rifle slings, steel helmets, emergency rations, field dressings—how do the men manage to lose these things? 1230: Cairo detachment arrives with Bren carrier and machine-gun platoons. Exchange Bredas for Brens. Assign anti-tank crew, two stretcher bearers, platoon cook.

14 JULY. El Amiriya. Air raid alarm. Reveille 0530; breakfast 0630 (be washed and shaved). Slit trenches. Platoon to move off at 0730 sharp; digging eight hours per day till well advanced. Dress: shorts and shirts, boots and puttees; carry rifles, groundsheets, sand bags and tools. Weapons: Bren gun, tripod and six magazines, anti-tank rifle, 2-inch mortar. 8-12 and 2-5, work! Stop at noon; march back for lunch at 1230. March back for dinner at 1900; dinner 1930. Section posts, communication trenches. Sleep in them.

So began my desert diary.

01 AUGUST. Saturday. Salt lake, Amiriya. Battalion move 0830, FSMO. Packs off in trucks. Bn start line at road junction three miles away. 30-minute sandwich ration and water halt at 1050. Company order of march: Company Commander's Jeep, 15-cwt truck, four 3-ton trucks for the men, 3-ton baggage truck, cook's truck last. Speed 7 mph. Intervals 150 yards minimum. Aircraft spotters on each vehicle. If attacked trucks stop, disperse, engage enemy with light machine-guns. Rendezvous with 21 Indian Brigade: map ref 450890 Barrani tomb 1600. Bde: ourselves, one Indian bn, coy Royal Engineers, field ambulance, 2nd New Zealand Division gunners. Overnight vehicle dispersal, tents. Bearings from pls to Coy HQ, and Coy HQ to Bn and Bde HQS, and vice-versa.

07 AUGUST. Alam el Bueib, Ruweisat Ridge. Bde intends to finish this line—then hold it. Bde: 1st Battalion Argylls, 2/8th Gurkhas, 104th Royal Horse Artillery less one battery, two troops NZ A/T gunners; A/A bty; ambulance. Bde HQ troops at Barrani tomb. Tasks: D Coy standing patrol 0715-1930 at Point 86 (one officer, one NCO and three men); B and C coys, ditto, at Pt 79; D Coy fielding sentries on east gap of mine-field, Gurkhas on west gap. A Coy plus one coy Gurkhas and carriers on anti-paratroop watch. Be off in 10 minutes from order to move. Dress: whatever we're in at the time—battle order—carry all weapons, ammo, mags, Mills bombs, Verey pistols and lights. Water: no reserve; go easy on the drinking, keep water bottles half full always.

14 AUGUST. Shamla tomb, Ruweisat Ridge, outside west gap in Bueib position: Coys to NZ posn if Jerry breaks through there. A Coy forward, B right, C left, HQ rear. D Coy to Amiriya. Care of equipment and arms: clean sand from weapons. Map reading: practise new map ref code. A/A sentries and camouflage—nets on vehicles for halts of more than 10 min-utes; disperse at cook house. Heat intolerable; bully beef and biscuit uneatable, seething with flies.

THE FIRST SOLDIER I SPOTTED IN THE WESTERN DESERT was a military policeman standing in a swirl of dust outside Alexandria, shouting at the traffic: 'Get a move on. We haven't got all bloody day!' Trucks packed with dead-eyed troops were retreating from the front and others, including mine, with wide-eyed innocents were heading for it. The road forked where the MP stood. I remember two signs: ALEXANDRIA, 7 KILOS and TO THE WESTERN DESERT. No distance was given to the desert. It was there. Vast and empty, except for drifting dust clouds that might be sandstorms, or stirred up by the jousting armies out there, 'in the blue' as we called it.

My first duty in the desert I am sure every infantryman who served in the Eighth Army remembered: I dug trenches. Lots of them. While fluid tank engagements had characterised the battles of 1941-42, the foot soldier's experience in the desert was more like the First World War. My company was set to work with 100 Indian pioneers who were digging communications trenches and field gun positions behind a minefield, part of defences being organised hastily in case the Afrika Korps broke the Alamein line.

After Wavell had crushed the Italians at Sidi Barrani in December 1940, the front line had swayed to and fro across the Egypt/Libya frontier. Since then, each side had attacked and counter-attacked, neither gaining a decisive advantage, although it looked as if Rommel might have one now. Tobruk had just fallen, a shambles that even Cairo's censors couldn't conceal. The garrison of over 33,000, including the Worcesters, surrendered. Fuel, ammo, and stores accumulated for the next offensive were destroyed or abandoned to the enemy. The Eighth Army retreated over 500 kilometres in eleven days. On 1 July 1942, General Auchinleck, then in command, made a stand at El Alamein, a desert railway halt only a couple of hours from Alex and Cairo.

The presence of Rommel and the Afrika Korps at El Alamein, less than 100 kilometres from Alex and Cairo, caused alarm and confusion.

The cities and the Suez Canal were vital to the war effort and to the security of the Middle East and the Gulf oilfields. Fifth columnists and enemy parachutists were rumoured to be everywhere. Curfews were imposed. In Alex, I recall being told to carry my service revolver at all times. The navy prepared to leave. The docks were mined for demolition to prevent their use by the enemy. In Cairo, the Embassy was besieged for exit visas. There was a run on the banks. Railway stations and shipping offices were swamped with evacuees desperate for tickets to the Sudan or Palestine, or steamer connections to South Africa. At GHQ, a bonfire of battle plans, maps and documents burned in the garden. Egyptians, waiting to see which way the wind from the desert would blow, were said to be ready to replace photographs of Churchill with those of Hitler and Mussolini.

Out in the blue, we were on edge most of the time as we dug defences, not knowing Rommel's intentions or where or when the Germans and the Italians would strike. The sounds of fierce battles reverberated from the front. Counter-attacks kept the enemy guessing Auchinleck's responses. He had none except to hold the line. On 27 July, there was a lull as the armies disengaged. Like everyone in the Eighth Army that month, I remember being showered with orders, counter-orders and false alarms. We returned to Amiriya on 15 August having heard a lot, but seeing no real action.

Amiriya was a transit camp for troops moving from Alex and Cairo to and from the Western Desert. Accommodation was in trenches or well-worn tents. There were no amenities, apart from occasional Naafi trucks. Despite the organisation's motto, 'Service to the Services', these usually ran out of goodies just as you got to them. Amiriya was a place of depressing impermanence and discomfort, billowing with sand. Salt lakes added a sting to the air and eyes. Infantrymen from the front mooched around brewing tea while they waited for orders. Tanks rolled by, stirring up clouds of dust. At casualty stations marked by Red Cross flags, stretcher cases lay under makeshift canvas shelters.

The battalion camped in a threadbare olive grove from which an Arab family squeezed a tenuous living. We were deployed for airfield defence. The Desert Air Force—the RAF and Commonwealth air forces in Egypt—had lost its forward landing grounds and regrouped at Amiriya. The airstrips had been bulldozed out of the desert and had no infrastructure, apart from tents and sand-bagged blast pens. Only the dust trails of aircraft taking off or landing, the sound of engines racing and the glow of recognition flares during night-operations indicated where the landing grounds were. Air-raid sirens went off all the time. I saw two Messerschmitt 109s scudding over, low enough to see the black crosses on their wings, then the bursting Bofors ack-ack fire and swooping Hurricanes. Occasionally, and often silently, the blazing smoke trail of a downed plane would end in a distant eruption of sand, or a white plume on the sea. We were jumpy because we had been told to watch for German paratroop drops. As nights fell, I saw searchlights switched on, their beams waving and criss-crossing in the dark sky over Alex.

16 AUGUST. Sunday. Alex to Cairo road. A Coy at landing grounds numbers 92 and 173, kilo 162-164. Company HQ and one mobile platoon in reserve; two platoons forward. Patrol lines marked by map refs and compass bearings. Patrols: two sections, two trucks patrol daily and at Stand-to.

18-21 AUGUST. Near Amiriya. Bn HQ at LG 87. Information: Forward LGs all on Alex to Cairo road. Danger of paratroops. Intention: Be on the lookout for paras and wipe 'em out. Two static coys do patrols: A Coy hold LG 92 and 173; C Coy LG 86 and 89 astride aerodrome near Bn HQ; B Coy mobile column (carrier pl and two A/T guns) south of Bn HQ; 2/8th Ghurkas on LG 90; 1/6th Punjabis on LG 98 and 99; Fighting French west of A Coy. Aircraft recognition signals: to be shown by friendly aircraft entering a prohibited area; approaching aerodrome; to establish identity when picked out by searchlights or fired on: 1700-2300 GREEN-GREEN; 2300-0300 RED-YELLOW; 0300-0800 GREEN-YEL-LOW; 0800-1700 RED-GREEN. Transport recognition signals: two flags on mast. Challenge with blue flag, waved in a circle. Reply with blue flag, waved horizontally. Practice alarm on 21st at Stand-to. Dress: battle order—steel helmets, respirators, all weapons! Warning system: half hour grace before attack.

The rumours of paratroop landings were unfounded, because after their losses on Crete the German paratroop divisions were used mainly as ground forces. They were still feared and respected. The Argylls got to know them again in Italy, of which more anon.

The 'flap' in July prompted Churchill to fly to Cairo with the Chief of the Imperial General Staff, General Sir Alan Brooke, to reorganise Middle East Command. They arrived on 3 August. Churchill sacked Auchinleck, as he had Wavell. The new Commander-in-Chief, Middle East was General Sir Harold Alexander, untainted by Tobruk or the retreat to El Alamein. The Eighth Army's new commander was Lieutenant-General B. L. Montgomery. He flew out from the UK as second choice. In a quirk of fate, the man intended for the job, Lieutenant-General Gott, was killed when his plane was shot down by 109s, on the same flightpath flown by Churchill the day before.

Montgomery had a reputation for being abrasive. Churchill had remarked: 'If he is disagreeable to those about him, then he is also disagreeable to the enemy.' One of Montgomery's first acts after he landed in Egypt on 12 August was to visit and move Auchinleck's forward HQ from fly-blown Ruweisat Ridge to the more bearable coastal sand dunes at Burg el Arab, where Eighth Army HQ and DAF HQ were now located. Montgomery was keen to co-ordinate tactical air support for the army. He was also planning to form a mobile Tactical Headquarters (Tac

HQ) for the front line. The Argylls were apparently among the units being considered to guard it.

Captain Tidmarsh, who was still my company commander, gave me the gen from Battalion HQ. My platoon had been chosen for a dummy run. I still don't know why. Perhaps because I was tall, smartly turned out and had grown a stylish moustache; or because I had adapted quickly to desert conditions and had knocked my platoon into good shape, with the assistance of my admirable regular army sergeant. I got Bloomfield to have the men wash thoroughly, shave closely and generally smarten up in case we met the army commander. A gobbled breakfast amid much speculation, then we loaded kit, weapons and ammo (less tents, since it would be a one-day exercise) into four trucks and set off for the rendezvous at kilometre 20 on the Alex to Cairo road.

We arrived at 0900, 22 August. In charge was Major Oswald, G2 Operations. He briefed me briskly on the day's play. Oswald had a couple of dozen vehicles and a colourfully-badged crew of officers and men: Tac HQ brass, liaison officers, signalmen, tankies and ack-ack chaps, all assigned a role—or like 9 Platoon, A Company, the Argylls, being assessed for one. So we spent the day practising out in the blue. It was all new to me: desert map-reading and manoeuvres, formation driving, ack-ack dispersal, setting up laagers. Because radio silence would often be maintained, flag signals had to be learned—Blue up: prepare to move. Blue down: Move. Red up: short halt. Blue and Red: Halt. Thus I was initiated into the craft of desert army travel.

One of the old hands gave me the basics of desert driving: how to read the sand, weaving between low dunes seeking hard ground, taking unavoidable patches of soft sand at speed to plow through. Metal sand mats and shovels were usually needed to unstick ourselves; letting air out of the tyres gave better traction. The sand crust could give way, throwing the steering wheel off course; a plunge at speed into a hidden wadi would take the axles off a truck. Broken axles, boiling radiators, sand in the carburettors, burst tyres—over the next four months I got used to them all. We had maps, but apart from the coast road and a parallel railway there was nothing on them except low ridges and wadis. The maps looked like Admiralty charts; indeed, sometimes we navigated like sailors, by the sun and stars. Flag signals heightened the nautical effect. Rendezvous was by a six-figure map reference within numbered military zones. The map references corresponded to white-painted and numbered oil drums that were anchored, like mooring buoys, on desert tracks by Field Survey scouts—when you could find them that is, the drums or the tracks.

The desert seemed to swallow all that entered it. Tanks and vehicles were camouflaged with nets. Men dug in to be as inconspicuous as possible. Standing on an area the size of a cricket pitch, it was possible not to realise that a company might be hunkered down all around. Compass bearings were taken to link positions whenever we camped; dials of stones were laid out pointing to section and platoon areas; distances were measured in paces to make contact easier at night. Even by day, without the bearings you could drive for a kilometre or walk for a few hundred metres and get completely lost.

I saw Montgomery for the first time when we were passing a line of stationary vehicles on the coast road the day after the exercise. He was standing in an open-top Humber staff car, his arms leaning on the windscreen as he scanned the horizon, like a hawk looking for quarry—a characteristic pose. He wore shirtsleeves, beret, and held a fly whisk. Entirely practical. No obvious brass. I took a quick photo. 'Monty', as we all called him, was visiting troops, dishing out cigarettes and pep talks, typical behaviour it transpired. Back at Amiriya, Ted Tidmarsh and the others wanted to know what he was like. I thought he radiated confidence and a magnetic personality.

On Ruweisat Ridge a few days later, Alexander inspected the battalion, accompanied by corps, division and brigade brass hats. I met him briefly, a suave former Irish Guards officer, armed with a revolver and aristocratic charm; stylish, dressed in breeches, high boots, sheep-skin-lined jacket, medal-ribboned tunic and red-banded cap. He had perfect manners and a record as a courageous soldier. In France in 1940, he had commanded the British 1st Division and the rearguard at Dunkirk where he was said to have been the last away. Alexander and his gang were upbeat, smiling, confident: already in the Monty mould. Word got around that Churchill too had been in the desert, visiting troops south-east of the ridge, flashing his V-for-Victory sign and chomping on a cigar. Great stuff! We needed it.

We knew little of Monty or Alexander. Bloomfield doubted if Rommel would be bothered. The Afrika Korps leader had acquired a legendary status among us as well as with his own soldiers. Even in deepest Abyssinia, reports of the 'Desert Fox' and his exploits had reached us. Auchinleck had observed: 'There is a real danger that our friend Rommel is becoming a kind of magician or bogey-man to our troops.' He tried to prevent Rommel being talked about, banning his name and substituting 'the enemy forces', an initiative that not only failed but also exposed his weariness and insecurity. Monty understood the Rommel factor. If he was intimidated by his adversary's fame and charisma, he didn't show it. He beat Rommel, not only on the battlefield, but also at the publicity game. Unlike Auchinleck and Wavell, Monty was a shame-less self-publicist with a gift for the memorable prop. Rommel's was a pair of captured British desert goggles. Monty took to wearing eccen-tric headgear, and adopted the army's casual, corduroy-and-suede-boots dress style.

Before Monty arrived, the German commander was probably the Eighth Army's most popular general. I certainly felt that our morale and self-esteem were boosted by the knowledge that we were fighting a dar-ing and honourable enemy. He had a reputation for 'fair play'. That virtually guaranteed him the respect of the British officer class. Perhaps we forgot about the régime he served. We didn't call Rommel or his men Nazis—just 'Jerries'. They called us 'Tommies' or 'Jocks'. Lest this seem too chummy—for men who were trained and sometimes required to kill each other and who often died horribly—I think that most of us wanted to believe that some decency could survive the absurdity, chaos and cruelty of war; indeed, many veterans of the fighting found the myths that embellish the campaign more comforting than the often grim reality. For men on both sides, the desert seemed a greater enemy. It stripped everything to essentials. We were alone, far from home, fighting a private war. There was no civilian population to complicate the contest. For both armies the Western Desert was a perfect battlefield.

Monty sought a rapport with the Commonwealth commanders: lieutenant-generals Sir Leslie Morsehead (9th Australian Division), Sir Bernard Freyberg (2nd New Zealand) and Major-General Dan Pienaar (1st South African). How frustrated they were can be gleaned from an exchange between Pienaar and a DAF liaison officer: 'If you've got to bomb my trucks, you might at least hit them. But you missed every bloody one!' After being shelled by British gunners he declared: 'My father fought the British in the Transvaal, and all I want to know is, what side I'm supposed to be on. Because if I'm on Rommel's, say so, and I'll turn around and have him in Alexandria within 12 hours. Just work it out and let me know as soon as you've decided.'

When Monty arrived at Auchinleck's HQ, the first thing he did was address the Eighth Army's sceptical staff officers:

> I want first of all to introduce myself to you. You do not know me. I do not know you. But we have got to work together; therefore we must understand each other and we must have confidence in each other . . . I believe that one of the first duties of a commander is to create what I call 'atmosphere' and in that atmosphere his staff, subordinate commanders and troops will live and work and fight.

I do not like the general atmosphere I find here. It is an atmosphere of doubt, of looking back to select the next place to which to withdraw, of loss of confidence in our ability to defeat Rommel, of desperate defence measures by reserves in preparing positions in Cairo and the Delta. All that must cease. Let us have a new atmosphere.

The defence of Egypt lies here at Alamein and on Ruweisat Ridge. What is the use of digging trenches in the Delta? It is quite useless; if we lose this position we lose Egypt . . . I have ordered that all plans and instructions dealing with further withdrawal are to be burnt, and at once. We will stand and fight here. If we can't stay here alive, then let us stay here dead.

Our mandate from the Prime Minister is to destroy the Axis forces in North Africa . . . And it will be done. If anyone here thinks it can't be done, let him go at once. I don't want any doubters in this party. It can be done, and it will be done: beyond any possibility of doubt.

Now, I understand Rommel is expected to attack at any moment. Excellent. Let him attack . . . we ourselves will start to plan a great offensive; it will be the beginning of a campaign which will hit Rommel and his Army for six right out of Africa . . .

Francis de Guingand, Monty's Chief of Staff, one of the few staff officers to keep his job after Monty took over, wrote:

That address by Montgomery will remain one of my most vivid recollections. It was one of his greatest efforts. We all felt that a cool and refreshing breeze had come to relieve the oppressive and stagnant atmosphere. The effect of the address was electric—it was terrific! And we all went to bed that night with a new hope in our hearts, and a great confidence in the future of our army.

One of Monty's gifts was to make every man know why he was fighting, what was expected of him and that the general relied on him. He would stand on a Jeep and talk to hundreds of men, making each one feel that his individual conduct mattered. Even those who never saw one of those performances—or who indulged in bursts of 'bellyaching', roundly condemned by Monty—felt his presence: by word of mouth; from pictures and quotes in the Eighth Army's newspapers; from each 'Personal Message from the Army Commander' printed before every battle and handed or read to every man. He saw us as individuals, not cannon fodder (he had been wounded in France in the First World War). We in turn never saw him as a member of a social class, other than that of the professional soldier. Since the war his reputation as a commander has taken some knocks. His arrogance and blatant self-promotion are undisguised in his memoirs, which I read after the war. But in 1942, he tore up GHQ's plans for retreat, and transformed the Eighth Army from a dispirited and confused miscellany into a confident, unified, battle-winning force.

On the day of Alexander's visit, we were told to get ready to move further up the blue. As this was likely to be an extended tour of action on the front line, I assembled my platoon and spoke to each man. I checked each name, rank, army number and age; each man's height, date of enlistment, rifle serial number, boot and headgear size, occupation in civvy street, religion, marital status, home address and next of kin, and made sure that each one of them wore his dog tag. Of the thirty men in my platoon, most were from Glasgow and Clydeside. Apart from Sanders and Bloomfield, only two were over thirty. Most were under twenty-five. Nineteen gave their mothers as next of kin. A few were regular army, a few were volunteers. Two-thirds had been drafted. They represented a cross section of the skilled and unskilled pre-war working class: miners, shipyard rivetters, stevedores, lorry drivers, farm labourers; an apprentice plumber, a chromium plater, a coat maker, a fishmonger, a carpenter. That roll call had a biblical resonance as they stood in front of me in the desert and confirmed who and what they were. One-third of the platoon had been unemployed before joining up—the poor bloody infantry in more ways than one.

Essentially, the Desert War was confined to an 800-kilometre-long, limestone coastal plateau no higher than 200 metres above sea level—a landscape of hard flat sand, loose stones and thorn bushes, rocky low ridges and shallow wadis, with none of the photogenic sand dunes seen in *Lawrence of Arabia*. Scattered settlements, the two-lane coast road and the Alex to Mersa Matruh single-track railway built by the British in the 1920s ran along a sea-level coastal strip no more that a few kilometres wide. At El Alamein, the plateau was only 60 kilometres wide, from the Mediterranean coast to the Qattara Depression. The depression was a dried-up sea bed 120 metres below sea level, covered with salt and shifting sand all but impassable to vehicles.

With the Mediterranean to the north and a southern flank that could not easily be turned, the Afrika Korps and the Eighth Army were forced to confront each other on the Alamein line. Auchinleck had fallen back, knowing it was the narrowest defensive position before Alex and Cairo. To proceed, Rommel would have to make either a head-on attack along the coast or a flanking manoeuvre to the south. Two low ridges, Ruweisat and Alam Halfa, helped secure the flank; a third, Miteiriya Ridge, near the coast road, was held by the enemy, as was Himeimat Ridge to the south, near the depression.

At the end of August, the Argylls joined 161 Brigade, 5th Indian Division on Ruweisat Ridge. Two of the brigade's battalions, the 3/7th Rajputs and 1/2nd Punjabis, were being relieved because of exhaustion and casualties, both evident when we reached the end of the track to the ridge and carried out the changeover. The battalion relieved the Punjabis, while the 4/7th Rajputs had been brought up from the Sudan to replace the 3/7th. The ridge was a long lizard-like feature that was a key point in the line. We were deployed along much of its desolate length. Its western end was scattered with burned-out tanks, ours and Jerry's. Our task was to dig in and defend it. Our accommodation was as expected: in sangars and foxholes, and trenches which often had to be drilled and blasted from the rock by sappers using pneumatic drills and dynamite.

We stood-to every dawn and dusk for enemy attacks. We were placed on Stand-by, then stood down as orders came and went. We changed positions to rotate with other units in our brigade. That was partly operational, but also because many senior officers had been in the trenches in the First World War and understood there was a limit to mens' endurance on the front line. It was a restless life, on Stand-to and Stand-by, never long in the same place, trying hard to reason why, accepting as cheerfully as we could our lot in higher command's scheme of things.

The first shock I experienced on the desert front line was the complete absence of four things normally taken for granted: freedom of movement, decent food, clean water, and secure shelter. Sangars were shallow holes piled with a semicircle of stones. They offered meagre protection from enemy fire and none from the blazing sun or the night chill. Dugouts were protected by sandbags and covered with sheets of corrugated iron. Mosquito netting and canvas were draped across the entrances. Inside these hovels, we slept like troglodytes on shelves cut out of the sand. Not that we always slept much or easily—we were frequently disturbed by bursts of shellfire. Cooking fires and lights were restricted. The tell-tale glow from cigarettes was concealed by cupped hands, lest it be spotted by the enemy. During the day, temperatures were often high enough to fry eggs on truck bonnets. Not that we did this often on forward positions: the risk of being shelled or machine-gunned more or less confined us to our holes during the day.

Artillery fire, ours and theirs, swished over our heads to explode elsewhere. Some shells came closer, forcing us to dive into our holes where we would lie, petrified, shaken by the concussion and peppered by shrapnel. When it was safe to raise our heads to see if we were all okay we tried to appear completely unconcerned about the stonk. I noted how experienced officers casually ignored shells bursting nearby, and steeled myself to copy their composure under fire, a most difficult pose to maintain. Apart from a few skirmishes and intermittent Italian fire in Abyssinia, this was my first sustained experience of frontline soldiering. I had not even been bombed. That soon changed. Ruweisat Ridge was easily spotted from the air and it attracted Stukas like flies. We were often dive-bombed at teatime: 1730. You could set your watch by those nuisance raids and we got used to them. But I will never forget the first time I was a Stuka target.

The plane appeared harmless at height, then peeled off into a near-vertical dive. I had been told about the sound effects—to terrorise their victims Stukas had sirens on their wings that shrieked louder the closer the planes came. They had the intended effect. I was transfixed. Bloomfield yelled: 'Get down!' and jumped into a foxhole. I leapt in after him and curled up in a ball, sand and rock an inch from my face. I felt that the Jerry was aiming only at me. I looked up. Just when I thought the plane would hit the ground, the pilot released a 500-kilogramme bomb and pulled up and away. The black crosses on the wings seemed particularly malevolent at that moment, as did the falling bomb. This all seemed to happen in slow motion—until the bomb screamed down, to burst with a deafening crash and an eruption of rock and sand . . . then silence, except for the fall-out of sand and pebbles pattering our position like rain. I looked around to check the number of tin hats that appeared from our holes as the smoke and dust blew away and shouted: 'Everyone okay?' No casualties. The men who had been on Crete had seen what Stukas could do to ships. But against smaller targets in the desert, they were less effective. Unless they scored a direct hit, or shrapnel caught you in the open, the bombs could land less than

100 metres away and, if you stayed down, you'd be shaken but you would survive.

Stukas were not particularly fast and were easy prey for our fighters. Those that eluded them faced a barrage of Bofors. Our own attempts to shoot down Jerry planes were unsuccessful. We had been given some ack-ack training at Omdurman, with Brens mounted on tripods. On Ruweisat Ridge none of us was angry, brave or stupid enough to stand up during an air attack to fire them. As for shooting down low-flying aircraft with rifles or tommy guns, we weren't in Hollywood. A 109 whizzing past at 500 kilometres an hour is gone by the time you aim. Given that a Hurricane's eight .303 Browning machine-guns were calibrated to fire 200 bullets a second to shoot down a Messerschmitt 250 yards away, our chances of bringing down a Jerry, even with Brens, required very lucky shots. I never saw one.

The Germans had more formidable weaponry on the ground. Rommel favoured dynamic, fast-moving warfare and he was better at it. He also had better equipment. The Eighth Army's tanks had been out-gunned by the Afrika Korps Mk III and Mk IV Panzers whose front armour defied the 2-pounder pop-guns used by our tanks and anti-tank infantry. The 2-pounder's range was 500 yards; the range of the German 50-mm anti-tank gun was 1,000 yards. Jerry's secret weapon was the 88-mm flak gun, which the Afrika Korps used as an anti-tank gun, to devastating effect. It fired a high velocity, 20-pound solid-shot shell over 2,000 yards that could penetrate 80-mm of armour. The Eighth Army's fast but mechanically unreliable Crusader tank had 40-mm of front armour. Also, our tank commanders' penchant for cavalry-style tactics—romantic, in a Charge of the Light Brigade manner—exposed their tanks to 88s in the open desert. Monty soon put a stop to that.

By the time of El Alamein, M3 Grant tanks shipped from the US to Suez, and their successor, the M4 Sherman, began to even up the score. Both had heavy armour and 75-mm dual-purpose guns that fired high explosive and armour-piercing shells. These tanks could thus be deployed in infantry-support and anti-tank roles. The obsolete 2-pounder was being replaced by a 6-pounder anti-tank gun; our 25-pounder field gun was a modern, versatile weapon. We also had the 3.7-inch ack-ack gun, a potential rival to the tank-busting German 88, had the army chosen to deploy it in that mode at the time. I saw plenty of them in the Canal Zone, but they would have been more useful in the desert. The Italian weapons were, with a few exceptions, like the Breda machine-gun, inferior to ours. This was just as well, because the Italians had more troops in the desert than the Germans.

Monty expected Rommel to attack before the Eighth Army was reinforced and re-equipped. Rommel's most likely strategy would avoid the strongly-held coastal sector at El Alamein for a flanking drive south of Ruweisat and Alam Halfa ridges, then a thrust to the coast road to cut off the Eighth Army, and a strike to Alex or Cairo and the Delta. To secure a passage he would have to capture one or both ridges. Monty set a trap. Both ridges bristled with anti-tank guns, infantry positions, hull-down tanks and artillery. Rommel's panzers would be lured forward and knocked out. Then the decisive battle at El Alamein would be fought. On 30 August, hurriedly-mimeographed Orders of the Day were distributed. We read these, bunched shoulder to shoulder, inspired by the clarity and confidence of Monty's message.

TO OFFICERS AND MEN OF THE EIGHTH ARMY
SPECIAL MESSAGE
1. The enemy is now attempting to break through our positions in order to reach CAIRO, SUEZ, and ALEXANDRIA, and to drive us from EGYPT.
2. The Eighth Army bars the way. It carries a great responsibility and the whole future of the war will depend on how we carry out our task.
3. We will fight the enemy where we now stand; there will be NO WITHDRAWAL and NO SURRENDER.

Every Officer and Man must continue to do his duty as long as he has
breath in his body.

If each one of us does his duty, we cannot fail; the opportunity will then
occur to take the offensive ourselves and to destroy once and for all the
enemy forces now in EGYPT.

Into battle then, with stout hearts and with the determination to do our
duty. And may God give us the victory.

B. L. Montgomery,

Lieutenant-General.

27 AUGUST. Thursday. Ruweisat Ridge. Scene of fierce battles not long
before, between the Germans and NZ and Indian divs. Met division and
corps commanders. MacDougall, C Coy on fighting patrol tonight. West
Yorks heavily shelled at midday. A desolate area, scattered with burnt out
tanks, our own and German.

28-29 AUGUST. Got some books from the padre. Heavily shelled at
2030. Arty shoot of ours brought down Jerry defensive fire. MacDougall
and C Coy on fighting patrol. More aircraft activity. Witnessed good
dog-fight—Hurricanes and 109s. One Hurricane crashed. Pleasant hour
after Stand-down, reading *Kenilworth* by lamplight in bivouac.

30 AUGUST. Sunday. Ruweisat Ridge. No info yet of Jerry's threatened
push. Heat and flies intolerable still. Another dogfight over the South
African positions at 1745. Three planes down—one pilot baled out.
Beautiful cloud effects in evening sky—majestic backdrop to swift fight
between puny mortals. Wrote letter card home and had short practice on
my harmony lessons (a correspondence course from Dad) in the afternoon. Jock Hamilton, A Coy platoon commander now in command of
the Bn A/T pl, visited us, with a bottle of whisky, and news of his
engagement. Party ended at 2200 to the sound of heavy gunfire.

31 AUGUST. Very heavy gunfire from soon after midnight till dawn. Air activity much increased during morning. Stand-to at 0330. Some talk of an enemy attack with tanks on the West Yorks' position. C Coy moved forward with A/T guns in readiness for emergency. Very cold world twixt night's retreat and dawn's advance.

Later. News of Jerry local attack confirmed. West York coy driven off posn which by counter-attack was retaken with eleven casualties. South African two-coy attack successful: fifty prisoners, all Italian bar one. New Zealanders also raided enemy lines and captured thirty Germans. 4th Armoured Bde and 7th Armoured Div engaging enemy armoured forces in the south, El Himeimat. Is this Rommel's final push? Much air activity all day. A/A batteries bagged two Stukas and a Messerschmitt. Steel helmets, binoculars, slit trenches the order of the day. Consequent on the attack on West Yorks, all minefields to be patrolled—rather an obvious precaution.

Mail. Shocked and concerned to hear Dad admits he feels the weight of his years. I pray God that he and Mum are spared further worry and trouble and that he will continue to bless and strengthen them and keep them safe. Had a few words with Shaw who is worked hard and busy with his duties as regimental signals officer.

01 SEPTEMBER. Visit from CO at 1000. Thirty Jerry tanks knocked out and twenty disabled out of ninety-five engaged. Our heavy armour not yet involved. (CO's arrival, incidentally, greeted by the bursting of an A/A shell in Coy HQ area!) Plenty of cloud in the sky today and a pleasant breeze blowing. Statistics show that upwards of 7,000 shells expended by our arty a couple of nights ago! Two pls of South Africans involved in a skirmish with the enemy last night; were almost surrounded, but fought their way back with fifteen casualties. Visited the Cape Town Highlanders, from coy of whom we may take over. Heard the full story of their patrol and enjoyed excellent hospitality. 'There's nothing like

Canadian Club' as MacDougall would say!

Good story of a Jerry who gave himself up to the South Africans: a schoolmaster fed up with Hitler and the war. A POW friend wrote to him saying he was well-treated and able to get books to read; so the schoolmaster just walked across no-man's-land and gave himself up in the sure hope that he'd be able to continue his studies. Drew pay from Bn HQ at 1900. Heavy A/A barrage against Jerry planes. A/A shells burst 150 yds away and a stick of bombs fell in Bn area—no casualties or damage. Some enemy planes brought down. Continued my harmony exercises today. Early to bed and a sound sleep.

02 SEPTEMBER. Heavy arty fire during the night. Air activity at 0700. More in the forenoon and a bit of bombing. One sleeps full and deep in the desert, except when the arty wallahs decide to have a shoot in the middle of the night. Orders: Bn HQ, A and C coys ready to counter-attack in any position of brigade area. Tank battles in the south. Enemy infantry digging in outside NZ box; NZ brought out light tanks; threat from the south; another attack may come in the north? . . or anywhere. Bn ready to move out at moment's notice.

Transport coming—three 3-tonners only. Dress: battle order; fighting kit only, picks and shovels, entrenching tools. See Sergeant Grant about collecting spigot mortar and ammo from Bn tomorrow. Popping in and out of slit trenches all day. Great activity in the air. Saw two more Jerry planes shot down. Had an amusing, impromptu music lesson with Sanders this afternoon. Wrote out some hymn and psalm tunes and did more harmony work.

Mail. More music, book on harmony and psalter on the way for me. Harold enjoying life in the RAF at Skegness, where he seems to be able to carry on with some of his social and church activities. Cecil still at home. Friends joining commandos and paratroops. Very heavy tank bat-tle in progress not far to the south. 'No withdrawal' order received today from Army Commander. 1945. Enemy southwest (8,000-10,000 yds) of Bueib—making for 891278—Bashaza. May have to take up posn tonight Point 79. Bed with boots on. Slept well, fully dressed. No emergency turnout.

03 SEPTEMBER. Spent good part of the day paying out the coy. Air activity as usual with plenty of A/A and occasional dogfights. Have not had much time today to meditate on the fact that this is the third anniversary of the outbreak of war. On this National Day of Prayer we think of the oppressed, homeless and miserable people throughout the world crying, 'How long, O Lord, how long?' and steel ourselves to our utmost endeavour to hasten victory. No news yet of battle in the south. Wrote a couple of aerograms to Dad and put in some more harmony.

1930. Jerry's armour on the way back in the south. Feint or retreat? Coy stands by again tonight for counter-attack role if needed on Pt 64. Cracked another bottle of whisky with Captain Tidmarsh, Hamilton and the sergeant major. Party interrupted at about 2130 by heavy bombing raid which continued for two hours. Flares plentiful. Slept until 0330 when Jerry came across and dropped bombs all round us and all over our sector until about 0600. One bomb burst in one of my areas. No casualties. Rotten feeling, huddling at the bottom of a slit trench watching the parachute flares, listening to the drone of planes, the whine of bombs and bursts of machine-gun fire.

04 SEPTEMBER. Tired this morning after noisy night. Comparatively quiet and idle day. Evidence of ground and air activity in the south after dark, but everything peaceful in our sector. Had much-needed undisturbed night's sleep.

05 SEPTEMBER. Jerry seems to have received a right good kick in the pants down south and lost ninety tanks. First round to us! Everybody

highly incensed at a single Jerry plane which dive-bombed our coy positions at 0700. Some narrow escapes in 7 and 8 pls but no casualties.
Cloudy sky and breeze-laden air today. Very pleasant, but time still hangs
heavy on our hands. Received word this afternoon that we move up the
line tomorrow night to take over from the 1/1st Punjabis. Felt happy this
evening. Mail arrived, also the canteen stuff. Fine letter and lesson 9
from Dad. Had two superb bottles of Canadian beer during and after
Stand-to. Slept well and peacefully and had pleasant dreams of Mum at
home.

06 SEPTEMBER. Sunday. Superb cloud effects in the sky this morning
which were again a backdrop for an aerial combat. Two Hurricanes and
three or four Stukas shot down. Quiet informal service in 9 Pl area.
Lesson: Psalm 91. God certainly in our midst in these open-air services.
Cool breezes still prevail and cumulus clouds pleasant to the eye. Wrote
weekly letter card in forenoon after church service. 1200. Move Order.

Move 1930, two vehicles. Route: Coy HQ - 7 Pl - gap - B Coy - Rajputs.
Order of march: Coy HQ, 9, 7, 8 Pls. Coy HQ pass through 7 Pl gap at
2130. Distance: as far as visibility permits. Dress: battle order, wearing
steel helmets, shorts, boots, puttees etc. Four mile march. Weapons: all
carried. Mags, Mills bombs, and Bren, tommy guns, clips etc. Feeding:
truck brings hot meal after dark. B'fast and lunch—cold. NO brewing up
of tea. NO fires at any time. Spare kit: two dumps; 1. essential
kit—ammo, spigot mortar, packs, blankets, picks and shovels, nets; 2.
non-essential kit—bivouacs, gun chests etc. Two trucks: one for ammo
etc., picks, mortar; one for packs, blankets and rations; third truck: spare
kit, bivouacs, gun chests.

1600. Ted returned from recce of Punjabi posn with pl commanders,
raging about unconcealed activity—trucks and troops all over the place,
making a fine target for the enemy. 'Criminal'. Prepared for a shambles
when taking over tonight. Bottle of beer saved from last night restored

him to a better humour and satisfied the thirst I had. The prospect of a one-hot-meal-a-day life not too pleasant. Bags of patrolling to do, I suppose. New experiences in store for many of us; I welcome them. Filled in income tax return. Paymaster's staff should act as officers' accountants and do this for us . . . we're busy enough dodging bombs and shells without having to bother our brains with tax forms. No sleep for any of us tonight. Takeover effected with comparatively little trouble. No interference from Jerry. Quiet if tiring night.

07 SEPTEMBER. Spent the day acquainting myself with the Coy posns and surrounding country, which is as grim and barren as anyone could wish to see. 1930. Orders: patrol with two officers, Scott-Barrett and myself . . .

The longer we stayed in the desert the more we became prisoners of the pesuasive normality of it all, as if no other life were possible. Every patrol, every move we made (unless forced by the urgency of the battlefield), was methodically typed out in advance at Battalion or Company HQ. A dispatch rider or runner would hand me a 'secret' envelope. I'd unfold the sheets of paper for another night's work. The text was always matter-of-fact, typical of the bureaucracy of war:

1 / A. & S. H. Patrol Order No.3. SECRET Copy No.2.

7 Sept. 42.

Ref. Map 1 / 50,000 El Alamein.

INFORMATION.

1. A Patrol from S. A. Div. will be operating to the North of Pt. 38 (879283) and along the Grid Line Northing [sic] 285, Westwards.

2. The Patrol for the night 7/8 Sept. will be provided by 'A' Coy.

3. Comd. Lt. Ward with Lt. Scott-Barrett and One Pl.

Tasks:

4. Act offensively and obtain enemy prisoners or identification as opportunity offers.

5. Report on posn. and type of enemy dispositions on Southern Edge of Shallow Depression ...

METHOD.

6. Time of Start: 2230 hrs.

7. S.P. : Area North of Pt. 37 - 'A' Coy. Area.

Arty Support:

8. No pre-arranged concentration.

9. Fire Support at call.

10. The Signal for supporting fire will be GREEN - RED - GREEN.

11. A Standing Patrol of One Sec. will be posted at the S.P. to look out for signals and assist if necessary.

12. Patrol will return not later than 0500 hrs. 8 Sept.

13. Report Bn. HQ immediately by phone and confirm in writing.

14. P.O.W. or identification will be sent immediately to Bn.HQ.

Dress and arms:

15. As arranged with O.C. 'A' Coy.

ACK.

Time of signature 1900.

By DR

(signed) Iain Scheurmier

Captain. Adjutant, 1st. Battalion, The Argyll & Sutherland Highlanders.

Distribution: O.C. 'A' Coy. Copy No. 1. Lt. Ward. No. 2. 161 Bde. No. 3. War Diary. No. 4 & 5. File No. 6.

I got used to being out in the desert at night, creeping across no-man's-land to probe enemy positions—the excitement of it, the cold grip of fear, the strange shapes and shadows. Leading a bunch of men, all similarly keyed-up, in arrowhead formation over rough, stony ground scattered with unexpected obstacles and shallow depressions. Fearful of bumping into an enemy patrol, or coming across mines or tripwires. Keeping silent, keeping distance, keeping alert. Straining eyes and ears, not knowing what to expect. The night sky lit with stars, flashes of tracer fire, flares and arty bursts. There was an eerie beauty about it all.

Equipment wasn't carried, except for weapons, ammo and compasses. We blackened our faces and put on balaclavas, battledress or shorts, and pullovers to keep out the cold. There was the usual here-we-go-again grumbling as we laced up our suede desert boots ('brothel-creepers', as we called them). We went out through gaps in the wire and stole slowly towards the enemy, periodically lying motionless flat on the sand to listen for voices, movement, the sound of a rifle bolt. Then we'd walk on and repeat the tactic, or drop to the ground when bursts of tracer fire whooshed past at head height, or flares shot up like fireworks, exploded, then burned as they fell.

One night we were shelled by our own artillery. Back through the wire, and having had only a couple of hours of sleep, I was pestered all morning by Royal Artillery gunners, battalion, brigade, and field regiment intelligence officers about the effect of the harassing shoot which we had witnessed and came close to being caught up in. I told them that next time they might consider harassing Jerry. On another occasion, our IO wanted a prisoner. Bloomie and I went out alone, and managed to worm our way among enemy work parties. We heard the Jerries talking, as we waited like cats to ambush a straggler. To be frank, we were relieved that none of the Jerries came our way. I still wonder what we'd have done if we'd met an armed patrol. Shoot, surrender, run like hell? We preferred to avoid surprise encounters and I'm sure Jerry felt the same.

08 SEPTEMBER. Tuesday. Patrol uneventful. Saw no sign of Jerry or of his wire or positions. Southern edge of depression definitely not occupied. Returned about 0400, reported and went to bed. Wakened at 1000

and told to write out report and go to see Bde intelligence officer. Had lunch at Bn HQ. One platoon B and C coys out on patrol tonight.

09 SEPTEMBER. Stop all unnecessary movement and undue exposure. Rations to be issued at night from cook's truck. Dress: men getting scruffy and untidy—even by desert standards. No relaxing. Shelling and air raids—get below ground (the men need little encouragement). Met MacDougall at B Coy in afternoon. Finished harmony lesson 9 today. Discovered that Lieut Rollo Charles, the officer in charge of the A/T guns in our area, is musical. Had a beer and a long chat with him in the evening, singing Mozart and humming Beethoven at each other for a couple of hours. Grand experience! 2/Lt McKinnon and 7 Pl out on patrol tonight. Visited 2 Section, 9 Pl at observation post out on Pt 37 at 2230. Heavy MG and arty fire to the north.

10 SEPTEMBER. Wrote a couple of aerograms to Mum and Cecil this morning, then went 2,500 yds out into no-man's-land on a recce with Bloomfield. Dust blowing and didn't see much. Got lost. Discovered the skeletons of three half-buried Indian sepoys. Covered them over. Strangely moved by this tragic sight. Had a tot of rum after dinner with Bloomfield in his dugout.

What we'd have done without the stimulating and restorative qualities of alcohol in those circumstances I don't know. It helped to make life tolerable. The regular beer and whisky ration (officially, one bottle of whisky per officer per month) kept the Eighth Army going as much as sugary tea, despite Monty's aversion to booze and tobacco. If anything went wrong, a cigarette and a brew-up were called for, and order and morale would be instantly restored. If the Germans could have bombed the distilleries of Scotland and Canada, and the tea plantations of India and Ceylon they could have won the war in weeks. Water—four to six pints per day per man—was brought up by truck from B Echelon at night. It always tasted brackish or chlorinated, or had been in petrol tins. Half was for cooking and tea; half for a wash and shave. Any left went into vehicle radiators. We were brought one hot meal a day, more often than not M and V, also by truck at night; otherwise hard tack and bully beef. The biscuits were more palatable soaked in sugar and condensed milk, a concoction that attracted flies. I rarely complained about food after the war.

Shortages of water, a diet that was as unappetising as it was monotonous, and disease carried by flies caused constant health complaints. Diarrhoea was endemic; desert sores from cuts and scratches, and eye and ear infections were common. Flies covered everything, penetrated everywhere. A chunk of bully beef would be seething with them before you could get it out of the tin. Rodents and reptiles often scurried about our blankets. I caught a chameleon and kept it on a string as a fly catcher. I was often woken, at night or while dozing during the day, by sand falling on my face. I'd look up to see lizards scuttling away. They were harmless, but we got into the habit of tapping our boots upside down in the morning to allow visitors to leave. Scorpions were the least welcome. Those we caught were put, two at a time, inside a petrol-soaked ring of sand, which was then ignited. Then we clustered round like schoolboys, and bet on which would sting the other to death. But we never got rid of the flies. The Senussi told us there had been none before the war. Now there were millions, breeding in latrines and on corpses. The dead were buried quickly, if conditions allowed. Latrines were soaked with petrol and burned. On forward positions, where movement in daylight provoked machine-gun fire and shelling, you didn't use latrines—you crept off with a shovel and the hope that Jerry snipers were inattentive.

We experienced an odd intimacy with the enemy—the sense that in our isolated, lonely battlfield friend and foe shared a similar fate. At times, it was difficult to tell the two sides apart. Each captured the other's rations, transport, equipment and clothing, causing occasional confusion on the battlefield. Nothing was wasted in the desert. The Germans drove our trucks and ate our rations (canned South African peaches apparently being preferred). We were partial to Italian food and wine. We prized Jerry's twenty-litre, steel petrol containers. These 'Jerrycans' were much more robust than our Egyptian-made, four-gallon tins, which leaked from shoddy welding. In a typically bungling—or inventive—British way, our petrol tin, useless as it was for its purpose, proved an ideal kettle and cooker: slice off the top, puncture the sides with a bayonet and fill it with a sand and petrol mixture; this would burn for about half an hour, over which a half tin with a wire handle could be suspended and filled with water—perfect for a morale-boosting three-minute brew-up.

Life in the desert had its lighter moments. Often, there were quiet days with no artillery or air activity. All of us tuned into the BBC, when our radios weren't set for artillery shoots or army communications. We would pick up the Afrika Korps signal and hear 'Lili Marlene', that sentimental, haunting melody that captivated soldiers on both sides. On quiet evenings, I'd follow compass bearings or pace out the distance to Mac or Shaw's positions for beer, whisky and chat.

On such nights, Bloomfield was in the habit of carousing with his crony, the CQMS, and usually returned quite late and half fu'. He always manage to wake me up by blundering into our covered dugout muttering: 'Duck the heid, Bloomie, duck the heid.' Thereafter, whenever the platoon was dive-bombed or shelled, we took to yelling in unison: 'Duck the heid, Bloomie,' as we scrambled for cover. I remember fondly another of his catchphrases. He'd come rushing up, calling out: 'Have you heard the latest, sir?' Sanders and I, all agog, would wait for the news expectantly. Was it an impending move, a panzer attack, the fall of Tobruk, or something equally important? 'What?' we would ask, and came the reply from a beaming Bloomfield, 'Treacle's up a ha'penny.' We relished such moments, for it was not often that 'Gloomy Bloomie' was in such jovial mood.

My harmony practice also provoked amusement. Prompted in part by my old singing teacher, Robert Watson, I had started taking postal lessons in harmony and counterpoint from my father—with the intention of becoming a professional singer after the war—and would sit in my tent or barrack when at the rear, or in my dugout at the front, working at music manuscript paper. I roped in Sanders for impromptu singsongs of psalm and hymn tunes and other exercises. I still have the complete librettos of Gilbert and Sullivan operas that I bought in Cairo. I learned many by heart. Of course, I am now struck by the absurdity: in the middle of a war, in the desert, walking around with a music score, singing with my batman.

Eccentric behaviour was not unknown in the desert. Nor was eccentric dress. Desert boots were an essential part of an Eighth Army officer's image, as were moustaches. The boots were soft, airy, and more comfortable than the regular army issue. A craft industry sprang up in the backstreets of Cairo to satisfy the demand for them. They were just one aspect of the Eighth Army's non-standard dress. The longer officers stayed in the desert, the more flamboyant their attire became. The classic outfit was ankle-high suede boots, silk scarves, shorts or corduroy trousers, wool or cotton pullovers and sheepskin jackets and coats. The style was later affectionately lampooned in 'The Two Types' cartoons by Captain W. J. P. Jones of the Army Newspaper Unit, whose book I have still.

Newspapers and magazines were passed around, each copy of the *Egyptian Mail* or *Eighth Army News* circulated until it disintegrated or was used as lavatory paper. Whenever I went to Alex or Cairo, I brought back reading matter for myself and the men. I read and re-read a Shakespeare anthology *The Ages of Man* that I bought in Cairo, along with the *Pocket RLS* and *Sonnets by Shakespeare* from home. I remember Mac, Shaw and I, hunkered down in my dugout, reading *Henry V* to each other on off-duty evenings. We especially enjoyed the scenes with the four captains: Fluellen, Gower, Macmorris and Jamy. We identified with their thoughts on war, and the play's themes of brotherhood, bravery and honourable old age. We were responsive to its stirring rhetoric and the fact that the play does not shy away from the horrors of war. I got to know some South African and New Zealand fellows among the anti-tank and ack-ack crews in our sector. They always shared their cigarettes, beer and chocolate. There was a tremendous spirit among all of us, despite our grumbles and complaints about the heat, dust and flies; about the poor food, water rationing and the dangers we were exposed to. We got used to all that, even to the bombing, shelling and strafing.

Much of the desert was clean and clear. Cool breezes tempered the heat and dispersed the flies. The sun and stars produced magical effects. Then nature would play its tricks, with mirages of Jerry tanks, or sandstorms. Neither goggles nor silk scarves, not even our gas masks, could protect us from the violence of a sandstorm: a cloud on the horizon, moving fast . . . then the wind rushing over us, oven hot, bringing blinding, stinging sand which covered everything and penetrated everywhere. It fouled carburettors, pitted windscreens, and even stripped camouflage paint off tanks. After the tempest moved on, we would sit spitting grit for the rest of the day.

The bizarre thing about our situation, apart from the spectacle of nature's mocking beauty and brutality, was that the pleasures of Alex and Cairo were only a couple of hours away. In this respect we were better off than the enemy soldiers, who were days away from Benghazi and Tripoli. Leave, or even the prospect of it, offered an interlude from the desert war's boredom and danger—a temporary return to comfort and sanity. Mac, Shaw and I fantasised about sleeping in real beds and

soaking in hot baths at Shepheard's and being groomed by Cairo's attentive barbers; or swimming at Stanley Bay, flirting with girls on the
Corniche; quaffing ice cold lager at the Cecil and gorging decent food
at the Union Club . . . But every time I headed back up the blue, passing the familiar sign on the Alex to Cairo highway—TO THE WESTERN
DESERT—and turning onto the long, black, coastal road, I always felt
a heightened sense that I was young, fit and alive. Grains of sand stick
to me still, such was the effect of the desert, and the nomadic life and
camaraderie I found there.

EIGHTH ARMY

Personal Message from the ARMY COMMANDER

1—When I assumed command of the Eighth Army I said that the mandate was to destroy ROMMEL and his Army, and that it would be done as soon as we were ready.

2—We are ready NOW.

The battle which is now about to begin will be one of the decisive battles of history. It will be the turning point of the war. The eyes of the whole world will be on us, watching anxiously which way the battle will swing.

We can give them their answer at once, "It will swing our way."

3—We have first-class equipment; good tanks; good anti-tank guns; plenty of artillery and plenty of ammunition; and we are backed up by the finest air striking force in the world.

All that is necessary is that each one of us, every officer and man, should enter this battle with the determination to see it through — to fight and to kill — and finally, to win.

If we all do this there can be only one result — together we will hit the enemy for "six," right out of North Africa.

4—The sooner we win this battle, which will be the turning point of this war, the sooner we shall all get back home to our families.

5—Therefore, let every officer and man enter the battle with a stout heart, and with the determination to do his duty so long as he has breath in his body.

AND LET NO MAN SURRENDER SO LONG AS HE IS UNWOUNDED AND CAN FIGHT.

Let us all pray that "the Lord mighty in battle" will give us the victory.

B. L. MONTGOMERY,
Lieutenant-General G.O.C.-in-C., Eighth Army.

MIDDLE EAST FORCES,
23-10-42.

7 MONTY'S BODYGUARD

Lieutenant T. R. Ward. 1st A & S H, M E F
Sunday 27 September 1942

My dear Dad,

A wee present for you, which if you don't like to accept as a fee for services rendered, you must as a small Christmas present from an admiring and loving son! I'm sure there are lots of things you need and would like and this should enable you to buy youself something.

I got an air mail letter from you the day before I came on leave, with a lot of cuttings and other letters enclosed which made good reading. Harold's letter was particularly interesting and amusing!

By George! it's good to be on leave—hot baths daily, leisure, first-class food, book shops, music shops, cinemas, concerts, 'long lies' in bed—no getting up for Stand-to at 0500! I go back to the 'blue' on Wednesday, refreshed and strengthened I hope, by the rest. It's time I was off to church now Dad. Thanks again for your letters.

Love to all,

Ray

I WAS IN CAIRO THAT WEEKEND IN SEPTEMBER 1942, on six day's leave, the first since being sent up the blue in early July. Some Jocks came with me, sitting on bare boards in the back of the truck. I can still hear them singing bawdy songs as we left Ruweisat Ridge. Only our speed keep the morning heat at bay. On the coast road, I shouted back to ask if the men fancied a swim. What a sight we were, racing to the breakers coming in from the Med, all white buttocks on otherwise tanned bodies. A tonic! We needed the break. We'd been living in slit trenches for weeks, periodically bombed, shelled and strafed; on patrol, on working parties, on Stand-by and Stand-to, poorly fed and plagued by heat, dust, thirst and flies. Furthermore, I had been promoted to full lieutenant and had just had a hectic week's introduction to life as a company commander.

Captain Tidmarsh had gone on six days' leave to Alexandria, leaving me in charge. Since I had been commissioned, I had been playing the officer: another role, like Captain Corcoran in *HMS Pinafore*. Now, it was serious.

15 SEPTEMBER 1942. Tuesday. Rudely awakened at 0700 and told I was to report to Bn HQ at 1000. Did so dutifully and discovered I had to attend A/T gun lecture at Div HQ with Ted and Jock Hamilton. Quite interesting and instructive to the uninitiated layman. Had a beer at the Royal Surrey HQ there. Wrote letters in afternoon. Had a gin with Ted later. He goes on leave tomorrow, as does Sanders. OC A Company eh?! Hope nothing happens while Ted's away. Had a shandy with Rollo Charles at Stand-to. Talk with Ted after dinner and received final instructions.

16 SEPTEMBER. Ted and Sanders away on leave. Slight shelling 600 yds north of Coy HQ at 1200. Air activity in afternoon. Spent a lot of time receiving, answering and sending messages. Feel tremendously important as OC of A Coy! No Argyll patrols tonight. Company Duties: 8 Pl, standing patrol on points 37 and 38; 9 Pl, one sec at new gap in minefield; 7 Pl, one sec on gap at Pt 37. Great how-de-do about strength states and rations. Sgt Grant moaning about being given short rations, based on wrong figures. Fixed the matter up with the Adj after waiting for phone line to be repaired. Had very sound sleep. Night undisturbed.

17 SEPTEMBER. Visit from CO this morning. Brig at points 37 and 38 with Capt Elder and Mac Hall. A couple of gins and a crack with 'wee Tattie' Shaw, who also visited me and brought a bottle of squash and news of D Coy's part in the Tobruk raid. Seemingly, Lieut McLaren was killed on board ship on the way back. Further details awaited. Cash requisition for 200 Egyptian pounds. 2/Lt Scott-Barrett fired off his wpn from Pt 38 at 1400. No shelling or air activity all day. Some mail arrived from Bn at 1630. Short visit from Rollo Charles at 1900. Evening snifter and a crack. Lesson 7, Schumann volume and text book on harmony arrived with the mail! Bad attack of diarrhoea after dinner. No patrols tonight. 7 Pl, standing patrol; 8 Pl, one sec on 37 gap; 9 Pl, one sec on north gap. NB: see CO about compressor. Binocs and compass for 9 Pl.

18 SEPTEMBER. Feeling a bit better this morning. Joyfully opened my parcel and lovingly gazed on contents. Must get cracking on lesson 7 as soon as I can. One sec 8 Pl started wiring at 1100, around 2-pounder near north gap back to 7 Pl area. A few enemy shells landed approx 1,000 yds south at 0900. Heavy machine-gun fire from South Africans at 0900. Worked on lesson 7 and studied harmony book in afternoon. Orders for next leave party. Two from A Coy, Sun 20th. C Coy on patrol tonight. 7 Pl, one sec at north gap firing white Verey lights; 8 Pl, one sec at 37 gap; 9 Pl, standing patrol at 37 and 38. A few drinks with the arty OP officer. McKinnion drew pay (200 Egyptian pounds) from Bn HQ.

19 SEPTEMBER. C Coy patrol retired approx 0400. One man lost. Found at 0630. Cpl Clark and McKinnon commenced paying out the Coy at 1100. Brig, CO and IO passed through Coy position at 1130 on forward recce. Wrote letter card and sent off lesson 7. Conference with CO at 1645. Dive-bombed by Stukas while at Bn HQ.

Points from CO's orders: 1. More activity wanted—offensive spirit. Daylight observation—patrols. 2. Three posts in front of carrier sec in hollow fwd of Pt 37 from first light. Two carriers in hollow (88022817) approx 200 yds west of 37. Third carrier, 800 yds fwd. 3. Starting 20/09/42, patrols of two men along edge of ridge from Pt 38, approx 1000-1200 yds. One section digging slits to accommodate A and C Coys. Standing patrols from respective pls, Pt 38, in hollow at 88022817, carrier in front. 4. Extensive wiring, starting from fwd positions. Double apron wire sited tactically and defensively, with mines at Pt 38 (wire coming up tonight to be carried out to Pt 38). 5. When slits completed in hollow, standing patrols headquarter there; two-man patrols operate from there. Pt 38 NOT to be occupied by day, but made proof against infantry attack and occupied at night.

General points: waken men up, stimulate curiosity, mental alertness, initiative etc. Cultivate offensive spirit. Ask questions—give short talks. Test NCOs and, if necessary, instruct them in topography and general knowledge, and general alertness and efficiency. Study patrolling—new ideas. Impress on men that a minefield is NOT an infantry obstacle!

Wiring to start as soon as possible on Pt 38. Unloading and carrying party from 7 Pl tonight. Sec from 9 Pl start digging in hollow tomorrow. Sgt Bloomfield to Coy HQ tomorrow at 0600. Meet Capt Fanshawe and 10 at Pt 37 at 0630 tomorrow—recce hollow . . . 9 Pl sec: two white lights at 0100, two white lights at 0330 and thereafter at half-hour intervals till patrols return. B Coy patrol—pass thro' A Coy at 2130. Wire for Pt 38 arrived 2100. Platoon starting wiring at 2300. Harassed all evening by phone calls. Had time for a couple of canned beers with Rollo Charles at my HQ. Rearrangement of sections at gaps. Saw Scott-Barrett at 2230 and sent him out to Pt 38 to get wiring started on the right lines. CSM sick and not much help.

20 SEPTEMBER. Sunday. Slept quite well considering. Recce'd hollow west of Pt 37 at 0630 with Lt Renny, Capt Fanshawe and Bloomfield. 50 yds of double apron erected by 8 Pl during the night at Pt 38. 9 Pl start

digging this morning. Activity from our arty from early morning. Two-man patrols start today from Pt 38. Scott-Barrett out on personal recce to within 600 yds of enemy wire. Exchanged shots. Dive-bombed by Stukas at 1700. Busy with messages, phone calls, visitors and orders till after dark.

L/Sgt Jennings refused to go out on patrol at 1915. Placed under close arrest. Thinks he has a grievance and is being overworked—while on Active Service and in the frontline, mark you! (Grievance and stubbornness magnified by the fact that, I think, he had had a few cans of beer.) Feel very disgusted, annoyed and angry with the whole wretched business. Wonder what Ted will have to say. Strange Sunday this! 7 Pl, one sec north gap; 8 Pl, one sec south gap; 9 Pl, two secs, 37 and 38. Secs from 8 and 9 pls wiring at Coy HQ from 2200 till 0100. Two aerograms from home today. Slept well.

21 SEPTEMBER. Heavy shelling from our arty early this morning and intermittently all morning. Digging fwd of Pt 37 cancelled. C Coy, I understand from Capt Fanshawe, taking up position fwd of Pt 37. B Coy taking over C Coy's positions today. McKinnon on standing patrol last night. Visited patrols by day. Tried Sgt Jennings at 1230 and remanded him to the CO. Scott-Barrett and nineteen men at concert party at B Echelon area at 1630. Warn guides for C Coy's truck at 1930. Great deal of movement by troops and transport through our coy area after dark. Working parties and compressor for C Coy sec out in front. Uneventful night. Slept well.

22 SEPTEMBER. Very heavy dew this morning. Thick mist till 0900. Coy area visited by Corps Commander, Division Commander, Brigadier and CO at 0800. 'Everything under control.' Ted due back tonight. Cash requisition to be at Bn HQ 0900, 23rd. Sgt Jennings for CO at Bn HQ 0900, 23rd. 8 Pl (two secs) patrol tonight. Duties: 7 Pl, two secs standing

patrol; 8 Pl, two secs fighting patrol; 9 Pl, one sec at north gap; Coy HQ, one sec at south gap. South Africans dive-bombed by Stukas at 1730. C Coy shelled rather heavily at 1830 by our own arty! Two casualties. C Coy withdrawn at 2230. Scott-Barrett on patrol. Sleepless night. Phone ringing all night.

23-24 SEPTEMBER. Ted arrived back this morning. Wrote some aerograms home. Going on leave tomorrow. Slept well . . . Bn HQ at 1100. Summary of Evidence, then Ho! for Cairo.

I had some sympathy for Lance Sergeant Jennings. He had won an MM on Crete, so may well have been justified in thinking he'd done his bit. But he wouldn't change his mind, despite pleas and threats from the CSM and Bloomfield. Perhaps he had simply had enough—of the shelling, the Stukas, the frightful noise. If so, his was not the only case of battle fatigue I had seen, or would see. In an earlier incident, another of my section leaders shot himself in the foot. Accidentally, he protested, while cleaning his rifle; said he'd forgotten there had been no safety cut-off. A likely story. Bloomfield was incensed. If the man wasn't malingering, he was evidently careless with weapons and a danger to the rest of us. I believe he was court-martialled. Jennings may have been reduced to the ranks.

With the memory of the upper and lower decks on the *Windsor Castle* still with me, I had resolved that I would not let the army's hierarchy get in the way of my relationship with my men. Remembering the poor private singled out by the drill sergeant at Stirling, I had vowed not to make a public example of any of them. Misdemeanours would be solved firmly but fairly. I tried to be sensitive to each man's mood and aware of my own. That proved difficult at times. With each platoon commander reporting to me, I felt tremendously important as OC of A Company. Of course, I had to justify this by setting an example, to maintain discipline and morale. I couldn't have let Jennings off the hook, even if I'd wanted to . . .

We were in fine fettle as we passed the Pyramids and crossed the Nile into Cairo, where we split up like a bunch of boys on the first day of school holidays. I wondered what the men would do—it was rumoured that Monty had closed the Berka.

I took a room at one of the services clubs. After the scarcity of water up the blue, to fill a bathtub seemed reckless; fresh bed linen felt hedonistic; to sip tea that didn't taste of chlorinated water or petrol was an almost forgotten pleasure. At Shepheard's, officers swanned about as usual. Newspaper boys weaved between the tables on the terrace. I sensed confidence in the air—Monty's doing. Soldiers on leave from the IBD wandered along the streets, pink as piglets. I tried to resist feeling superior—the suntanned desert veteran.

It may have been on that occasion that I was approached by one of Cairo's elderly Arab guides. Before I could wave him away he magically procured a taxi driven by his son. They were agreeable, chatting in animated, passable English all the time, the guide directing us from mosque to mosque. We entered alleys no wider than the car, overhung with enclosed, arabesque balconies which, I imagined, promised seduction behind their patterned screens. Nothing was veiled at ground level: the lanes were lined with open shopfronts whose fragrant and foul goods spilled out onto the street. Deformed beggars reached out as we passed a beautiful mosque; snake charmers lifted basket lids and poked sticks at their cobras. Tinsmiths hammered away in the heat at what looked like the flimsy petrol cans we got at the front. I had the thought that, if that wasn't sabotage enough, their sons might be in the basement, with printing presses churning out anti-British propaganda. I thus passed through Old Cairo with feelings of Grand Tour nostalgia and loathing. At the Citadel above the city's domes and minarets, the wind brought flurries of desert dust like snow.

I found my men, as arranged, at the railway station, relieved that none had gone AWOL. On the drive back to the battalion, the road was thick with military traffic, the macadam humming: staff cars, Jeeps, armoured cars; trucks loaded with camouflage netting and ammo; convoys of petrol and water tankers; quad tractors towing 25-pounders, and Scammell transporters loaded with brand-new Sherman tanks. Cheery troops packed into trucks we overtook gave us the 'thumbs up'. Signposts to training camps, airfields, field depots, LAD workshops and POL dumps seemed to have sprung from nowhere. Spirits were high after the success of the Battle of Alam Halfa. We knew now that Rommel had shot his bolt, and preparations were going ahead for our big offensive.

In the desert to the south, an elaborate deception was deploying fake tanks, bogus supply depots and a dummy pipeline and railway. The Luftwaffe was allowed to photograph these decoys, to make Rommel think the offensive would be away from the coast and later than Monty planned. The ruse succeded: Rommel was in Germany on leave when the Battle of El Alamein began. The subtefuge was masterminded by a London music-hall magician, Jasper Maskelyne, serving with the Royal Engineers (he had previously built bogus docks at Alex to lure enemy bombers away from the real thing).

The battalion was resting behind the lines on Ruweisat Ridge. At Company HQ, Captain Tidmarsh was pacing about waiting for me.

'Ray! Glad you're back. You won't believe this,' he said, handing me a sheet of orders:

SPECIAL MISSION. MOST SECRET. Square 475916. Area south of Conical Hill. South of Main Road. Report to GSD Branch, Main 8th Army. GOC (Army Commander) Bodyguard.

'Monty's bodyguard?'

'You leave tomorrow. Keep it under your hat.'

A Company's 9 Platoon, which I still commanded, had been selected as Infantry Guard at Eighth Army Tactical HQ, Monty's mobile
command. Perhaps that day we went swanning about near Amiriya with
Major Oswald in August got us the job; or because my week as temporary OC, A Company had passed without disaster. Even so, I flipped
through my Field Service Pocket Book that afternoon, re-read the orders
and briefed Sanders (who was the platoon runner and back-up wireless
operator as well as my batman) and Bloomfield about our new job—and
the trucks, petrol, oil, water, stores, rations, weapons and ammo we'd
require, to be picked up from B Echelon.

I must say, I was excited by the unexpected assignment, if not entirely happy about again leaving the battalion and my friends. But at Tac
HQ there would be novelty, more responsibility, better food, slightly
cooler weather and fewer flies, as Monty preferred it to be located by
the sea. I said goodbye to Padre Smith who was leaving. That night at
Company HQ, Mac, Shaw, and Ted laid on a bit of a party for 'Monty's
bodyguard'. My diary entry that day ends with me 'rolling home by the
light o' the moon.'

On the morning of 2 October I assembled the platoon. Bloomfield
appeared smartly with my list of equipment and ordnance, and checked
each section. The Jocks thought we were about to go on a raid behind
enemy lines. In addition to each man's rifle and bullets (50 rounds per
man and 20 rounds in clips), each section was equipped with a Bren,
with 21 magazines, spare barrel, spare parts pack, cleaning rod, oil and
tripod, plus a tommy gun and four mags. Section 9 still had a captured
Italian Breda machine-gun, with a tripod, spares and ammo strips.
Platoon HQ—myself, Sanders and Bloomfield—had a 2-inch mortar,
with one box of smoke bombs and three of HE, a .55 anti-tank rifle
(completely useless, replaced later by the Piat gun), four boxes of .303
and two of .45 calibre ammo, and 68 hand grenades and a box of det-

onators. I had my .38 service revolver, the platoon compass, field glasses and a Verey pistol. All of this was standard equipment, but as we stood around armed to the teeth and grinning, dressed in our shorts, battledress jackets, scarves, balmorals and desert boots, we looked like a crew of desperadoes about to start a small war.

02 OCTOBER. Friday. Sat around waiting for transport to take us on our 'special mission'. Left for Burg el Arab at 1230, arrived 1530. Kept hanging around until 1800. Settled down in position with the Royal Tank Regiment's Tac HQ Tank Protective Detachment (squadron of Grant tanks and armoured cars).

Conference at 1730. Admin and 'interior economy' discussed with Major D. J. Coulson 6th RTR: petrol, water (bottles and cans: six 2-gallon cans per truck, and 15 per platoon); cooking, rations (at RTR cookhouse), mail (censored), canteen (stamps, airgraphs); day leave (10 men?), sea bathing (dangerous here); discipline, dress (shirts on), boots, dhobi; strength states (for rations), nominal roll (for pay), pay (rates of), leave passes; blackout, ARP; sentries, slit trenches, latrines. Pay parade at Platoon HQ at 1745. Pay books. Payout at RTR office truck 1800; remainder at 0830 tomorrow. Reveille 0600; rifle and line inspection 0900. Start messing tomorrow breakfast with RTR.

03 OCTOBER. Burg el Arab. Messing now with RTR. Likely to be semipermanent job, this. May last for six months. Eight men on day's leave to Alex. Exercise on Tuesday. Spent morning discussing domestic problems etc., seeing about rations, petrol, pay etc. Slit trenches and latrines dug in section areas. Wrote a letter card home this afternoon. Rained slightly today. Thunder and lightning storm too! A pleasure to witness natural and elemental activity in the sky instead of the usual 'air activity'. RTR mess for dinner before going to bed at 2215.

△ General Montgomery by his Grant tank at Tactical HQ, El Alamein, October 1942. *'He tore up GHQ's plans for retreat, and transformed the Eighth Army from a dispirited and confused miscellany into a confident, unified, battle-winning force.'* ◁ Cover of a War Office/Ministry of Information propaganda book celebrating Monty's victory over Rommel's Afrika Korps.

THE EIGHTH ARMY

▷ 'Steady, boys, steady!' Sporting Club, Alexandria, June 1942: MacDougall, Ward and Second Lieutenant Pyper. ◁ Ray Ward washing, desert style. ◁ Walter Sanders. ▽ Buglers of the Sudan Defence Force and Argylls mounting guard on the promenade outside the Governor's Palace, Khartoum, January 1942.

'I imagined the men of Kitchener's army suffering similar discomfort as they prepared to crush the Islamic uprising of 1898.' 1st Battalion, the Argylls assault training on the plain at Omdurman, January 1942. ▷ Ack-ack drill (Ray Ward with tripod-mounted Bren gun). ◁ Officers watch as the men tackle an obstacle course. ▽ 'Fix bayonets. Slope arms. Quick march. Charge!' Canvas and straw dummies simulated the enemy.

◁ 'My first duty in the desert I am sure every infantryman who served in the Eighth
Army remembered: I dug trenches. Lots of them.' The infantryman's war: foxholes in
the Western Desert, 1942. △ Italian PoWs at El Alamein, November 1942.
▷ A knocked-out Sherman tank, El Alamein. ▽ The corpse of a German gunner
rots among the debris of an 88-mm anti-tank gun position.

△ Lieutenant Ray Ward, as acting company commander, Ruweisat Ridge, September 1942. ◁ Sergeant Bloomfield in the Western Desert, winter 1942. ▽ *'The first shock I experienced on the desert front line was the complete absence of four things normally taken for granted: freedom of movement, decent food, clean water, and secure shelter.'* MacDougall at his dugout, Ruweisat Ridge, August 1942.

◁ Marble Arch, Libya, built in 1937 on Mussolini's colonial Via Balbia, December 1942. ▷ 9 Platoon, 'A' Company, 1st Argylls with Montgomery at Tac HQ, 24 December 1942 (Lt. Ray Ward, with Sergeant Bloomfield by his side, is on Monty's right). ▽ Monty, snapped by Ray Ward on the Western Desert coast road.

◁ Cover of the Eighth Army guide to Sicily. △ Port Said, 5 July
1943: An Argyll on the *Duchess of Bedford,* en route to Sicily.
▽ Major MacFie (centre) and Soviet delegates, Mena Conference, November 1943.

04-05 OCTOBER. Rifle inspection at 0900. Sergeant Bloomfield on day pass to Alex with nine Jocks. Bloomfield and three other ranks missing from returned leave party . . . Truants not back at Reveille or b'fast; turned up eventually at 0900 looking very sorry for themselves. Plausible and credible story best forgotten. Gave the three other ranks the 'berry' of their lives. Sorry for Bloomie, as I can imagine his feelings. Couldn't find it in me to be too hard on him. Major Coulson preferred to wash his hands of it. Gave them all another dressing down and started again from scratch with Bloomfield. No more trouble likely from the others. 1700. Briefing for tomorrow's Tac HQ exercise. Heavy rain and thunder storms in evening. Camp flooded.

06-07 OCTOBER. Rev 0630. B'fast 0715. Haversack rations drawn. Out for day and night. Trucks report to section areas at 0800. Trucks loaded with complete kit, lock, stock and barrel; water and petrol. Dress: battle order; respirators and steel helmets slung. Men ready to move off at 0830. Spent day 'out in the desert' manoeuvring etc. with RTR. NCOS working very well. Quite successful day. My job in this show is 'Camp Commandant' of all things; provide guards, sentries, police, guides etc. Wouldn't mind a Jeep and another pip! Dinner at laager in the field. A drink with Sgt B in laager posn in the evening . . . Rev 0515. Moved off in Desert Formation at 0545. Mighty cold morning. Heavy dew and thick mist until 0830. Back to own area at 1000. Rest of day on interior economy.

08-09 OCTOBER. Spent day in Alex. Lunched at Union Club. Went shopping and saw an American flick. Met three RTR blokes by arrangement in the evening at the Cecil. Had a few drinks then dinner at Pastroudis. Saw another flick and returned in their 8-cwt at midnight. Grand crowd in the 'tankies' and am beginning to get on well with them. Major Coulson a grand chap—very kind and helpful to us. Two-day scheme starting on 12th . . . Saw about pay in the forenoon; an after-noon swim with four other chaps. Mail on the way for us! Hundreds of our bombers and fighters in the sky today. Must be something on. Rumours of a captaincy for me.

Standing Orders: 1. Division of Tac HQ by groups as follows: Army Commander, signals, G2 Ops Major Oswald, Camp Commandant Captain Adams, and RTR. Group comds will report for orders daily to the Armoured Command Vehicle at 2000. One representative from each group to travel with advance party. 2. Road movement: all vehicles to have numbers painted, indicating order in column; vehicles to be spaced 100 yds apart by day (interval at night dependent on state of moon); vehicles to halt off road.

11 OCTOBER. Sunday. Quiet lazy day. Read, wrote and slept most of the time. Two-day scheme starting tomorrow. Wrote to Capt Tidmarsh.

12-15 OCTOBER. Orders for Scheme 0930. Leave 1400. Meet Main Party Tac HQ at road at 1420. Route to 520875 (35 miles south-east). Normal order of march. Ourselves behind Tac HQ. 0900, 13th. Join up with 10 Corps. Exercise begins at 1100, ends at 1600. Laager: night of 13/14th. Return morning 14th. Carried out my Camp and Provost duties. Practised set-up for Infantry Guard. Strength: Guard Comdr, NCO and nine men; period of duty 24 hrs, 1900-1900.

Posts. By day: one man at traffic control point at track junction, one man at track junction near GOC's caravan, one A/A sentry with Bren behind ACV. By night: armd cars at traffic control point, one sentry at GOC's caravan, one sentry at ACV, one prowler. Infantry Guard Comdr responsible for posting and relieving of sentries by day and night; also responsible for traffic control, dispersal of vehicles. Guard will sleep near ACV; by day will stand by in platoon area with the rest of the men. A drink with Bloomfield and a good night's sleep under the stars . . .

Rev 0615 sounded by Bren bursts. Off again at 0800. Very dusty trip to new posn. Many vehicles stuck. Platoon HQ truck conked out. Given a scout car for rest of the exercise. Had a drink in the ACV with Major Oswald, G2s and G3s . . . Recce'd new position near Alamein in forenoon. Returned by 'Jeep', fell behind chasing stragglers. Thorough wash after settling down. Conference at 1400 with Coulson, G2 and G3 on moves over the next few days. Interior economy in afternoon. Bed early, troubled sleep.

16-18 OCTOBER. Tac HQ battle position, El Alamein. Dust storm started at 1430 and continued all day. Heavy rain in evening. A bad night for all, especially guards. Had a drink with Lieutenant Clark, A/A Troop Commander. Overnight rain . . .

Morning spent digging out vehicles and weapons pits. Violent rainstorm all morning. Whole place and everyone in a sorry mess. Decided the matter of guards and sentries with Oswald. Duties: police posts and prowlers, ack-ack sentries and Bren gunners; sign posts, mark location of ACV, Army Commander's caravan, Officers' Mess, G2 Ops, Signal Corps etc.; stop and disperse visitors' cars, establish identity of visitors. Plan of Tac HQ, camouflage nets, armbands. Informed at 1400 by Oswald that we (the infantry pl) will remain behind with 28 Signals to improve and complete excavations and clean up the area for return of Tac HQ on Wed [Monty touring the front line]. Blast! No more day trips to Alex now. Very cold tonight. Had a game of chess with 'Nobby' Clark.

19 OCTOBER. No improvement in weather yet. Still cold and rainy. Got men started on digging tasks. Weather better by lunch time. Compressor arrived at 1045 and kept busy till 1700. Men worked very well at digging. Good job done. No mail yet. Good food we're getting at cookhouse. Men well-pleased . . . Another busy day for everybody. No time to do any reading or writing. Some shelling going on in forenoon. Digging

programme well in hand. Should be finished tomorrow. Bloomfield in a 'mahleesh' mood; merits the nickname 'Gloomy Bloomie' today all right. Split a bottle of beer and had a desultory chat with him tonight. Went back to Burg el Arab after b'fast to see about mail, NAAFI goods etc. No mail or beer yet. Kept awake by a desert rat scurrying about in my bivvy.

20-21 OCTOBER. Part of 30 Corps HQ (Lt-General Leese) moved in beside us. 7 Section on interior economy this morning, rest of platoon finishing off final tasks—slit trenches, cleaning up area after rain . . . Tac HQ in part, armd cars and ack-ack moved up this morning. Oswald well-pleased with work done by my platoon. Fixed up signposts before dark. Wrote letter card home. Had dinner in mess with other Tac HQ officers. All leave stopped. No one will be allowed on the road back to Alex, Cairo and the Delta. Great anticipation of and confidence about the imminent offensive.

Tac HQ was a compact unit formed to enable Monty to conduct the forthcoming offensive from the battlefront, not from GHQ Cairo or some other safe position behind the lines. Unit commanders were kept on their toes, always half-expecting the army commander to turn up at the front to see things for himself, as indeed he did. As the infantry guard commander at Tac HQ, I found myself responsible for round-the-clock protection of the camp: identity checks, admittance or refusal to visitors, traffic management, signage, marking the route to Tac HQ from the nearest corps centre line, vehicle dispersal, camouflage, sentries, and infantry defence against surprise attack—tasks repeated each time Tac HQ moved and a new camp was set up as the army advanced. I quickly noted and got to know the unit's composition and its staff:

EIGHTH ARMY TAC HQ: General Montgomery, his batman, his staff and liaison officers, cipher and signals staff, drivers, mechanics,

an electrician, cook and orderlies (12 officers and 70 other ranks).
TRANSPORT: One Armoured Command Vehicle, Monty's personal
caravan, five staff cars, seven Bantams and 15 trucks (five for commu-
nications). DEFENCE: Tank Protective Detachment, B Squadron, 6th
Royal Tank Regiment (10 Grant tanks, seven officers, 43 ORs); 6th
South African (two armoured cars, one officer, seven ORs); 1st
Armoured Light Aid Detachment workshop (13 ORs); D Troop, 113
Light Anti-Aircraft Battery, Royal Artillery (six Bofors ack-ack guns,
tow-trucks, one officer and 40 ORs); Infantry Guard, 9 Platoon, A
Company, 1st Argyll and Sutherland Highlanders (one officer and 32
ORs, four platoon trucks).

The desert army relied on wireless communication, often with distant HQs. There had been no core to the network. Signals were often
distorted, depending on weather and topography. In previous battles
communications had frequently failed. The ACV, a customised,
armour-plated truck with staff inside controlling the army's wireless
web, was designed to solve this problem. It was the Eighth Army's nerve
centre in the field. Monty, whose initiative it was, often issued orders
over the ACV's radio telephone. His caravan had a wood-panelled study
and map room with, it was said, a picture of Rommel on the wall. I
never saw the inside: the closest I got to it was to check up on my sentry permanently posted outside.

Major Oswald made it clear that Monty detested interruption and
most visitors, other than his Chief of Staff, Freddie de Guingand, and
a handful of divisional and air force commanders, were barred, not only
from the caravan, but also from the camp. Even the C-in-C, General
Alexander, rarely visited Tac HQ, preferring to leave Monty in complete control. Their relationship was a key factor in the success of the
campaign. Alexander dealt with diplomacy, for which his upper-class
background and charm were suited, and he had the wit to let Monty,

the hard-nosed professional soldier, plan and direct the battles without GHQ's interference.

I was ordered to refuse entry to anyone arriving at Tac HQ without authorisation. This made me obsessed with security and I often woke in the early hours to check the sentries. They were generally good lads and alert, but, to keep them so, I passed on a story that Italian marines had been captured after landing to sabotage the railway behind our lines. I told them that, in November 1941, commandos had made a daring (if unsuccessful) raid Rommel's HQ; that raids by the Long Range Desert Group and the SAS might give the enemy ideas. I reminded them that in September our own Captain McFie and D Company had taken part in a combined operations raid on Tobruk—with marines and army units by sea and the LRDG overland—to destroy installations and shipping, and divert attention from Alamein. (As Shaw had alluded earlier, that raid didn't go well. The Argylls were not landed, but were bombed at sea on the way back to Alex. One of the navy's destroyers was sunk by shore batteries and another, along with a cruiser, by Stukas. 'Loose lips' did sink ships: rumours of the raid had circulated in Palestine and Egypt before it happened.)

I got to know Monty's staff and liaison officers. I expected them to be foppish cavalry types (the *aide-de-camp*, Captain Poston, was an officer in the 11th Hussars). In fact, they were delightful fellows—young, handsome and confident. After my experience on Ruweisat Ridge, I thought they lived pampered lives. They had their own mess and bar, mobile showers, camp beds, sheets, pyjamas, changes of clothes, good food and servants. They were certainly not the 'donkeys' of the General Staff in the First World War. All had been hand-picked by Monty. They were intelligent, well-educated and efficient fellows. Bloomfield called them 'Monty's boy scouts'. Each morning they drove off in their Bantams to liaise with frontline units, reporting back at sunset for dinner and debriefing. In the evenings, Monty relaxed in his mess tent with his acolytes. I'd hear bursts of laughter ripple out into the night air, as my men and I patrolled the perimeter and the sand dunes.

Monty, a stickler for discipline in most other ways, wore corduroy trousers, pullovers and unconventional hats. He sported an Aussie bush hat that glittered with the badges he pinned on each time he visited a different regiment. After taking possession of his personal Grant tank, he took to wearing an RTR beret, adding his general's badge to it. He claimed the effect on morale was worth two divisions. Like the bush hat, the beret became a trademark. So did the tank.

Tank gunners, wireless operators and drivers were regular soldiers, but the commanders still tended to be cavalry types who spoke the lingo of the Light Brigade—Monty's tank was referred to as 'the army commander's charger'. Major Coulson, more of a realist than a Light Brigade type, showed me round one of the Grants. While Cairo was in a flap after the fall of Tobruk, the RTR had been in action, caught up, as Coulson said, 'in the bloody confusion of armoured warfare': the smoke from near misses, the brew-ups (not tea), Stuka attacks, the deadly 88s and fast-moving panzers. The Grant's disadvantage, he explained, was that its 75-mm gun pointed forward from the tank's hull, not from the revolving turret, which had a 2-pounder. [The Sherman, which was arriving from the US in increasing numbers, solved this problem, with a 75-mm gun in the turret.]

I climbed onto the 28-ton monster and levered my way inside. The interior was as I imagined a submarine's would be: cramped, hot and smelling of sweat and oil. Bundled sleeping bags (crews slept outside), water cans and rations were stowed in any spaces left free by steering levers, engine gauges, radios, gun breeches, grenades, Browning machine-gun belts and racks of brass-cased shells. The Grant had a speed of 26 mph and a range of over 100 miles. Coulson's Grants were diesel but most ran on petrol, as did Shermans. They were death-traps when hit. I envied the tankies' courage but not their occupation. If this was how the modern cavalry went to war, it was not romantic. After that, I never complained about joining an infantry regiment.

22 OCTOBER. Thursday. Talk by Major Oswald this morning about the Army Comdr's plan for the forthcoming battle. Zero Hour: 2200 Friday 23rd; arty: 800 guns (4.5 inch, 5.5 inch and 25-pounders) for half an hour; mine lifting and attacks all along the front. Main attack in the north: the 9th Australian, 51st Highland, 2nd New Zealand and 1st South African divisions—they break through and establish a bridgehead; 10 Corps tanks then pass through. Diversion in centre by 4th Indian Div; attacks in the south by 50th, 44th, and 7th Armd divs and the Free French Bde. Intention: to destroy the enemy in North Africa. Phase 1. Arty and aerial bombardment. 2. Infantry attacks and establish bridgehead. 3. Infantry pushes on to objectives, mopping up, and tanks pass through. 4. Tank battle? . . . Start guard and sentry duties proper at 1900, armd cars and ack-ack tps assisting. Wonder what the Argylls' objective will be tomorrow night.

23 OCTOBER. Our thoughts all day about 2140 hrs tonight, when the arty barrage starts one of the biggest and most decisive battles in history. Surprise visit by General Montgomery to our mess during tea. Cheerful, keen-eyed, wiry wee man. Looks and feels very confident. Had a chat with Lieutenant-General Leese, commanding 30 Corps, whom I had shown over A Coy's posn north of Ruweisat Ridge five or six weeks ago.

Lieutenant-General Sir Oliver Leese, a casually-dressed Old Etonian and former Coldstream Guards officer, walked about the desert with the air of a county squire out on his estate. He was a bluff, good-humoured, let's-have-a-crack-at-Jerry type. He handed me a printed sheet of paper and told me to read the text to my men. The message was read by or spoken to every soldier in the Eighth Army:

EIGHTH ARMY

PERSONAL MESSAGE FROM THE ARMY COMMANDER

1. When I assumed command of the Eighth Army I said that the mandate was to destroy ROMMEL and his Army, and that it would be done as soon as we were ready.

2. We are ready NOW.

The battle which is now about to begin will be one of the decisive battles of history. It will be the turning point of the war. The eyes of the whole world will be on us, watching anxiously which way the battle will swing. We can give them their answer at once, 'It will swing our way.'

3. We have first-class equipment; good tanks; good anti-tank guns; plenty of artillery and plenty of ammunition; and we are backed up by the finest air striking force in the world.

All that is necessary is that each one of us, every officer and man, should enter this battle with the determination to see it through—to fight and to kill—and finally to win.

If we all do this there can be only one result—together we will hit the enemy for 'six,' right out of North Africa.

4. The sooner we win this battle, which will be the turning point of this war, the sooner we shall all get back home to our families.

5. Therefore, let every officer and man enter the battle with a stout heart and with the determination to do his duty so long as he has breath in his body.

AND LET NO MAN SURRENDER SO LONG AS HE IS UNWOUNDED AND CAN FIGHT.

Let us all pray that 'the Lord mighty in battle' will give us the victory.

B. L. Montgomery.

Lieutenant-General, G.O.C.-in-C., Eighth Army

Middle East Forces

23-10-42

23 OCTOBER, *continued*. Thought of all the poor devils in the infantry, lying up all day in the heat and discomfort of their slit trenches, keyed up for the greatest trial of their lives. Guns start dead on time all along the front. A most impressive sight and awe-inspiring in its implications. Watched tanks of the armoured brigade moving up the road for the breakthrough. Stood with Sergeant Bloomfield and toasted A Coy, the Argylls.

Bloomie and I stood on a sand dune with Leese and his staff. The sunset had been ominously red that evening. Now a full moon was up, lighting the sea to the north with a steely sheen. The desert, reflecting no light, was completely blank. Yet thousands of assault troops were waiting out there. In the silence, you could hear your heartbeat—or was it the ticking of the wrist-watches we kept our eyes on?

2140. 23 October 1942.

800 guns roared along a 20-kilometre front. We stood paralysed in a panorama of muzzle flashes, flares and arcing streams of tracer, in thrall to the unstoppable terror. Seconds later, the ground shook as the concussion rolled over our mound. Even at our distance, the noise was indescribable and the ground fairly shook under our feet. The flashes lit and coloured our faces red, pink, deathly white.

Over the racket, Leese, breathing fire like an old warhorse, turned to Bloomfield.

'Don't you wish you were up there at the front, Sergeant?' he bellowed over the din.

Bloomie, who had already had a go at Jerry at Sidi Barrani and Crete, answered sturdily and honestly.

'No, sir.'

Leese didn't hear, or ask me. Just as well because, although I would have felt bound to answer 'Yes indeed, sir', I was as happy as Bloomie to be where we were—with the brass hats, the usual spectators.

At 2155 the bombardment stopped as abruptly as it had started. I was then aware of the dust and the smell of cordite that drifted over our position, and the glow of fires on the horizon, where the Germans and Italians must have been sheltering or dying in their pulverised gun emplacements and trenches. Five minutes later, the guns boomed again—a creeping barrage, moving forward in front of the infantry. What a job for the poor fellows lifting mines, with thousands of shells screaming overhead. What a job for the poor bloody infantry following the sappers' white-taped tracks through the minefields. In the distance, I saw tanks lit by gun flashes, rumbling forward for the breakthrough. Searchlights arced across the sky. At 2200, waves of aircraft screamed over to lay smoke and bomb enemy batteries and communications.

During this commotion several Scammells carrying new Grants for the RTR lumbered into camp unannounced, alarming my sentries. Bloomfield and I dashed to the dispersal area to sort things out, the ground lit by flashes of artillery as we ran. We got the tanks parked. The crews dismounted and stood mesmerised as we were at the spectacle. The second barrage continued until 0300. When it ceased, the distant sounds of battle drifted towards us. There was heavy dew when I crawled into my tent. I slept fitfully and had horrid dreams.

24 OCTOBER. Morning news: 7th Armoured Division in the south encountered greater opposition than expected at second minefield. Very successful in the north where the main attack is. Infantry divisions of 30 Corps gained second objectives and 10 Corps establishing itself in appointed positions. Had a chat with Coulson, whose tanks are now up. General Alexander C-in-C visited Tac HQ in forenoon. Went across to RTR mess for dinner with Clark and Lieutenant Cazalet (SA armd cars). Went to bed early after a crack with Sanders and Bloomfield.

25 OCTOBER. Getting fed up with having nothing to do when so much is being done elsewhere. No sign of any mail yet. Bombing during the night, plenty of air activity by day. Battle situation obscure.

Alexander and his Chief-of-Staff, General McCreery, had come up from Cairo to see how the battle was progressing. In the early hours of the following morning, Leese (30th Corps) and Major-General Lumsden (10th Corps) were led into the camp by de Guingand for an urgent army commander's conference, their tension not just the result of a Jerry air raid when they arrived. Vague communiqués were issued, my only gist of what was going on. What I remember most from our disengaged position by the sea was the din of more bombardment: the flashes and crumps of artillery at night; the columns of smoke across the battlefield at dawn and swarms of Hurricanes and Kittyhawks over-head. I remember Monty watching his aides speed off in their Bantams, or setting off in his tank to see things for himself. Two 10th Hussars arrived with Ritter von Thoma, an Afrika Korps general they had cap-tured in no-man's-land. Monty insisted the exhausted Jerry dine with him. Highland Division replacements slogged up to the front. Red Cross trucks passed by, going in the other direction. I began to feel ill at ease in the midst of these momentous events, wondering how my battalion was doing while I was compelled to mooch around at Tac HQ.

26-28 OCTOBER. Lingered over the teapot after b'fast, as usual, won-dering what to do with myself today. Did a little work with the platoon this morning, straightening out a few domestic and administrative points. Footered about a bit, visiting sentries and then had a good swim before lunch. [Amost everyone at Tac HQ swam, although I never saw Monty in the sea.] Still no mail. Swim with Clark before tea.

Still fierce fighting in the battle area but situation still rather obscure. Thinking and dreaming a lot about home these days. Fresh bread, butter

and honey for tea in the mess today! Gorged myself silly. Most enlight-
ening hearing the talk of G2s and G3s in the mess, delightful chaps.
Clark came in for a lot of back chat for the sins of A/A gunners, i.e.
shooting at our own planes. A couple of games of chess after dinner and
so to bed. Quite a lot of bombing again during the night. Pretty ineffec-
tual, I gather.

Visited Clark's battery HQ at 'Bombay Road' in the forenoon to pass
the time and called in at the RTR mess on the way back. Good to see the
regular flights of bombers, eighteen at a time, on their way over to Jerry,
who must be feeling rather sick by now. Spent a pleasant hour or so on
the beach in the afternoon. Wrote a letter to Shaw at the Bn. Heard that
the 4th Indian Division moved up a bit, taking over positions the South
Africans captured. Wonder how the Bn is faring . . . Fifty Jerry tanks
knocked out yesterday and a good bag of aircraft by the RAF. Everything
going satisfactorily, according to communiqués. Probability of big tank
battle in a day or two.

30-31 OCTOBER. Great air activity in the morning. Sky full of our
bombers, fighters and fighter-bombers. Passed the day somehow. Had
another swim. The water of the Mediterranean quite bracing, with huge
breakers rolling over the sandy beach. Played chess with Clark . . . Took
a truck and set off with Bloomfield on search of our Bn which we found
not far from here, midway between Ruweisat and Alamein. Bloomie
wants to get back to it. Good to see friends again. Went to B Echelon
and missed mail by a short head. Back about 1800.

01-05 NOVEMBER. Wrote a letter card home and did a bit of harmony
study. Swim before lunch. Had a beer with Bloomie after dinner. 0105.
We watch bombardment that precedes final push. 0540. One of my sentries put under close arrest by G3 for being asleep at his post. Bad show.
Got a bit of a rocket at the ACV. Got the NCOs together and gave them

stick—must tighten things up and exercise more control . . . Headache and bouts of sweating and shivering. Had a swim before tea. Very cold. Still no mail . . . Battle going well and Jerry on the run; talk of moving from here soon. Sentry tried by Major Coulson at 1730. Through my intervention, the charge is dealt with under Section 40 of the Army Act—28 days' Field Punishment. Mail arrived at last! Sixteen airgraphs, six postcards and eight letters. After dinner, read till my head swam. All well at home. Cecil in the Royal Marines . . . Sentry off under charge of Bloomfield to Amiriya. Spent the afternoon replying to letters. May move tomorrow. Terrific traffic on the road, moving west for the past 48 hours. G1 of main Jerry HQ put in the bag. Rommel pulling out—fast.

06 NOVEMBER. Bloomie and escort turned up this morning. Traffic too intense to attempt return journey last night. Wrote letters in the forenoon and afternoon. 1430. Two tps of tanks move out for El Daba. We move to Mersa Matruh first thing after breakfast tomorrow! Good bags of prisoners, guns and material etc. Rommel has definitely been routed this time. May spend my 26th birthday in Tripoli yet!

8 MARBLE ARCH

The battle is going very heavily against us. We're simply being crushed by the enemy weight. I've made an attempt to salvage part of the army. I wonder if it will suceed. At night I lie open-eyed, racking my brains for a way out of this plight for my troops. We are facing very difficult days, perhaps the most difficult that a man can undergo. The dead are lucky. It's all over for them.

Rommel, letter home, 3 November 1942

The enemy has just reached the breaking point and is trying to get his army away. The Royal Air Force is taking a heavy toll of his columns moving west on the main coast road. The enemy is in our power and he is just about to crack. I call on all the troops to keep up the pressure and not relax for one moment. We have the chance of putting the whole Panzer Army in the bag and we will do so.

General Montgomery, 4 November 1942

07 NOVEMBER 1942. Saturday. Tac HQ, El Alamein. Moved off for Mersa Matruh at 0800. Reached a point eight miles this side of Fuka at 1200. Stopped for half an hour for lunch. Very slow moving thereafter. Solid stream of traffic of six miles long or more. Vehicles tip to tail near Fuka. Well-seen Jerry has no planes! Passed about 4,000 prisoners on their way back. Innumerable burnt-out enemy vehicles—hundreds of them—and many damaged planes. Jerry must have suffered terrific losses in this push. Quite a number of black, bloated bodies of Germans about the battlefield. Traffic jams are terrific, more than Ascot or Derby Day

must ever have been. Arrived this side of 'Smuggler's Cove' road just
before dark. Fixed up sentries and saw the platoon fed.

08 NOVEMBER. Outside Mersa Matruh. Vehicles of Tac HQ sorted out
and personnel settled down. Heard that Mersa Matruh was clear, so went
there with Nobby Clark and Philip Cazelet to see what we could find.
We were almost the first people there. Saw a few prisoners and Senussi.
Picked up a camp bed and chair for myself, a knife, a camera, cigarette
lighter, cigars, and numerous odds and ends. Quite a lot of drink too:
brandy, liqueurs. Found a truck load of Jerry Christmas mail.

THE REMNANTS OF THE AFRIKA KORPS were escaping into
Libya. Tac HQ was not far behind, Monty directing the chase with
his aides, who each day scampered off in their Jeeps to check the army's
progress. Traffic on the coast road was impassable in places so we often
drove across the desert, after we by-passed El Alamein's minefields. It
was a wonderful feeling moving in Desert Formation, in parallel
columns like ships in a convoy. The armoured cars scouted several kilometres ahead of the main group: a G3 navigator, two tank troops and
Monty's tank 400 metres up front; the ACV, the army commander's
caravan, car and trucks in the centre; ack-ack on the flanks and my
four trucks bringing up the rear.

Every member of Tac HQ felt the frisson of victory. A marvellous
esprit de corps existed in the Eighth Army at that time. At Mersa Matruh,
some New Zealanders warned me about Jerry booby traps. The Kiwis'
accents reminded me what a glorious hotchpotch the Eighth Army was.
At various stages there were French, Greeks and Poles, but the accents
I heard that day were from all parts of the British Isles, the Dominions
and the furthest outposts of the Empire.

We hadn't seen much of the battle, but as we drove forward we saw
its grim aftermath. Fighter-bombers whizzed low overhead, flying west

to strafe and bomb Rommel's retreating columns. At El Daba, three 109s were captured intact, so quickly had Jerry pulled out. The rest of the airfield was a tangle of burned-out Messerschmitt and Stuka skeletons—dead engines, twisted propellers, fuselage fragments, broken wings and tail fins strewn around as if hit by a tornado. Thousands of Italian prisoners trudged east in long, bunched columns to captivity. There were fewer Germans. The fleeing Afrika Korps abandoned its ally and took its trucks, leaving three Italian divisions stranded in the desert. What was left of the 15th and 21st Panzer divisions escaped, but with fewer than fifty tanks.

Up ahead of us it rained for two days. The road was clogged with vehicles. Desert tracks ploughed into furrows of loose sand during the initial chase turned to mud. Tanks and armoured cars speeding forward to cut off Jerry's retreat got stuck, or ran out of fuel. Wadis became swamps. We passed the flooded wreckage of the Afrika Korps—a sea of discarded equipment—empty Jerrycans, ammo boxes, helmets, gas masks, water bottles. Sodden bundles of fabric turned out to be corpses; mangled clumps of metal materialised as panzer carcasses, their tracks peeled off like apple skins. Gun turrets lay upside-down in the mud. Makeshift German cemeteries appeared like islands in the quagmire—a few mounds of stones, each planted with a white-trimmed Iron Cross and swastika, with rank, name and dates As we passed these stranded *mementi mori* someone shouted: 'You started it, Jerry!' Privately, I was saddened by those sights. Odd that I should have felt that in some way the dead Jerries were comrades too.

10-12 NOVEMBER. Left at 0700 for Sidi Barrani. 1300. Arrived at kilo 111 and established Tac HQ. Pleasant spot, again by the sea. Fixed up guards, signs etc. Had a swim before tea. Before dinner, heard a recording of Churchill's speech and of the combined British and American landings in French Morocco and Algeria. Good show! . . . Went on an abortive shooting expedition with Clark 25 miles south of Sidi Barrani. Only game we saw, either feathered or four-footed, was a brace of pigeons, which we missed. Had a swim and wrote a letter card home before tea. On to Buqbuq tomorrow . . . Left at 0830. Arrived at new site and got settled in by lunchtime. No Germans now east of Tobruk!

At Mersa Matruh, a mosque and some single-storey adobe buildings were unscathed; others were looted and wrecked. The little harbour, the haunt of sponge fishers before the war, was littered with debris. Sidi Barrani was a pile of rubble, dating back to Wavell's campaign in January 1941. Bloomfield fell silent as we passed through it. He remembered the place well.

Monty's intensive troop training and build up of weaponry before the Battle of El Alamein had ensured that Rommel was outnumbered in men, tanks, artillery and aircraft by a factor of about two to one, and eventually outfought. At first, the offensive did not go entirely according to plan, but the Eighth Army had enough reserves to win what turned out to be a First World War-style battle of attrition. Monty would have had to have been a spectacularly incompetent general to have lost it. Had Hitler given Rommel a fraction of the Nazi resources deployed on the Russian front, the scorecard might not have been to our advantage.

In a message to the troops on 12 November, Monty boasted:

In three weeks we have completely smashed the German and Italian Army, and pushed the fleeing remnants out of Egypt, having advanced ourselves nearly 300 miles up to and beyond the frontier.

The following enemy formations have ceased to exist as effective fighting formations: PANZER ARMY: 15 Panzer Division, 21 Panzer Division, 90 Light Division, 164 Light Division. 10 ITALIAN CORPS: Brescia Division, Pavia Division, Folgore Division. 20 ITALIAN

CORPS: Ariete Armoured Division, Littorio Armoured Division, Trieste Division. 21 ITALIAN CORPS: Trento Division, Bologna Division.

The prisoners captured number 30,000 [10,000 were German], including nine Generals. The amount of tanks, artillery, anti-tank guns, transport, aircraft, etc., destroyed or captured is so great that the enemy is completely crippled.

[Estimates vary, but 10,000 to 20,000 Germans and Italians were killed, wounded or missing. The Eighth Army suffered 13,500 casualties, including 2,500 killed. Today, at El Alamein War Cemetery, the Commonwealth War Graves Commission tends 7,367 British, Commonwealth and Empire graves and 603 cremated remains from the desert campaign. The Alamein Memorial, opened by Field Marshal Montgomery on 24 October 1954, lists the names of 11,874 soldiers and airmen who have no known grave.]

On the radio, we heard Churchill's address at the Lord Mayor of London's luncheon on 10 November. He congratulated Alexander and Monty for their 'glorious and decisive victory . . . fought almost entirely by men of British blood from home and from the Dominions'. Speaking to the troops at Tripoli on 3 February 1943, he predicted:

After the war when a man is asked what he did it will be quite sufficient for him to say, 'I marched and fought with the Desert Army.' And when history is written and all the facts are known, our feats will gleam and glow and will be a source of song and story long after we who are gathered here have passed away.

That was stirring stuff—it moved me then and it still does now. Few of us thought that the Battle of El Alamein would be the swan song of the British empire—the last truly British imperial victory of the war.

On 15 November church bells chimed across the UK to celebrate the victory, the first time they had rung since the ban in 1940. In retrospect, they had a hollow ring. After Alamein, the strategy of the war was influenced increasingly by the Soviets and Americans. Great Britain was no longer the dominant world power. The pride and nostalgia that I and other veterans of Monty's Eighth Army feel is tinged with that loss.

15 NOVEMBER. Sunday. I seem to have been on the move practically every Sunday since July. Set off at 0645 with two sections to do a bit of traffic control at Halfaya and Sollum. Traffic incredibly thick. Road bombed several times and some trucks damaged. Corporal Pate and his truck fell behind and took the wrong road. Passes reminiscent of Abyssinia. 'Brewed up' in an escarpment. Rained as we neared Bardia. Couldn't make Gambut by dark. Halted 10 miles this side of site with 8 Sec. Had a hot dish of M&V and dossed by the roadside for the night.

16 NOVEMBER. Wakened at 0530 by slight rain. Packed up and left for Tac HQ at 0645. Found the place in a shambles. 7 Section truck driver ruined a wheel running with a punctured tyre. Got him fixed up with a spare. Had b'fast, a wash and shave and moved off again at 1130 for Martuba. Had lunch at Tobruk. Raining most of the day. Stopped near Gazala for the night. Mosquitos very bad. Good dinner and a few drinks in the mess.

17 NOVEMBER. Tobruk-Martuba. Very cold, damp and dark at 0530. Rained heavily at 0630. Move held up by business at the ACV. Column moved off at 0830. More vehicle trouble. Platoon HQ truck jiggered. My vehicle on tow to an armd car. Petrol tanks full of water! Got my fitters on to my truck at first halt. Had the engine cleaned out.

At Tmimi, I saw a Bren carrier and a 3-tonner, within five minutes of each other, blown up on mines. The sight of sudden death and destruction left me strangely unmoved. Watched Jerry bombing the road a few miles farther on. Found out later that the officers' mess truck had been destroyed. Cook and mess corporal, both good chaps, killed. Other casualties also among vehicles and personnel. Traffic held up for hours. Stopped short of Tac HQ site for a meal with the ack-ack chaps. Slept by the roadside. Gloomy Bloomie behaving dreadfully. Losing confidence in him. Had a sip or two of Kummel with Clark and so to a damp bed.

18 NOVEMBER. Martuba. 26 today! Miserably cold and wet at six in the morning. Heavy rain during the night. Got into HQ for b'fast and spent the morning getting our house in order. Very strong wind. Got hold of a 40lb tent from camp commandant. Made myself a very snug home. Still feeding at the men's cookhouse. 1600. Delivered a short homily on discipline, responsibility, control etc., to the section comdrs. Not much of a birthday this!

At Sollum, the road twisted up Halfaya—'Hellfire'—Pass. Rommel had pulled back from the heights, which was just as well because Hellfire Pass was jammed with what seemed like every vehicle in the Eighth Army crawling forward in low gear. At the top, we had to pull off the road when a couple of Junkers 88s flew over. They dropped their bombs on the snake of single-file traffic wriggling through the dust and haze on the coastal strip below. I thought of Major Coulson and the RTR chaps, who had been left down there to return to Amiriya because there was now no danger of ground attack. The ack-ack gunners stayed with us. As usual in such circumstances, we wondered where the bloody hell was the RAF.

At the Egyptian/Libyan frontier, we passed Fort Capuzzo, the first of several almost comical *Beau Geste*-style Italian forts we would see on Mussolini's Via Balbia, an 1,822-kilometre, paved road from Tunisia to Egypt opened in 1937. Our route would take us through Cyrenaica and the 'Jebel'—the Jebel al Akhdar, the upland area inland and west of Tobruk—to 'Marble Arch' on the border of Tripolitania. The road had many new signs: BOOBY TRAPS . . . DANGER MINES . . . TOBRUK UNDER NEW MANAGEMENT. Tobruk—what was left of it—was a tangle of abandoned gun emplacements and war junk scattered around its defences; the town a heap of rubble; the harbour blocked by dozens of wrecked ships.

The Jebel was dotted with identical stucco settlements and white farmhouses—Mussolini's attempt to re-colonise Cyrenaica, the breadbasket of the Roman empire. All were deserted and the fields were abandoned, as if a plague had swept across the land. Oddly, I found many strange wildflowers there, sprouting among piles of circular metal canisters—Teller mines 'de-loused' by our sappers—which lay dumped by the roadside. Jerry half-tracks and trucks that had run out of petrol, or been hunted down and strafed by Hurricanes and Kittyhawks, lay nose first in the ditches. The airstrips at Martuba had been captured on 12 November, but low cloud now limited DAF operations. Rain, Jerry rearguards and demolitions held up the chase.

Tac HQ had driven about 800 kilometres in ten days—over the same ground that the Eighth Army had retreated across in June, and in about the same time. Monty has since been criticised for not having pursued Rommel with more speed and vigour. But the weather changed for the worse and, because of its extended line of supply and the fact that the port of Tobruk was wrecked, the Eighth Army ran short of ammunition and petrol. Indeed, the Afrika Korps had experienced similar constraints when Rommel raced for the Nile.

With things bogged down, Monty flew to Cairo to meet Alexander. Leese at 30 Corps was left to prepare the next moves. At dinner after Monty left, there was a tremendous party in the mess. We made merry on Italian wine and brandy, had great arguments about 'war aims' and peace projects, poetry and music, and chess battles. God knows what the men thought. Bloomfield told me the Jocks resented the fact that while they were restricted to five Players per day, and a niggardly ration of beer, Tac HQ's Officers' Mess was evidently not short of booze and tobacco.

As if to make the point, four privates went AWOL. In Derna for a drink, seemingly. Dirty scoundrels! When they turned up, I got them a forfeiture of seven days' pay from the commandant, a light punishment, considering. Three other men failed to return from water fatigue. The first to report back was charged and awarded ten days' deprivation of pay. The other two appeared in the company of MPs. Involved in a case of assault and robbery against a native, it seemed. At a line-up, they were pointed out as assailants by two Arabs and placed under close arrest. One of them was on sick report (VD) with evacuation recommended by the MO. He was flown back to Egypt. I felt sorry for the other chap, who obviously had been led astray. Another man received an airgraph, dated 24 September, telling him that his wife, mother of their three children, was going to have a child by another man and was in England with him. German propaganda tormented our troops with this sort of stuff and here was the real thing. The platoon's outgoing mail was censored, by me and then passed to the G3. Generally, the men gave little away that would have been of use to Jerry, or about what they felt, to those at home.

28 NOVEMBER. Bit of a head this morning. Heavy rain till lunchtime. Inspection cancelled. Wrote a letter card to Cecil. Orders for move tomorrow: Rev 0600; trucks loaded; b'fast 0645; h'sack rations. Order of march: ACV, ops, A/A tp commander, one gun, and Free French, Jocks, armd cars, fitters, Camp. Route: Martuba-Di Martino-Marava-Barce-Socra-Benghazi. Lunch, mid-day. Laager: Marava. Watch out for mines. A/A defence, 100 yd intervals. Section commanders at 1430. Issue move orders. Beautifully mild and sunny afternoon, like a spring day at home.

29-30 NOVEMBER. To Marava. Another Sunday on the move. Left at 0745. Very slow journey in forenoon owing to heavy traffic. Beautiful country in parts, wooded and hilly, with grass and meadowland and thick banks of wildflowers. Platoon HQ truck on tow from lunchtime. Laager for the night 12 miles past Marava in pleasant spot of grassy, wooded hillside . . . Barce-Benghazi. Heavy mist and dew this morning. Everything soaked! Traffic manners and discipline on the road are still non-existent. Yanks and RAAF on the road, looking like hoboes. Big hold-up at the pass before Socra. Stopped for lunch on the coast road at 1200. By-passed Benghazi and reached the site of Tac HQ on top of the escarpment beyond Benina at 1530. Windy, bleak moorland country.

01-02 DECEMBER. Benina-Regima. In the wrong place, apparently. Moved on to proper posn a mile away after b'fast. Spent day settling down. Had a glorious bath and change of togs! Sgt Mars and 9 Section on guard at ACV . . . Regima. Heavy dew this morning and pleasant nip in the air. Inspection at 0900.

Went to Benghazi after lunch with Clark and visited field cashier. Approached road into the town from the escarpment, unaware that it was steep and winding, in top gear in my 15-cwt truck. Couldn't change down in time. Endured a terrifying run, braking and lurching all over the road before it levelled out. Went on to Nobby's Bty HQ and got shamefully drunk on Canadian Club whisky. Reached camp miraculously in safety after another dreadful drive. Lost my balmoral when it blew out of the truck. Had Bloomfield and Mars in my tent afterwards and fierce arguments ensued.

03 DECEMBER. Felt like death this morning. Incapable of rising till about 0900. No inspection. Borrowed a balmoral from a cpl. Felt better as day advanced. Major Oswald in expansive mood in the mess, telling stories of army life in Egypt and the desert at the beginning of the war.

Benghazi had fallen on 20 November, the fifth time it had changed hands during the Desert War. The Casa Municipal was back in Eighth Army hands; the Royal Navy's HQ was the marbled Banca d'Italia. On the esplanade, a twin-domed cathedral had survived air raids. The harbour was destroyed like Tobruk, and Massawa. A smouldering tanker lay split in two offshore. After the frightening run in, I calmed down by driving slowly along deserted avenues lined with the first four-storey buildings I had seen since Alexandria. I saw few people as I weaved around disabled trams. There was no water and no electricity. Nobby and I were only in the city to find the Naafi stores and draw pay. The stinking sewers did not tempt us to linger.

Monty returned on 10 December. Major Oswald told me he'd heard that the Argylls might be moving to Iran or Iraq. I asked him when. He didn't know. I told him as politely as I could that we were all fed up with the assignment, longing to get back to our battalion and that my men's morale was suffering. (I cheered them up a bit with football—the Argylls versus the 2nd Derby Yeomanry—on an expanse of salt flats where they played like school boys, with haversacks on the ground as goal posts.) Nobby Clark, the ack-ack commander, left to rejoin his battery which had been detached at Benghazi. He had been a good companion, yet I never saw him again. All of us at Tac HQ understood we had been brought together by chance. We relished our camaraderie—we could not have been sustained without it—but few of us sought or expected any permanence in war.

Tac HQ was now 50 kilometres south of Beda Fomm, where Wavell's army had routed the Italians in February 1941. At El Agheila, 130 kilometres further on, Rommel was expected to make a stand. El Agheila had been the limit of Wavell's advance, and of Auchinleck's against Rommel in November that year, before the calamitous retreat to El Alamein. Now the 7th Armoured (the Desert Rats), 2nd New Zealand and 51st Highland divisions moved up as Monty prepared for another set-piece battle. But Rommel, about to be outflanked, lived up to his nickname and escaped into Tripolitania. The Afrika Korps had neither the tanks nor the fuel to counter-attack, as it had done successfully eleven months before.

On 18 December, I moved off with Tac HQ's advance party for Marble Arch, a fabled monument much talked about but never seen by us. And what a sight it was—a monumental Fascist folly visible from miles away, astride the road on the Cyrenaica /Tripolitania frontier. Its Latin inscription, commemorating Mussolini's visit to North Africa in 1937, was already fading. Nothing else now remained of the Italian African empire it represented, on that barren border of salt marsh and sand stretching away.

We bivouacked by the roadside, hungry and cold. Next morning, Oswald and I found a new site near the sea for Tac HQ and settled in. I found a Jerry food dump to which we helped ourselves, careful to check for booby traps. As we ate, Oswald said our relief should turn up soon. Monty's lot arrived at 1700, along with the rest of my platoon. Brass from Eighth Army HQ dined in the mess that night, their visit accompanied by sporadic ack-ack fire.

As I made my usual rounds of the sentries, I sensed that out assignment was about to end. Soldiers and tanks had been streaming through Marble Arch, among them the 7th Battalion, the Argylls on their way up the line. I chatted briefly with some of the officers. When I told them I had been with Tac HQ since before the Battle of El Alamein, one recalled Monty's tremendous bombardment, and hearing the skirl of the pipes as he advanced. 'Seems a long time ago,' he observed. In the past few days, twenty of his men had been killed by landmines, near an airstrip where Spitfires and Dakotas were now landing. The transport planes droned in, heavy with cargo: 45-gallon drums of aviation fuel and ammo for the fighter squadrons; mail and Christmas rations for us. The 7th Argylls pushed on.

There was still no sign of our relief and our hopes of getting back to the battalion in time for New Year were fading fast. Then, at lunch time on the 24 December, our relief platoon turned up. I completed the change-over quickly and we prepared to leave for Alex.

I had asked Monty, through his *aide-de-camp*, if he would pose for a photograph with my platoon as a parting gesture. He accepted! He'd do it after an afternoon address to the officers. He was in a cheerful mood and gave an entertaining and edifying talk. I got Bloomfield to smarten up the men and assemble them in three ranks near the beach. Monty, wearing battledress and his non-regulation two-badged beret, was amiable and talkative. He thanked me for the platoon's three-month tour at Tac HQ. Then, hands clasped behind his back and head angled to look each man in the eye, he inspected the platoon, stopping occasionally to speak to a few of the men. The low sun lit his face and cast long shadows of 9 Platoon across the sand.

'The light's going. We'll never get this picture,' Bloomfield muttered.

I think Monty heard this. He turned to me and said, 'Right, let's get on with it, lieutenant.'

We took our places in the centre of the ranks.

I had arranged for Captain Geoffrey Keating of the Eighth Army Film and Photographic Unit—its photos and film *Desert Victory* made Monty and the Eighth Army famous—to use his camera and my own, so I could get prints for the men. When Monty heard this he told Keating: 'See that the pictures are published in the Glasgow papers.' Photos taken, Monty paused and turned to me: 'Good show,' he said. We gave him three cheers as he left.

Captain Adams, the camp commandant, gave me a copy of the officers' mess Christmas Dinner menu. I got the chaps to sign it as a souvenir, had a few drinks with them and dished out Christmas beer and Naafi cigarettes to the men.

We drove away from Marble Arch on Christmas Day. If we thought having been Monty's bodyguard would give us special privileges we were mistaken. At Tobruk, we had to squeeze into filthy railway boxcars for the journey east. We arrived at Amiriya at midnight on 31 December and spent the night at a transit camp. What a way to celebrate Hogmanay! Early on New Year's Day 1943, I organised some MT and got the platoon back to Alex at 0930, where we found our battalion at Mustapha barracks, on security duties.

At the Battle of El Alamein, the Argylls had been dug-in with the 4th Indian Division on Ruweisat Ridge. Attacks were ordered, then cancelled when it was clear that Rommel was retreating. Apart from PoWs they saw no enemy. When the battalion did push forward, the CO was nearly killed and his driver wounded when their Jeep hit a Teller mine. A carrier was destroyed in the same way and six men wounded. The Argylls were then relegated to battlefield salvage. Back in Alex, the battalion's security duties were relieved by the usual recreation—in cafés, bars and restaurants, or the pool at the Sporting Club. The battalion football team won the Alexandria Services League final. All this while the Eighth Army was battling its way through Tunisia to the final defeat of the Afrika Korps.

On 23 January 1943, the Eighth Army entered Tripoli, three months to the day from the first barrage at El Alamein. Churchill, Alan Brooke, Alexander and Monty took the salute on city's seafront as the pipes and drums of the 51st Highland Division marched past (a fitting revenge for its humiliating surrender, to the then panzer division commander Rommel, in France in 1940). Rommel left North Africa and returned to Germany, but not before delaying the Allies in Tunisia. On 7 May 1943, scouts from the Desert Rats entered Tunis. The Afrika Korps and Mussolini's army in North Africa were trapped at Cape Bon. Around 250,000 Italians and Germans surrendered. In Tripoli, Alexander reported to Churchill:

Sir, the orders you gave me on August 10, 1942, have been fulfilled. His Majesty's enemies, together with their impedimenta, have been completely eliminated from Egypt, Cyrenaica, Libya, and Tripolitania. I now await your further instructions.

♣

In March 1943, the battalion moved across the Sinai to a tented camp at Hadera, on the Palestine coast 50 kilometres north of Tel Aviv. There, we began training for the invasion of Sicily. Because the plan was secret at that time, we weren't told what all the fuss was about.

The Argylls were to form the nucleus of a new combined operations formation, 33 Beach Brick, one of several such teams that would land, defend and distribute all the paraphernalia needed to sustain a seaborne invasion of enemy territory. No. 33 Beach Brick was organised around an infantry battalion (1st Argylls), plus two infantry companies of the Frontier Force Rifles (Indian Army), Royal Artillery gunners (ack-ack), Royal Engineers (sappers), RAF and Royal Navy liason officers, and officers and men from the army's medical, signals, pioneer and transport corps: a total of 125 officers and 2,056 men commanded by our CO, Lieutenant-Colonel McAlister.

In mid-May, we had a dry run—literally—when we moved to Aartouz, near Damascus. On a Syrian desert plain, we went through the motions of disembarkation, landing and setting up positions with 17 Brigade, 5th Infantry Division, much to the bewilderment of those Bedouin who saw us. The plain was east of Mount Hermon and at night the wind from its snowy peak was perishing cold. The training was meant to be as realistic as possible, so we slept in the open on hard ground, clad only in khaki shirts, shorts and pullovers. I recall kipping down with our signals officer, Lieutenant Johnnie Scott-Barrett. He and I had roughed it on night patrols on Ruweisat Ridge. Here, we found ourselves unrolling army maps and wrapping them around ourselves, trying to keep warm.

We rewarded ourselves in Damascus on the second night of the two-day scheme, spashing out in a French restaurant. At a cabaret later, we were greeted by the memorable spectacle of a belly dancer wobbling like jelly. After the surrender of the Vichy régime in Syria and Lebanon in mid-1941, much of Palestine and Syria was militarised, with army camps and soldiers everywhere (the esplanade at Tel Aviv flowed with Forces personnel looking for off-duty seaside fun). But Damascus, with its central mosque and covered souk, seemed entirely Arab in character: the same city that Allenby and Lawrence entered in 1918 after defeating the Turks.

The drive up from Palestine had been via Nazareth, Tiberias and the Sea of Galilee. I would have loved to have stayed there awhile, in those older places where farmers were working in the fields and fishermen at their nets on the shore. While in Palestine, I had climbed Mount Carmel, for the view of bay with the ancient city of Acre and the mountains of Lebanon on the other side. In Syria, one of the best sights was the snow on Mount Hermon, the first I had seen since I left the UK in January 1941. Indeed, I was begining to enjoy being a tourist, when a telegram from Cecil caught up with me, with the news that in April my father had died. He never recovered from shock he got during the blitz on Glasgow two years before.

I took the news badly and recall the sympathy I received from Mac and Shaw. My first thoughts were for my mother, left to cope alone because her four sons were now in the Forces. She managed, with help of friends and neighbours, the parish minister and her own faith and courage. When I got back to Alex, I arranged for a draft from my pay to be sent to her every month. I also found my father's obituary waiting in the mail. He had been a reserved, God-fearing and remote figure in my youth. When I went overseas he became a faithful correspondent sending letters, newspaper cuttings and music lessons. His words were a source of comfort and inspiration. So too our musical bond. He would never hear the outcome of all those harmony lessons he sent me in the desert. I found it difficult to continue with them without his coaching.

At the end of May, the battalion moved to an isolated camp at El Shatt, tents in the desert, near Port Tewfiq. Officers went on courses at Combined Operations at Kabrit, or kept the men training. I was promoted captain and second-in-command of A Company. I also got a new CSM. This was Jimmy Stewart, the abusive instructor from infantry training at Stirling. He had joined the battalion, became a sergeant and had been promoted. I got the measure of him by reminding him of my recruit days in Balaclava Squad and told him to be sure to treat my men with more respect and consideration than he had done us. I added: 'Don't complain, you're the one who told me to apply for a commission.' I had no trouble from him after that.

On the night of 8/9 June, we boarded a troopship and steamed south to the Gulf of Aqaba for a final and more realistic exercise with 17 Brigade. We joined a flotilla of warships, transports, and tank and infantry landing craft off the shores of the Sinai desert, where our activities would be unobserved. Over two days, infantry companies, mortar and machine-gun platoons, ack-ack gunners and sappers swarmed ashore. Every man got to know his position in the landing craft and his role and responsibilies on the beach. To maintain secrecy after the exercise we were confined to the camp, a sure sign that something was on. Monty visited us. There was the now familiar inspection and pep talk, but no clue as to our destination.

On the 29th, we woke to see five ships offshore: *Duchess of Bedford, Monarch of Bermuda, Bergensfjord, Dilwara* and *Sobieski.* We spent the day embarking. My ship was the *Duchess of Bedford*, a 20,000-ton Canadian Pacific liner built in 1928 at Clydebank. Requisitioned by the Admiralty in 1939, she now looked the worse for wear. So did the others. Oily smoke issued from their funnels and rust reddened their grey paintwork. I recognised the *Duchess of Bedford* from the convoy that had taken me from Liverpool to Egypt in 1941. She had brought Canadian troops to the UK in 1940 and made three voyages to Suez via the Cape. In January 1942, she evacuated refugees from Singapore and then landed troops during the invasion of French North Africa. The crew, seasoned sailors to a man, was nonchalant about this record, a reminder of the Merchant Navy's unsung part in the war (the ship's gunners had sunk a U-boat in the North Atlantic, with the 6-inch naval gun on the liner's stern). Now the *Duchess of Bedford* was loaded with stores and equipment, A Company and 1,100 other armed men. We stowed our gear and lay on our bunks, panting in the heat.

At sunset on 30 June our convoy formed up slowly in single line ahead to enter the canal. At that point, we knew we were not going to India or Burma, the subjects of speculation. It was now obvious that our training was for an invasion somewhere in the Mediterranean—we had already painted over our vehicles' desert camouflage in olive green. Suez disappeared in the hazy gloaming as we began a night passage of the waterway. By morning, we were anchored with dozens of other ships under a cloud of barrage balloons in the harbour at Port Said. Shore leave was forbidden. We idled away the time leaning on the ship's rail, smoking as we watched sweating stevedores, self-important port pashas and Egypt's ubiquitous peddlars pestering soldiers on the quaysides. A lighthouse rose like a minaret above the town; the reflection of the white-domed Suez Canal Company building glittered on the water. In those docks and gleaming architecture, I glimpsed Liverpool's waterfront grandeur, when I had embarked on the *Windsor Castle,* two and a half years before.

9 THE SHORES OF SICILY

Captain T. R. Ward. 1st A & S H, M E F
Saturday 17 July 1943

My dearest Mum,

You will no doubt have received the letter card I wrote you with the
startling news that I am in Sicily. At the time of writing it all we
knew was that we were allowed to mention that important fact, but
since then the censorship regulations have been relaxed and we are
now able to write in general terms about the landings, and of places
visited in the past. These latter are many and include a few you don't
know about.

First of all . . . the invasion as it affected us, and as I saw it, and a
little about the island itself and how we are living . . . We have been a
long time preparing for this show . . . and knowing what was coming
off had to exercise strict self-control when writing letters, in case anything should leak out . . . I've had a grand time on board ship and an
uneventful voyage across the Mediterranean. The RAF and the Navy
saw to it that we were not molested in the slightest and, but for the
warlike preparations on board and the protective screen of destroyers
all round and planes above the convoy, one might have been on a
Mediterranean cruise. Our own convoy was a most inspiring sight,
but paled to insignificance when we met up with others. The whole
sea seemed to be full of ships, and I felt proud to be with such an
armada and taking part in such a glorious enterprise.

As D-day approached I could feel a growing tenseness in the atmosphere and by midnight on 9 /10 July all were keyed up and ready for
disembarkation. It was an eerie feeling, clambering down the ship's

side into our landing craft, and then stealing through the water past dark silent shapes of other craft, lit up by sudden flashes of naval guns in the distance and the gleam of fires caused by bombing ashore. The period of waiting and suspense was annoying but soon I was too busy with the job on hand to worry about anything else. Our craft stopped some distance from the beach, and at 0515 hours on the morning of Saturday 10 July yours truly might have been seen wading through five feet of clear cold Mediterranean to the shore of Sicily! That was only a week ago, and already, according to the latest news, a third of the island is in our hands and good progress is being made in all sectors. As I've said before this Eighth Army of ours is a magnificent organisation and I feel proud to belong to it.

The Italian PoWs I've come across seem to be a war-weary, dispirited lot, and no doubt are quite relieved to be in our hands. We exchanged greetings with the local population, and it is not unusual to be met with a 'V' sign from a small boy, and greeted a with polite *Buon giorno* from country men and women. One cannot help feel sorry for these people who have been bombed out of their homes and in some cases have had to evacuate their farms, but they are suffering far less than the people of Britain have done, and they have brought it all on themselves . . .

It's now about seven in the evening, and I can just see the sun through a clump of olive trees on a hill . . . it is singularly calm and peaceful at the moment. I'm sitting at a table by our olive tree, stripped to the waist and brown as a berry enjoying a bar of chocolate and a cigarette out of our excellent 'compo' rations, a mug of tea by my side and, thank goodness, no planes overhead! Ants are crawling up my legs and spiders dropping down my back, but these are friendly little creatures and do no harm. Neither do the little lizards that scuttle about among the grass and rocks. There's an almond grove over the wall at my back, and a vineyard farther up the road and a bucket of water by my side, waiting for me to have a wash!

Sanders is still with me, and cooking for our Company HQ, is in his element. At the moment he is brewing up the tea and getting the dinner ready, cheerful as ever. This pleasant spot we are in could be somewhere in Blighty . . . country lanes, stone dykes, trees and grass all lend to that impression, though of course one doesn't find olives, almonds, tomatoes, lemons, grapes and pomegranates growing all over the place at home. Our rations are superb. I should think that we are the best-fed army in the world. We are able to supplement them now and again with potatoes, onions and tomatoes, and we had a stroke of good fortune on the second night after our arrival when a chicken and rabbit appeared unexpectedly at our HQ. By George, the chicken broth and rabbit stew we had for dinner tasted like the food of the gods!

As you will have gathered from all this Mum, I am doing exceedingly well and am in fine fettle. We had an orgy of washing the other morning, and you should have seen me scrubbing away at my shirts and socks, etc. I should make a good wife for somebody when I get home! . . .

Who would have imagined, three years ago, that I would have travelled so far and seen so many wonderful places by the middle of 1943? And my travelling days are not over yet, I should imagine. I could talk of Abyssinia and Eritrea, Egypt, Khartoum and the Sudan, Palestine, the Western Desert and Cyrenaica, but I must leave something for another letter. Alexandria would be subject in itself! . . .

I trust everything is still well with you my dear Mum, and that you are still receiving my letters regularly . . . rest assured that I am doing well, and grateful for it too.

Look after yourself and keep well.

Love and blessings,

Ray

WE SAILED FOR SICILY ON THE MORNING OF 5 JULY 1943, passing the kilometre-long breakwater and the statue of Ferdinand de Lesseps, the builder of the Suez Canal. Then he and Egypt slipped away astern as we cleared the mole in the early light. Several destroyers pranced around as we turned west. The tension I had experienced in the first weeks of the voyage on the *Windsor Castle* returned—in an emergency, what ladder do I climb, what deck should I be on, what's the quickest way out of here? The battalion assembled in companies on deck for action stations and boat drill. Then we were inspected and stood in silence, waiting to be briefed by the CO and his staff.

The only sounds were the ship's engines and the sea.

'At ease, gentlemen,' he ordered. 'Let me tell you what we've all been waiting for.'

Then we heard his electrifying news.

'We are going to invade Sicily and knock Mussolini out of the war!'

The Allied invasion of Sicily was code-named Operation Huskey. Convoys were already en route from Egypt, French North Africa, North America and the Clyde, to converge off the south coast of the island. Our ship would join the invasion's Eastern Task Force (Eighth Army, Monty), whose troops would land on the south-east coast, secure the beaches, capture local airfields and press north to Catania. A Western Task Force (American Seventh Army, Lieutenant-General George S. Patton) was also at sea and would land to protect Monty's left flank. Paratroops were to be dropped to grab bridges and airfields, and commandos and SAS with two-man kayaks were approaching the beaches by submarine, to land and sabotage coastal guns, and flash signals to guide us in. Air support would be overwhelming. Enemy airfields in Sicily and Italy were being bombed,and fighters were aloft to keep enemy planes away. Battleships were steaming towards Sicily to shell enemy positions on the shores.

[The armada was the largest in history: 2,590 warships, troopships and landing craft; 1,614 British ships, including six battleships and two aircraft carriers; 945 American vessels, among them five cruisers and forty-eight destroyers. There were 31 ships from the free forces of Belgium, Greece, the Netherlands, Norway and Poland. 160,000 soldiers, 600 tanks, 1,800 guns and 14,000 vehicles were landed. There were seven infantry divisions (three British, three American and one Canadian); an American armoured division, and three armoured brigades (two British and one Canadian); commandos, US rangers, and airborne troops; 3,500 Allied warplanes based in North Africa and Malta provided the air cover. Defending the island were 230,000 Italian and 40,000 German troops, coastal guns, artillery, tanks and aircraft. Churchill and Roosevelt had agreed on the scheme at the Casablanca Conference in January 1943 and their staffs thrashed out the plan.]

EIGHTH ARMY
PERSONAL MESSAGE FROM THE ARMY COMMANDER
To be read out to all Troops
1. The time has now come to carry the war into Italy, and into the Continent of Europe. The Italian Overseas Empire has been exterminated; we will now deal with the home country.
2. To the Eighth Army has been given the great honour of representing the British Empire in the Allied Force which is now to carry out this task. On our left will be our American allies. Together we will set about the Italians in their own country in no uncertain way; they came into this war to suit themselves and they must now take the consequences; they asked for it, and they will now get it.
3. On behalf of us all I want to give a very hearty welcome to the Canadian troops that are now joining the Eighth Army. I know well the fighting men of Canada; they are magnificent soldiers, and the long and careful training they have received in England will now be put to very good use—to the

great benefit of the Eighth Army.

4. The task in front of us is not easy. But it is not so difficult as many we have had in the past, and have overcome successfully . . . the combined effort of the three fighting services is being applied in tremendous strength, and nothing will be able to stand against it. The three of us together—Navy, Army and Air Force—will see the thing through. I want all of you, my soldiers, to know that I have complete confidence in the successful outcome of this operation.

5. Therefore, with faith in God and with enthusiasm for our cause and for the day of battle, let us all enter into this contest with stout hearts and with determination to conquer. The eyes of our families, and in fact of the whole Empire, will be on us once the battle starts; we will see that they get good news and plenty of it.

6. To each one of you, whatever may be your rank or employment, I would say: GOOD LUCK AND GOOD HUNTING IN THE HOME COUNTRY OF ITALY.

B. L. Montgomery,

General, Eighth Army.

July 1943.

I had always thought of the Mediterranean as a calm sea but it was choppy south of Malta when our convoy of twenty ships, escorted by a cruiser and eight destroyers, joined more troopships, landing craft and warships. We had a few air-raid alarms during the voyage but saw no enemy planes. Now RAF fighters flashed overhead.

As we approached Sicily on 9 July gale force winds swept the sea. Before the war our ship had been nicknamed 'the drunken duchess' and we found out why. The *Duchess of Bedford* was built for the shallow approach to Montréal and had a relatively flat keel, a design feature that caused the ship to roll at sea. This quirk was amply demonstrated in the storm's heavy swell. By dusk, we were wallowing 60 kilometres off the coast and feeling hellish. In the mess, we were given a spoof menu:

SPECIAL BREAKFAST FOR SICILIAN TOURISTS
Stewed Fruit of the Island. Oats, Rolled by Commandos.
Fresh Fish (Knocked unconscious by the first L.C.A.)
Grilled Breakfast Bacon, Fried Eggs (Next issue from Café Royal,
Palermo). Breakfast Rolls, Soda Scones, Marmalade, Tea, Coffee.
TO ORDER: Marsala Wine, Pistachio Nuts, Seven Days' Leave for
Milan Cathedral and Il Duce.
N.B.—Do not fail to visit the famous ruins of Syracuse, especially the
brand new lot, created by that Cultural Society, the RAF.
HAPPY LANDINGS—GOOD LUCK. Keep your feet dry.

I leafed through my copy of the army's *Soldier's Guide to Sicily*, an unitentionally amusing diversion. The cover showed a fist pointing to a silhouette of the island—a symbol of our invasion fleet and the knock-out blow we were expected to give the enemy. Inside there was a Monty-style special message from Dwight D. Eisenhower, General, US Army, the Allies' C-in-C. That was followed by clichéd tourist information, dated photographs and an over-inked and completely useless map. The text included some idiosyncratic observations:

Sicily has a long and unhappy history that has left it primitive and undeveloped, with many relics of a highly civilised past. Saint's Day feasts with their odd mixture of operatic songs and pantomime are a feature of the Island . . . The Sicilian lives on pasta with tomato sauce and a little meat, sardines, tunny fish, cheese or olive oil to add a variety of flavours; oranges, lemons, almonds are plentiful; Marsala wine, is the popular drink . . . Crime is highly organised in all grades of society; 'gangsterism' in the USA had its origins in Sicilian immigration. Morals are superficially very rigid, being based on the Catholic religion and Spanish etiquette of Bourbon times; they are, in fact, of a very low standard, particularly in agricultural areas. The Sicilian is still, however, well known for his extreme jealousy in so far as his womenfolk are concerned, and in a crisis still resorts to the dagger.

Thus, we expected a land of opera singers, saints, violent menfolk and gangsters, living in a land plentiful with food, wine, and ruins of antiquity. We were to see plenty of ruins in Sicily but they were not the historic kind.

The invasion of Sicily began in the early hours of Saturday, 10 July. The swell eased and the night closed in. No lights showed on the *Duchess of Bedford* or on any other ships. We were about 15 kilometres south of Syracuse and about 15 offshore when we waited to disembark. I sat smoking in the dark with Mac and Shaw in one of the *Duchess of Bedford*'s formerly plush lounges, studying aerial photographs and sketched plans of the beach, and a card printed with Italian road signs, while waiting for the call to muster the men. They were cooped up inside the bowels of the ship, their faces lit by dim red blackout lights. The atmosphere was charged with the nervous chatter of recruits disguising their apprehension and the introspection of those who knew what war was like. To add to our jolly mood, every man was given anti-malaria pills because the plain north of the beach was mosquito-infested.

A disembodied command came over the Tannoy: 'Crews will man boats.' The ship suddenly came alive as each man, laden with fifty pounds of kit, and weapon in hand, shuffled along the passageways and up ladders to the muster stations on deck in a pre-planned sequence for disembarkation. I prepared to clamber down one of the scrambling nets heaved over the ship's rail to a landing craft alongside. The air was thick with the stench of vomit, the ship's fuel oil and salty air. Looking down, I saw a hundred peelie-wally faces: the Jocks shoulder-to-shoulder in the craft, many of them seasick.

The sea was swept by searchlights and speckled with sporadic flashes of naval gunfire. Shells whizzed and arced over our heads and burst like fireworks on the coast. Multiple fluorescent streams of projectiles fired from 'rocket ships' hit the shore with explosive crackles and flashes. Aircraft droned above the masts and funnels of the armada. 'Give 'em Hell lads,' we cheered, hearing but not seeing the planes. Some were Dakotas, whose pilots turned back when faced with enemy ack-ack, and many of the paratroops they carried were dropped over the sea and drowned; troop-carrying gliders crashed and sank, having been released prematurely by their tow-plane pilots. I saw the shipboard flashes of our own ack-ack, which shot down more of our planes that night than enemy flak. The Allied paras who did land on the island found themselves in isolated groups. Only a few of the gliders landed on target.

At 0245, assault troops of the 6th Seaforth Highlanders and the 2nd Royal Scots Fusiliers stormed the beach in front of us. They knocked out two enemy pillboxes and pressed inland to occupy the village of Cassibile, a kilometre and a half inland. They found little difficulty on the beach, but it took three hours to overcome Italian resistance at Cassibile. Then they pressed on to Syracuse, the nearest port and their objective. The Argylls' landing was preceded by a navy commander and one of our officers, Major Provan, in a pilot boat. The first detachments of 33 Beach Brick included Captain Macalister Hall and Lieutenant Rome, who went ashore to direct obstacle clearance—mines, barbed wire and tank traps. Almost immediately, one Jock was killed stepping on a mine. Macalister Hall was wounded the same way and evacuated. (Subsequently, he was posted home, as an instructor to an OCTU, then served with the 7th Argylls in North-west Europe until the end of the war).

At 0515, my LCI grounded in the shallows and the landing ramp splashed down. Clutching my tommy gun, I plunged down the ramp into the cold surf. The navy's bombardment, the spluttering of the LCI's engines, me shouting to the men, 'Come on, come on!' and the sounds of battle from Cassibile were deafening. But now, my memory of wading ashore in that pre-dawn pallor comes back to me like a scene in a silent film: hundreds of men holding weapons and equipment above the waist-deep swell as they struggle ashore; sporadic enemy fire erupting in the water; shells from the navy's big guns exploding and fires glowing in the ominous gloom beyond the beach; a streamer of black smoke drifting over the scene and dawn breaking over the Mount Etna massif.

The landings achieved complete surprise. It was not until after the war, in the film *The Man Who Never Was,* that I learned of the elaborate hoax—a Royal Navy submarine carrying a corpse kitted out with a navy officer's uniform and a briefcase containing bogus plans, which was released and washed ashore on the Spanish coast, where it was found and the plans passed to a German secret agent—that successfully duped Hitler into thinking that the target for the invasion would be Greece.

We saw no enemy on 'George' beach, as ours was identified, apart from groups of Italians surrendering, clearly relieved that their war was over. The beach was divided into three contiguous sectors—Green, Amber and Red—along 1,500 metres of deserted sandy shoreline enclosed at either end by rocky arms. By 0830, Beach Brick HQ had been set up in an orchard a short distance inland from Green beach. Our immediate job was to get the constant stream of men, tanks, trucks and equipment dispersed in camouflaged parking areas and storage depots or flowing inland. Anything left exposed on the beach was vulnerable to air attack. At first light we were strafed by two Jerry fighters, which caused no damage. I saw them climb away, glinted in the rising sun which promised a clear, hot day.

A glance out to sea revealed the epic scale of the invasion. There were hundreds of vessels—warships, troopships, tank and infantry landing craft—so many that I gave up counting. Beachmasters with semaphore flags directed craft approaching the shore. The beach was awash with LCIs and LCTs, their ramps crashing in the surf; thousands of soldiers wading ashore; Jeeps, trucks and tanks surging through the surf. Barrage balloons floated above the fleet and a string of them was raised to protect the beach. Ack-ack batteries were dug in. Spitfires based in Malta provided initial air cover. To the fighter pilots George beach must have looked like an ant hill. From my point of view it was like an enormous construction site.

Our work was dirty, hot and round-the-clock: sappers cleared and marked dispersal trails and exit lanes; mine-clearing tanks rumbled inland. We laid steel mesh tracks, erected signs and directed traffic. We marked out zones for RAF and army ammo, fuel and stores; set up vehicle assembly areas and vehicle 'de-waterproofing' and 'drowned vehicle' parks (tanks were waterproofed to a depth of six feet; other vehicles took their chances, and we had to winch some stranded trucks out of the surf). The American-designed DUWK amphibious vehicles, which could carry twenty-five soldiers or three and a half tons of supplies, proved indispensable. They shuttled between the ships and the beaches, driving out of the surf to depots and distribution areas we organised, or to the front line where they caused traffic jams on the narrow Sicilian roads. We employed Italian prisoners as labour. They were willing workers, keen to show a turncoat sincerity.

The German attitude did not change. During the day we were interrupted by hit-and-run air attacks by Messerschmitt 109s and Focke-Wulf 190 fighters, the latter a new type we hadn't seen before. They came in at low-level, often pursued by our fighters, flying across my line of sight. Eight of our men were killed that first day, by landmines or Luftwaffe attacks; others were nearly buried alive in their slit trenches when bombs burst. At 'all clear' we jumped up to dig them out. Occasionally our ack-ack sent Jerry planes flaming into the sea. We cheered every one.

Enemy air activity over our beach decreased after the first day, but one raid caught us on the hop. We barely saw the planes, which swept over at head height as we scrambled for cover. Bombs burst nearby, shaking the ground and showering us with sand. I peeped above my foxhole and counted heads as they emerged from the dunes. Someone was missing. I ran around our positions and was horrified to find Captain Tidmarsh, my esteemed company commander—a most excellent officer, commissioned in the field, hero of Sidi Barrani and Crete—cowering in his slit trench literally shaking with fear. Ted had seen more action than most of us and he'd reached breaking point: bombed and shelled once too often. He should have been evacuated, but on the beach—impossible. I helped him to his feet.

'Thanks Ray. I'll be fine,' he murmured.

As company second-in-command, I found myself burdened with more responsibility as I tried to take some of the weight off his shoulders. He recovered slowly. Pride and a sense of duty made him carry on, but he was never the same man again. Nor was I. The incident still shocks me.

Despite the air attacks, over 11,000 men, 500 vehicles and 90 tons of equipment and stores passed through George beach in the first 24 hours of the landings. In the first 48, over 8,500 vehicles came ashore in the Eighth Army sector, with similar activity in the American zone, 100 kilometres to the west. Opposition from the five Italian coastal defence divisions had been paltry. Their soldiers were not frontline troops; many were part-timers; most threw away their weapons and gave themselves up or walked home. The four Italian infantry divisions and two panzer divisions (the Hermann Goering Panzer Division and the 15th Panzer Grenadiers) in Sicily were not at the beaches. That was a lucky break because some of the panzer units were equipped with the formidable Tiger, a new tank first encountered in Tunisia, which outgunned the Sherman. They counter-attacked one of the American beachheads but were scattered by gunfire from US Navy cruisers. Our beaches too continued to be covered, by the Royal Navy's big guns. Their shells, directed by artillery spotters at inland targets, whistled over us during the first day. U-boats sank six ships and damaged an aircraft carrier and two cruisers. Ten enemy submarines were sunk. The Italian surface fleet stayed in port. The Luftwaffe attacked a hospital ship, despite the vessel being illuminated and painted with Red Cross markings. Off the American beaches, a ship loaded with munitions was hit, exploded and sank in seconds.

South-east Sicily was taken in three days. Monty arrived with Tac HQ from Malta on the 11 July. The port at Syracuse was opened on the 14th despite bomb damage, although congestion in the town's narrow streets restricted movement. George beach was kept open and we were kept at work. We saw the 1st Canadian Armoured Brigade's tanks clanking ashore; the 78th Division disembarked, with the 8th Argylls who we piped ashore. The 7th Argylls also landed on Sicily, with the 51st Highland Division. Air cover over the beachhead improved on the 13th when the Desert Air Force arrived to operate from captured airfields on the island. [Despite having left North Africa, the DAF kept its name and gave close air support to the Eighth Army until the end of the Italian campaign.] I watched Kittyhawks and Spitfires landing on a dusty airstrip bulldozed across a vineyard at Cassibile. The battalion was not bothered by the Luftwaffe after that.

On 27 July, our beach brick duties ended abruptly when we were ordered to the front line. Captain E. V. Lees RN, Senior Naval Officer, Eastern Landing Force, sent a signal to our CO:

It is with real and heartfelt regret that the Navy in 'George' has to say *au revoir* to our comrades of the Argylls . . . One and all have pulled together to make a team which has done a job which will go down in the history of combined operations as a standard at which to aim. It may be equalled, it may even be exceeded, though I doubt it, but we have together done something of which every officer and man may justifiably be very proud . . .

After a hasty clear out, the battalion's thirty-five officers and 598 men set off in Jeeps, trucks and Bren carriers. We drove through the debris of Cassibile and the untouched streets of Noto, whose baroque buildings sheltered gangs of starving children. Along the coast to the north of us, a fierce battle raged for control of a vital river bridge near Catania. But we skirted the Catania plain and drove towards the puffing cone of Mount Etna. Monty had ordered us to join the 51st Highland Division which was holding the line in the Sferro hills south of the volcano.

The rolling countryside, progressively bleak and hilly, was dotted with austere and melancholy villages, many undamaged, each punctuated by the dome or campanile of a baroque church. Villagers would peek out of doorways and watch us, sometimes with welcoming smiles and gestures while their children begged for chocolate. Over the next ridge Jerry would be waiting to shoot at us. That harsh, rocky hill country and its narrow lanes favoured defence. Every hill town and church campanile was a potential enemy observation post. Olive groves, vineyards, hedges and drystone dykes provided perfect cover for ambush; mountain glens and wadis, cover for enemy movement—and our own, once we learned to play the game. The German tactics, which held us up all through the Italian campaign, were simple and effective: Jerry played hide-and-seek, defending a line or position, then moving back to another each time we advanced, making us pay a heavy price in casualties for every village, river and mountain ridge.

The Germans were led by the skilful and decisive Field Marshal Albert Kesselring. Units of the German 1st Parachute Division (which had fought in Norway, the Low Countries, Crete and on the Russian front) were parachuted in from bases near Avignon to reinforce the panzer divisions. That quick deployment was an all too typical German response and their paras were crack troops. Monty's advance on the Catania plain was held up. The 51st Highland Division was counter-attacked in the hills. The 1st Canadian Division, pushing towards the western slopes of Mount Etna, and the Americans, who had reached the north coast, also encountered tough opposition.

We had to approach our new position on foot, trudging up farm tracks in the prickly-pear cactus country of the hills. The heat and dust were as intense and uncomfortable as the desert. We were used to that. We wore our desert outfit 'khaki drill' shirts and shorts. But our tactics that had worked in North Africa proved unsuitable for Sicily's terrain—and for the German resistance we met. Monty's set-piece offensives were less successful in Sicily and Italy despite the now well-practised artillery and air support. The Eighth Army was not used to footslogging. We had trucks in the desert. Since the army had, in its wisdom, not provided pack animals for hilly Sicily, we had to carry everything ourselves. At every rest stop, we slumped exhausted in the shade of olive groves, ditches or drystone walls.

That night, we filed silently up a steep track to take over a front-line position from the 7th Royal Marines, formerly of 31 Beach Brick, who were in the sector with the 1st and 7th Black Watch. Our job was to protect the Black Watch start line and flanks for the 51st's night attack in the Dittaino river valley. At 0400 on the 29th we hunkered down on the unforgiving ground. At dawn we found we were almost completely exposed to the sun and, if we moved, Jerry machine-guns on a hill a kilometre or so away. We crouched baking in our sangars, eyeing the enemy across stony slopes. Lizards scuttled in and out of the rocks. There was no relief from the heat and our thirst. The following night, the track we had come up on was shelled.

At 2350, 31 July, an artillery barrage lit up the hills. The battalions of the 51st advanced in the dark to the other side of the valley. From our vantage point, I saw streams of tracer and bursts of shellfire and heard the crackle of small arms and echoing explosions. Shell bursts bloomed and died, silhouetting the hills and ridges like theatrical sets all along the front. I watched, fascinated, as if in some vast auditorium. The Highlanders took the hills. The division's reserve battalion, the 7th Argylls, passed through our positions, prompting some sardonic wit and banter. The enemy withdrew in the morning. We heard later that, at midday, a German infantry and panzer counter-attack had been broken up by some well-directed artillery stonks. By 1800 all was quiet. Jerry retreated over the Simeto, the next river, and eventually to Messina on the north-east tip of the island. As the sun set we sat on our hill, with the lizards, among the stones.

A few days later, we took over positions from the 7th Battalion 1,500 metres up on another ridge. Again no shade, not even a breath of air—but no spandaus, since it was now a quiet sector. There was a stream in a shaded wadi below us. (How odd that we still spoke of 'wadis', a nostalgia for the desert, I suppose.) Groups of us took turns to strip off and sprawl in its shallow, pebble pools—paradise! At the same spot, I took a pot shot with my revolver at a black mamba slithering through a hedge close to my bivvy. I missed it but startled Sanders. We were befriended by a trio of hungry ragamuffins. I even remember their names: Michele, Alfredo and Salvatore. They approached us cautiously like sparrows, snatched food from our hands and scampered away. But they always came back and hung around the camp cadging food and chocolate, which we bribed them with to bring us eggs and tomatoes. We picked and ate bunches of sour grapes. Some of my Jocks broke open some casks of immature wine in a farmhouse cellar and got hopelessly drunk. In Catania, MacDougall, Shaw and I had our first taste of Marsala. A bottle split between us in a café fairly went to our heads. In the circumstances, the food and wine of Sicily tasted like nectar.

Our CO, Ronnie McAlister, had hoped the battalion would play a fighting role with the 51st. He was disappointed. We were recalled to form another beach brick, in preparation for the coming invasion of the Italian mainland. The Jocks didn't mind, nor did I. Life on the beachhead was hard work but it was preferable to risking life and limb in an infantry attack.

We were based for a couple of weeks north of Catania, which had fallen on 5 August. There was a round of military parades, film shows and football matches to keep the troops occupied. Officers could wangle visits to Catania. It was an austere place of black lava façades, with a baroque cathedral at its core. I remember it as the first Italian city I saw. Mac, Shaw and I drove along Via Garibaldi to Piazza Duomo where the cathedral had narrowly escaped being hit by bombs, or gunfire from the *Warspite*, one of the battleships offshore. The locals, however, seemed happy enough. I was not brought up a Catholic but I was moved to visit the Duomo, and sat through Mass. I doubt that many soldiers there noticed the tomb of Vincenzo Bellini, the composer. How absurd, I thought, that we were fighting these people.

At a dried-up fountain in the centre of the piazza, hung a sign: THIS TOWN IS OUT OF BOUNDS TO ALL H.M. AND ALLIED FORCES, UNLESS ON DUTY. As always in a newly liberated city, security had to be enforced. Frankly, we really shouldn't have been there that day. There had been some looting and civil unrest—Fascist offices trashed; scores settled. No evidence of the Mafia, though. That was in the American sector where, notoriously, Italian-Americans in army service, some of whom were gangsters, were used as liaison officers. Mussolini had repressed the Mafia. The Yanks brought it back.

We took a Jeep as far as we could drive up Mount Etna and then struggled up a few hundred feet of lava-strewn screes. The reward was a panoramic view, with the mountains of Calabria across the Straits of Messina. In 1860, Garibaldi saw the scene after he liberated Sicily and prepared to lead a 10,000-strong army across the straights to Rome, the route the Allies would follow. As we drove back to Catania we passed landowners' villas, some now commandeered by British officers. The contadini in the fields took little notice of us unless we asked for help, which they invariably gave. We were surprised at the frequent kindness of the poorest people. They offered us wine and blessings despite the war on their doorsteps. Their stone-built farmhouses provided accommodation and cover for both sides. Many had been wrecked by stonks. The peasants bore this disruption with a fatalism and dignity. These people had been used to hardship and misfortune for generations. Sicily had known many invaders and occupiers: Greeks, Romans, Arabs, Crusaders, Bourbons, Garibaldi, Mussolini, the Germans and now the Yanks and us. I daresay we were more welcome than some—we had seen Fascists beaten and arrested—but I felt, recalling the fading beauty of Noto, that the island would remain the same after we moved on, crumbling in poverty and aristocratic decay. I don't believe we changed much in Sicily, except to add to the ruins that were already there.

The campaign in Sicily ended on 16 August when Messina fell to Patton's forces, beating Monty by a few hours. Patton, who had liberated the capital, Palermo, on 22 July, was jubilant, but the Allies failed to trap the enemy. The German rearguard had melted away from Messina on the night of the 15th. Over the previous days, 40,000 German and 62,000 Italian troops, with guns and vehicles galore, had escaped to the mainland. Royal Navy captains and commanders, perhaps recalling the abortive attempt to force the Dardanelles in 1915, when several battleships were sunk by Turkish mines, were reluctant to expose their big ships to mines and E-boat attack in the narrows. The Allied air forces, on that occasion, were equally ineffective.

The remoteness of Allied high command in Algiers contributed to that fiasco. There were other problems. Eisenhower was inexperienced and his deputy Alexander lacked what Monty called 'grip'. In Sicily, operations were bedevilled by rivalry and suspicion between Monty and

Patton, although they had much in common: both were inspiring leaders and neither was publicity-shy. Monty was known for his eccentric headgear; Patton strapped on pearl-handled revolvers. Later, in Italy, Patton's sucessor, Lieutenant-General Mark Clark, became paranoid about what he thought was British one-upmanship, despite Alexander's charm. Monty's contempt for the Americans was unconcealed: the Yanks were vulgar Johnny-come-latelies; they thought the British were patronising snobs.

There was a fundamental disagreement about strategy. At the Casablanca Conference, Churchill had persuaded Roosevelt to help knock Italy out of the war. He was suspicious of Soviet intentions in Central Europe and the possibility that the Red Army would occupy Berlin and Vienna. An Anglo-American advance up Italy to the Alps might counter this threat. Churchill was also aware that the Mediterranean was the only theatre where the British still played the senior role. The Americans thought an invasion of northern France was the best way to crush Hitler. For them, the Mediterranean was a sideshow, with a fading British imperial script. As they had every intention of succeeding that empire after the war, they were disinclined to prop it up.

The Italian campaign was thus launched by reluctant partners with incompatible aims. Unfortunately for us, the Allies' year and a half slog up the mountainous length of Italy was opposed by a clearly-focused, resourceful and determined enemy. Whatever the American and British politicians and generals thought about each other, most of those in the poor bloody infantry who did the fighting, suffering and dying—whether under American or British command—felt mutual sympathy and at times respect.

❦

On 2 September, south of Messina, the British 5th and Canadian 1st divisions prepared to embark for the invasion of the mainland. On a calm sea, hundreds of landing craft, DUKWS and destroyers milled around. These preparations were impossible to conceal from Jerry. While we waited on the beach we were attacked by three bombers, but they sheered off without dropping bombs, scared off by the curtain of ack-ack fire that was raised. As they vanished into the darkness over the Italian shore, I saw the sea splattered with falling shrapnel. Unusually, there was hardly any enemy artillery fire from the mainland, as there had been a few days before.

We boarded our landing craft and cast off at 1900. At 0335 on 3 September 1943—the fourth anniversary of the start of the war—the night exploded with an 'Alamein barrage', a ferocious 600-gun bombardment. The sky sang with shells from Sicily as we chugged across the straits in the dark, watching in frozen fascination as the barrage straddled the enemy coast. All this turned out to be a complete waste of ammo. When we hit the beach at 0615, four kilometres north of Reggio di Calabria, our landing was unopposed. We were slightly dazed by the silence after the profligate bombardment. If someone had bothered to recce the beaches, I thought, or checked aerial reconnaissance photos, the shelling of an undefended coastline should surely have been avoided. But Monty had the firepower and there was an inevitability in its use.

On the first day some Jerry planes evaded our fighters and strafed and bombed the beaches. One of our men was killed and five were wounded. Such statistics sound heartless, but those anonymous men, and others I have mentioned, were not in A Company. I neither knew them nor their names—the infantryman's interest and loyalty being confined to his own small group.

The Germans chose not to defend Calabria, preferring to concentrate further north towards Naples. We saw no Jerries but we bagged

Italians—hundreds of the blighters, whose white flags had been waved the moment we landed—an instant labour force. In the first hours of the invasion we dealt with constant streams of soldiers and vehicles landing. Over the first three days, 5,300 vehicles passed through the beachhead. Monty landed on the first morning, no doubt to see the results of his bombardment.

On 8 September we heard that Italy had surrendered. We were neither surprised nor triumphant at this news. From my experience from Eritrea onwards, it was obvious that the Italians were ambivalent about their part in the war. Neither we nor the Germans took them seriously—although Kesselring did take the precaution of disarming the Italian army within days of the surrender. Many Italian soldiers deserted and fled to the countryside, as did many Allied PoWs. Mussolini, deposed by his own government after the Sicily landings and under house arrest in the Abruzzi mountains, was freed in a German glider and parachute raid and spirited north to form a puppet régime that continued the war. On 9 September, the Eighth Army's 10th Corps and the American Fifth Army's 6th Corps landed at Salerno. On the Adriatic coast, Taranto was taken after a seaborne landing. The 78th Division landed at Bari. By the end of the month, the strategic airfields at Foggia had been captured. 'Rome by Christmas,' the generals said. For a while, that seemed likely.

We were relieved of our beach duties in mid-September and spent a month on the Calabrian coast north of Reggio, reorganising and retraining. I recall being astonished on one exercise in the country to see peasant women with baskets full of grapes—the wine harvest in progress. Something else sticks in my mind—the sad fate of my company commander, Captain Tidmarsh. He had gone out one evening, recklessly and injudiciously, with Jimmy Stewart and another warrant officer on the prowl looking for wine and women. They ended up at a farmhouse, where they were attacked by the outraged father protecting his daughter. Fortunately, the contadino did not use a dagger. At first, the incident seemed trivial. But poor Ted suffered a severe blow to the head and he was flown home for treatment. He had just been decorated—an MC, a periodic award for his service in the Middle East. As second-in-command I took temporary charge of A Company, adding considerably to my responsibilities and worries. Sanders, loyal and cheerful as ever, was a boon. As for Ted, I never saw him again.

In mid-October we moved by road and rail to Taranto. We were not surprised on arrival to be ordered to the docks. Throughout the war the battalion's postings and tasks were unpredictable and often unconventional. We thought we might join the 51st Highland Division with the 7th Argylls, returning to the UK to train for the D-Day landings in Normandy. Instead, we sailed back to Egypt.

The ship was the *Llangibby Castle*, a Clyde-built Union Castle Line vessel. During the voyage, I learned that the *Windsor Castle* had been sunk off Algeria in March by a torpedo-bomber, but stayed afloat long enough for over 2,500 troops to be rescued by other ships. Otherwise, our passage to Egypt was uneventful and we arrived at Alex at the end of October. After two weeks at Sidi Bishr we moved to Mena camp outside Cairo, for security duty at the Mena House Conference. This was attended by Churchill, Roosevelt, Chiang Kai-Shek, Alan Brooke, Lord Louis Mountbatten, a Russian delegation and assorted chiefs of staff, admirals, generals, *aides-de-camp*, politicians, interpreters, reporters and cameramen. The setting was Mena House Hotel, built as a royal lodge for Khedive Ismail, where Prince Albert, Napoleon III and Empress Eugénie were guests when they visited Egypt in 1869 for the opening of the Suez Canal.

We cordoned off the hotel's forty acres of jasmine-scented gardens, and stood sentries at the main gate. Mena bristled with troops, tanks and ack-ack guns. Bren carriers scurried about in the shadow of the Great Pyramid, shooing curious onlookers away; the RAF had an observation post on the pyramid's summit. Our guards wore kilts and sporrans and performed their ceremonial Changing of the Guard with a special swagger to impress the Ruskies, Chinese and Yanks. Officers were given passes to eat at the hotel and use its amenities. Captain Jim Sceales was assigned ADC to Chiang Kai-Shek. I had the unusual experience of finding myself standing next to Mountbatten at the urinals in the gents' lavatory.

'Fine fellows, your chaps,' he said.

'Yes, indeed, sir. Thank you, sir.' I agreed, surprised that I found my voice and that he had bothered to speak to me. He was generally popular figure, if over-promoted as chief of Combined Operations, who had been the captain of the destroyer HMS *Kelly* when it was bombed and sunk off Crete.

The bigwigs left after a few days, Churchill and Roosevelt flying to Teheran for a conference with Stalin. When we returned to Alex, I was astonished to meet my brother Cecil, a second lieutenant in 42 Royal Marine Commando. He had joined up in 1942 and was commissioned at Thurlestone OCTU in Devon. In mid-November 1943, he sailed from Gourock, en route to the Far East. His ship was bombed in the Med and was now in the Western Harbour at Alex for repairs. The last news from me had been my letter to our mother, from Sicily. He had tracked me down, having phoned around various camps on the off chance of finding the Argylls. I saw that he'd been promoted. He laughed. His CO, thinking it a slur on the Royal Marines for one of his officers to have a younger brother a captain in the Argylls had made him a full lieutenant, to maintain the Marines' honour.

Mac, Shaw and I (and Lieutenant Pyper, who must have come over from some Indian unit) took Cecil and a fellow marine officer, David

Keith Hardy and some Forces girls we knew, for drinks at the Cecil Hotel. Then we gorged ourselves on a lavish Christmas dinner at the Union Club: fish, turkey, ham, pudding, mince pies, fruit and Turkish coffee. Marvellous! We enjoyed some music-making together, Cecil and I playing the piano and singing as we had done at home. Shaw and Mac joined in, Mac playing a violin he had acquired on his travels. I remember writing out on manuscript paper the notes of the 'Eton Boating Song' for Hardy's benefit, which he sang with great gusto. Apparently, he had planned to be an assistant choreographer in a ballet company, thought again and enlisted in the Commandos. That evening we strolled along the Corniche without a care in the world. As usual, the euphoria didn't last—we inhabited a world of abrupt and unpredictable highs and lows. A few days later Cecil and Hardy rejoined their ship and sailed for Bombay.

Cecil never said much about his war. The memory of any unpleasantness was disguised by cheery banter, which I was always happy to go along with. He'd laugh when recalling Calcutta, where he and Hardy penned a music column in *Jungle Book*, the magazine of the 3rd Commando Brigade, South-east Asia Command. He managed to play cricket occasionally and used to send me photos that always showed him in the company of attractive girls, evidently taken at some palm-fringed beauty spot or hill station. He joked that the only time he was wounded was in India, when he fell off a motorbike. But I do know that in 1944, Cecil's 42 Royal Marine Commando trained near Goa, for jungle warfare, and on India's east coast for combined operations. It went into action with the 3rd Commando Brigade against the Japs in the mangrove swamps, paddy fields and mountainous jungle of the Arakan on the Burmese coast in January 1945. The 3rd Commando Brigade experienced some of the toughest, close-quarter fighting of that campaign, against a '*Banzai*-screeching, suicidal enemy'.

Many of my battalion's men with long service overseas were repatriated at the end of 1943. Those of us who remained moved to a desert camp near Suez to absorb and train replacements, some from the HLI and the Cameron Highlanders. It was then that I had another surprise encounter. We were packing up ready to move off. I was supervising the loading of trucks and the clean-up of the area, urging the men to get a move on. I became aware of a Jock standing nearby, gazing at me intently. I was just about to give him a bawling out when I noticed, to my astonishment, that it was none other than Willie Rankine, elder brother of Davie. He was a private in the Camerons, standing there in his battledress and balmoral, with a big smile on his face. Willie was as surprised as I was. He knew I was in the Middle East, but little expected to come across me as he did. I knew he was in the Camerons but had little idea he was in Egypt.

Our meeting was brief, unfortunately, as I was about move off and his battalion had just arrived to take over the camp. I commiserated with him on his brother's death in June. Davie had been a private in the Royal Army Ordnance Corps and I had met him in Cairo shortly after he arrived in Egypt earlier in the year. Later, I heard that he had contracted typhus and was in hospital in Alex. But I hadn't been able to find out how he was, because we were at the final stage of preparation for Sicily, and my movements were completely restricted. I didn't know of his death until we returned to Egypt, to Mena House. I managed to send Sanders to seek out his grave and take a photograph, which I had sent to his mother. Willie and I brought each other up to date with other news, then bade farewell with a handshake and an exchange of smart salutes. He went to Italy with the Camerons' 2nd Battalion, but I didn't come across him there and we didn't meet again until after the war. The Rankine brothers and the Ward brothers were the mainstay of the Baldwin Cricket Club before the war and we had known each other since our boyhood days. Those coincidences, meeting Willie and Cecil such a long way from home in such times, still amaze me.

At the end of January, the battalion entrained for Port Said for immediate embarkation on the *Dilwara* and sailed for Taranto. The ship was
modern and, having been designed specifically as a troopship, relatively comfortable. The passage was routine, apart from a moving ceremony.
The CO and the padre, Rev. A. C. Dow, gathered the battalion on deck
to commemorate the 150th Anniversary of the Raising of the Regiment.
Kipling's 'Recessional' and the 91st Psalm drifted across the Med as
we stood in silence and prayer. It was 1100 hours, 6 February 1944. The
following day we sighted the shores of Sicily again. We were returning
to the war.

Part Two

10 THE GUSTAV LINE

The Middle East my father left in February 1944 has changed so much in sixty years that I'm not sure my visiting Egypt, Palestine and the Western Desert, or East Africa would add much to his memoir of those places, beyond a now-and-then travelogue. Mussolini's art deco buildings still decorate Asmara and appear as a curiosity in newspaper travel sections. The obelisk from Aksum, looted by the Italians and re-erected on a Roman piazza, was returned to Ethiopia in 2005. Perhaps Massawa looks the same: in the late-twentieth century, it was bombed by the Ethiopian air force during wars with Eritrea, and the old governor's palace wrecked. The stretch of the Nile my father sailed on has been flooded behind the Aswan Dam. And the Holy Land? If he were able to go back he would be appalled, as I would be for him.

As for the louche, cosmopolitan glamour of Alexandria and the starch and snobbery of British imperial Cairo and Khartoum: these have been erased completely since the 1940s and I have no sentiment for them. Shepheard's Hotel was destroyed by fire during anti-British riots in 1952; the statue of Ferdinand de Lesseps at Port Said was toppled by Egyptian nationalists in 1956; Cairo's nineteenth-century opera house burned down in 1971. The Cecil Hotel in Alexandria is now part of a French chain. The Western Desert remains the same—littered with millions of Afrika Korps and Eighth Army landmines which still kill or maim the unlucky or unwary. Away from the minefields, the Desert War is well chronicled. There are even package tours from London to Egypt's Mediterranean resorts that take in El Alamein. Having read my father's account of 'the perfect battlefield', I don't think I need the tour.

The Italian campaign is a different story. My father wrote:

After a month spent reorganising and training for our new combat role, we sailed for Italy. There, we exchanged the joys of Alex and the warmth of Egypt for the unexpected rigours of an Italian winter. It took some getting used to. The battalion joined 19 Brigade, 8th Indian Division, with which we were to serve for the next year and a half, up the length of Italy from the heel to the Po valley, until the end of the war.

Churchill called Italy 'the soft underbelly of Europe', hoping it would provide a swift route to Berlin. But for the Argylls, and every other Allied soldier who fought there, the Italian campaign was neither swift nor soft. We faced determined, often ferocious German opposition. It was the most eventful, action-packed and harrowing period of my war service.

Italy was where he returned after the war: not physically, but in dreams and nightmares—and in periodic, late-night revelations to me when I visited Glasgow during his retirement years. Italy was where his wartime ghosts were and, for over fifty years, they visited him often and uninvited. Italy was where he saw his men die.

When he retired in 1981, we talked about a trip to Tuscany. It never happened. At the time, I was working in London, and then moved to Vancouver where other priorities seemed more important. I did send him newspaper clippings of items about the war, of which there were many, especially around Remembrance Day. But my father remained unwilling to confront his wartime memories, until late in life. I was unwilling to share that emotional journey with him, until now. So I shall travel to Italy for him, and to satisfy my curiosity about the Battle of Monte Cavallara—to find the graves of his fallen comrades whose fate haunted him until the day he died.

ON 8 FEBRUARY 1944, the *Dilwara* steamed between two break-waters into the bowl-shaped lagoon of Taranto's outer harbour. In 1940, torpedo bombers from the aircraft carrier HMS *Illustrious* had attacked Taranto, sinking three battleships, a blow from which the Italian Navy never recovered. Most of its ships were now in Allied hands, having sailed to be surrendered at Malta. The damage we saw as we sailed in was the result of more recent air attacks. A battered ancient *castello*, the Italian naval HQ, guarded the entrance to an inner lagoon. The water-front was lined with crumbling, ochre-coloured palazzi, many displaying bomb damage. It was in one of those grandiose hulks that MacDougall got us mixed up in a bar room brawl.

I had seen plenty of inter-service and regimental rivalry in Alex and Cairo but had always managed to avoid getting involved. Mac, Shaw and I were with some South African and Rhodesian officers who had just joined the battalion, drinking in a hastily-established officers' club. The club was more like a wild west saloon and, sure enough, a scrap started. Mac, who had a Highland soldier's temperament—his often courteous and inoffensive exterior concealing a talent for violence—was at his belligerent best. It didn't take him long to bristle at some bois-terous junior officers just off the boat from Blighty. He pushed his way over, picked the biggest one out and told him he didn't know how to wear the kilt. The big man's pals surrounded Mac. I went across to try to cool them off. One of them, not realising I was on a peace-keeping mission, laid a hand on my shoulder and tried to pull me away.

'Take your hands off me!' I shouted.

I told him twice and, when he refused, floored him with an upper-cut. His pals piled in. We ended up on the floor, like a rugby scrum.

At that moment, two senior officers appeared.

'What the bloody hell's going on?'

We were separated quickly and peace was restored. Mac, Shaw and the 'Zulus' (as we called the South Africans and Rhodesians) loved it.

After that rumpus, I became known as a 'hard man', a reputation that did me no damage.

Shortly after we arrived, A Company was placed on Stand-by after reports of rioting in the city, provoked by food shortages. None of us looked forward to crowd control. In the event, we were stood-down a few days later. The battalion spent three weeks under canvas at a staging area at Taranto, training and re-equipping for combat duty with the 8th Indian Division. Carriers were taken over from another regiment; Jeeps, 15-cwt trucks and 3-ton lorries from Egypt were picked up at the docks. On the 12th, the CO went off to Eighth Army HQ at Vasto on the Adriatic coast and toured the division's front line—a sure sign that a move was imminent. We left Taranto at 0500 on the 25th, checking our route cards. We had full tanks of petrol and 100 miles reserve for the 300-kilometre drive north, up the Adriatic coast and into the mountains of Abruzzo to locate the 8th Indian. I was with the advance party (the CO, adjutant, company commanders and other officers), followed at intervals by the main vehicle party (subalterns, NCOs and men) and a rail party (tracked vehicles, mortars and 6-pounder A/T guns and all their crews).

I rode with Major W. H. Lossock, my new company commander, who had originally joined the battalion from the London Scottish Regiment in 1940. There was no sign of the war in the bare orchards, olive groves and secretive hamlets we passed. The only other travellers we saw were a few Italians on bicycles or horse-drawn carts and carriages, who were forced off the road as we passed. Poverty, shortage of petrol and the Germans' habit of commandeering serviceable vehicles had relegated civilians to the transport of the nineteenth century. At Bari, we edged forward along streets packed with army vehicles and off-duty British, Indian, New Zealand and Canadian soldiers. Normal chaos had resumed after a German air raid on the port in December when over a dozen ships had been sunk. At Foggia, muddy airfields were churned up by planes which threw up showers of spray as they took off. We arrived at Campomarino sometime that afternoon, with 50 kilometres still to go. We pushed on, crossed a Bailey bridge over the Sangro river and turned away from the sea, into the foothills of the Abruzzi whose peaks were ominous and snow-capped. A blizzard on Hogmanay had left three-metre-deep drifts across the mountain battlefield. 'Sunny Italy', Lossock observed.

We overtook dozens of mules led by Indian soldiers, plodding in single-file columns along the side of the road. Red Cross tents, bivouacs, tanks and trucks were scattered along the valleys. At every hamlet, troops clustered around braziers and steaming cookhouses, drinking tea and stamping their feet to keep warm. The CO stopped to report to Divisional HQ at Lanciano, a stone-built hamlet that looked and was medieval, with amenities to match. We then left our vehicles and tramped up to billets in stone-built farms and houses in and around another primitive hamlet, Castelfrentano.

Conditions were rustic: earth floors and open-hearth fires, which tourists today might find charming. Sanitation was inadequate. Local water had to be boiled. Since the contadini put up with these living conditions and were friendly, I thought it churlish to complain. All the way up Italy, we encountered hardy peasants who worked the land in return for spartan accommodation and half the fruit of their labour (the other half went to the landowner at harvest time). The Germans usually stole their pigs and cattle. We were grateful for the straw that had been left because we slept in the empty byres. We fortified ourselves with a nightly ration of rum and kept fires roaring day and night (mindful of a Brigade HQ order not to cut down olive trees or telegraph poles).

The village was in full view of the enemy, so movement during the day was restricted. Tracks were given sinister nicknames: 'spandau road', 'suicide ridge.' A curfew was in place from 1900 and a blackout strictly enforced. The farmhouses kept out the bitter cold, but not enemy shellfire. Fortunately a policy of 'live and let live' was being observed. If we refrained from shelling German-held houses, Jerry would also refrain from deliberate destruction of those in our own lines. Life outdoors was miserable, especially for those stuck in frontline sangars and trenches. It was pretty awful too for the Italian guides and the Indian muleteers of the pioneer platoons. They had to make nightly treks, often harassed by small-arms and shell fire, to bring up supplies to the forward positions. We got a crash course in mountain warfare, learning the tricks of survival and, worst of all, loading and handling our temperamental pets. It still amazes me that while we were fighting a twentieth-century war, mules were our lifeline in the mountains throughout the Italian campaign.

On the 29th, the CO, Major MacFie and I toured the Sangro front. The road was strewn at random with rusting debris and temporary wayside graves left over from Monty's late-November offensive. Burned-out tanks lay slumped like drunks by the roadside. We crossed several Bailey bridges, which had been pushed over gaps where the original spans had been destroyed by Allied bombing or by the Germans. Those Bailey bridges—Meccano-like steel trusses, each section of which could be carried by six sappers and bolted together—became a feature of the Italian campaign. We couldn't have advanced without them. For the moment, though, the forward troops were making do, stuck in foxholes or sheltering in tumbledown, shell-damaged farmhouses. Life for Jerry was probably much the same.

In the Sangro battles of a few months before, the 78th British and 2nd New Zealand divisions had forced a crossing of the river and established a bridgehead in the Gustav Line, the position to which the Germans retreated after being expelled from Sicily. The line, partly fortified and defended by panzer, paratroop and infantry divisions, zig-zagged across the breadth of Italy from the Adriatic to the Tyrrhenian Sea. The offensive had been a desert-style big push, with infantry, armour and close air support. But torrential rain, winds, low cloud and hilly country changed everything. Rivers burst their banks, tanks got bogged down and the DAF was frequently grounded. Flanking attacks in the foothills of the Abruzzi—where the 8th Indian Division, which had arrived from the Middle East in September 1943, was fighting—made little progress. The Kiwis encountered dogged German resistance when they tried, throughout December, to seize the hill town of Orsogna. Another tactical target, the town of Ortona on the coast, only fell to the 1st Canadian Division after heavy street and house-to-house fighting. The advance stalled and the Eighth Army, and the Germans, dug in until spring.

At the end of December, Monty had been recalled to the UK, where he was promoted to command the Allied armies that were preparing for D-Day. At Vasto, he had issued a final message to the army he had made famous.

EIGHTH ARMY

PERSONAL MESSAGE FROM THE ARMY COMMANDER

To be read out to all Troops

1. I have to tell you, with great regret, that the time has come for me to leave the Eighth Army. I have been ordered to take command of the British Armies in England that are to operate under General Eisenhower—the Supreme Commander.

2. It is difficult to express to you adequately what this parting means to me. I am leaving officers and men who have been my comrades during months of hard and victorious fighting, and whose courage and devotion to duty always filled me with admiration. I feel I have many friends among the soldiery of this great Army. I do not know if you will miss me; but I will miss you more than I can say, and especially will I miss the personal contacts, and the cheerful greetings we exchanged together when we passed each other on the road.

3. In all the battles we have fought together we have not had one single failure; we have been successful in everything we have undertaken. I know that this has been due to the devotion to duty and whole-hearted co-operation of every officer and man, rather than to anything I may have been able to do myself. But the result has been a mutual confidence between you and me, and mutual confidence between a Commander and his troops is a pearl of very great price.

4. I am also very sad at parting from the Desert Air Force. This magnificent air striking force has fought with the Eighth Army throughout the whole of its victorious progress; every soldier in this Army is proud to acknowledge that the support of this strong and powerful air force has been a battle-winning factor of the first importance. We owe the Allied Air Forces in general, and the Desert Air Force in particular, a very great debt of gratitude.

5. What can I say to you as I go away? When the heart is full it is not easy to speak. But I would say this to you: You have made this Army what it is; you have made its name a household word all over the world; you must uphold its good name and its traditions. And I would ask you to give to my successor the same loyal and devoted service that you have never failed to give to me.

6. And so I say good-bye to you all. May we meet again soon and may we serve together again as comrades in arms in the final stages of this war.

B. L. Montgomery,

General, Eighth Army.

Italy, 1 January 1944.

General Alexander, now Commander-in-Chief, Allied Armies in Italy, appointed Monty's understudy, Lieutenant-General Leese, to command the Eighth Army. This was the same gung ho Leese who had stood with Bloomie and I as we watched the Alamein barrage. For Leese, promotion couldn't have come at a worse time. Before Alamein, Monty had taken over battle-weary, cynical, and demoralised troops who had lost faith in their generals. He moulded them into a well-trained, superbly-organised, efficient fighting force that won its battles. Now he was gone, and the Anglo-American strategic focus shifted to North-west Europe.

During the week we stayed at Castelfrentano we were inspected by Major General 'Pasha' Dudley Russell, the 8th Indian Division's CO, and Brigadier T. S. Dobree, CO, 19 Brigade. We put on a bit of a show but it must have been clear to them that we were neither finding it easy to acclimatise to the fierce weather nor getting the feel of this different country. Having been used to khaki shorts and short-sleeved shirts for so long, we were now laden down with battledress, leather jerkins, winter boots, gloves, scarves, balaclavas and gas capes. Every man in the battalion would have given a year's pay to have been back in North Africa, footslogging through the hot dry, desert day.

Russell, nicknamed Pasha because of his bushy black moustache, swagger stick and confident manner, was a Kiplingesque professional soldier, a type now extinct. During the First World War he had served with the Royal West Kent Regiment and been wounded in France. He was transferred to the Indian Army and won an MC during Allenby's campaign in Palestine. He campaigned on the North-west Frontier and, by 1939, was the CO of the 6/13th Frontier Force Rifles. He had served in East Africa, with the 5th Indian Division in Eritrea and Abyssinia, and negotiated the Duke of Aosta's surrender. He had also been in the Western Desert and won our affection by wearing desert army shorts, except in the coldest weather. Dobree, 'The Wee Briggie', a Royal Artillery subaltern in the First World War, who had served recently with the Indian Army in the Middle East, East Africa and India, was also a former desert army officer.

The 8th Indian Division's three brigades (17th, 19th and 21st) were scattered across the hilly front line, somewhat disorganised after the

Sangro river offensive. The 1st Argylls had been moved up to relieve
19 Brigade's 1/5th Essex Regiment, which had lost almost 100 men in
the recent fighting. The brigade's other infantry battalions were the 6th
Royal (Scinde) Battalion 13th Frontier Force Rifles and the 3rd Battalion
8th Punjab Regiment. The 53rd Field (Bolton) Regiment (25-pounders)
and the 14th Canadian Armoured (Calgary) Regiment (Sherman tanks)
provided the brigade's artillery and tank support. Each Indian division had a British or Commonwealth artillery and armoured regiment
attached; each Indian brigade had a British infantry battalion. The 8th
Indian's senior officers were British as were those who led its brigades,
regiments and battalions. I never met an Indian officer above the rank
of major. Altogether something of a relic from the Raj, I thought, like
the division's CO.

This was the first time in the war that the 1st Argylls were attached
permanently to an infantry brigade, and the battalion would remain
with the 19th until the end of the war. After years of being moved
around from unit to unit and place to place, we welcomed the posting.
There was some muttering among the Jocks about being in the Indian
Army, a feeling that service with colonial troops was a demotion. But
the Indian Army attracted the cream of British officers and superb fighting men.

Those Indian soldiers—Dogras, Gurkhas, Mahrattas, Pathans,
Punjabis, Rajputs, Sikhs and others—were recruited mainly from the
tribal lands of northern India, Nepal and what is now Pakistan. The
similarity of the 6/13th Frontier Force Rifles and the 3/8th Punjabis
to the traditional composition of Scottish Highland regiments was striking. All the men were volunteers (although some may have been coerced
by poverty and village elders). Their code of personal honour was root-
ed in tribal, village and family pride, not solely in service to the Raj or
the East India Company. They were as proud of their martial heritage
and regimental traditions as any Scot. The Indians were loyal, courte-

ous and dignified with friends—and ferocious fighters of enemies. The politics of Indian nationalism, which caused unrest in India during the war, did not affect their conduct in the Italian campaign, despite propaganda leaflets inciting mutiny that the Germans lobbed over our lines. We got on well with them and grew to admire them as if they were our own. I thought they were wonderful men.

At dawn on 8 March, an overcast, cold, wet and miserable day, we moved to the front line, initially to relieve the 1st Royal Fusiliers (17 Brigade). Because of the atrocious weather the front was static, except for nightly patrols by both sides to contest no-man's-land. The battalion set off at 1000 hours, companies at 20-minute intervals on the eight-kilometre approach march to the Fusiliers' positions, crossing the Moro river and up a narrow, muddy track near the village of Poggiofiorito. We were burdened with full kit—shovels, steel helmets, weapons and ammo—and wore gas capes to protect us from the rain. We reached our assembly area, a slippery, rocky hillside. There we sat or lay flat out, exhausted, until fortified by a hot meal and a tot of rum. Then the battalion dispersed across a couple of square kilometres of hills. A Company moved off to its frontline positions, centred on a scattering of isolated farm buildings much knocked about by shellfire. The pouring rain turned to snow. The relief was completed by 2245.

As company second-in-command I was left behind with a section of Jocks to bring up rations, water, ammo and other stores by mule train. Over the next few hours, this task was accomplished in pitch darkness, lit sporadically by flashes of star shells, artillery explosions, and tracer fire. Our progress was punctuated by the rattle of Jerrycans and ammo boxes carried by the mules and by the curses of the muleteers as we climbed. When we reached Company HQ, I found a scene of confusion. Our positions were hardly a line, more an inter-connected series of strongpoints facing a similar one on the German side. The takeover from the Fusiliers had not gone smoothly and nobody seemed to know exactly where they were or what they were doing. To make matters worse the Fusiliers had left mines and booby traps scattered around the area, unmarked. And there was snow on the ground.

We started unloading the mules which, typically, refused to stand still. I grabbed one by the leash. It snorted and shied back . . . A sudden flash and an almighty bang and I found myself lying on my back, semi-conscious in the mud and snow, feeling as if the mule had kicked me. It had trodden on a booby-trapped grenade, taken the full force of the blast, and now lay whimpering and dying in a heap of boxes. Anything within 20 yards of a grenade exploding will be hit, and I was closer than that. 'What a pathetic way to go', was what went through my mind as I shivered in shock. Then I heard voices coming near. Lieutenant W. A. Dunn, one of A Company's platoon commanders, appeared out of the gloom and peered at me closely through a swirl of snowflakes. He helped me up and we staggered through the blanketed entrance of Company HQ, where I collapsed at the feet of my horrified company commander. It was a bad start to the night's operation for him. A worse one for me.

Two Jocks had also been wounded and were sitting in the snow moaning. The other casualties were three bottles of whisky I had brought up for Lossock and his subalterns.

'Sorry we can't give you a dram,' Dunn said, after establishing that I would live. I'd been hit by shrapnel in the upper and lower left leg.

I raised myself on my elbow and stared at him.

He nodded. 'All gone. Blown to buggery.'

The ever-resourceful Sanders produced some field dressings and patched me up as best he could. Lossock called for stretcher bearers. I had seen men hit before but didn't know, until that moment, that the pain can be delayed. Adrenaline shoots through the system like a drug. I was also pretty numb from the cold as we set off down the hillside. Dunn shouted after me, 'Good luck, Ray. You owe me a whisky.'

I was stretcher-borne, the two others walking wounded. One of them had been hit in the body, and by his groans was having a painful journey, as were the two Indian stretcher bearers. I don't know how they managed with their burden on that fearsome track in the dark. How they must have cursed me! I felt I should give up my stretcher to the poor devil with the stomach wound, but he was not seriously hurt and I couldn't have walked, even with assistance, and I was beginning to ache. I was stretchered into a casualty clearing station at Battalion HQ and dumped on a couple of wooden trestles. A medic came over and gave me a shot of morphine and cleaned and bandaged my wounds. Ronnie McAlister, our experienced, well-respected CO, looked down at me with sad eyes full of sympathy. He was a fine, gentlemanly, kind-hearted man, with whom I had got on well in the desert. Perhaps he was not ruthless enough for the job, for he was to be replaced by Lieutenant-Colonel Freddie Graham, of whom more anon. I was mad at the Fusiliers for not clearing their booby traps. (I told Shaw afterwards that I knew now the indignity he felt from having been shot by one of our sentries in Abyssinia.) Anyway, I was glad to be out of the line and away from the hateful hills of Poggiofiorito. But my ordeal was far from over.

I still had to face an interminable journey by ambulance, driven through the night on rutted, shell-holed roads by a mad Indian driver, to an Indian Army field hospital. What a relief it was to get into a comfortable bed with clean white sheets, after roughing it in the mountains. The wounds in my leg were giving me gyp, and I suppose I was suffering from the effects of after-shock, aggravated by the horrors of that nightmare journey by stretcher and ambulance. All I wanted to do was sleep, but I was kept awake by the chatter of nurses and doctors. I told them rudely to shut up and give me some peace. This couldn't have endeared me to them. One nurse got her own back by giving me an enormous enema. This had a most explosive and turbulent effect on my bowels, which had been constipated for a week.

I was operated on a couple of days later and bits of shrapnel were dug out of my leg. One piece was missed by the Indian surgeon and left inside my upper leg, as I discovered some years after the war. After he had operated, the surgeon asked me if there was anything I would like. I replied, 'Yes, a glass of whisky please.' He gave a loud laugh and told a nurse to let me have it.

Waking up the next morning, I heard voices of children at play outside. Having been so long accustomed to the company of soldiers and the noise of battle, the happy sound fell on my ears with such moving novelty and clarity that I almost wept. I don't remember much else about my stay at the field hospital or how long I was kept there, except that I soon began to miss the battalion around which my life revolved. And I had forgotten to ask Sanders to give me my oilskin wallet, which had all my letters and writing materials. No one at home or even at the battalion now knew where I was. It always took some time for a casualty's whereabouts to be passed on. Mail took a long time to catch up. When it did, I had been moved 150 kilometres south, to a British army hospital at Barletta. I imagined the shock my mother got on the doorstep when she received the dreaded War Office telegram:

GOVERNMENT ABSOLUTE PRIORITY. 7.15 LIVERPOOL OHMS PTY.
PRIORITY CC A. WARD 99 KNIGHTSCLIFFE AVE. GLASGOW W3. REPORT
DATED 12TH MARCH 1944 RECEIVED FROM CENTRAL MEDITERRANEAN
AREA THAT CAPT. T. R. WARD ARGYLL AND SUTHERLAND HIGHLANDERS
HAS BEEN WOUNDED. THE ARMY COUNCIL EXPRESSES SYMPATHY.
LETTER FOLLOWS SHORTLY. UNDER SECRETARY OF STATE FOR WAR.

The letter was addressed to my late father.

The War Office, Casualty Branch
Blue Coat School, Church Road, Wavertree, Liverpool 15

20 March 1944.

Our Ref./08/2927/W (Casualties)

Sir,

In confirmation of War Office telegram dated the 17th March, 1944, I regret to have to inform you that a report dated the 12th March, 1944, has been received by telegraph from the Military Authorities in the Central Mediterranean that your son, Captain T. R. Ward, The Argyll and Sutherland Highlanders, has been wounded.

No particulars as to the nature of the wound or the name of the hospital to which your son has been admitted have been furnished. If, however, he becomes seriously ill as a result of his wound, further reports will be received by telegraph which will be telegraphed on to you. In the absence of such a communication, it can be assumed that Captain Ward is making normal progress in which event you will, no doubt hear from him in due course about his wound and progress.

In the meantime communications for your son should continue to be addressed to him at his unit, where arrangements exist for their redirection if necessary. Will you kindly notify this office of any change in your address, in case further reports are received.

I am, Sir,

Your obedient Servant,

[signature illegible]

I felt a bit of a fraud at Barletta, having my modest wounds dressed daily by attentive nurses. Especially as in the next bed to mine there was a young fellow in the RAF, who had suffered severe burns to his hands and face in a plane crash. His cries and groans were heart-breaking to hear as he had his wounds dressed, twice daily. He must have suffered terribly. As he got better, I wrote letters home for him, to his dictation, in which the brave fellow made light of his condition. We all made much of him in the ward, trying to cheer him up and take his mind off things. I don't know how good a recovery he made; he must have been scarred for life. For me, the hospital became an agreeable billet for the two months I stayed there until my wounds healed. The weather improved. Some of us convalescents recovered sufficiently to stroll on a causeway, refreshed by sea breezes blowing in from the Adriatic. I also amused myself by reading, writing, compiling cryptic crossword puzzles and playing cricket with fellow patients, with a rolled-up paper ball and a walking stick—an activity that may have confirmed English eccentricity to any Italians who saw us.

At the end of May, I was ordered to report to the Infantry Base Depot at Benevento, 50 kilometres north-east of Naples. After a bone-crunching two-day drive, with many hold-ups and diversions in the mountains, I arrived at the town. The United States Army Air Force had bombed the place months before. Piles of rubble remained uncleared. Most of the people were still in mourning, dressed head-to-foot in black. In a pre-war Baedeker I had aquired, Benevento was noted for its eleventh-century cathedral. The façade now stood like a stage set, the rest of the building having collapsed. A Roman triumphal arch had survived the air raid, as if to mock Mussolini, and us. The town, home of Strega liquore, was now the source of much of the toxic hooch that was sold to Allied troops on the streets of Naples. Starving women and children camped outside the IBD, begging for food and clothing. In the surrounding countryside, gangs of Neapolitans foraged for food. The war had forced Mussolini to introduce rationing in 1942. In Naples, the system had imploded and been replaced by a black market that locals couldn't afford—the price the Italians were now paying for Mussolini's ill-judged entry into the war.

Naples had been liberated at the beginning of October 1943, after American Fifth Army and British divisions broke out of the Salerno bridgehead. The Allies headed for Rome. But the advance had been halted at Cassino, where the Germans held high ground and a mountain-top monastery overlooking Route 6, the main road to Rome. In January 1944, American and British troops had landed at Anzio to turn the Cassino flank. But instead of a quick advance, the beachhead was consolidated by a cautious American commander, Lieutenant General J. P. Lucas. Kesselring, caught on the back foot, moved swiftly to counter the threat. The Germans bombarded the boxed-in Allied bridgehead for the next four months.

I managed to visit Naples, a trip that plunged me into depression and horror. Arriving at Stazione Centrale, which had been partly wrecked by Allied bombing, I saw a peasant child trip on the platform and fall under a moving train. The boy was sliced in two. The hysterical mother turned and leapt at me, pounding me in the chest as if I was to blame for the boy's death, for the air raids, the war. Two Carabinieri pulled her away and I escaped, shocked, with a feeling of helplessness at the slow inevitability of it all. The smoke-filled station was so crowded with civilians and soldiers that the mother and I may have been the only witnesses to that pointless tragedy.

Outside the station, Piazza Garibaldi was a sea of hustlers, many of them ragged urchins like the boy under the train. The mother had probably brought him in from the country to join this crowd. Now she had lost her bread winner. I was pawed at by aggressive beggars: 'Inglese, Americano, Canadese, Scozzese?' they yelled. It was as if every rat had emerged from the sewers, sniffing the cigarettes and chocolate that the victorious Allied soldiers brought. I sidestepped several hawkers who lurched to intercept me and sprinted down an avenue of grim, Risorgimento-era façades. Naples had been off-limits because of air raids, anarchy and disease since it had fallen to the Allies. Now, there were plenty of off-duty soldiers milling around. I found an army club in the bomb-damaged salons of the Royal Palace, and had a stiff drink at the bar.

Before they fled north, the Germans blew up the city's electricity and sewerage systems. The Central Post Office was destroyed by a delayed-action mine that killed many civilians. The port, bombed by the RAF and the USAAF, became a target for the Luftwaffe, because the Bay of Naples was packed with Allied supply ships and naval vessels. Barrage balloons were tethered to most of them. Mount Vesuvius smouldered in the background, having erupted spectacularly in March. The superstious Neopolitans were not alone in seeing that as a sign of divine displeasure.

I don't think I walked along a single street in Naples without being solicited by the dignified and the depraved: impoverished bourgeois *signori* sat outside their apartment buildings, selling heirlooms and jewellery; rapacious street children hovered around waiting to pick pockets. I recall entering the Galleria Umberto, its vaulted iron and glass roof twisted by bombs. Beneath this limp debris, the bawdy banter of British squaddies echoed from the bars while American soldiers strode by, arm-in-arm with garish tarts. The arcade, shorn of its pre-war pretension, was evidently a black market and everything was for sale: sex, cigarettes, alcohol and pilfered Allied supplies, especially blankets, medicines and rations. Army stuff that wasn't stolen by the recently-liberated citizens of Napoli was bartered by Allied troops, rear echelon men and administrators. I don't know if AMGOT indulged this illicit activity or simply couldn't stop it. The Military Police, I am sure, learned never to leave their Jeeps unattended. I saw one spiv selling what looked like parts from army lorries.

Outside the galleria, I found myself in front of San Carlo opera house. I was amazed to find it open, with uniformed flunkeys at the door. That evening, amidst the gilded stucco of San Carlo's eighteenth-century auditorium, I sat with an audience of Allied officers and the city's melancholy bourgeoisie, all seeking refuge and consolation in Puccini and Mozart. Perhaps Naples had always been a city of extremes: poverty and Puccini; tenements grimmer than those in Glasgow's slums;

baroque façades on streets as squalid as Old Cairo's; the sparkling bay and the azure of the sea towards Capri; the Grand Tour beauty of the setting.

I was uneasy when I got back to Benevento, not just because of what I had seen in Naples: I was worried that I might not get back to the battalion. That was the fear of many of the officers in transit at the IBD. Those who had become detached, as I was, could be sent wherever the army's pen-pushers thought they might be needed, not necessarily to their original regiments. This happened all the time, the casualty rate among junior officers in the infantry being so high. We had officers and men from practically every unit in the Eighth Army posted to us at one time or another, a trend that increased as the war in Italy dragged on. I didn't want to be cast adrift in this way and made up my mind that if it came to the bit I'd cut loose and hitchhike back to the battalion.

While I had been luxuriating in a comfortable hospital bed at Barletta and hanging around the IBD at Benevento, the war in Italy had entered a new phase. The Argylls completed an unpleasant tour of duty in freezing cold at Poggiofiorito, patrolling and being shelled and mortared. I heard later that two of my men were killed and one wounded when a shell hit the farmhouse where they were sheltering. Two other Jocks were wounded when a sentry threw a grenade in the dark, after they failed to respond to his challenge. Another was killed and three wounded when their platoon was mortared. They had been perched, safely they thought, on the blind side of a terraced hill, which ninety-nine times out of a hundred couldn't be hit. Then the hundredth bomb arrived. The battalion was relieved by the 4/16th Punjabis in April. Later that month, the 8th Indian Division was trucked across the Abruzzi to the Cassino front, where the Argylls and the 14th Canadian Armoured

Regiment began intensive training for river crossing. The exercises, on the Volturno river, were watched by Lieutenant-General Leese. An offensive to capture Monte Cassino was about to be launched.

Route 6 from Naples to Rome enters the Liri valley below Monte Cassino, where an enormous Benedictine monastery sprawls on the summit, commanding the surrounding countryside as effectively as Stirling Castle guards the Forth valley. From the mountain top, German artillery observers brought down shellfire on anything moving on the highway. With the Allies stuck at Anzio, Monte Cassino and the town below had to be seized and the Liri valley penetrated before Rome could be liberated. Three previous offensives had failed, all with heavy casualties to American, New Zealand, British and Indian troops. The German units included the 1st Parachute Division. During the second battle for Cassino, it fought the 4th Indian Division and the 2nd New Zealand Division (which Rommel had regarded as the Eighth Army's best) to a standstill.

On 15 February, the monastery was carpet-bombed by B17 Flying Fortresses and other American planes. Despite post-war reconstruction of the ruins, the bombing remains controversial. It was less so to the Allied infantryman crouched in his foxhole, with the seemingly impregnable monastery looming over the battlefield like an all-seeing spectre. The Germans claimed they were not using it for observation—but they held the heights around it. They removed its books and artworks to the Vatican for safe-keeping and told the abbot to leave. Warning leaflets were dropped by Allied aircraft, but the abbot stayed with his monks and about 200 refugees from the town. Most of them were killed in the raid. The bombs created a summit strewn with rubble, ready-made for defence—which the Germans promptly occupied.

The final battle for Cassino began at 2300 on 11 May with a Monty-style artillery barrage. Monte Cassino was to be captured and German resistance in the Liri valley crushed by overwhelming force. The Argylls' part in the great assault was to cross the Rapido river at the entrance to the valley and secure a bridgehead for 19 Brigade's tanks to pass through. From what I heard later from my friends, it was a grim show.

Mac and Oxborrow had been the 'beachmasters' at the river crossing. They spoke of confusion in the dark during the approach march, lumbered as they were with assault boats; trying to follow white tape lines marking the route, some of which had been blown away by the shelling; smoke from the barrage reducing visibility to zero in places. The river was only about 15 metres wide but the crossing was a nightmare, with many boats holed by enemy fire or swept away in the fierce current. Battalion HQ and A Company (Major Lossock) were forced by a deluge of enemy shells to take cover in ditches on the near bank. Those who crossed—B Company (Major W. P. Elder), C (Major Sceales), and D (Major Hunter)—found themselves stranded the next day, with no tank support, on open ground criss-crossed by ditches and sown with mines. The 6/13 Frontier Force Rifles gave covering fire from the near bank, but the 14th Canadian Regiment's tanks had yet to get across. The Argylls were pinned down for 24 hours by Jerry machine guns, artillery and Nebelwerfers.

Shaw, then the Regimental Signals Officer, and a sepoy signalman, Fakir Khan of the Brigade Signal Section, laid a phone line while under fire to alert Brigade HQ that the battalion was cut off. A Jerry counterattack was broken up by artillery, but there was no choice but to withdraw. Major Elder, the bridgehead CO, evacuated his men, including the wounded, back across the Rapido on the only remaining boat, or across a Bailey bridge that, too late to assist the Argylls' assault, had been carried on top of a Canadian tank driven straight into the river. Elder won an MC. Later, an Argyll platoon was found on the enemy bank, having got through to the 3/8th Punjabis' bridgehead on the right. It was through that salient that Argylls recrossed the river on the 14 May.

Despite their dogged resistance, the Germans lost the battle. The Free

French (the North African, Corps Expéditionnaire Français), secured the hills to the west; the American 2nd Corps advanced along the coast. The 4th British and 8th Indian divisions forced the Rapido crossing. Monte Cassino was captured on the 18th by soldiers of the 2nd Polish Corps. Within a few days, the Germans were streaming in retreat up the Liri valley, pursued by British 78th, 6th Armoured, and Canadian 1st divisions. To the north, the Allies broke out of the Anzio beachhead, threatening Kesselring's line of retreat.

The Battle of Cassino cost the Argylls two officers and nineteen other ranks killed and three officers and seventy-six other ranks wounded. Jock Hunter, who had helped me organise the Battalion Highland Games at Khartoum, was killed leading his company; Jim Sceales, was wounded and *hors de combat* for three months; Bill Dunn, who had been with the battalion since El Alamein, and who had helped me up from the snow at Poggiofiorito, was also wounded. His war was over, because he had stepped on a 'Schu' mine. I found him by chance in a hospital at Benevento.

I smuggled in a bottle of whisky for him.

'Thanks, Ray. You remembered.'

'How could I forget?' I grinned, sharing the irony of the situation.

We drank to our survival. I remember how he complained about the pain in his foot, which wasn't there.

My posting back to the battalion came through in the last week of June. The day before I left, in another of those unexpected, coincidental wartime meetings, MacDougall, now promoted to captain, turned up at the depot. We had a lot to talk about.

There was a new CO, Lieutenant-Colonel F. C. C. Graham, who had arrived from India at the end of March to replace Ronnie McAlister (who returned to the UK and saw service in North-west Europe and then at HQ Scottish Command).

Mac told me that when the Eighth Army moved up the Liri valley the Argylls got a taste of the Germans' infuriating and deadly rearguard tactics: SP guns (self-propelled, like tanks) shelling the roads; snipers in the woods and villages; hit-and-run combat groups armed with spandaus and mortars (often backed up by SPs or tanks); the occasional Jerry plane dropping anti-personnel bombs; blown bridges, booby-trapped buildings, trees blocking mined roads. He reminded me to drive and march warily and to take with a pinch of salt assurances of Royal Engineers that particular tracks had been cleared.

'Of course, you know all about booby traps, Ray.' he added.

Mac had seemed preoccupied and told me why.

While leading D Company, he had been caught up in one of those delaying actions Jerry was so good at. Mac was confronted in open country by well-positioned and camouflaged SPs and spandaus. With no immediate artillery, armoured or air support to back him up, there was little that he or his men could do. Any movement attracted accurate enemy fire. So D Company very sensibly scuttled into the ditches on both sides of the road and everyone kept their heads down for the rest of the day. Two Canadian tanks trundled up the road but were knocked out trying to reach Mac and his men. Eventually, C Company and a troop of Canadian tanks arrived, by which time Jerry was pulling out, allowing D Company to move on after dark.

The delay was holding up the brigade's advance. Back at Battalion HQ, Lieutenant-Colonel Graham was getting stick from Wee Briggie Dobree. When Graham, at some risk to himself, went forward to investigate he took it out on Mac.

'What's up? Are you on strike?' he asked, casting a disdainful look towards the Jerry postions.

Mac, completely fed up and certainly not needing flak from the CO shouted back: 'No, sir. I'm waiting for a bus!'

More harsh words were exchanged. Graham told Mac he shouldn't have allowed himself to be pinned down in the first place, should have shown more spirit and dash.

Mac swore: 'Spirit, dash? Well, that would have been a bloody stupid sacrifice.'

The CO sacked him on the spot.

My sympathies were with Mac. It was easy for those back at Battalion HQ to criticise the men at the sharp end. Mac especially. He was a hard, thrawn man but good in a tight corner. I opened a bottle of officer-ration whisky I'd been saving and helped him drown his sorrows. He was in limbo at Benevento, awaiting a posting. As I left, he gave me a glimmer of his old self, saying he'd never live down the indignity if he were to be transferred to an English regiment. It would be some time before I saw him again.

On 4 July 1944, the day that Rome was liberated, I boarded a train for Spoleto with an other officer and a draft of forty-five new men. Our train steamed slowly along a repaired track. We were packed into cattle waggons, so I saw little of the passing and increasingly hilly landscape as we moved into Umbria. Images flitted by like a slide show: picturesque Narni, unspoiled . . . Terni, extensively and not accurately bombed by Allied planes, probably American . . . Spoleto, where the area around the station had been devastated when a German ammunition train exploded, but sparing the old town above.

I found the Argylls camped in olive groves on the slopes below Spoleto. The battalion had just returned from Assisi, which it had liberated on 17 June. The Germans had retreated, but only after losing off some spandau fire at the approaching Jocks. To the din of church bells—and there are many churches in the town of St Francis—the Argylls and their vehicles were engulfed by crowds cheering 'Viva i Scozzesi'. During this emotional civic outburst, C Company, which had been first into the town, reached Porta San Francesco below the bulwarks of the Basilica, when a Jerry mortar stonk landed, killing one Jock and wounding three. Some unfortunate civilians were also killed as they scattered for cover. The Argylls mopped up the area but Jerry, as usual, escaped to the north.

I had a happy reunion with Shaw and Sanders but not, alas, Sergeant Bloomfield, who had been posted home after long service overseas. (He returned to active service, was wounded in Normandy and invalided back to Scotland.) Shaw had been promoted captain. He introduced me to a new officer, Lieutenant Stephen White, who had been posted to the battalion from the Kosbies after Cassino. Since hearing Mac's tale of woe I hadn't been looking forward to meeting Lieutenant-Colonel F. C. C. Graham. But Mac's nemesis, a tall, black-moustached figure who strode around with a deer-stalking stick, turned out to be a likeable and admirable chap—a 'soldiers' soldier' who quickly gained the respect and affection of all officers and men.

Freddie Graham had been born in Helensburgh, my father's home town, and we got on well from the start. He had joined the army after Eton in 1927, trained at the Royal Military College, Sandhurst, and served with the Argylls' 2nd Battalion in China, Hong Kong, India and on the North-west Frontier, and with the 1st during its peace-keeping duties in Palestine. He moved to Cairo, as a staff officer. In 1941, he was the Commando Brigade major with 'Layforce', which was landed on Crete just as the retreat was in full swing. Graham and his colonel, Robert Laycock, narrowly escaped being captured. Evelyn Waugh, who featured the fiasco on Crete in his novel *Officers and Gentlemen*, was the brigade's intelligence officer. After the remnants of Layforce were evacuated, Graham was posted to the 14th Infantry Brigade. He served in the campaign against the Vichy French in Syria, had been at Tobruk during the last few weeks of the siege and then sailed for Rangoon. Fortunately for him, the brigade's troopship was diverted to India when

Burma fell to the Japanese. He was appointed to the India Central
Command Training School at Agra. But, as he told me, he preferred
active service. After two years behind a desk he had jumped at the
chance to get back to the Argylls.

The battalion had another new arrival. Graham had noticed a 12-
year-old Italian boy hanging around Battalion HQ. It was not unusual
to find Italians in our camps (some worked for us), and children often
hung around, scrounging for food like stray cats. What intrigued the
CO was that this boy wore some articles of regimental uniform, including a balmoral, and always saluted him smartly. It turned out that Luigi
Miniotti—'Wee Toni'—had been adopted by the Jocks and had been
with us for some time.

He was an orphan. His parents and sister had been killed when a
Jerry shell destroyed their home during the fighting around Frosinone,
on the road from Cassino to Rome. The boy had wandered off, terrified and exhausted. One of our cooks, Private Leitch, found him alseep
in a ditch and gave him some food. When the battalion moved on Wee
Toni pleaded to be taken along. Leitch kitted him out in battledress and
showed him how to salute. Pipe Major McGlinn taught him the bugle
and the pipes. He picked up some English, which he spoke with a
Scottish accent. When he was given his own kilt he asked me what it
meant. I told him: 'It means you're a Highland soldier. One of us.'
Freddie Graham said the boy should be sent to the Red Cross, but Mrs
Leitch in Glasgow had, apparently, agreed to foster him, so he stayed.
I think we all understood the redemption our new mascot offered us.

I didn't get back to my old A Company, which I had first joined as
a platoon commander in Egypt three years before, but was appointed
second-in-command, D Company (Major Scheurmier). That was a disappointment, but I made sure Sanders came with me. He cheered me
up by telling me how the QM, Lieutenant A. W. 'Dodger' Brown, had
almost led his Jeeps into Arsoli, unaware that the enemy was still there.

Only the timely intervention of a Bengal Lancer, who had taken cover in a ditch, prevented the battalion's rations being delivered to Jerry. Then, when the Argylls entered the town the following day, the CO was welcomed by an elderly lady sporting army boots, a sunbonnet, a grey skirt and a red shirt, who introduced herself as 'Signora Garibaldi', and claimed to be a relative of the famous Italian patriot.

Shaw and I managed a day trip to Rome with the battalion intelligence officer, Captain George Rome. The streets were full of soldiers from all the Allied nations—British and Indian, Canadians and New Zealanders, Free French and Poles—on sightseeing trips as we were. And of course, GIs. They were thick on the ground and a great attraction for Italian women and girls of all classes, especially street-walkers, and urchins on the scrounge for chewing gum and chocolate. We stood on a bridge over the Tiber and admired the Grand Tour vista, saw the Colosseum and the ruins of the Forum. We visited St Peter's, where I was at once mesmerised and repelled by its splendour. On the piazza outside, we mingled with black-cloaked priests and pretty girls, who seemed taken particularly with our kilts and sporrans. Of course, we couldn't resist taking photographs of ourselves. Rome and such places were a novelty, for most of us had never been abroad before.

The people of the Eternal City were glad to see the last of the hated Tedeschi and grateful that their historic buildings had been spared the destruction so common elsewhere. Since they seemed to despise everything about Naples and the south, they evidently thought it fitting that their superior world of Vatican intrigue, political duplicity and snobbery should be preserved. At Piazza Venezia I saw the balcony where Mussolini had appeared in newsreels I had seen before the war, when Il Duce had been dismissed in Britain as a pompous buffoon preening himself as he harangued the crowd. But he was the dictator of a Fascist state that persecuted or murdered political opponents, and whose armed forces had brutally conquered Abyssinia. Now we were here, the Romans could scoff with impunity at his motto: MUSSOLINI HA SEMPRE RAGIONE (Mussolini is always right).

Across the piazza was the 'Wedding Cake' memorial erected in honour of King Vittorio Emanuele II, which I assumed wrongly to be one of Mussolini's monuments. I knew little then about art and architecture to benefit fully from seeing many Italian places rich in such treasures. That applied to most of us I expect, except to the appropriately-named George Rome, who had been a student of architecture at Cambridge before the war. In any case we were too much involved in the making of modern history to be all that interested in the culture of the past. We saw too much of the ravages of war in desecrated churches and towns and villages devastated by bombs and shells. Death and destruction stalked the length and breadth of Italy like a medieval pestilence, making a mockery of venerated ancient sites.

At dawn on 8 July, we got a 'move at once' order, to support the 6th Armoured Division, which was fighting on the road to Arezzo. Practically the whole brigade was advancing up Via Flaminia, that most beautiful of Italian roads, the Roman route of pilgrims and legionnaires. We crossed the Tiber and passed below Perugia. Lake Trasimeno shimmered in the distance and disappeared in a thunderstorm. Heavy rain slowed the advance and allowed the Germans to regroup. Beyond Cortona, we took over from the 7th Battalion, the Rifle Brigade, on a hill north-east of Castiglion Fiorentino. The town's castle had been given to Sir John Hawkwood, the English mercenary who commanded the Florentine army in the fourteenth century. Later, in Florence Cathedral, I saw the fresco of him, painted by Uccello in 1436. Hawkwood, who inspired Conan Doyle's novel *The White Company*, was a reminder that the campaign of 1944 was not the first to lay waste to Tuscany.

Our new position could only be reached by Jeep or on foot, so the trucks were left by the road. Our job was to neutralise enemy artillery observation posts from where shelling was being directed at the 6th

Armoured's tanks on the main road. Sergeant Ellison won an MM for leading a patrol which stalked a Jerry OP and captured the spotters and their radios. That night, Lieutenant White led a patrol to ambush another enemy OP. But they were spotted and shot at. One Jock was killed and another wounded. It was a short but typical tour of duty. The 6th Armoured was able to press on. We were relieved by a Kiwi battalion and returned to Spoleto. Jerry was now in full retreat. We left for Siena on the 18th. As usual, the move was preceded by an Operational Order that was typed up and circulated to all officers. Those of us with long service greeted these missives with sardonic resignation: 'Here we go again, the Agile and Suffering Highlanders.'

The pursuit continued for the next month or so, until Florence was liberated in August 1944. This was a period of constant movement, in brilliant summer weather. We had long since discarded our battledress, gloves, scarves and leather jerkins for more comfortable and familiar khaki shirts and shorts. We criss-crossed Umbria and travelled through Tuscany, being trucked but often marching to new assembly areas, to relieve or support other Allied units. The countryside was cultivated. At rest stops we supplemented our rations, foraging for food as soldiers have done through the centuries. Contadini unlucky enough to have been caught up in the campaign had little left to barter after the retreating Germans came and went. Some of our Jocks too were not averse to pillage, if they thought they could get away with it. The battalion was involved in minor skirmishes with Jerry rearguards, but as second-in-command of my company, I was mostly back at either A or B Echelon, organising delivery of rations and supplies to the forward platoons. I was little involved in any of these actions or patrol activity, but came in for a fair amount of shelling.

It seemed that almost every bridge in Umbria and Tuscany had been destroyed, either by our own air forces or blown by Jerry. These demolitions were sometimes covered by small but skillful enemy rearguards.

Diversions and hold-ups were constant, until Bailey bridges could be erected by the division's Royal Indian Engineers. Refugees and their ox carts added to the congestion. Several thousand vehicles were required to transport an army division and they were often funnelled onto the same route. When the traffic did move, the landscape was animated by plumes of dust thrown up by trucks and tanks, or shellfire from both sides. Dust trails on the white gravel roads were easily spotted. Signs said: DANGER, NO TRAFFIC IN DAYTIME BEYOND THIS POINT . . . ROAD UNDER SHELLFIRE . . . DUST MEANS DEATH, and we would be held up until Jerry artillery could be cleared by tanks or fighter-bombers.

Many villages in our path were wrecked: roofs holed by shell fire; walls blown away by bomb blasts, exposing rooms like dolls' houses; streets blocked by rubble from buildings that the Germans demolished to detain us. Some villagers greeted us with *vivas* and vino, while boys ran forward, pointing to where Jerry had planted mines. Other places seemed completely deserted, until we passed through them. Then, looking back, we would see the people emerging from their hiding places like goblins. Outside one village that had been completely destroyed by bombs, I found a priest and his flock cowering in a cave. Some were dead, the rest were starving. Concerned about typhus, I made my men stand back but gave the priest what food we could spare. Those refugees in the cave still return to haunt me, like a Goya etching from *The Disasters of War*.

The Germans should never have been allowed to hold up the Eighth Army around Arezzo and Lake Trasimeno. They could have been beaten on the road to Rome, but a chance to bag the German Tenth and Fourteenth armies was squandered.

Kesselring's forces had retreated up the Liri valley, pursued by the Eighth Army. The Germans were also forced to withdraw from Anzio when the Americans and British finally broke out from their Gallipolilike torture on the beachhead [the indecisive Lucas having been replaced by the forceful Major-General L. K. Truscott]. Lieutenant-General Mark Clark, the Fifth Army commander, had agreed to Alexander's plan that the Americans should cut off the German retreat from Cassino. The Germans would then have been caught between the Fifth and Eighth armies and squashed. But Clark, whose war was as much a contest with the British as it was with the Germans, ignored Alexander's intentions. Instead of cutting Route 6, he ordered one of his divisional commanders, Major-General Truscott, to head for Rome. The German Tenth and Fourteenth armies squeezed out of Alexander's trap.

Clark was obsessed with Rome and wanted, above all, to get there before the British. Alexander, the country gentleman and Guards officer sitting in the gilded salons of Caserta, the Italian Versailles where he had located his HQ, was too polite or politically shackled to discipline his subordinate. As C-in-C of the Allied armies in Italy, Alexander commanded Americans, British, Canadians, French, Indians, Italians, New Zealanders and Poles. His diplomatic skills were well regarded and necessary. He also had Churchill, who felt the Mediterranean was a British show, breathing down his neck. But the forfeit was his failure to assert authority when it mattered. Alexander waited until 1962, in his memoirs, to publicly castigate Clark; even then, he did so in the mildest of terms: 'If he had succeeded in carrying out my plan the disaster to the enemy would have been much greater; indeed, most of the German forces south of Rome would have been destroyed . . . I can only assume that the immediate lure of Rome for its publicity value persuaded him to switch the direction of his advance.' Clark should have been sacked on the spot. Monty would have been furious. Truscott was dumbfounded.

Clark's entourage included a fifty-strong public relations team and he ensured that, on 5 June 1944, he was photographed in his Jeep on the avenue to St Peter's square and on foot ascending the steps of the

Capitol. He held a press conference and declared: 'It's a great day for the Fifth Army.' He didn't mention the Eighth. Clark's fame and folly were eclipsed by the Allied invasion of Normandy the next day. Thanks to his insubordination and vanity [among his souvenirs was a 'Roma' road sign which he later kept in his garden], thousands of Allied soldiers would be killed or wounded when the Germans regrouped on the Gothic Line in the Apennines north of Florence, in the winter of 1944. After D-Day, the war in Italy really did become a sideshow—except for those who remained fighting there.

11 TUSCANY

We're the D-Day Dodgers, out in Italy—
Always on the vino, always on the spree.
　　Eighth Army scroungers and their tanks
　　We live in Rome—among the Yanks.
We are the D-Day Dodgers, way out in Italy.

Hamish Henderson. *Ballad of the D-Day Dodgers*, 1944

SIENA, SEPTEMBER 2004

I am in Siena, following my father's route to the River Arno, and across the Apennines to the Po valley, where the Italian campaign and his war ended in May 1945. From the top of the Cathedral Museum, a panorama, punctuated by the campanile of Palazzo Pubblico, unfolds across terracotta-tiled rooftops. Siena looked much the same on 3 July 1944, when the campanile's bells chimed and Sienese packed Piazza del Campo to welcome their liberators, the Free French. To the north, the Tuscan landscape rolls away towards Florence and the Arno, the route the Argylls took in that heady summer of 1944.

My father always said that period was exhilarating, when the Argylls, almost unopposed, pursued the Germans to the Arno and were the first unit in the Eighth Army to reach the river, at Empoli. Freddie Graham wrote in the battalion history: 'Kesselring's "Nazi supermen" were in retreat ... the hunt was up.' On reaching the banks of the river, 'the 91st had won the race!' My father remembered that pursuit almost as if it had been a fox hunt—with the inconvenience of being shot at and shelled. He recalled Tuscan villas with statuary and classical gardens, and the scenery looking like a Renaissance painting, which it still does. I leave the museum and cross to the Duomo where, preceding the pageantry in the Campo, the French held a thanksgiving service. In the presence of frescoes, statues, saints and superstition, I experience, as perhaps they did, that powerful Italian continuum—of armies, whether soldiers or tourists, mere ripples in an eternal flow...

Among my father's papers in the German ammunition box, I found two letters—two old soldiers who never met sharing memories and a rekindled camaraderie. My brother Brian had been best man at a wedding in London. The bride's father had been a major in the US Army. When Brian told him our father had served with the Argylls in Italy, he was astonished when the American replied that he too had been there—and had come across the 1st Argylls in Tuscany while seconded as a liaison officer to the 8th Indian Division ...

71 Whittingehame Drive
Glasgow
5 October 1983

Dear Brian,

What an extraordinary coincidence, your meeting with someone who served as a liaison officer with the 8th Indian Division during the war in Italy in 1944.

As a mere company commander in the 1st Argylls I had few dealings with Brigade or Div. HQ but your American friend would have known Major-General 'Pasha' Russell, a legendary figure whom I met a few times, and Brigadier Dobree, affectionately known as 'The Wee Briggie', whom I last saw in October 1944 at a shell-torn, hilltop hollow in the Apennines north of Florence where he had come to visit my company after the Battle of Monte Cavallara; he would know too Lieutenant-Colonel Green, CO of the 6/13th Frontier Rifles, and

Lieutenant-Colonel Sanderson, CO of the 3/8th Punjabis, and, of course, my own CO, Lieutenant-Colonel Freddie Graham, as he then was. You may remember meeting him when you were a boy and he was a Major-General, at a parade in George Square, Glasgow many years ago.

A list of place-names in Umbria and Tuscany, where we spent some hectic months on the move during the summer of 1944, will no doubt awaken memories in the mind of the former liaison officer of many shared experiences. When you write to him in America, it will be sufficient to mention Spoleto (where I rejoined the battalion, after a stay in hospital and convalescent depot, when it was enjoying a short-lived rest period), Assisi, Perugia, Arezzo, Siena, Poggibonsi, Certaldo, Castelfiorentino (where we took over from the Free French amid much confusion), Empoli on the River Arno, and Florence.

My recollections of that period are both clear and confused. Tension, exhaustion, and lack of sleep must have dulled the senses. Memories of the following few months are of mines and mortars, mules and mountains—Monte Abetino, Monte Cavallara, Monte Cerere and Monte Grande—malignant monsters every one.

These names should mean something to your friend, as they do much to me, and also those of such places as Marradi, Borgo San Lorenzo, Frassineto, and San Cassiano. So too should Pisa, Lucca, and the Serchio Valley, where our 19th Brigade was sent urgently halfway across Italy, in support of an American unit, the US 92nd Division when it was driven back by the Germans at the end of December 1944. That was a novel interlude in our mountain campaign. We missed out on Christmas, I remember, but were relieved just in time to bring in the New Year in some style at Lucca.

He will remember too, as I do well, the stalemate in the Gothic Line and the rigours of that horrible winter; the preparations for a spring offensive (Bagnacavallo, Russi, Lugo), the final battle on the

River Senio (scenes from which I still remember vividly forty years on), Ferrara, and VE Day celebrations like ours at Costa di Rovigo.

The mere recital of these names brings back memories, which should help me with the book I'm trying to write. Pass on then, Brian, my greetings to your friend, as one old soldier to another, who shares his pride in having served with one of the finest formations of the Allied armies in Italy. The enclosed story of the 8th Indian Division and other papers (which he may keep as I have copies) will no doubt be of interest if he hasn't seen them already.

Dad

305 Spruce Street
San Francisco
12 January 1984

Dear Mr Ward,

It was very generous and thoughtful of you to send to me that brochure about the 8th Indian and the communiqués which brought back so many memories.

I first met the officers of 19th Brigade HQ—and I do remember Brigadier Dobree with affection—in the languorous summer heat of 1944 when you relieved the French north of Siena. My 88th Infantry Division went into the line south of Volterra, after a brief respite following our assault on Rome, and I was sent off to 'liaison' with our right flank—the French.

I entered Siena with their forward elements—no opposition. I was stunned to find the Sienese taking their evening strolls around the town square as though nothing had happened in 400 years, which may be how they felt about us foreigners fighting in Italy.

Your people welcomed me with great courtesy, and I would drive, back and forth between 19 Brigade and my own Division HQ, frequently bringing a goose or a duck picked up en route at some farm. The brigade mess would turn it into a delicacy and that's where I first learned about Indian food, which I still like, at least the hot curry and beer aspect. We would recline on meadowed slopes in the afternoon sun (as you remember, the Germans were withdrawing to the Arno without resistance) and eat curried duck and drink beer. I thought I was in Heaven.

When we reached the Arno I walked across the little dam, upriver where your troops crossed, and wandered around Florence, which I had known as a child. Then we pushed north against the Gothic Line; the 1st British Div. relieved you on our right flank, so I never saw your troops again. I kept a division patch which is sewn, with some others, on a scarf I still wear around here. We fought north to Monte Grande losing over half our regimental strength, then, in the spring of 1945 we—and you—broke out of the mountains into the Po valley. I was in the mountains again, heading for the Brenner Pass, when the war ended for us.

I have been back to Italy several times, but only in 1968 did I make an effort to return to my battlefields. With my wife and daughter (whose marriage your son so ably supported) I rented a farmhouse halfway between Florence and Arezzo, where we spent a month, walking and riding in the countryside, then spent several days and nights in Florence to 'do' museums, etc. I had several experiences, astonishing to me, that showed the permanence and impermanence of war.

When I showed the places to my daughter where the houses had been demolished, the roads torn up, the trees shattered, I found that we were looking at a countryside completely restored, bucolic, beautiful. Nature and man had returned to normal. Yet, on the first night that I slept at that farmhouse, behind those thick stone walls that you remember, I woke in a screaming nightmare of the war returned.

Writing to you about those distant places, I am reminded of a passage in Archibald MacLeish's great poem, 'Conquistador', in which the old soldier, Bernal Diaz, contemplates a history written by some monk too young to have been born when Cortez took Mexico:

I fought in those battles! These were my own deeds! . . .
These were my friends: these dead companions: . . .
I was young in that country: These words were my life: . . .

Perhaps some day we shall meet. I sincerely hope so.
Best wishes for a Happy New Year.
John Hale Stutesman

I FIRST SAW SIENA FROM SOME DISTANCE AWAY after a long day's drive, its hilltop domes and campanili caught in late-afternoon, terracotta sunlight. As was usual during our transit, radio silence had been maintained and vehicle unit signs concealed. A flash flood had washed away a Bailey bridge, causing diversions which disorganised our staggered convoy. It took until midnight for the battalion to straggle in to a bivouac below the city walls. In the morning, I saw the Fascist-era railway station, which had been bombed. Its clock tower still stood, with the timepiece stopped—which seemed to me a fitting comment on Mussolini's régime and his boast that he made the trains run on time.

Siena was now a staging post for the Allied advance. Thousands of soldiers and vehicles were passing through or around it. Shortly before we arrived, Generals Alexander, Leese, Clark and Juin [the French commander] had attended a service at the Duomo, and watched a tattoo of tanks, troops and Sienese pageantry in Piazza del Campo, to mark Bastille Day and the city's liberation by the 3rd Algerian Infantry Division. We were well aware that, while we were camped outside, army brass and AMGOT administrators were now enjoying the city's most

luxurious palazzi and hotels. As a frontline soldier I viewed such privilege and its beneficiaries with a mixture of envy and contempt. Siena
had come through the war with little damage. Its medieval streets and
piazzas were packed with Sienese chattering like starlings, as they celebrated their freedom. I also recall the stillness of the Tuscan dawn,
broken by the benign, hourly chime of the Duomo's venerable bells.

Our stopover at Siena was brief. An operation order for our next
move, to a concentration area behind the front line, had been issued
the day before we left Spoleto. The order didn't specify where, but it
was obvious that the battalion would be in action soon:

... 3. Transport:

(a) Coy Tpt i.e. one Jeep and trailer, one carrier, two 15-cwts per Coy will
revert to Coy control w.e.f. 1300 hrs 18 July, 1944.

(b) The Q.M. and M.T.O. will issue sandbags to vehicles on the normal scale
so that floors can be properly sandbagged as protection against mines.

(c) Camouflage: It is expected that there will be an increase in enemy air
and artillery activity in the near future. The importance of camouflage is
again stressed. Coy Comds will ensure that Nets are in good condition and
it is the duty of ALL officers and NCOs to check drivers for failing to
camouflage correctly ...

Landmines and artillery were indeed a hazard, but the Luftwaffe
failed to appear. Allied fighters had established air superiority, allowing
our bombers and fighter-bombers to range at will across the skies of
central and northern Italy, destroying roads and bridges, strafing trains
and sinking coastal and river traffic as far north as the Po valley and the
Venice lagoon. But wars are won or lost on the ground. The Germans
still managed to move their troops around.

We left Siena at 0900 on 20 July, and marched up Route 2, through
the bottleneck at Poggibonsi and then, passing San Gimignano, to an

assembly area near Certaldo, where we were to take over from the Free French. The plan was that our brigade, with 21 Brigade and the 2nd New Zealand Division on our right, would clear the German positions in the high ground south of the Arno between Empoli and Florence.

The Eighth Army used maps reproduced by army cartographers from pre-war Italian originals. Each sheet was a maze of printed contours, twisting roads and places we had never heard of. Units frequently became lost and sometimes stumbled unawares into enemy-held positions. We rarely knew where we were. Every hill town, except San Gimignano which has a unique skyline, looked the same. The Free French never did know where they were. To find them, the CO, IO, and company commanders had gone ahead in the Jeeps to recce the new sector. The carriers and trucks (loaded with mortars, machine-guns, ammo, Jerrycans of petrol and water, rations, equipment and stores), company cookhouses and a mobile bath unit followed later. We walked. The battalion was led temporarily by Major MacFie, the second-in-command, with companies following at intervals. Mine, D Company, the HQ company, brought up the rear.

The march was in blistering heat, but through pleasant countryside and along quieter roads. I got off to a bad start. I missed a turning and, after marching for about a kilometre, realised there was no one in front of me. Amid some disgusted rumblings from the ranks, I checked my map, about-turned and took the right road. Then I spotted a track that seemed to offer a short cut. Later, as we were resting for a 10-minute break by the roadside, who should appear but Major MacFie at the head of the battalion. The other companies passed amid jeers and catcalls from my Jocks. Taking the short cut after my blunder redeemed me in the eyes of my men, and they were now in a better humour. I felt able to give them a pep talk before we marched off again. 'You've stuck it out well so far,' I told them, 'so let's continue in the same way. We're going to march like soldiers, not straggle in like a bunch of Chinese irregulars.' So we did, and entered the appointed assembly area in some style, heads held high, and rifles at the slope. The CO watched our arrival with approval and was very impressed. Did my standing with him no harm at all. Not for long, though.

During the march, the men had been smothered in stour raised by passing traffic. Some of them, against orders, had drunk too freely from their water bottles, which soon became empty, and they were parched with thirst. There were many stragglers and some fell out by the way-side, with sore feet and heat exhaustion. As my luck would have it, Pasha Russell passed us. His Jeep slid to a halt. When the dust cleared, I saw him looking back, appalled at the sight of such a rag-tag Fred Karno's army. Later, he gave Wee Briggie a roasting. This was passed on, with increasing severity all down the line: to our CO, company commanders and finally to me and my long-suffering Jocks.

Every few kilometres, we passed ruined villages—the calling cards left by the armies of both sides. Places that had existed peacefully for centuries had been abruptly visited by death and destruction, which had then departed as rapidly as they had arrived. Hill towns, previously familiar only to locals and art history *cognoscenti*, appeared with sudden brevity on army communiqués and newspaper headlines. The town of Poggibonsi had the misfortune to be a rail and road junction and was a scene of utter desolation after American bombing. San Gimignano's cluster of medieval towers, which were suspected Jerry OPs, had been shelled by French artillery. Each side blamed the other for the damage. Miraculously, the towers survived.

After the war, I read that Kesselring claimed that he tried to prevent Italy's historic cities and towns becoming battlefields. Assisi, Orvieto, Rome, Siena and others were indeed spared by timely German evacuation. But Kesselring's concern to save Italy's heritage was no less expedient than ours. The French gunners at San Gimignano followed the Allied commanders' stated policy towards Italy's historic monuments: they weren't worth the death of a single Allied soldier. I don't believe we were gratuitously destructive, but if there was an enemy sniper or artillery spotter in a Renaissance campanile we got the air force or the artillery to hit it. Apparently, we employed Monuments, Fine Arts and Archives officers armed with lists, compiled from pre-war Baedeker guides, of monuments to be protected, and repaired if damaged. They operated at battalion and company levels and worked with Italian museum curators and conservationists. There was only a handful of them in Tuscany at the time. A list of protected monuments was circulated. I never saw it and I never met a single MFAA officer.

The battalion, supported by tanks of the 14th Canadian Armoured Regiment, marched along Val d'Elsa towards Castelfiorentino, 50 kilometres north of Siena, but more than that on the route we took, in glorious weather. We had orders to relieve the 2nd and 4th Moroccan divisions of the French Expeditionary Corps, which had fought its way through the hills west of Siena, often leading the Fifth Army's advance. The French were being withdrawn, along with an American corps, for an invasion of the south of France.

The Moroccan troops were French-officered, mountain tribesmen: les Goumiers Marocain. They helped restore the French army's reputation with the Allies, particularly with the Americans who equipped them and under whose command they fought. Like the Gurkhas and tribesmen from the North-west Frontier in the Eighth Army, the 'Goums' were adept at aggressive patrolling, ambush and skirmishing. Some of them were mounted on tough little ponies. The Goums also acquired a fearsome reputation, like our kukri-wielding Gurkhas, and were rumoured to bite the ears of any Germans they captured. The Italians accused them of looting and rape. Our Indian soldiers, who were highly disciplined, were sometimes mistaken for them by frightened civilians. I saw no evidence of Goum, Indian, or indeed Scottish war crimes—which is not to say there were none.

Certaldo's medieval hill town rose on our right like a fresco, slightly cracked here and there by the DAF and French artillery. We moved on past fields cratered by shells and bombs, not knowing if the French held Castelfiorentino or which parts of it [like Certaldo, it has an historic upper and modern lower town]. The hills to the west had evidently been shelled by both sides. On the 22nd, south of the town, we found the Moroccans, a piratical-looking bunch, dressed in striped *djellabas*, baggy gaitered trousers and turbans. Their French officers sported stylish uniforms and kepis. Their garb and manner reminded me of the haughty Italians we had captured in Abyssinia and confirmed my antipathy towards *La Gloire*.

There was a language problem, which our Scottish accents and their pantomime gestures hardly overcame. The garbled Italian we had picked up—and used as a *lingua franca* between the Punjabis and Indian frontiersmen and ourselves—was disdained by the French. The situation was not helped by the fact that their HQ officers didn't have a clue where their forward troops were. Nor did they seem to be expecting us. The relief was a fiasco.

Graham sized up the ground—a two-kilometre-wide valley with low hills on both sides—and agreed tactics with the company commanders. A Company (Major Sceales) crossed the local railway line and the River Elsa to hold the flat ground on the river's west bank. C Company (Major Oxborrow), supported by the Canadians' A Squadron tanks (their B Squadron was with 6/13th Frontier Force Rifles who had advanced with us), went into the hills east of Castelfiorentino. B Company (Major Elder) was led into the town by French guides—and promptly shelled by Jerry, and forced to hole up under fire for the rest of the day.

The next morning, D Company (Major Scheurmier) went into the line. We rode in on tanks, having passed through 6/13th's positions in the hills, dismounted and managed to make contact with Elder's beleaguered Jocks. Then Sceales' force re-crossed the river, passed through us and linked up with Oxborrow and the Canadians. D Company pushed forward along the main road to Empoli. Sappers filled in a 'blow' in the road to let the tanks cross. Jerry shelled us off and on all day. Two Jocks were wounded in an ambush, when grenades were thrown by some Jerries hiding in a house. We flushed them out and shot the lot. Their bodies were searched for orders, letters or diaries, to be passed to Captain Rome. Next day, Elder's men captured an OP manned by Panzer Grenadiers, but the shelling continued. Three Jocks were killed and three wounded . . . Similar engagements happened all along the front as the Eighth Army advanced to Florence and, on the Adriatic coast, to Ravenna: each skirmish a small part in a relentless machine; each death grieved by some family in the Punjab or Perthshire or, I should imagine, Prussia.

Company HQ was set up in a villa beyond the town. Wireless communication, not always reliable in the hilly country, was re-established with the tanks and Battalion HQ, and telephone lines run out to the forward platoons. They were on watch for Jerry counter-attacks and I got them organised, with clear fields of fire and fixed lines. The CSM drew up duty rosters for signallers, drivers, cooks and runners; platoon commanders issued food and blankets, rations and ammo. But Jerry made no attempt to retake the town.

I recall returning from the platoons and parking the company Jeep outside the villa, just as an A Echelon lorry pulled up with a cook and a driver, who started unloading bundles of stores. They worked silently and fast, spurred on by an understandable desire not to linger unnecessarily in a dangerous spot so near the front line. As always in the wake of the infantry and exploiting its success came brigade's sappers with Bailey bridges and more mine detectors; then artillery, armoured units, petrol tankers and supply trucks: all the paraphernalia of a mechanised army on the move. Military police taped out routes, posted signs and directed traffic. Later would come the HQ groups, the field hospitals, the store depots, the mobile workshops, and the maintainance and supply units that would turn what had so recently been a front line into a safe and comfortable rear area—where staff officers could study their plans and men grumble if disturbed from their attempts to be as decently idle as they could be with impunity.

We stayed at Castelfiorentino for three days. Graham then got permission from Russell to push on in what was becoming a race to be the first Eighth Army unit to reach the Arno. Ten kilometres to our right, 21 Brigade [5th Royal West Kents, 1/5th Mahrattas, 3/15th Punjabis, 12th Canadian Armoured Regiment] and the New Zealanders were advancing in Val di Pesa. Further east, the 24th Guards Brigade and the 6th South African Armoured Division were in the Chianti hills and would be soon within sight of the great dome of Florence Cathedral. We were heading for Empoli, 25 kilometres west of Florence.

On a side road beyond Castelfiorentino, we surprised some Jerries who ran away leaving Teller mines scattered beside holes that had just been dug. This road seemed to offer a short cut, so we followed it. The scenery was entrancing: avenues of cypress trees leading to fairy tale villas, clusters of umbrella pines, cornfields in the valleys and vines on the hills. There was also the luxury of feasting on almonds and the fruit which grew in abundance in that fertile land. But it was a deceptive Arcadia, disturbed without warning by the whistle and crash of artillery and stuttering bursts of spandau fire; by our dives for cover and the stomach-churning fear as we lay in ditches, under the searching shadow of the grim reaper. Then Jerry would scarper and silent, golden Tuscany would bewitch again us as if nothing had happened.

Bivouacs were set up in the shade of olive groves. Under camouflage netting, we would spread out maps and aerial reconnaissance photographs on the bonnets of our Jeeps and plan the next day's advance. We would eat, then chat and smoke in the gloaming. A sentry's sudden challenge would be followed by a chorus of Italian. Partisans. They'd come in slowly, two by two, ducking under the olive branches. We'd give them food and quiz them for intelligence. I remember one telling us he'd see some Tiger tanks in the next valley. These armoured beasts out-gunned anything we had. If they couldn't be stalked with anti-tank weapons it was prudent to take cover and call up tank, artillery, or air support. But the only Tigers I saw, until towards the end of the war, were dead ones causing traffic jams. Sappers had to be sent forward with bulldozers to push the wrecks out of the way.

Orders for the next day were issued after dark—in my memory, in moonlight, the harvest moon that shone on friend and foe alike. Then we would hear thuds of distant shellfire and see the glow of falling flares in the north-east, where the battle for Florence had begun, the eerie illumination flickering across the landscape onto our parked vehicles and faces as we stood watching quietly.

We were now at Monterappoli, on a ridge far ahead of other troops and dangerously exposed on our flanks. Our advance had been so rapid that our artillery couldn't keep up—as we discovered one lunchtime, when we were stonked by Jerry. The tankies were understandably reluctant to move forward into territotry that we hadn't yet cleared, so air support was called down. I watched, mesmerised, as flights of Spitfires strafed and bombed the enemy batteries. There were no more stonks after that. By late-afternoon, we found ourselves on the slopes overlooking Empoli and the Arno plain. In the distant late-afternoon haze, I saw the ridges and peaks of the Apennines spanning the horizon. Then I head shooting. Scouts from C Company had surprised a German patrol and one of our men was killed. The Jerries tried to surrender, changed their minds and ran into a row of vines, where the Jocks shot two of them. One of our patrols, tipped off by partisans, captured seven Jerries resting in a house; another lost one man in a skirmish.

The next morning, 29 July 1944, A and C companies reached the mined and booby-trapped southern outskirts of Empoli. Jerry tanks were reported in the area but none was seen. Between us and the Arno, the Germans had demolished buildings and blocked the road under the Florence to Pisa railway tracks, west of the station where fires were burning merrily. Positions were established along the line of the railway. As usual, the station area had been bombed and we could see several large craters, in which we suspected spandaus were concealed. C Company stole round the eastern flank, crossed the railway and followed a tributary of the Arno. At midnight, the Jocks reached the Arno, the first Eighth Army unit to do so.

A Company established an OP in the tower of an abandoned cement factory on the south side of the tracks east of the station, a vantage point from where enemy movement at the station and in the town beyond it was noted. My company and the anti-tank platoon moved into line on the left flank, near the road under the train tracks. A Company was in the centre; C occupied orchards to the east; B was in reserve. Our mortar platoon had a good but exposed position on the forward slopes of the foothills behind us. Taking advantage of A Company's OP, which Jerry never spotted, the CO planned an attack. This was intended simply to let Jerry know the Argylls had arrived, but not actually to cross the river since one battalion was not strong enough to do so, or to hold a bridgehead. Anyway, Florence had to be liberated and the army reorganised before any further advance could be contemplated.

On the 31st, a troop of our Canadian tanks moved up behind the cement factory. Machine-guns were placed to fire point-blank into the enemy flanks. We synchronised watches and waited. Then our mortars opened fire. Bombs arced over our heads, exploding around the station and on the piazza behind it, where some Jerry vehicles had been observed. The Shermans rumbled up to the railway tracks and fired every weapon they could bring to bear; our machine-gunners picked off Germans as they ran away. The firefight was over in a few minutes. Ten Jerries were killed. There were no Argyll or Canadian casualties.

Next day, Brigadier Russell toured our positions, walking around with Graham, both men showing a commendable disregard for the occasional enemy stonk.

We held the line for the next few days, being shelled sporadically during the day, and foraying forward to the river at dusk to flush out enemy patrols, which had a habit of hiding by day in houses north of the Arno and crossing at night to probe our defences. We were in quite a vulnerable position on a wide front into which the Germans could have counter-attacked, but our action at the station must have deterred them, as did DAF Spitfires buzzing across searching for targets. Both sides settled to routine reconnaissance and desultory exchanges of mortar fire. One Jerry stonk disturbed Battalion HQ which was located behind the line, scattering men caught in the open and killing an unlucky corporal. The CO was outraged and came up to tell us to get the mortar, but its crew had moved position after firing. Later, a subaltern was shot by mistake during a platoon change-over and died of wounds. In that instance I didn't have to write the letter of condolence to the next of kin. I am sure that whoever did glossed over the circumstances of the death. You couldn't tell parents that sons died in such stupid and pointless ways.

Up in the hills to our right, four kilometres north of Montespertoli, a New Zealand patrol made an astonishing discovery 2,000 metres from enemy lines. The Kiwis entered Montegufoni, a sixteenth-century Tuscan villa belonging to Sir George Sitwell. Inside the house, they found groups of refugees—and a horde of Renaissance paintings from the Uffizi Gallery, including Botticelli's *Primavera* and Uccello's *Battle of San Romano*. Artillery was still crashing overhead when the 3/5th Mahrattas occupied the property. BBC correspondent, Wynford Vaughan Thomas, and War Office public relations writer, Major Eric Linklater, saw the treasures and broadcast the story. Many of Florence's finest artworks had been dispersed to the countryside until the war moved on. On a visit to the city a few months later, I discovered that Michelangelo's *David* had been too heavy to move and was entombed in brick for the duration.

On the morning of 4 August, the 3/8th Punjabis arrived to take over our sector; they in turn were relieved within a few days by the New Zealand Division's Maori Battalion. We had been keyed up to take part in an assault on Florence, but Alexander ruled that out to save the city from damage. Eighth Army units which had liberated its neighbourhoods on the south bank of the Arno were halted. We left the front line and marched to a rest area in the hills, before taking up new positions in the Arno valley just east of Florence. We passed through the Kiwis' sector. It was obvious there had been more severe fighting there than we had experienced. Many of the villages we drove through were wrecked. I recall stopping at a villa whose grounds were being used as a rest-stop. The villa was undamaged. Then I turned a corner and was confronted by two panzers stranded in the garden, where they had been knocked out by Allied tanks.

The Germans still occupied Florence. Shaw and I set off in a Jeep for a shufti but we only got as far as Impruneta. The main piazza was chock-a-block with tanks, trucks and Allied troops. The local church had been bombed and partly destroyed. Back at our camp near Greve, we had some comic relief when a troupe from ENSA turned up. The players were led by Will Fyffe, the Scottish comedian and pantomime star. Fyffe, who arrived in a Jeep, was wearing a kilt—an entrance that brought back memories of the theatres in Glasgow where we were more used to seeing him perform. Fyffe and his gang were invited to supper in the Officers' Mess. Some of the Canadians, who were quartered at the nearby Castello Vicchiomaggio, joined us. Chianti and nostalgia soon flowed. The party ended with a rousing chorus of Fyffe's most pop-ular song, 'I Belong to Glasgow', echoing into the night.

The battalion took over from the 14th Sherwood Foresters on 13 August. Our new position was at Bagno a Ripoli, south-east of Florence. The German rearguard had begun to pull out of central Florence on 11 August, sniped at by partisans. Germans and Fascists still held the northern part of the city centre, as we could hear—the crackle of small-arms fire from street fighting continued for several days. The Eighth Army's task, like the Fifth's downstream from Empoli, was to hold the south bank of the Arno, send patrols across to probe enemy lines and keep the Germans guessing about Alexander's next move. Since the Arno was low and could be forded, we sent a platoon across to the north bank to ferret around. Our artillery had OPs in the hills behind us. Thanks to intelligence brought back by Sergeant 'Buster' Keatings and Private Brady, who went on a 12-hour recce into enemy territory, Major Ivan Kridge, the 53 Field Regiment's liaision officer, directed his gunners to accurately shell Jerry positions. Not in the city, though: that was strict-ly forbidden on Alexander's orders. Three of my Jocks were wounded by return fire.

Battalion HQ was in a hilltop villa two kilometres from the Arno and three from Florence. The villa's owner, Count Pietro Lamberto Lamberti, was pleased to be of service and wandered about aristocrat-ically, pointing to the views from his estate, which were fabulous: the river, the city's domes and campanili and the Apennines beyond. He also pointed to the Arno bridges, all destroyed by the Germans, except for Ponte Vecchio. Brunelleschi's great terracotta dome was centred in a panorama animated by puffs of smoke from enemy artillery, located in the hills around Fiesole, which continued to shell the city and the Eighth Army on the south bank. Oltrarno, the district directly across the river from the centre, was crammed with refugees from demolished buildings and street fighting. Signs by the river warned: BEWARE

ENEMY SNIPERS. A few weeks before, Lamberti had been to Teatro Verdi to hear the *Barber of Seville*. Now, the city was cut off. For nine days Florentines had been prisoners in their homes, with little food and no public services. Allied aircraft had dropped leaflets. Some had fluttered down into the count's garden. He extracted one from his breast pocket and translated the text:

GENERAL ALEXANDER:
SPECIAL MESSAGE TO THE CITIZENS OF FLORENCE
The Allied Forces are advancing on Florence. The city's liberation is near. You, citizens of Florence, must unite to preserve your city from destruction and defeat our common enemies: the Germans and the Fascists. Prevent the enemy from exploding mines that might have been placed under bridges, public buildings and other key points in the city. Protect the telephone and telegram exchange and all other means of communication.

Lamberti wondered how Alexander expected fearful and untrained civilians to do such things. Didn't we know that the very day the leaflets floated down the Germans had evicted all residents from their apartments on the banks of the Arno and neighbouring streets, under the pretext that the Allies might bomb the bridges? All other citizens were told to stay indoors or be shot. Dozens of historic buildings either side of Ponte Vecchio were evacuated. Then the Germans dynamited the lot, along with water mains and power lines. On the evening of 3/4 August, they blew the bridges. The Uffizi gallery was damaged by the blasts; the Vasari corridor that led from the gallery across Ponte Vecchio to Palazzo Pitti was partly destroyed. The destruction of the bridges seemed completely pointless, because the Germans were pulling out anyway, and Eighth Army sappers soon put a Bailey bridge across the river.

Life at Battalion HQ was quaintly civilised. Count Lamberti was charming and the red wine from his cantina was excellent. Over glasses of this we all toasted the liberating 'Inglesi', as older Florentines called foreigners, a relic of the Grand Tour. The eighteenth-century villa was also a relic of that era. I remember the gilded furniture, chandeliers, family portraits, bookcases and billiard room—and the Jerry shells that landed fitfully in the garden. 'What a mess Italy's in now,' Lamberti complained as the German shells exploded. 'How unsociable,' he added, shaking his head.

On 23 August we left the unflappable count, his wine and the beautiful setting. We were relieved by the 2nd Royal Scots and the 1st Hertfordshires. A stonk delayed the change-over. At that moment, Captain Rome had been questioning two ladies of, as Freddie Graham put it, 'doubtful character', who had crossed through the lines from Florence and been nabbed by one of our patrols. What were they—prostitutes, refugees or spies? It was well known that German intelligence sent Italians through our lines. These 'refugees' would hang around and then scarper back to the enemy lines. The count was amused and solicitous to the ladies as only an Italian aristocrat could be. When I returned to Florence on leave, I often thought of likeable Lamberti as I strolled around. I half expected him to greet me from behind the arcades and booksellers' carts in the main piazza, but I never saw him again.

EIGHTH ARMY

PERSONAL MESSAGE FROM THE ARMY COMMANDER

To be read out to all Troops

You have won great victories. To advance 220 miles from Cassino to Florence in three months is a notable achievement in the Eighth Army's history. To each one of you in the Eighth Army and in the Desert Air Force, my grateful thanks.

Now we begin the last lap. Swiftly and secretly, once again, we have moved right across Italy, an army of immense strength and striking power: to

break the Gothic Line. Victory in the coming battles means the beginning
of the end for the German armies in Italy.

Let every man do his utmost, and again success will be ours.

To those who go temporarily under command of the great Fifth Army:
your role is vital to our success. You will win fresh honours, and the Eighth
Army will be proud when you come back to us. Good luck to you all.

Oliver Leese,

Lieutenant-General,

Tac H.Q. Eighth Army,

Italy, August 1944

The Gothic Line was a formidable barrier across northern Italy. It
ran along the Apennines from Carrara to Ravenna, and had been con-
structed by German labour battalions since the fall of Rome. It was not
a continuous barricade but a series of fortified ridges, mountain tops
and passes, 25-50 kilometres deep, guarding the few main routes across
the Apennines from the Arno to the River Po. There were artillery and
mortar emplacements, pillboxes, barbed wire, trenches, machine-guns,
SP guns and, on the flat strip on the Adriatic coast, tanks. The line was
incomplete in August 1944 and should have been breached then, but,
because of the emphasis on the campaign in North-west Europe, the
Allies' did not have the resourses in Italy to complete the job.

Alexander had planned to throw the combined might of the Eighth
and Fifth armies directly against the Gothic Line while the Germans
were still disorganised. But the Fifth Army had been weakened by the
withdrawal of three American and four French divisions for landings in
the south of France, which took place on 15 August near St Tropez. That
lost Alexander the Goums and other French mountain troops, who
would have been more usefully deployed on the Apennines than in
the Rhône valley. Looking back on this, I wonder if high command had
any notion of the conditions we would be faced with in the mountains

during that winter of 1944. We had experienced some mountain warfare in Abyssinia and in the Abruzzi, as had our Indian comrades, but
the Goums were equal masters of the art.

At a meeting at Orvieto airfield early in August, Leese had suggested a two-punch attack: the Eighth Army providing the main assault
along the Adriatic coast to Ravenna and into the Po valley, with support from the Fifth Army through the Apennines to Bologna. Leese's
focus on the coast was influenced by the difficulties of a mountain campaign. There were few roads. Tanks would be at a disadvantage in the
mountains, the passes were well defended and the terrain would make
it difficult to support out-flanking manoeuvres. He favoured a set-piece
attack using artillery, tanks and infantry on the flat coastal ground. His
tactical thinking was stuck in Monty's desert mould. The delay caused
by replanning the offensive lost the Allies the best weather. Alexander
sold the two-punch plan to Clark, by agreeing to lend him an Eighth
Army corps to strengthen the attack in the mountains. When the Eighth
Army was secretly switched to the Adriatic coast, the British 13 Corps
(1st Infantry Division, 6th South African and 8th Indian divisions) was
placed under Fifth Army command.

We read Leese's message with disbelief. We were used to being moved
around, but we felt the Eighth Army had abandoned us. Leese's fine
words—vital role, fresh honours—I had heard before. Despite the fall of
Florence, most of us had begun to feel left out of things: the Normandy
landings, Monty's thrust through northern France, the liberation of
Paris on 25 August. Shaw and I agreed that the morale of the old desert
army had begun to drain away. When the fall of Rome had been eclipsed
by news of the Normandy landings, I remember hearing a BBC radio
news bulletin: 'D-Day has come. Early this morning, the Allies began
their assault on Hitler's European fortress.' No mention that the Eighth
Army had begun the assault in Sicily a year before. We even found ourselves mocked in the UK as 'the D-Day dodgers'. This was from a

comment allegedly made in Parliament by Lady Astor, suggesting that soldiers in the Eighth Army were swanning about in sunny Italy. Our response was a sardonic song, sung to the tune of the desert favourite 'Lili Marlene'.

On 31 August the Argylls waded across a weir at Pontassieve and marched into the Mugello hills, which the 8th Indian Division was ordered to capture as a prelude to the offensive. Meanwhile, it seemed that I might be promoted, because Freddie Graham sent me on a course at the Company Commander's Tactical School at Benevento (where my former company commander, Bill Lossock, had been transferred as an instructor).

The course was a stroke of good fortune for me, because I missed the first major engagement the battalion had with the Germans in the Gothic Line, at the Battle of Monte Abetino. It was no picnic apparently and cost the battalion dearly. I was well out of it on the course, which was an enjoyable and rewarding break: lectures, demonstrations and tactical exercises by day, with all the comforts of a well-run mess in the evening. I must have impressed the commandant, Colonel Buchanan-Dunlop of the Cameronians, for he wanted me to join him on the staff of a tactical school he was being posted to in the UK. Tempting as that prospect was, and despite the colonel's inducement that he could wangle a home posting for me, my loyalties lay with the battalion. I turned down the offer.

FLORENCE, SEPTEMBER 2004

I'm at Castello Vicchiomaggio, near Greve, in the area where the Argylls and the 14th Canadian Armoured Regiment rested after the fighting at Empoli. I discover that the Canadian HQ was at Vicchiomaggio, a classic Tuscan estate set in a landscape similar to that which my father described: 'The scenery was entrancing: avenues of cypress trees leading to fairy tale villas, clusters of umbrella pines, cornfields in the valleys and vines on the hills.' As my father found at Villa Lamberti, one of the few perks in the Italian campaign—for officers, that is—was the power to commandeer the best properties.

I have to visit a friend, to explain a mystery I've solved. It's late afternoon. The air is hot and dry. I drive down a gravel road and park the Jeep by an olive grove at Buon Riposo, a villa that my wife Porta and I have rented before. On the terrace, we are met by Piero, the charming owner. He's wearing an artist's smock and looks like a Renaissance painter.

I first visited this place on holiday from Vancouver with Porta in 1996. My father would have loved it. In waning sunlight, we had stood on the terrace, where the view over the Florentine hills is enchanting. Piero had said it was different in August 1944: his father had told him about the war—and the two knocked-out German tanks in the garden. Then we entered the villa, through a pair of old wooden doors. The vestibule was lit by coloured glass; the hall was tiled; a skylight upstairs let milky light filter down to the ground floor. The air was cool. There was no sound. I was embraced by a benign and irresistible feeling that I had been there before. Porta and I sat in the garden in the evenings, listening to the owls and watching the bats flutter among the trees. The unexplained déjà vu joined me every time.

Now, I have the 1st Battalion history with me. The Argylls are the first Eighth Army unit to reach the Arno, where they engage an enemy rearguard at Empoli. After a week of fighting, they are relieved and pulled back from the front line, to the Florence sector. I show Piero a passage on the next page, which I came across in Scotland a few months before. I experienced a frisson of recognition then and it makes me shiver again. Piero catches my eye and crosses himself. The Argylls have moved to a rest area. The view over the Florentine hills is enchanting. There are two knocked-out German tanks in the garden. It's called Buon Riposo.

At nearby Impruneta, the annual Fiera di San Luca, once an agricultural fair but now a carnival with market stalls, food and a funfair, is taking place in the piazza. We have timed our trip to be here for it and because my father was here in 1944. Then, the square was crammed with Eighth Army trucks, tanks and sections of Bailey bridges for the autumn offensive on the Gothic Line.

At first, I have no sense of the war here, until I enter the medieval Basilica di Santa Maria, where a small display of photographs shows how the sanctuary was completely wrecked by American bombers in July 1944. No one then or now can explain why Impruneta was bombed. It wasn't even on the front line at the time. My father told me that American pilots were known to jettison their bombs indiscriminately rather than return to base with a full load. At Impruneta, the damage seems to have been random: the church's loggia, clock tower and campanile were not hit. After the war, the town's tile and terracotta makers, whose ancestors supplied tiles for Brunelleschi's dome on Florence Cathedral, had no shortage of work restoring damaged monuments and churches, including their own.

That evening, I watch the flashes of the Fiera di San Luca fireworks on the horizon, the distant explosions sounding like the artillery fire from Florence that my father heard. The thought of Canadian tanks also having been here reminds me that the closest I've come to a battlefield experience was, bizarrely, at a regimental dinner in Vancouver, in the Officers' Mess of The British Columbia Regiment, Duke of Connaught's Own. My invitation was a reward for having sketched the regiment's HQ, Beatty Street Drill Hall, and written a Remembrance Day piece in my column in *The Vancouver Sun*. Canadians take the remembrance of the two world wars seriously: those were times when the nation came of age. The piece was also written with my father in mind, so I can blame him for what followed.

The Duke of Connaught's is a cavalry regiment. In the Second World War, in North-west Europe, its men rode into battle in tanks. But on Mess Nights, they bring out their Charge of the Light Brigade lances. I was the 'Honoured Guest'. Dinner was followed by toasts: the Queen, the

Regiment and the Fallen. Then, the Honoured Guest was invited to 'play the game', with one man the horse and the other the lancer. I was the lancer. We charged forward. My 'horse' fell as I threw my lance, impaling me briefly on the weapon.

My father wrote to me after my brother told him about the incident:

I have been at a few regimental dinners and mess nights in my time and know very well what rough and tumble and crazy high jinks spirited young men can get up to. I won't elaborate, but I appreciate how difficult it must have been for you to refuse to join the revelry, especially, as I suspect, the drink was flowing freely. I bet the Duke of Connaught's men all sobered up pretty quickly when it happened. We will no doubt hear your own detailed blow-by-blow account of the affair of 'The Broken Lance', by phone, or when you come over.

Had Beatty Street Drill Hall been Balacalva, I would not be editing this memoir. Fortunately, my punctured lung, torn muscle and fractured ribs were patched up promptly at the city's St Paul's Hospital. I thus gained an unwelcome insight into how my father may have felt that night in March 1944, when the mule sprang the Fusiliers' booby trap at Poggiofiorito, and he found himself flat on his back on the Gustav Line.

From Vicchiomaggio, it's about 20 kilometres over the hills to Florence. At Impruneta, I pick up the road taken by the South African 6th Armoured Division's tanks to the southern outskirts of the city where, at dawn on 4 August 1944, Shermans of the Imperial Light Horse, Kimberley Regiment drove down Viale del Poggio Imperiale, the tree-lined avenue that leads to Porta Romana, as I do now. I drive along the narrow canyon of Via Romana to Palazzo Pitti, where the one-way system prevents me from driving straight on to the Arno. The South Africans carried on, expecting to reach the river at Ponte Vecchio, until they found their way completely blocked by demolished buildings, heaps of rubble and German and Fascist snipers firing from the far bank.

General Alexander, mindful of the Monte Cassino controversy, hoped to avoiding street fighting and damage to Florence by crossing the Arno east and west of the historic centre, a pincer movement to encourage the Germans to leave before they were trapped. They too had stated that Florence was essentially an 'open city', thus excluding it as a military target. Kesselring had withdrawn most of the garrison troops from the city centre at the end of June. But all through July, German troops retreated through Porta Romana, across the sixteenth-century Ponte Santa Trìnita and through the *centro storico* towards the Apennines, where the Gothic Line defences were been prepared. The Americans had already bombed the rail yards east of the centre. Alexander would have been perfectly justified, militarily, had he chosen to bomb the German vehicle columns on the Arno bridges and in the bottlenecks around Piazza Duomo. He didn't, but historic Florence was not entirely spared.

The one-way route takes me from Ponte Vecchio to Ponte Santa Trìnita, where I'm stuck in traffic outside an old palazzo. In 1944, the Eighth Army's traffic was stuck here too, because, as my father saw, the Germans had blown up the bridge, and all the others crossing the Arno except for Ponte Vecchio. A plaque on the wall the palazzo notes the disaster. I cross the river and find my way to Mercato Centrale, where I leave the Jeep in the parkade under the cast iron and glass market hall.

It's a short walk to Largo Alinari. In a courtyard hidden from the street, I enter Alinari Archives. I want to see photographs of the city in 1944 and Fratelli Alinari, founded in Florence in 1852, must have some. I'm shown into the library where I wait surrounded by shelves brimming with bound albums of pictures of pre-war Florence. An attendant brings me a series of large black-and-white prints that show, in incriminating detail, what happened on 3/4 August 1944: Ponte Vecchio stands in limbo between two rubble-strewn shores; dozens of dazed Florentines survey the destruction;

Ponte Santa Trìnita looks to have been vaporised.

I walk back through a city that now seems forbidding and austere, passing Palazzo Strozzi, whose rusticated bulk survived German shelling. The Duomo and the Baptistry escaped near misses; San Lorenzo, Santa Croce and the Uffizi Gallery were all hit; shells glanced off Giotto's Campanile. I picture my father on a day's leave, browsing the book barrows in the arcades of Piazza della Repubblica. He bought an art guide, 'Galleria degli Uffizi, Firenze', illustrated by Alinari. I still have the guide and the book barrows are still there. He was unable to visit the Uffizi, which remained closed until 1947 because of the blast damage caused by the demolitions around Ponte Vecchio. I correct myself for becoming too affected by all this. Florence is a masculine city with a violent history. The Medici statuary outside the fortress-like Palazzo Vecchio—the equestrian bronze of the bellicose Grand Duke Cosimo I, the imperialistic Neptune fountain, Hercules, Perseus beheading Medusa, and *The Rape of the Sabine Women*—is more bloodcurdling than any image I've seen from 1944.

Ponte Santa Trìnita was replaced within days by the Royal Engineers. Their Bailey bridge was regarded with some affection by Florentines until the mid-1950s, when Ponte Santa Trìnita was rebuilt, in the old style. Now, the river scene looks like the pre-war photographs I have just seen at the archives. The areas around Ponte Vecchio were rebuilt on the medieval street plan and have so mellowed that few tourists know that South African tanks rolled down Via Romana; that Nazi and Fascist snipers shot at Florentines who stumbled across the rubble of Ponte Santa Trìnita to the Allied side of the river; that partisans fought in the streets; that thousands of starving refugees from the demolitions sheltered in the courtyard and royal apartments of Palazzo Pitti, or camped among the statuary, parterres, grottoes and dried-up fountains in the Boboli Gardens.

On Via dei Gondi I find another plaque recalling the war, on the north wall of the Palazzo Vecchio, the side that tourists ignore. Florence, where Mussolini had entertained Hitler in 1938, had been a Fascist stronghold before and during the war. The inscription, by Piero Calamandrei, an anti-Fascist chancellor of Florence University, commemorates the city's salvation:

ON THE 11TH AUGUST 1944, FREEDOM—THE SOLE DISPENSER OF SOCIAL JUSTICE, NOT GRANTED BUT RECONQUERED AT THE COST OF DESTRUCTION, TORTURE AND BLOOD THANKS TO THE RISING OF THE PEOPLE AND TO THE VICTORY OF THE ALLIED ARMIES—HAS TAKEN HER PLACE IN THIS PALACE OF OUR FATHERS, ABOVE THE RUINS OF OUR BRIDGES, FOR EVER

Aerial reconnaissance photo: Monte Cavallara 5/10/44

12 MONTE CAVALLARA

I leave Florence, to follow the Argylls' march up Route 67, the Florence to Forli road, into the Apennines after the Battle of Monte Abetino. I hope to find Monte Cavallara, where my father led A Company, and won his Military Cross, in a deadly fight with Germans on 7 October 1944.

At Bagno a Ripoli, I see Villa Lamberti on its hill. Upstream is the weir near Pontassieve where the battalion waded across the Arno. On the road into the Sieve valley, the bewitching Tuscany of olive groves and vineyards, cypress avenues and Renaissance villas peters out after Dicomano. The scenery and the dampness I feel as the road climbs remind me of Scotland. I have my Jeep, for the back country's gravel roads. In 1944, when my father was promoted major and company commander, he was assigned a Jeep and a driver. But Tuscan mud is tenacious, and the weather and terrain during that winter in the mountains were so bad that most of the time he and his men walked. The road steepens as I drive past the village of San Godenzo. Like many in the mountains, it was demolished by the Germans to impede the Allies' advance. Only the eleventh-century Romanesque church was left standing, spared demolition because the parish priest told the German commander that the bishop who built it was Bavarian.

Above the rooftops of rebuilt San Godenzo, the road corkscrews up into pine and chestnut woods. This terrain inspired Dante who, banished from his native Florence in 1302, sought refuge in San Godenzo before trekking over the Apennines to political exile. His journey gave him imagery for the *Inferno* and I can see why. It's been raining up here and waterfalls and mountain streams gush down rock faces and splash across the road. The crags gape with black grottoes; the peaks are masked in cloud. Curtains of wire mesh are pinned to the slopes to prevent rockfalls. I pass road signs showing deer prancing, but my main worries are the dizzying drops at every bend. In 1944, the signs on Route 67 warned of additional hazards: BAILEY BRIDGE 100 YARDS . . . BEWARE BOOBY TRAPS . . . DANGER MINES.

Just when I think the climb can't get any steeper, I round a bend and see another sign: PASSO DEL MURAGLIONE, M 907. I pull over at a viewpoint. The pass is one of the highest in the Apennines. Ridges and summits float like islands above valleys drowned in morning mist. The trees beside me rustle in a gust of the wind—the Tramontana, the icy wind that, according to local myth, induces fatigue and depression. A hundred metres on, before the road plunges into an unseen glen, there's a caffè/tabacchi. In the centre of the road I see what looks like a Gothic Line fortificatio: the massive curving wall that gives the pass its name. A plaque on top of the wall notes the construction of the road by Granduca Leopoldo II in 1836. He built the wall as a refuge for his carriages from the wind that blasts the pass.

A dozen leather-clad bikers rumble up from Forlì, exhilarated by the wind and the winding road. They park outside the café, take off their helmets and lean on BMWs and Ducatis. The scene dissolves before me into an image of the 600 men of the 1st Argylls with their weapons, and 200 mules and Indian helpers, on a 10-minute rest stop. I steer my Jeep down from the pass and negotiate more hairpin bends before reaching San Benedetto in Alpe, a village at the bottom of a ravine. I turn left and climb, following the cross-country trail the Argylls took to Marradi. It's rough and single-track for most of the way. When the Argylls were here it was passable only on foot. My father wrote:

> During the battles on the Gothic Line, ground was gained not by massed assaults on broad fronts but hill by hill, pass by pass, foot by foot in countless, isolated engagements, where the leadership of company and platoon commanders and NCOs, and savvy deter-

mination and courage determined success or failure. We had artillery support, but rarely from armour. Both sides tried to deploy tanks in the mountains, but even tracked vehicles—even those driven by the courageous Canadians of the 14th Armoured Regiment—could not negotiate the mud on the steep, slippy slopes. Low cloud prevented air strikes on enemy positions.

The Gothic Line was an infantryman's war.

I look around at the forbidding landscape, trying to cross the chasm that separates me from my father's experiences here. I've had a relatively easy drive in fair weather. What was it like in 1944 for the Jocks and the Indians, or for the Germans who were waiting for them? To imagine it, as my father wrote, you had to have been here then. For over fifty years, he carried the burden of what he saw on the Gothic Line. The Battle of Monte Cavallara, when A Company seized the summit and took 30 per cent casualties, was the event he always returned to in later life when he felt like talking about the war, which wasn't often.

I HAVE BECOME A VICTIM OF WRITER'S BLOCK RECENTLY, and don't quite know how to proceed with these memoirs. Perhaps I am reluctant to awaken memories of our experiences in the Gothic Line during that dreadful winter of 1944 . . .

The Battle of Monte Abetino was a foretaste of what was to come. During attacks by the Argylls and the 3/8th Punjabis, two of our officers were killed, two were wounded and two reported missing—plus nine other ranks killed and seventy-two wounded or missing. One of those who died was D Company's commander Major Jim Sceales. I had known him since 1941, when he had joined the battalion at Asmara. I met his father, General G. A. Maclaren Sceales, at the Balaclava centenary celebrations at Stirling Castle in 1954. He questioned me about the circumstances of his son's death, but I could tell him little more than the battalion history related: that under heavy enemy mortar and machine-gun fire, Sceales had led two platoons to seize Monte Abetino, but he had been hit and killed after they took the summit. The Germans regained the position for a short time, partly by confusing the Jocks with an old trick: 'Thik hai [all right], Johnnie, it's your Indian friends,' they called out as they approached. Only six Jocks got away. Sceales' grave was found later. The Germans had buried him, taking the trouble to put a wooden cross on the grave. General Sceales seemed comforted when I told him what a fine officer his son had been.

One of those missing was Major 'Rab' Caldwell (who had joined the battalion when I did, after Crete). In command of A Company, he had gone forward on a recce with one of his platoon commanders, Lieutenant Jack, and a risky undertaking it proved to be. They ran into an enemy patrol. In the confusion, the young subaltern managed to get away and hid in the undergrowth. There he lay, with his heart in his mouth, till the Germans gave up their search. When the coast was clear he made his way back to the battalion and reported what had happened. Rab was captured and spent the remainder of the war as a PoW, first at Mantua and then at Stalag 7, Moosburg, Bavaria. At a reunion many years later, he told me how he had looked up from his hiding place to see a pair of Jerry boots and the muzzle of a schmeisser. The Jerry actually said to him: 'For you, the war is over.'

When I returned from Benevento in mid-September, the battalion was at Cistio, east of Borgo San Lorenzo, in the midst of a hasty reorganisation made necessary by the losses it had suffered recently. I was promoted major and was delighted to be given command of A Company, which I knew so well, and had served with for so long. I had no illusions about the fact that the vacancy had opened because of casualties, and Caldwell's capture.

The 8th Indian Division had cleared the Sieve valley and Borgo San Lorenzo, where we rested for a week before trekking further into the mountains. Some leave to Florence was granted, but not for me. I didn't request it, having just been given responsibility for the well-being and leadership of 100 men. When I took command of A Company, I found there were very few left serving with it whom I had known since our desert days. There was Sanders, of course. But apart from a scattering of men in the three platoons, most were newcomers. Casualties had been so heavy in the Italian campaign that men had been drafted in from other British and Commonwealth regiments. There were new officers, including a few odd bods who failed to fit in or make the grade. There was one gem of a chap however, the thoroughly reliable and good-natured Captain Steve White, a platoon commander with the company, promoted as my second-in-command. He lifted everyone's spirits with his jokes and cheerful banter. Some new men were unwilling recruits, but most learned to muck in together in difficult conditions and became loyal Argylls. Backsliders, shirkers and moaners were soon taught the error of their ways. God knows, they had plenty to moan about during that autumn and winter on the Gothic Line.

The Apennines are ruptured by gloomy glens, claustrophobic passes, knife-edge ridges and formidable peaks rising to 1,500 metres. These features lay across our line of advance. They were ideal for defence, but not to attack. Kesselring's strategy was to hold, until the last moment, the heights that commanded the roads and passes, then to withdraw to similar points further north. We were only too familiar with these tactics, but they cost many lives to overcome. Every move on the front line provoked mortar stonks, machine-gun fire and shells from 88s. Frequently, we found ourselves facing men of the German 1st Parachute Division. These soldiers, now deployed as infantry, were motivated by their *esprit de corps,* battle honours and professionalism. Some may have fitted the fanatical Nazi profile, but I never saw that. Nor did Alexander. Of the battles at Monte Cassino he had remarked: 'Unfortunately, we are fighting the best soldiers in the world. What men! . . .'

Can the ordeals and sufferings of the Jocks and Indians in the terrible conditions on the Gothic Line be imagined? Not really. No one can imagine them, who had not been there, and endured them. The weather was atrocious—the fiercest Italian winter in living memory. We were wet and miserable for days on end; bone-weary, loaded with kit and weapons, struggling up and down mountainsides, amid shell bursts, bullets and mortar bombs; then going through the same thing again the next day or night, suffering from the cold, snatched sleep and exhaustion, without the comfort of regular hot meals or dry blankets. Changes of clothing were rare. Trench foot and frostbite were as much a threat as enemy fire. 'Foot inspection' was a daily routine. We squatted in stinking latrines. At least there were no flies. As usual, supplies had to be hauled up by mules. We lived in and out of holes in the ground or ruined farm buildings, sustained by whatever creature comforts I could scrounge, and by our necessary nightly tot of rum and occasional beer and cigarette rations. And one hot meal a day if we were lucky, otherwise bully beef and hard tack.

Small wonder there were desertions, even among the Jerry para boys. Germans, who evidently lived in waterlogged squalor like us, occasionally came through our lines. Some claimed to be Austrians, as if that would get them better treatment. They didn't get it, or deserve it. I remembered newsreels in 1938 showing crowds cheering Hitler and his troops when they entered Vienna. A few of our Jocks deserted to escape the dangers and hardships of their existence. There were many more AWOL cases, we heard, among the GIs. Deserters sought anonymity in Florence, Rome and Naples, where the Military Police of the Eighth and Fifth armies were kept busy rounding them up. They were men the who'd had enough of a war that seemed endless. Men who 'took a powder', in the graphic phrase of Steve White. Others expressed their feelings in ugly, mutinous mutterings, alarmingly prejudicial to good order and discipline, if they were to be taken seriously. But many more revealed almost superhuman powers of endurance, with a quiet determination to stick it out to the end, and more often than not a cheerful courage and fortitude that lifted my spirits as their company commander.

Our brigade had been in reserve at the start of the main offensive in the Apennines, which had begun on 13 September with a deafening artillery barrage that was heard for miles all along the Gothic Line. The Americans met with fiercer resistance than did the British, but soon the outer defences of the line were breached and the Allies advanced to its main positions. On 21 September, we received a warning order to move the next day to a concentration area at San Godenzo, prior to going into the front line. I remember that because White and Oxborrow had their leave in Florence cut short.

The battalion moved along the Sieve valley to Dicomano, from where we were to follow up assaults by the division's 17th and 21st brigades. Dicomano had been visited by American bombers earlier in the year. Much of what remained had been blown up by the Germans. Some of the townsfolk, who had been evacuated, had returned to pick over the rubble of their homes, a pathetic sight. Tanks of the 6th Armoured Division, held up by the condition of the road ahead, were parked here and there outside the town. There was much activity: army vehicles rumbled in and out of ammo and petrol dumps, water points and LAD workshops; soldiers hung around cookhouses, tents and mobile bath units; wounds were being treated in an abandoned Jerry dressing station, rolls were being called, billets were being found, blankets and packs unloaded and weapons cleaned; cigarettes were smoked, yarns were exchanged, tea was being brewed and tired limbs rested—all the lazy-seeming confusion attending the reorganisation of infantry companies and tank squadrons after marching or fighting. When we arrived at our bivouac for the night, we were greeted by the snorts and shuffles of 200 mules and their Indian muleteers, who were waiting to carry the battalion's food, ammo and equipment up the most tortuous stretch of Route 67 (Star Route in army code), to San Benedetto in Alpe.

Reveille was at 0500. As we prepared for a march into the mist, we stood around smoking in quiet groups, stamping our feet around the steaming cookhouse braziers, clutching mugs of piping hot tea while the muleteers checked the animals and their loads. At dawn, the battalion assembled and moved off, a long line of men and mules disappearing into a 10-kilometre-long valley towards San Godenzo. This village had once clung picturesquely to a steep slope. It now looked like a quarry. Jerry demolition crews had blown it to pieces in an attempt to block the road. Only the church had been saved. Negotiating a path that had been bulldozed through the village, we followed the road as it twisted tightly left and then right as it climbed out of the ruins. A 17-kilometre sequence of hairpin bends rose to a high pass before the road dropped down to San Benedetto.

Higher and higher we tramped, followed by our mule train. Each time I turned to check on my men, I saw it snaking up below. We climbed out of the woods and layers of valley mist. At each new bend the edge of the road to my right dropped out of sight into a vaporous abyss. When we reached the crest of the pass we were rewarded with a rest stop and a grand view of distant ridges. The road turned through a gap and spiralled down towards San Benedetto, a desolate alpine hamlet in a gorge of the Montone river, where our column made a left turn up a steep track (Planet Route) that led to Marradi. This was 20 kilometres away, where the Lamone river, and the road (Sword Route) and railway from Florence to Faenza squeeze through a gap in the Apennines. Other 8th Indian Division units [the 1/5th Gurkhas, 1st Jaipur Infantry, 1st Royal Fusiliers, and the 1/12th and 6/13th Frontier Force Rifles] had seized the ridges and summits that lay south of Planet Route, so our left flank was protected. But hills on the right of the track were in enemy territory. Our task was to clear them to secure the road.

Platoons leap-frogged one another from hill to hill, the basic rule of this type of warfare being to deny the heights to the enemy. We occupied the high ground north-east of the road—Monte Susinelli, Monte Bruno, Monte del Cerro and Monte Bufalo—and sent out patrols, but these were uneventful except for the weather, which turned windy and wet. Battalion HQ, which someone without any desert experience had unwisely sited in a wadi, was washed away, leaving the CO and his staff sloshing and squelching, knee-deep in mud. The rest of us sat in hilltop sangars, cold, miserable and soaked to the skin. D company was driven off one hill, not by the enemy, but by torrents of lashing rain.

We spent the next couple of days patrolling hills and dead-end valleys. I recall being shot at as we occupied one of the peaks. We dived for cover as spandau fire zipped over our heads. Someone hollered: 'Where the bloody hell did that come from?' Echoes off the slopes made it almost impossible to pinpoint the source of the firing straight away. We called down arty shoots, but the low cloud prevented us from observing the results. At one point, an enemy platoon and one machine-gun pinned down the whole company. That was a typical situation. In pouring rain that night, before we were obliged to locate and silence the spandau, we were very pleased to be relieved by the Jaipurs. Formalities over, I sent the men down the muddy track and followed with the last platoon.

Near Marradi, we entered a cultivated, pine-scented valley. Spirals of wood smoke rose from Botteghette, a sodden hamlet close to an isolated monastery. Battalion HQ was set up and billets for officers were found in the hamlet. The men bivouacked nearby. We dried out for three days in the vast kitchens and commodious cellars of stone farmhouses that were typical of the region. There was no electricity, just wood fires and oil lamps. Furnishings were spartan, except for occasional heirlooms and religious imagery—faded photographs, a treasured piece of china, or heavy, ornate furniture from a more prosperous era. Images in every home I entered in Italy showed divided loyalties: pictures of the Madonna, saints, Garibaldi, and family portraits seemed as significant as any of Mussolini. The Fascist state never quite suffocated Italy's regional diversity, local identities and family-centred culture. The peasant women gave us what food they could spare and we shared our rations with them and their children. Cigarettes guaranteed the men's co-operation.

We were placed in brigade reserve. Not for long, though. Marradi had been captured on 24 September by the 1st British Infantry Division, which then veered off to the north-west, to Castel del Rio, to secure the Fifth Army's right flank. The 8th Indian Division was pushing northeast, to clear the hills that overlooked the Marradi to Faenza road. On 3 October, we got a warning order to attack Monte Bicocche, above the hamlet of San Adriano, north of Marradi. The CO took A and C company commanders on a recce to Popolano, two kilometers down the road. We were met by Lieutenant-Colonel Buchanan of the Royal Fusiliers. It was a sunny day, for a change, and we got a good view of the territory—the kilometre-wide Lamone valley and hills rising steeply on either side. Buchanan told us the valley was exposed to enemy fire, so a direct approach would be costly. Major 'Bob' Taylor of the 14th Canadian said the ground was unfavourable for his tanks. He could give supporting fire at San Adriano, but not for long—a Jerry SP had been shelling the area. Brigadier Russell joined the confab. He agreed that an infantry assault through the hills to the right of the road seemed to offer the best chance for success. The 3/8 Punjabis were in position ready to clear the Jerries out, he told us, but another feature, Monte Cavallara, an 800-metre-high Jerry strongpoint, two kilometres east of Botteghette, was in the way.

After receiving orders from Russell and Dobree on 4 October, Freddie Graham held a company commanders' conference in one of our farmhouses. The battalion was to take over from the 6/13th Frontier Force

Rifles and capture Monte Cavallara. Until it was taken, the advance of the whole brigade was stalled. Lieutenant-Colonel Green, CO of the 6/13th, said his men had attacked Cavallara twice, and been repulsed. It was vital, Graham emphasised, that it be taken—'at all costs'.

A Company was given the job.

I spent the evening at Company HQ, another dilapidated but watertight farmhouse whose tenants, an elderly couple, survived in this bleak environment, with the tenacity of old age. My platoon commanders, Captain White, Second Lieutenant Lindsay and Sergeant Taylor talked quietly, shadows from an army hurricane lamp and a blazing log fire flickering on their faces. I passed my cigarette and whisky rations around and explained the situation. Like Steve White, Andrew Lindsay was an Edinburgh lad, but a newcomer to the battalion. He'd never been in action.

'I don't think I'll survive this show,' he interrupted, ominously.

He seemed full of foreboding. His blunt statement dismayed us all.

'Don't be daft,' White laughed. 'You'll come through it. It'll be a walkover. Jerry'll skedaddle before we get to the top, as he usually does. We'll find the position empty.'

We tried to cheer Lindsay up, partly to take our minds off the taboo he'd broken—we never let our feelings and fears show in that way—but neither White's encouragement nor the whisky could lift his spirits.

His morbid talk put a bit of a dampener on the proceedings, but we shrugged it off as best we could and prepared ourselves for the business in hand. I was too concerned about my own duties and responsibilities to worry too much about what the Fates might have in store. I was convinced that I would come through the attack alive and well, and indeed survive the war. Most of us believed someone else would get it. I don't think we could have continued otherwise. If your number was up, you didn't want to know when. At every death, publicly and piously mourned, those of us who survived crossed ourselves privately with the thought: 'Poor bastard. Glad it wasn't me.'

At 1100 the next morning, the Argylls left the shelter of Botteghette and climbed through the woods, the CO, IO, and company commanders leading the way. Mules followed with their usual burdens, but we carried much of the stuff ourselves. We separated to trek to our respective positions. I saw Graham's single file of men one moment there, the next, gone, only to reappear blundering further away on the hillside. He set up a forward HQ at Grilleta, a kilometre south-east of Cavallara, and Battalion HQ at Rovoleta, one and a half kilometers away. B Company, and D Company (Shaw was second in command) were hunkered down in nearby valleys, with a company of Jaipurs attached to the battalion forward of B's position. I trudged on, passing some of the 6/13th men coming down. The flatter slopes had been cleared for pasture but we avoided these tempting, easy-to-cross open spaces: experience had taught us that they would be covered by Jerry machine-guns set to fire on fixed lines. An eerie silence lay over the scene, broken occasionally up ahead by the crack of bursting flares as night fell. Because of the terrain, and the fact that the relief had to be done in the dark to avoid enemy detection, it took us 10 hours to complete the change-over.

In the morning, I awoke in a cloud of mist unable to see a thing. As the vapour eddied away our position was revealed. We were sitting in slit trenches and sangars almost level with a precipitous, switchback ridge whose contours wriggled away for a kilometre either side of Monte Cavallara, its highest point. A reverse slope partly cleared for pasture was hidden from view. Gullies plunged away on either side of the ridge, with some tree cover. Beyond a defile directly in front of me, the scrubby face of the ridge rose to Cavallara, about 300 metres away.

There were four significant features, identified by their height in metres: Point 756, with some tree cover, held by A Company; Point 759, 250 metres to my right, occupied by C Company; Point 744,

Monte Cavallara itself; and Point 685, 300 metres beyond it. Points 744 and 685 were occupied by the enemy, who had previously withstood the 6/13th's direct assaults along the ridge. Expecting yet another attack, Jerry was jumpy, judging by the sporadic machine-gun and mortar fire directed our way all day. A and C companies were heavily shelled and one of my men was killed and another wounded. The Jaipurs were mortared. The fire was returned with no results observed.

Graham went to see the 3/8th Punjabis' CO, Lieutenant-Colonel Sanderson, whose battalion was poised to pass through our lines and take another feature, Monte Casalino, two kilometres north-east of Cavallara—if our assault cleared the way. Graham studied a vertical air photograph of the area and, taking advantage of mist as he returned, made a recce to find out if there was a fresh approach to the enemy position. He spotted a wadi on the north-west side of Cavallara, up which an attack might be mounted. At a company commanders' briefing, he explained his plan. A Company would move down into some thick scrub at the foot of the wadi at first light the following morning. C Company, led by Major Oxborrow, would then engage the enemy with mortars to make Jerry think the attack was coming along the ridge. Artillery fire would add to the deception. The stonks would end with smoke bombs to cover my company's attack.

Back at Point 756, I crawled into Company HQ's slit trench to explain the CO's plan to my platoon commanders. I sketched our assault route on a copy of the air photograph and detailed the disposition of the platoons. We synchronised watches, then drank each other's health with a tot of rum. Final checks were made of weapons, ammo, rations and equipment, and we settled down for the night. A pretty miserable one it was too for us all. It rained intermittently and we sought what shelter we could in our trenches and sangars. I lay there on my groundsheet, wrapped in my gas cape, watching the rain dribble down into my soggy trench.

We woke before dawn. The platoon commanders passed round a rum ration and cigarettes to the men who sat quietly holding their rifles, waiting.

I checked my watch. 0500.

'Okay lads, this is it. Good luck. Let's go!'

As quietly as we could, we made our way down the hillside to wait at our starting point in the trees, unobserved by the enemy. No bayonets, lest they snag on the foliage or rocks and make a noise.

Imagine, if you can, my company of 100 men, filing down a steep slope in intermittent rain, with weapons, ammo, steel helmets and haversack rations, knowing they would shortly be ordered to attack a strongly-held enemy position, wondering if they would come through it alive—the poor bloody infantry, grumbling and cursing, but kept going by loyalty to their regiment and their pals. There I was, in command of them all, required to lead them into battle, responsible for their well-being and their lives. Nothing in my background had prepared me for immediacy of this—certainly not the Company Commander's Tactical School at Benevento.

0700. 7 October 1944.

The artillery and mortar concentration erupted. Looking up, I saw explosions and smoke straddling the ridge. I gave the command: 'Company will advance!'

It was a three-platoon attack: Taylor on the right, Lindsay on the left and White in the centre. Company HQ—myself, the CSM, Sanders, a signaller and stretcher bearers—bringing up the rear. I'll never forget the cheerful, confident thumbs-up I got from Sergeant Taylor. He was a regular soldier, who had been posted to us from another battalion some time previously and who had made a good impression on us with his reliability, efficiency and authority.

We got off to a bad start. Though fortified by the tot of rum, the men had their confidence and morale shaken when a stray mortar salvo from

C Company fell amongst us as we set off. One of the bombs, which failed to explode, struck my signaller on the belt webbing in the small of his back and put him out of action. Luckily, the wireless set, carried in a haversack, was undamaged. Sanders, who knew how to operate it, strapped it on and secured the microphone round his neck. As he did this, the three attacking platoons, having fanned out in the wadi, charged the hill.

The mortars and arty ceased firing, and C Company's smoke shells began to fall, covering the summit in clouds of bilious haze. The farther we in Company HQ struggled up the slopes, it became clear that there was a fierce battle up ahead. As we approached the top, the sounds of confused shouting came through the smoke screen—and the rattle of machine-gun and small-arms fire, and the bangs of grenades exploding. Gasping for breath at the top, I found the position cleared of Germans, the remnants of whom had withdrawn to positions further down and beyond the ridge.

0730. The hill was ours, but at a cost.

It was shockingly clear that all three platoons of A Company had suffered heavy casualties. I had already passed some walking wounded making their way down the hill to the regimental aid post, but at the top, bodies lay about everywhere—some Germans, but mostly those of my Jocks. The stretcher-bearers had their work cut out, picking them up and tending the wounded. Two of my platoon commanders had been killed, and the third wounded, and there was scarcely an NCO left alive or unscathed.

Taylor had led his platoon with great dash and courage, and though wounded, was foremost in the attack, shouting encouragement and tossing grenades, setting a fine example to his men. He was evacuated, never returned to the battalion and, to my regret, I never saw the brave fellow again. Lindsay's prophecy was fulfilled: he was dead, killed while leading his men, firing a Bren gun from the hip. My most shocking and saddest moment of that morning was when I came across Steve White among the wounded. He had received a burst of machine-gun fire in the body and was lying semi-conscious, his mangled guts spilling out on the ground. I carried two water bottles, one filled with water, the other with rum. I gave him a swig of rum, which I hope brought him some comfort in his dying moments. I'm still torn by having left him there, to the care of the stretcher-bearers. But more urgent duties had to be done.

The men were suffering from shock and demoralised by the carnage and the deaths of two popular officers. I had to re-animate their fighting spirit and keep them busy, turning the position to all-round defence in case of enemy counter-attack. We had three prisoners but they refused to talk, so I sent them under escort to Battalion HQ. Sergeant McKeown, one of the two senior NCOs who had not become casualties, kept a cool head and was a great help at this critical time. Lance Corporal Callaghan roused and encouraged his section and I promoted him on the spot.

By 0830, we had consolidated our position. As the smoke and mist began to clear, we came under machine-gun and small-arms fire from Jerry's back-up position, Point 685. The bullets caused a bit of alarm at first, until we realised that we were quite safe if we kept our heads down in a hollow at the top of the hill. But the enemy fire was a nuisance, preventing free movement and observation. The spandau had to be spotted and put out of action if possible.

With this in mind, I set off armed with grenades and a tommy gun, cautiously working my way from cover to cover along the ridge. I took Sergeant Pate with me, leaving McKeown in charge of what was left of the company. Pate, like McKeown, was a Glasgow man who had been with A Company since 1941, through the campaigns in Abyssinia, the Western Desert and Sicily. He wasn't over-anxious to come with me, but as things turned out he didn't regret it. We didn't spot the spandau, but it spotted us. A rattling burst of fire sent us scuttling for cover. Pate got a bullet in the foot. After recovering from the initial shock, he could barely conceal his relief. His wound was a minor one, but sufficiently disabling to put him out of action. I'm afraid I didn't show him much sympathy, not that he wanted any, as I pulled out a field dressing. Keeping out of Jerry's line of fire, I helped him limp back to the company's position, then cursed inwardly as I watched him hobble his way down to the safety of the RAP—another NCO gone from my much-reduced company.

Pate and I had been so intent on stalking the spandau that neither of us heard the cries of some wounded men lying out of sight over the crest of the hill, one of them moaning for his 'mammy'. I crawled up to the edge of our position to see where they were. No sooner had I put my head over the top than there was a burst from the spandau. A volley of bullets hit the ground in front of my face. I tumbled back down the slope in a heap and lay still at the bottom. Everyone thought I had been hit. So did I. Then I realised I had only been blinded temporarily by the dirt thrown into my eyes. Reluctantly I had to admit that any attempt at rescue would be suicidal.

The poor fellows lying outside must have been far gone, for their cries soon ceased. I could see the effect of this on my men's faces. I went round, talking quietly to each one.

I remember a shivering Jock saying: 'A bit of a jam, sir.'

'We'll get out of it,' I replied, patting his shoulder, not sure at that moment quite how we would.

Somehow the indomitable Sanders managed to rustle up some makeshift snacks and hot tea, a blessing that calmed us all.

Then came the first blistering mortar stonk. I was on the wireless to Battalion HQ at the time, my eardrums ringing with the explosions, shouting to George Rome, the adjutant.

'There's another one. Did you hear that?'—I yelled into the mike, so as to leave them in no doubt about our situation.

The stonk went on for some time, and the men, only just begining to recover from the ordeal they had been through, were badly shaken. So was I when I had another miraculous escape. A young Jock, crouching next to me, got a bomb splinter in the neck that almost decapitated him. He gurgled and quickly bled to death. No point in calling for a medic.

As the bombs rained down, some of the men screamed obscenities back and, had I given the order, I think they might have rushed the Jerry position themselves. But another stonk kept our heads down. This was almost too much for us to take. We were jittery too, at the thought of a Jerry counter-attack. Mercifully it didn't materialise, but our situation, with the company strength so severely depleted, was sufficiently vulnerable for Russell, who came up from Division HQ at midday, and Graham to act. This they did by ordering two B Company platoons to attack Point 685, through our position.

When B Company's Jocks eventually turned up at 1600, they were greeted with derisive banter:

'Where have you been? . . . We've done our bit . . . Finish the bastards off . . . and get that fucking mortar!'

The men of B Company, seeing our sorry state, appeared not to be too keen to get the mortar. They were shaken too, when another stonk fell amongst us just as they were assembling to go over the top. Their officers and NCOs did their best to restore order. It was vital that further delay be avoided, as by this time C Company's mortars were firing smoke bombs on Point 685 to cover the attack. The leading platoon went over the crest and started off with some spirit, accompanied by our shouts of encouragement and covering fire. I was rather put out at seeing their company commander berating some reluctant heroes and actually pushing and kicking them over the edge. I felt he would have done better to go over himself and shame them into following him.

Both platoons surged on and overran Point 685 after a fierce fight. Jerry counter-attacked twice, then all was quiet.

Just before dusk, Second Lieutenant 'Pitch' Christopher, one of our Zulus, arrived back with the remnants of his platoon. Since we had heard nothing after the shooting stopped, I was never so pleased to see anyone in my life. B Company had beaten off the counter-attacks but, with only thirteen men out of his thirty left unscathed, he realised he didn't have enough strength to hold the position. He had lost sight of his fellow platoon commander, Second Lieutenant Smith, whose men were nowhere to be seen.

Christopher had arrived as I stood contemplating the body of a German, one of three killed in our initial attack. He was young, barely out of his teens, lying on his side beside a spandau and belts of ammo. I salvaged some of his belongings: identification and family photographs, the usual stuff. I was filled with sombre thoughts about the untimely deaths of so many young men, on both sides, whose lives had been sacrificed, and wondered how many more were to die. None of us had much sleep that night and what little I had was interrupted by disturbing dreams.

At dawn, I sent a patrol out into the mist. There was no sign of the enemy, but it came across Smith and his men, a pitifully small number, all wounded, lying around Point 685. The remainder of his platoon was dead or missing. Smith had heard the Germans moving about below him during the night, but no attempt was made to recapture the position, so he sat tight. I sent a second patrol to reinforce Point 685, but there was no further sight or sound of Jerry.

According to some Italians, who had seen the Germans pulling out after the battle, the enemy's casualties included their company commander, who had been killed by our artillery. I took no satisfaction at that small consolation for our losses. The attacks by A and B companies had cost fifteen men killed and forty-four wounded. Of those, two officers and ten other ranks killed and twenty wounded were A Company men. The dead were laid to rest at a makeshift cemetery in a pine grove at Vonibbio, a nearby hamlet. Padre Dow conducted a brief ceremony. We stood in silence as a piper played the lament.

The day after the battle, we got our first hot meal for ages and a chance to wash, shave and tidy ourselves up. And thank our lucky stars that we had survived an ordeal, the memory of which would remain with us for the rest of our lives. The brigade's arty chaps set up an OP on Point 744. Just another hill for them, thanks to the poor bloody infantry. The CO came up for a shufti, with Russell and Dobree. Russell said that our 'very excellent performance' had enabled the Punjabis to get their objective and forced the enemy to fall back, aiding the advance of the brigade'. Actually, it took a week of fighting by Punjabis and Gurkhas to force the Germans off Monte Casalino. We stayed on Monte Cavallara for several nights before we were relieved by the Jaipurs. The Jocks of A and B Companies were exhausted and subdued as I led them down the mountainside to Botteghette.

Shaw, Rome and others laid on a party in our honour: an extra beer ration and a hot meal for the men and stronger drink for the officers. Reaction to shattered nerves, relief that it was all over, thoughts about the casualties we had suffered—thoughts about the taboo Lindsay had broken—and grief, especially about the loss of my good friend Steve White overwhelmed me, and I couldn't enter into the spirit of things. All I wanted to do was to get out of my muddy battledress, stained with the blood of the poor Jock who'd got it in the neck, and sleep. I'd had little or none for week and was utterly drained. Overcome by the heat from the blazing fire in the farmhouse kitchen, the fumes of tobacco smoke and the drink, I lay down on my makeshift bed, flat out. I recall Shaw bending over me and saying, 'Look at this, chaps, Ray's passed out like a light.'

I slept the round of the clock.

MONTE CAVALLARA, SEPTEMBER 2004

At Popolano, the hamlet two kilometres north of Marradi where the
Argyll officers discussed tactics, I turn off the Faenza road onto a white
gravel track. The weather has cleared, but the drive through the mountains from Florence has taken much longer than I expected, just as the
Allied troops found every time they moved positions in the Apennines
in 1944. The Italian map I have confuses me with its closely-drawn contours—a graphic representation of the tangled terrain over which the
Argylls marched and fought.

The aerial photograph I have, which my father used to plan the attack
on Monte Cavallara, isn't much help either. It's a larger scale than the
map and the landscape has changed since that time. In the photo, the
ridges and summits are bare, and rocky screes spill away. Only the gullies
and lower slopes are wooded. Contadini, charcoal burners and woodcut-
ters used to clear the hills. Few of these people live here now: the flight
to the cities in the decades after the war saw much of the land abandoned and reforestation has reclad the hills. I unfold the map on the
hood of the Jeep. I am shouted at by an old woman dressed in black, an
apparition from the 1940s. She thinks I'm stealing chestnuts, which lie in
drifts by the side of the track. I drive on.

The aerial photo is sunlit and seems to have been taken around mid-
day, probably during the only break in weather the reconnaissance pilot
got. The shadows are barely long enough to pick out the features. I lean
on the Jeep re-reading my father's account of the battle to confirm the
location. I realise I've over-shot. A glimmer of late afternoon sun picks
out the details he described: the switchback ridge, the reverse slope
partly cleared for pasture, gullies plunging away on either side of the
ridge, with some tree cover.

Monte Cavallara is a kilometre away, slightly higher than the wooded
hillside to the north-east where I am. I scan the ridge with binoculars

trying to picture what happened here. Points 685 and 744 are visible; Points 756 and 759 are hidden behind the ridge. I curse myself for leaving it too late in the day to explore these features on foot. The ridge is too steep, even for the Jeep. Trying to get closer, I drive up a rocky track. I don't get far. The surface is unstable and I don't see anywhere to turn. Suddenly, the confusing topography becomes clear. Across a deep gully—the wadi from which A Company emerged—I see the summit of Monte Cavallara through a screen of pine trees, 300 meters away.

After backing down the track, I try to make out the pine grove at Vonibbio, the hamlet where my father buried his men, but it looks to be back where the old woman shouted at me. Anyway, the dead would have been reburied in a Commonwealth War Graves Commission cemetery, probably at Florence.

I read my father's notes:

> The Battle of Monte Cavallara was not a big show; just a routine attack with a limited objective; wishful thinking by the brass to seek a breakthrough at that time in that part of the line. Cavallara was typical of the swift and deadly actions, fought by the infantry in the Fifth and Eighth armies, that were necessary to win the Italian campaign. Like them all, it was known to, and is remembered only by the men who took part.

Freddie Graham wrote, in a Regimental Letter of 22 October 1944:

> We have been in the thick of it again, operating in the mountains (some mountains too!) and spent a very unpleasant fortnight in foul weather and plenty of Boche about . . . Everyone was soaked to the skin . . . Transport was almost entirely by mule pack and even man-pack at times . . . The position to be attacked was a 'two pimple' hill stinking with spandaus . . . A Company, under com-

mand of Major Ray Ward, was detailed to capture the first domi-
nating pimple . . . The attack went in, and thanks to superb
leadership and the greatest dash on the part of the troops, was
completely successful. As soon as the first pimple was captured all
Hell was let loose on A Company, and they were also heavily shot
up from pimple No. 2 . . . Two platoons of B company, under
Captain Graham Wood, were rushed up to deal with this. The
distance was only some 300 yards and under cover of smoke B
company went for it like 'Tigers' and got it . . .

The landscape I look at now is silent, with nothing—no monuments,
no graves—to tell of what took place here on 7 October 1944.

On the way back to Florence, I stop at the Commonwealth War
Graves Commission cemetery. It's on the north bank of the Arno, five
kilometres east of the city, between Route 67 and the river. It is beautifully maintained. The Cross of Sacrifice, common to all CWGC burial
grounds, and row upon row of white headstones stand in a field of grass
and cypress trees, in an atmosphere of soothing solemnity. I walk slowly
along the rows, looking for Argyll badges engraved on the markers. I
soon find Major Sceales and the other Argylls killed at Monte Abetino,
but not the men of Monte Cavallara. I leave, wondering where they are.

After the battle, A and B companies were merged under my father's
command. He made a list of the casualties for the record and also
because company commanders had to write letters of condolence to
next of kin. I found the list, and letters from those who replied, among
his papers.

18 Henderson Terrace
Edinburgh
7/11/44

Major T. R. Ward

Dear Sir,

I thank you with all sincerity for your letter, dated 15th October relating the circumstances of my oldest son's death in action under your command. Truthfully, the blow has been heavily-felt by both of us, but I must say, the information of his meritorious death has in some measure been a comfort to our feelings.

I was glad he was popular with his fellow officers and men and apart from your letter, I have had others from his CO, Padre, and also from nine men of his platoon.

To all ranks of your esteemed battalion please accept our best wishes and heartfelt thanks for all the information. We will follow your wanderings and battles with the enemy with the utmost interest and pray that the end is not too far distant when you shall all return to normal.

May God be with you all.

Yours very sincerely,

A Lindsay

6 Niven Street,

Maryhill, Glasgow

25/11/44

Dear Sir,

Please accept my grateful thanks for your kind message of sympathy. It's a great relief to my mind to know that my poor son was not left long to suffer and also to know that he got reverent burial and is laid beside his fallen comrades.

In my great grief I feel proud that he was worthy of such high praise from you but I know Charlie would do his duty. If anything he and his fallen comrades did has been a help to those who are left to carry on, or if it was the means of saving other precious lives, they haven't died in vain. It was hard luck he was not spared to see the victory he was so sure of but God willed otherwise.

It was a terrible blow to his father and me. He was all I had to live for and he was one of the best and kindest, his only worry being away was that I would not be here when he came home. He was two months in Italy before I knew he was abroad . . . I know I will never get over his loss but I know too I'm only one in thousands.

I had a very nice letter from the Chaplain, Rev. Dow and a card of sympathy from the King and Queen. I think that was a great honour. No one could do more for me in my grief than give me their sympathy. It has helped me a lot and I'm very grateful to you and may God help and sustain you all in this terrible struggle and it will be my daily prayer that you don't lose any more brave men till it's finished.

I'm sorry if I've trespassed too much on your time. I know it's not all your own. I'll close now thanking you again for your message and wishing you and your men all the best of luck.

Yours gratefully,

Mrs Scullion

21 Boleyn Road,

London N16

9/11/44

To Major Ward,

Many, many thanks for your letter of 23/10/44. You have no idea what a relief it was to learn how my husband met his death. I was beginning to imagine so many terrible things. I shall always be thankful to both you and the Padre for the lovely letters that you wrote. They are letters I will always keep and be proud of.

I suppose it is quite natural for every wife to think that her husband is the most wonderful man in the world, and I was no exception, but it is quite another thing to learn how much his Major and comrades thought about him and I feel terribly honoured and proud. You'll never know how much your letter means to me and also to my husband's family, and how it helped us to know that he died bravely and without suffering. Once again I thank you from the bottom of my heart.

Good luck to all of you fighting out there and may God bless you and keep you safely and give you the courage and strength to finish this awful war very soon.

Yours sincerely,

Doris Barrett

126 Rhymer Street,

Glasgow

7/11/44

Dear Sir,

I'm writing to thank you for the letter you sent me concerning Patrick Monaghan 14401085. Your letter in a measure did help and comfort me a little as I had all sorts of thoughts about his death. To know that he was well liked and brave gave me consolation. He was so young to die as I can remember him still at school when war was declared and never dreamt that he would be in it.

My Mother and Father died when I was seventeen and I was left with seven: three brothers and four sisters. Patrick was the youngest and through all the years we have been a happy family. I don't know why I am telling you this but I want you to know that Patrick was a good boy.

After his brothers joined up and he was of age he followed in the footsteps of his brother William who was in the A & S H and is now a prisoner of war. Patrick joined the A & S H and was so proud of his regiment. I know he wasn't afraid and I'm glad he died as he would have liked, with his boots on, those boots he was always so proud of and was always polishing.

I remember all these things and how he always wore his cap when home on leave. From the first thing in the morning till last thing at night he wore his A & S H bonnet and nothing would persuade him to leave it off. We all miss him and these little things I'm telling you show how much he loved the Army and give us some comfort.

I don't expect an answer as you will be too busy but I just want to say that I hope you have every success in all your engagements and avenge the loss of my brother Patrick and his comrades.

Thanking you once again.

I remain yours sincerely,

Mrs J Booth

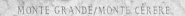

MONTE GRANDE/MONTE CERERE

ON THESE MOUNTAINS DURING THE ITALIAN CAMPAIGN, ON
DECEMBER 12, 1944 THE TROOPS OF:

1ST BN. THE ARGYLL AND SUTHERLAND HIGHLANDERS

3RD BN. THE 8TH PUNJAB RGT.

6TH ROYAL BN. (SCINDE) FRONTIER FORCE RIFLES

OF THE 8TH INDIAN INFANTRY DIVISION

REPULSED SEVERAL DETERMINED ATTACKS BY THE
GERMAN 1ST PARACHUTE DIVISION
AND DESPITE HEAVY CASUALTIES
THE GROUND WAS HELD.

SHABASH

IN ONORE DEI COMBATTENTI ALLEATI
INSIEME AI SOLDATI E PATRIOTI ITALIANI
NELLA LOTTA DI LIBERAZIONE.

The battlefield memorial, Monte Cerere, October 2004

13 THE GOTHIC LINE

BATTALION ROUTINE ORDERS

by Lieutenant-Colonel F. C. C. Graham commanding, 1st. Battalion
The Argyll and Sutherland Highlanders (Princess Louise's)
C. M. F. 16 October 1944

737. Order of the Day—by Lieutenant-Colonel F. C. C. Graham.

The Battalion has recently completed a period of campaigning rendered extremely unpleasant by the continuous presence of the enemy and the almost continuous failure of the weather. This period culminated in the attack of A and B Coys against two very strong enemy positions. These attacks were pressed home with the greatest gallantry and all the objectives were captured. These actions will go down in the History of the Regiment as two of the most glorious episodes. Unfortunately the heavy losses sustained rendered it necessary to amalgamate A and B Coys and B Coy temporarily loses its identity. The amalgamated Coys will be known as A/B Coy. This is no reflection on a very gallant Company but is occasioned purely by necessity.

We have every reason to be proud of the last ten days' work. Training will continue with a view to further conquests.

738. Day Leave to FLORENCE.

The Battalion has been allotted 78 Day Leave Passes to Florence.

Leave will commence tomorrow, 17 October 1944.

1. Curfew Hours: (a) Civilians and Other Ranks 2200 hours to 0600 hours (b) Officers 2300 hours to 0600 hours.

The above Curfew Hours does not apply to Day Leave personnel who will be clear of Florence by 1900 hours.

2. Dress: Other Ranks: Battle Dress (done up at the collar), Balmorals and Gaiters. If in possession of Collar and Tie they may be worn.

Officers: Battle Dress with Black Shoes, or Kilt and Battle Dress Blouse, or Trews and S. D. Tunic. Scarves will NOT be worn. Glengarry may be worn.

3. Entertainment & Amenities: See Appendix B to this Order.

4. New type special Day Leave Passes will be issued with this order and will be used at all times by personnel proceeding to Florence on Day Leave.

[Signed] G. H. S. Rome, Captain.

Adjutant,

1st. Battalion, The Argyll and Sutherland Highlanders

AFTER THE BATTLE OF MONTE CAVALLARA, I took command of A/B Company, with Captain Graham Wood of B Company as my second-in-command. Wood had trained at the OCTU at Dunbar shortly before I was there and had been overseas since 1940. He was a junior intelligence officer at GHQ Cairo before joining the battalion in the Western Desert. He had landed on Sicily and served throughout the Italian campaign.

The battalion tramped back to Botteghette on the night of 13/14 October. On the 15th, we marched into Marradi, then waited for transport to take us out of the line. The town's narrow streets and tight piazzas were lively enough with troops and trucks, but it was a dismal place to hang around. People had taken to the hills to join the partisans after the Germans tried to press gang them as forced labour. Marradi's main industry had been a silk factory, now in ruins after an American air raid earlier in the year. The factory was a legitimate target, as the silk thread was spun for parachutes. The railway had been hit and bridges blown. Apparently, when winter set in, Indian soldiers billeted in the derelict factory and the manager's villa burned the office paperwork and the furniture to keep warm.

We returned to Cistio for nine days of rest, leave and training. The mobile bath unit was a godsend as normal standards of cleanliness and hygiene were impossible to maintain in the mountains, where rules about washing and shaving had been relaxed. Stress and exhaustion washed away as I stood naked in the open-air shower. Then there was the bliss of crisp, fresh clothing, and feeling clean and civilised after weeks in mud-stained battledress. An ENSA tour, led by the Hollywood film actor Brian Aherne, entertained us. His anecdotes about playing alongside Marlene Dietrich and other stars were a great hit in our makeshift mess. Halfway through the show, Aherne and his troupe were thrilled to bits when they heard the sound of artillery in the distance. Something to talk about, no doubt, when they got back home.

Day trips to Florence were organised. The 'liberty' truck drivers amused themselves by competing to clock up the fastest trip. We had an early start and we got there in record time.

Florence had taken on a new lease of life after the Germans left. Apart from the destruction of the Arno bridges, the city had been spared the worst of the war. The Uffizi Gallery was closed because of blast damage when the bridges were blown, but the Duomo and Baptistry were open. Statuary outside the Palazzo Vecchio had shed its protective covers. Cafés, shops and street stalls were open. I bought postcards and a Uffizi catalogue from a book barrow in an arcaded piazza. I was amazed by the normality of it all—despite the presence of soldiers of many races and uniforms. Headdress of every description bobbed to and fro: American forage caps, New Zealand bush hats, brass hats, tin hats, Sikh turbans, glengarries and balmorals. As proud Argylls we wore our kilts, and strutted through this pageant adopting a disdainful air towards any mere gunners, sappers, signallers or Yanks. Military vehicles of all kinds rumbled along the Renaissance streets or were parked in the piazzas. Florence was a through route to the mountains. Army road signs—STAR ROUTE, SWORD ROUTE, ARROW ROUTE, ALL TRAFFIC THIS WAY—were everywhere.

The Florentines were still suffering food shortages and there was evidently poverty and hardship. Musicians stood at street corners playing flutes or violins; ragged children—tiny figures lost in the wartime life of the city—hung around cafés begging for food. We lucky conquerors had a slap-up lunch at a Forces club in a commandeered palazzo, whose frescoed salons had become an army canteen. Then Shaw and I engaged a fiacre to take us across the Bailey bridge, up to Piazzale Michelangelo. Rubble around Ponte Vecchio was still being cleared, but the city skyline looked as it did in pre-war postcards I had bought. On the piazzale, dozens of Allied soldiers strolled around or had their photographs taken. Our driver stood smoking and chatting to colleagues. A few months earlier, they had no doubt taken German officers up to view the same beauty spot.

Back at base the next day, I had to preside at a Court of Inquiry, after an accident while grenades were being primed on a training exercise. Through carelessness or incompetence by the NCO in charge, one of the grenades went off, killing one man and wounding two others. I also had to hold Company Office, one of those out-of-the-line chores which I disliked, held usually in some dim farmhouse, lit by oil lamps. Some soldiers who when in action were courageous and reliable managed to fall foul of authority whenever relieved of the obligatory, life-saving discipline of the battlefield. Cases of Conduct Unbecoming, AWOL, or minor breaches of army etiquette or regulations were common. I held the men with a light rein when battles were being fought. But I knew when to draw it tightly.

'How many have we got?' I would ask CSM Stewart.

He would brief me on each case, march the offender in and then stand to attention beside the farm kitchen table at which I sat. At times, I rather enjoyed the theatricality of it all. On one occasion, three Jocks, back from a day trip to Florence where they had been arrested, fighting drunk, appeared before me. Because they were a good-natured trio, and because I remembered I had been involved in similar misbehaviour at

Taranto, I had some sympathy for them. Nobody had been hurt in the affray, a street fight with a bunch of Yanks. I asked them who won.

'We did, sir.'

'Save it for Jerry,' I said, and dismissed them.

The CSM marched in the next offender, a wee Jock up on a charge of having a dirty rifle and of insolence to a superior officer.

Suddenly a dishevelled figure rushed in, brushed aside the sergeant-major and the Jock, and stood before me in a very agitated state. This was one of my rookie platoon commanders. He had got drunk while in charge of a day leave trip to Florence, failed to turn up at the agreed rendezvous, missed the truck bringing the men back and was still absent by breakfast time.

'Reporting back, sir. Got lost. Most terribly sorry about this. Let you down. Came to report as soon . . .'

'Get out,' I roared. 'What the bloody hell do you mean by bursting in here while I'm holding Company Office? You look like a tramp. Get out and clean yourself up. I'll hear your explanation later.'

'Sorry, sir,' he groaned, hopping from one foot to another.

He retreated apace, then pulled himself together to essay a swinging salute, then turned and fled. Just then I noticed a sly smirk on the face of the wee Jock who was waiting to be sentenced and doubled the punishment I had intended awarding him.

The errant platoon commander had just been posted to the battalion from another unit and had already fallen foul of me. He caused trouble by compensating for his insecurity with a hectoring manner that antagonised his sergeant and NCOs. He was all for training exercises and inspections, but his men were at the stage of not being able to care less about the war. His openly admitted ambition was to kill Germans and it was no secret that he coveted medal ribbons and even wound stripes. He was a square peg in a round hole. If one could have been found, his men would gladly have thrown him into it.

The maverick subaltern's men called him, among other less com-plimentary and more obscene names, Holy Willie, because of a book he read constantly which they mistook for a Bible, but which was actu-ally a manual of infantry tactics. I had been keen once, but I found the new man's enthusiasm tiresome and pathetic. I told him to go easy on his platoon, especially after his sergeant had complained about being bawled out in front of the men. I told him that his sergeant was a good soldier and could help him; that he should show a proper respect for his NCOs; that his men had had a rough time, and even if they didn't seem keen they would do their duty if they were treated fairly. That had been my experience, but I wasn't sure this youngster was willing to accept advice. I asked Graham to take the him off my hands. D Company was short of a junior officer. The CO said I'd have to make out an official report. I didn't want to damn the man completely, so he stayed.

On 25 October, the battalion went back into the mountains, as 19 Brigade's reserve on Sword Route. We were based at Popolano, the tum-bledown village on the banks of the Lamone river, just north of Marradi where Major Taylor of the 14th Canadian had said the ground was unfavourable for his tanks. If anything, it was now worse. And our quar-ters were far from luxurious, but they were infinitely more comfortable than slit trenches in the open. That respite was a brief one. A/B Company was ordered forward to secure an undamaged railway bridge near San Cassiano, another miserable, soaking hamlet, eight kilometres down the valley, and to plug a gap in the front line between the 6/13th and 1/12th Frontier Force battalions.

Two days later, we were ordered to relieve the 1/5th Mahrattas and 3/15th Punjabis in the hills to the west. Enemy shelling was infrequent and patrol activity non-existent. Not so the rain, which persisted for days on end. Jeeps and carriers slithered and spun up to a dead end four kilometres off the main road, where we found RSM McGuigan waiting with sepoys and 100 mules. We transferred and trudged up to relieve the Indians. Mules were indispensable in the mountains, but although we appreciated their value to us neither the animals nor their handlers got much sympathy: we were no better off ourselves, being but beasts of burden like them at times. One night, I recall a man losing control of his mule, and the animal slipping and disappearing into a ravine with its load, accompanied by the noise of tumbling Jerrycans. Suddenly, we were lit up by the searching brilliance of two flares, followed by a shower of abuse on the unfortunate handler's head. Then silence, except for the rain.

On Hallowe'en, we shivered in our eyries, drenched by a 10-hour downpour in bitterly cold winds. In the first week of November, it snowed. Freezing cold nights in the open in slit trenches and dugouts made for conditions which, I imagine, Scott of the Antarctic would have been familiar with. Fortunately, there was at least one substantial farmhouse in each company area. The men, in small groups at a time, spent a night under cover to dry out and get a comfortable sleep before returning to their troglodyte existence. Wood and Padre Dow worked wonders in preparing roaring fires and Scotch broth and tea by the gallon for the men, who came in exhausted, caked in mud and soaking wet. Our only benefit was that we qualified for a 'high altitude ration', which gave us extra tea, sugar, milk and chocolate, and a daily issue of rum that became not a luxury but a necessity.

The Allies' autumn offensive in the Apennines had met with limited success. The Germans resisted for a time, then it became clear that they were following an all too familiar pattern. Positions would be captured at great cost, then the enemy would withdraw to more prepared defences, and the same tactics would have to be repeated all over again across the ravines and ridges that obstructed our advance. When the weather worsened, everything stuttered to a halt, like the First World War. The landscape was different from Flanders but in that Italian winter of 1944, more casualties were caused by trench foot than by enemy action.

I worried about some of the new men we had been sent. Few of them had any infantry training or frontline experience. Some were teenagers straight off the boat. Others were ack-ack gunners, artillery chaps and older rear-echelon men. Such transfers were a commonplace towards the end of the Italian campaign, as the Allies were short of infantry. These recruits, no matter how keen—and not all were—were potential liabilities. Often, they turned up at night, just as we were about to go on patrol, and had to be assigned to platoons without us even knowing their names.

Not all of them adapted. I recall a new CSM whose army life had been led in the sheltered cosiness of the peace-time band, followed by spells in the battalion orderly room and the quartermaster's stores. He was mild-mannered and deferential with little presence and less authority. I found I had to do his job for him in training and drill. He cultivated a waxed moustache, in the classic image of the rank, but was NBG as a sergeant major. Another man, a novice platoon commander, arrived as my company was about to start a particularly dangerous mountain sortie. He was in his mid-30s, an old man to the rest of us, and physically unfit. He'd been transferred from some rear-echelon unit and had no infantry training: a lame duck. He protested that he wasn't even used to marching—never mind the rigours of an infantryman's life in the mountains. He was completely useless to me and a hazard to the men he was supposed to lead. Securing a hilltop position, we were barely halfway up when I saw the wretched man on the point of collapse. Sanders, who wasn't too happy about our present assignment, grudgingly relieved him of his pack while I carried his rifle. We eventually got him up the hill where his platoon stood watching and waiting in silence. The next morning I found him lying shivering in his bivvie well after Reveille. Three times, I ordered him to get up. He refused.

'Sanders,' I said, 'I'm going to piss on this man if he doesn't move. NOW!'

The man heard me and he still didn't get up—so I unbuttoned and carried out my threat. Sanders walked away shaking his head. I spoke to the CO and had the bugger RTU'd. I came across him sometime later at a transit camp. With memories of the subsequent heroic endeavours of the men he had failed, I blasted him with a volley of abuse, recrimination and contempt. I'd had a drink or two and felt a bit ashamed of my outburst afterwards. What became of him I don't know. At the time I didn't care.

In mid-November we were relieved by the 6/13th. There followed another brief respite in Popolano (where, on the 18th, Sanders, bless him, produced a bottle of whisky for my 28th birthday). Then we took over from the Punjabis in the mountains to the east of San Cassiano and in San Cassiano itself. It was thought that San Cassiano was now unoccupied, but when A/B Company probed the road towards it we were shot at from the far side of a blown bridge on the edge of the village. We dived into the ditches by the side of the road, none of us particularly keen on a direct assault. Since there was no urgency to clear the place, I got the mortar platoon on the wireless, gave them the co-ordinates and asked them to lob some bombs over. The small-arms fire soon stopped. The main threat now came from mines and booby traps. I remember picking my way along a taped track supposedly cleared, when one of the men in front of me trod on a Schu mine that blew his foot off. D Company in the hills lost three men in one day, all to landmines.

I sent patrols to check our flanks in the wooded hills that sloped down on our left and on the flat land across the river on our right. Partisans had told us that Jerry had some SP guns in the village, although we hadn't seen them or been shelled. That night, I was woken by engines and gears crashing. A German voice gave orders. Some minutes later, I heard grenade explosions, the crakle of small-arms fire and angry shouts, then silence. The next morning a deserter, a Russian in Nazi service, came through our lines and indicated that Jerry had pulled back further down the valley after being ambushed by the partisans.

We walked in single file into the village, weapons at the ready, eyes peeled for snipers as we stepped over rubble and broken roof tiles. There were no shots. Most of San Cassiano's buildings—200 metres of abutting, dun-coloured houses on both sides of the road—were in a bit of a mess as a result of shellfire. The Germans had also been thorough in their demolitions and looting. I did a bit of looting myself. To the victor the spoils. A villa outside the village was almost completely ransacked. I checked for booby traps. None. Scarcely a stick of furniture was left—chopped up for firewood I expect, including a piano. Anything of value had been spirited away. Other contents were scattered about all over the place. Among them I found some opera scores which I felt no compunction about taking. I imagine the owner was conductor of the local choir and operatic society. His precious scores could have come to a worse end and fallen into worse hands than mine. Reading and playing from these brought me great pleasure for years after the war—and the memory of the anonymous choirmaster and the ruins of San Cassiano.

A/B Company stayed in the village while the rest of the battalion occupied hilltop positions on a two-kilometre front directly east. To the north, the Lamone river gushed though a landscape that relented towards Faenza. The valley broadened and became more cultivated; the flanking mountains softened to foothills that dissolved somewhere in the distance into the vast Po plain. For a short time, the weather improved and there was so little activity that the CO organised a pheasant-shooting party with some Italians, who turned out to be alarmingly trigger-happy. When he got back, he said the hunt had been 'a more dangerous sport than chasing the Boche'.

Captains Ward and Shaw in Rome, July 1944

◁ Previous page: The Two Types; Eighth Army cartoon characters by W. J. P. Jones.
△ The CO, 8th Indian Division, Major-General 'Pasha' Russell (in shorts), and C-in-C
General Alexander (left), Italy 1944. ▽ Canadian Sherman tanks and traditional
transport, Sicily, July 1943.

△ 'I even remember their names: Michele, Alfredo and Salvatore. They approached us cautiously like sparrows, snatched food from our hands and scampered away.' Children of Sicily, August 1943. ▽ 8th Indian infantry street fighting, Lugo, Italy, April 1945.

'Siena had come through the war with little damage. Its medieval streets and piazzas were packed with Sienese chattering like starlings, as they celebrated their freedom.'
Via di Città, Siena, 3 July 1944.

△ Siena's Palazzo Pubblico seen from the Cathedral Museum, 2004. Siena looked much the same on 3 July 1944, when the campanile's bells chimed and the citizens welcomed their liberators, the Free French. ▽ *'The Arno bridges, all destroyed except for Ponte Vecchio.'* Aerial view of Ponte Vecchio, Florence, August 1944.

△ The Jocks liberate Ferrara after crossing the Po di Volano ◁ (Ray Ward, hand on hip, far right) 23 April 1945. ▷ Ward, Shaw, and MacDougall, Costa di Rovigo, 11 May 1945.

The 1st Argylls' Pipes and Drums, Pisa, 25 January 1945

△ 1st Argylls, Lucca, 3 January 1945. Front row: Lieutenant-Colonel Graham (centre), Majors Ward (fourth right), Wood, Kelway-Bamber, MacFie (third, fourth, fifth left), Capt. Rome (fifth right). Middle row: Captains Scott-Barrett, Hamilton, Candlish (second, fifth, sixth right). Back row: Lts. Holyoake, Christopher (third right, right).

▽ 1st Argylls and 6/13th Frontier Force Rifles, Foligno, June 1945 (Lt-Col Graham, seated, second row, fourth left).

I had my own brush with local characters in the woods around that time. Sanders and I had been out on a recce in the company Jeep and had taken a short-cut, not sure if we were still in friendly country. I rounded a bend and skidded into a barricade of rocks and trees. Four fierce-looking men, all bearded and clad in nondescript uniforms, jumped out from the trees. Each carried a wild assortment of knives, pistols, bayonets and grenades, and wore bandoliers slung over their shoulders. Each had a rifle or submachine-gun in his hands. To my surprise, they were accompanied by a dazzlingly attractive young woman, wielding a Sten-gun. All seemed eager and ready to fire at the slightest provocation. A villanous-looking ruffian sprang forward and dug me in the ribs with the muzzle of his gun. With a jerk of his head he motioned me to get out. 'Scozzese,' I shouted, pointing to my uniform. Another partisan came forward and saluted me with a smile.

As in France, the resistance groups gave a boost to national self-esteem. As the war worsened for the Germans, and despite brutal reprisals by the Waffen SS and other units, increasing numbers of Italians found the courage to join the partisans—communists, nationalists, malcontents, romantics, students, peasants, soldiers and factory workers (and some Allied PoWs on the run). Encounters with these motley bands of guerrilla fighters became a feature of the campaign in the mountains and later in the towns and villages on the Po valley.

At the end of the month we got a warning order to assist the 6th Armoured Division in the Santerno river valley. As usual, the company commanders took a couple of Jeeps and set out for a recce. We drove to Castel del Rio, where we crossed a gorge spanned by what must have been the highest and most spectacular Bailey bridge in Italy. That was as nerve-racking as the drive had been: 20 kilometres as the crow flies, but for us a bone-rattling 40 kilometres over an atrocious mountain road that twisted and climbed into the cloud base. In places, the road had been washed away. We passed groups of sappers at work, shoring up the verges with logs. A traffic jam blocked the approach to the 6th Armoured's positions and we were forced to halt behind a line of vehicles drawn up at the roadside.

'What's up?' I asked a soldier who was sitting on the running board of his truck.

The answer came in the form of a Jerry stonk that burst abruptly up ahead.

'Come on, we only die once,' I shouted to Sanders, and signalled to the other Jeep, and we sped derisively past the stuck trucks before the next stonk landed. When we got to the 6th Armoured HQ, we were told that things were under control. Exasperated, we drove back, to find that the orders had been cancelled. Battalion HQ then received another urgent summons. This one was not a false alarm.

We were sent to reinforce the 1st British Infantry Division's 2nd Brigade in the mountains east of Route 65, the main Florence to Bologna highway, where the 1st Division was holding a vital part of the Gothic Line against German paratroops. This was Kesselring's last line of defence in the mountains. The Fifth Army's US 2nd Corps (85th, 88th and 91st divisions), which had broken through Il Giorgo and Futa passes in September, had been stopped in this sector by the enemy and the weather. After liberating Marradi, the 1st Division had relieved the US 88th early in October. General Clark, the Fifth Army commander had issued a frank assessment of the situation:

Throughout the war the Germans have fought with unvarying determination, and have employed every means at their disposal to defeat us. They now know that the Allies will accept nothing but unconditional surrender with its consequent disastrous effect on the Nazi military machine, prestige and aspirations. Therefore, we may assume that from now on the German army and the German people will fight with the ferocity of an animal at bay which knows that it has no alternative but to stand and slug it out. We of the Fifth Army have encountered this form of fanatical resistance during out recent break through of the Apennine position.

There was no recce this time: we upped sticks immediately. After yet another hellish drive to Castel del Rio, and a hazardous ascent on the evening of 3 December—on foot after the Jeeps bogged down—we approached Frassineto, a hilltop hamlet 20 kilometres south-east of Bologna.

The battalion took over from the 6th Gordon Highlanders on a two-kilometre-long mountain. There were two summits linked by a ridge, Monte Grande furthest west and Monte Cerere. Directly to the east of and slightly below Monte Cerere was Frassineto, where we were based. We were joined on the 6th by our old friends, the 3/8th Punjab Regiment and 6/13th Frontier Force Rifles, who took over positions on Monte Grande and Monte Cerere respectively. The Punjabis found several American tanks and SPs stranded on Monte Grande, manned, in a static role, by crews from the Canadian 11th Armoured Regiment. Our Canadians of the 14th Armoured stayed at Marradi. The terrain, weather and blown bridges prevented their tanks being moved either forwards or sideways. They would certainly have had difficulty on Monte Cerere.

The three-kilometre climb from the jeep-head to Frassineto took five hours. The steep and winding tracks were slushy and knee deep in mud in places; the land littered with shell craters and limbless trees. Intermittent explosions boomed and echoed across the valleys as we approached the hamlet, which was wrapped in a veil of fog. When it lifted the next day, we saw a valley to the north and a final roll of hills occupied by the Germans barring the way to Bologna. If the weather had been clearer we might have seen the domes and towers of the city, or the Alps across the Po plain. Behind us in the San Clemente valley, 1st Division's HQ and base area was crowded with camps, supply dumps, maintenance depots and vehicles. The front was thinly manned because of the scarcity of reinforcements, and vulnerable to counter-attack. A retreat from San Clemente would be a serious setback. Facing us was the 3rd Battalion, 1st Parachute Regiment—the para boys of the 1st Parachute Division. We knew them well. We were about to get to know them better.

Frassineto was a group of houses and farm buildings at the end of a north-east facing spur, in full view of the German positions. It stuck out like a sore thumb. And like any sore thumb, it attracted more than its fair share of hard knocks. These came from artillery shells, machine-gun bullets and mortar bombs. Worst of all was the fire from an 88. This gun damaged most of the buildings we occupied. The ever-methodical Sanders calculated that our position attracted around 150 mortar bombs and thirty shells each day. The spur was open on both flanks and dangerously exposed at the front. This made movement impossible in daylight. The only safe place to be was in the cellars.

The battalion's precarious position was no more than 500 metres square. I was in command of A/B Company at Frassineto, on the end of the sore thumb. C Company (Major Oxborrow) and forward HQ were in dugouts and slit trenches on the knuckle; D Company (Major C. G. Kelway-Bamber and Shaw) was at the wrist, at Casa Nuova, a farm on a rise below Monte Cerere. Despite the proximity of our posi-tions, the lie of the land and Jerry observation meant we could reach each other only by dangerous or circuitous routes along steep, slippy tracks. My men in the forward positions were constantly on edge, always on the alert for enemy patrols. The enemy-held road below our posi-tions was 'tankable' and had to be watched by two A/T crews. To add to the discomfort, the slits filled with mud and water, which froze at night. In the open, with only one blanket per man, conditions were sheer hell. I recall getting on the wireless to Battalion HQ to complain, contrasting our sorry state with the relative comfort at HQ behind the lines, where I knew there were blankets galore. More came up on the next mule train.

A/B Company HQ was in the substantial cellar of a shell-battered farmhouse where I spent most of the daylight hours in a constant fug of cigarette smoke, fumes from the fire and oil lamps and cooking. There I had time to catch up on lost sleep, broken by bursts of shellfire, and somehow managed to do some reading and letter-writing. The men occupied themselves cleaning their weapons, drying their blankets and dreaming of home.

While we were there, the CO passed on news that A Company's awards for the Battle of Monte Cavallara had come through. I was awarded the Military Cross (Immediate Award), as was B Company's Lieutenant Smith; Wood also got an MC (Periodic Award). I had put forward Sergeant Taylor for a Distinguished Service Medal, and Sergeant McKeown, corporals MacLaren and Callaghan and privates Alexander and Goodfellow for Military Medals. All were granted. I should have put Sanders up for an MM. Throughout the ordeal he had operated the wireless while under fire, and his cheerful presence raised the spirits of the men. But he was my batman and I thought I'd be guilty of favouritism. Anyway, Cavallara now seemed to have happened a long time ago.

The Wee Brig came up one day and declared that we had to dig in—as if we didn't know that by now . . . said he wanted more wire and trenches. Just what we needed. It was raining all day. Fewer Jerry stonks, though, all of which the Brig missed. One of my company's slit trenches received a direct hit, killing two Jocks and wounding another. Then a Jerry deserter walked in, a para, a cheeky blighter. He wouldn't talk, except to say that when we were captured we didn't say much, so why should he. Somebody should have shot him.

Each evening, I would button up my leather jerkin and prepare for my nightly round. The round was necessary because Jerry shelling disrupted field telephone lines and our radios were unreliable. It was also vital for morale that the men see their company commander out in the forward positions. I'd find them huddled in their slit trenches, gripping their rifles with numb fingers, gazing out, alert for enemy patrols. I'd give them a few words of encouragement or share a sardonic comment and move on. It was always a chancy business. There were many incidents in the mist—men shot by scared sentries, or taken prisoner when their positions were overrun. I recall watching a line of PoWs being marched along a mountain track on the other side of the valley, too far away for me to intervene. One night, an enemy patrol clashed with a D Company post and was repelled with grenades, which wounded one of the Jerries who lay moaning out of sight. He was dragged in but died before he could be interrogated. Shaw sent out a patrol but it was spotted, after a jumpy Jock fired his tommy gun, giving the position away. Jerry charged and one of D Company's men was killed and three taken prisoner in the ensuing scrap. The patrol leader managed to get away. Later, another of my men was killed and two wounded by Jerry mortars.

A Company spent a week out on the sore thumb. That was considered enough for any company and we were mighty pleased when our turn came to be relieved. When C Company marched up we were too tired even for banter. We were a sorry-looking lot when we came off that dreaded spur, bleary-eyed, muddy, unshaven and unwashed. We moved only a couple of hundred metres, to forward HQ on the knuckle below Casa Nuova. At least it was in a relatively safe spot, even though it was exposed and we only had dugouts for shelter. We barely had time to settle in.

0700. 12 December 1944.

We were shaken by a German attack. It came out of the blue, at dawn, through a thick mist. The whole of the brigade's front line was shelled.

At that moment, I was in my dugout, stark naked and enjoying the luxury of a thorough wash, the first for weeks. Machine-gun bullets whistled about. Mortars thudded. Shouts, and MG and small-arms fire were coming from Casa Nuova. I scrambled into my clothes. I couldn't see a thing in the smoke and mist but I shouted to the signaller to get Battalion HQ on the wireless. I still remember how simple sounds were curiously magnified in the throbbing air: the crackle of the wireless; the scrape of the match a sergeant struck to light a cigarette to calm his nerves; the rattle of stones dislodged from a dugout; the sporadic shouts in the mist. We were in a tight corner.

D Company's forward platoon had been overrun, with some men killed and others captured. Casa Nuova was being attacked. So was Frassineto. Jerry attacks on the Indians' positions were successful, initially. The 6/13th's forward platoon was forced back from the flanks of Monte Cerere. Another Jerry foray was directed to the tip of the Frassineto thumb, where paras rushed uphill through a smoke-screen, but were driven back by C Company's Bren and mortar fire. D Company's forward HQ at Casa Nuova was overrun. Lieutenant Alan Reid and Sergeant Reid led a rearguard action, killing several Jerries. Subsequently, they were awarded an MC and MM respectively for their courage. But the farmhouse, visible against the sky through the drifting mist and the smoke of shell bursts, was captured.

My weary men realised the danger and, like the good soldiers they were, they buckled to and prepared themselves for whatever might be in store. For all we knew as we peered out into the void, we ourselves might be rushed by the para boys. That didn't happen, but we came under steady fire from Casa Nuova. I shouted orders to organise a sound defensive position, putting on a show of calm confidence, as did my platoon commanders and the NCOs. Even my crackpot subaltern put up a good show. He began to earn my respect and that of his men, by showing an admirable coolness under fire and organising his platoon efficiently. In fact he was in his element, under fire for the first time. He was so eager to get to grips with Jerry that he kept urging me to let him rush the Germans with his platoon. I couldn't allow that, as we had been ordered to hold our ground. In any case his Jocks would probably have mutinied had he tried.

We gained some relief when one of the 6/13th machine-gunners, Havildar Tara Sing, kept the enemy pinned down at Casa Nuova. The 6/13th counter-attacked and broke the enemy's grip on Monte Cerere. The para boys at Casa Nuova, who ran up to stem the retreat, were caught in the open by Tara Sing, firing at point-blank range. By mid-morning, dead and wounded Germans lay all over the place. Their commander, according to a radio intercept, reported that if he wasn't reinforced he'd have to withdraw.

Encouraged by this and the courage of the 6/13th, Freddie Graham ordered D Company's reserve platoon to counter-attack. This order only got through because Shaw's signaller, Corporal Laing, had repaired field telephone lines while under fire. Every mortar in the battalion then plastered the enemy positions for over half an hour. D Company's men leaped from cover and dashed across a stretch of open ground to recapture Casa Nuova. We gave covering Bren fire, and a blast from a Piat anti-tank gun. I still remember following the flight of the hurtling bomb as it flew straight through a window of the farmhouse and burst with a shattering explosion inside. This had a great effect, causing the Germans to panic. They were on the point of withdrawing when the D Company platoon rushed them. The platoon took three prisoners. Five dead Jerries were found at Casa Nuova, killed by our Piat bomb.

Also found at Casa Nuova was D Company's Lance Corporal

McDade, whose eardrums were still ringing from the blast. When the paras had burst in, he and a Middlesex Regiment mortar observer had scrambled under the floorboards, where they hid for the rest of the morning. Later, the mortar observer's officer reappeared, having been taken prisoner, and escaped by pushing his escort over a cliff. Further down the hill, more men emerged from their original positions. They had been cut off by the initial attack, stayed put and took pot shots at any Jerry that came their way. The only casualty suffered by A/B company was Private McKnight, who had the skin torn off the tip of his nose by a stray bullet. I can still hear him yelling blue murder with the pain of it. The image that stays with me, however, is of Red Cross flags and stretcher-bearers from both sides picking their way over the hillside looking for the wounded. The truce didn't last long.

The following morning, Jerry lobbed some smoke bombs into Frassineto as we stood-to. We replied with mortars and small-arms fired into the mist. But no attack came. We were kept on edge over the next few days by the unwelcome attention of a high velocity gun, fired from a very long range, possibly a railway gun in the Po valley. We were used to artillery shells wizzing in and crashing, and mortars arcing up and over with a lazy whoosh, taking their time to find and kill you. But that big gun was frightening. Its shells came in like an express train, hitting the ground with a stunning blast followed by a fierce gust of air, scattering shrapnel, stones and mud across 100 metres. None of our OPs located it for our gunners or the air force. C Company captured a Jerry para, who had wandered into their position, completely drunk. He was given some rum and talked. He knew nothing about the high-velocity gun, even when shown the huge craters it made, but did reveal that his company had suffered twenty casualties.

On our last day at Frassineto, two Jocks were killed out of the blue, when that one-in-a-hundred chance hit demolished the house they were sheltering in. On 17 December, we were relieved by the 2nd Battalion,

The Sherwood Foresters. Coming down off that hill was the worst descent I ever experienced. Several men got stuck in mud up to their waists and had to be hauled out. As the last platoon blundered in the dark, the rain streaming off our faces, I heard the corporal yell at a Jock in front: 'Hey Jimmy. Where the fuck's the Bren?'

The Jock, who'd either lost the gun or left it behind, swivelled round, knee-deep in mud, bristling with anger and frustration.

'Where the fuck's the Bren? Fuck the fucking Bren, the fucking fucker's fucked!'

What a release of tension that was.

Given the ferocity of the battle, our casualties had been light: three men wounded; one officer and twenty-six other ranks missing, all from D Company, believed captured. The company was so depleted that it had to be augmented temporarily by a platoon from the 1st Battalion, the King's Shropshire Regiment. The much-feared Jerry paras, however, had been repulsed with heavy losses. Forty dead paras were picked up between the 6/13th's and D Company's positions; the Indians took ten prisoners; the retreating Germans carried many wounded away with them, only to be caught in mortar and shell-fire as they went. It was reckoned that the Battle of Monte Cerere cost the 1st Parachute Division some 200 casualties along 19 Brigade's front.

Subject: Congratulatory No. G/11/169

H.Q. 19 Ind. Inf. Bde. Field

14th Dec. 1944

[to] C.O. 1st A. & S. H., C.O. 8th Punjab, C.O. 6th R. F. F. R. O.C. C Company 5th R. Mahrattas, O.C. B Company 3rd Field Ambulance

Commander 8th Indian Division has sent a letter expressing his delight and that of the rest of the division in the successful defeat of the German attack on 12th December. He wishes to congratulate all ranks on seeing off some of the best German troops in Europe and inflicting very heavy casualties on them. Well done! Commander 13th Corps has also sent his congratulations to the brigade.

T. S. Dobree

Brigadier

Commanding 19th Ind. Inf. Bde.

The bravery of the 1st Argylls, the Frontier Force Rifles and the Punjabis, fighting side by side, had beaten off the best Jerry troops on the Continent. The enemy prisoners blamed lack of artillery support and reinforcements and the effects of our accurate counter-barrage, for their failure to exploit their initial success. I suspect also, that the men of the 1st Parachute Division were as tired of the war as we were. There had been desperation in their doomed assault.

On the 18th, the brigade arrived back in the Sieve valley, where we had four days' rest in the vicinity of Villa Frescobaldi. Day leave to Florence was organised. Pipe Major McGlinn composed a tune to commemorate the Battle of Monte Cerere. The COs of the Argylls and the Frontier Force Rifles exchanged a characteristic correspondence:

1st Batt. The Argyll and Sutherland Highlanders, C. M. F.

20th Dec. 1944

[to] Lieut.-Colonel G. Green, D.S.O., O.B.E.

Commanding the 6th (Royal) Battalion 13th F. F. Rifles

Dear Jimmy,

I ought to have written this before but you realise that, like you, we were all pretty tired and things were apt to be forgotten. My battalion are acutely conscious of what your battalion did for them on the 12th December. Alone we could not have done it, and the marvellous support we got on our left was typical of what we chaps expect from our old friends. I hope this is recorded in our regimental histories. I wish we could have had a really good party during this time of rest (?) but it will have to wait until our New Year Party at which I hope you will be present. Our thanks from all ranks of the 91st Highlanders.

    Yours,

    Freddie Graham

6th Royal Batt. (Scinde) 13th F. F. Rif. C. M. F.

22nd Dec. 1944

[to] Lieut.-Col. F. C. C. Graham

Officer Commanding, 1st Battalion, The Argyll & Sutherland Highlanders

Dear Freddie,

It was so good to get your letter. It's not us who should be congratulated by you, but the other way on. For if your chaps had not so gallantly counter-attacked and restored the situation on our right then indeed we would have been in a pretty pickle. But knowing that you were there we had no qualms. This battle has only made the two battalions feel even closer than they did before. I hope that our battalions are given to serve the rest of the war alongside each other. A merry Xmas and still more a Happy New Year to you all.

    Yours sincerely,

    Jimmy Green

We were not given much time to recover from the Battle of Monte Cerere. Our rest at Villa Frescobaldi was interrupted by move orders, cancellations and abortive recces of new positions. We were welcomed at one jeep-head, where we were to take over from the South Staffordshire Regiment, by a blistering mortar stonk. The South Staffs' CO had been pinned down in his forward HQ for a fortnight. The area, at Monte Calderaro, was under constant Jerry observation—another

Frassineto, even receiving attention from the same long-range gun. As Freddie Graham put it, 'We looked around at each other in grim despair while the mortar bombs thudded outside.'

Happily for us, a message from Brigade HQ came through: 'Recce parties Argylls rejoin battalion forthwith.' We skedaddled as fast as we dared, driving down to Castel del Rio and through a blizzard on the way back to Borgo San Lorenzo. The battalion was gone by the time we returned. Another order was waiting. It took us halfway across Italy, to reinforce another Fifth Army sector. We found the battalion at Lammari, a village four kilometres north-east of Lucca. The rest of 19 Brigade arrived in the area in dribs and drabs, and all units were settled in by Christmas Day. It was my fourth Christmas away from home. The weather improved with crisp, clear frosty air and the first sunny skies we had seen for weeks.

There was no war damage inside the medieval walls that encircle the little city of Lucca, the birthplace of Puccini. It had been occupied by the Germans but they withdrew before the Americans arrived on 5 September. We weren't there for a rest cure, though. On Christmas Day, we were put on three-hours' readiness. On Boxing Day we were ordered into the mountains again. Intelligence reports from partisans indicated that the Germans were about to launch an attack. The 8th Indian Division was moved 20 kilometres up the Serchio valley to bolster up the US 92nd Division, threatened by the Germans, and not expected (as proved to be the case) to put up much resistance to a determined attack. The move was made just in time.

The weather was fine, if bitterly cold. We thought we had seen the last of the cursed mountains. What we saw now was not promising—the snow-clad peaks of the Apuan Alps stretching away to the north, and west towards Carrara where the marble quarries Michelangelo knew glistened in the sun. After long spells of fighting the enemy in harsh conditions, my battle-weary Jocks didn't take kindly to this turn of events, especially as it meant coming to the aid of the Yanks. The 3/8th Punjabis led our advance up the valley; the 6/13th on the right; the Argylls on the left flank.

The 92nd Division's men were inexperienced, having only arrived in Italy in August, and were strung out on a 30-kilometre front near Barga. The 92nd was the only black American frontline division in Europe. Racial prejudice did not help its morale. Most of its senior officers were white, many from the former slave-owning southern states. The American military was still segregated, to an extent I neither experienced in the 8th Indian Division, nor in the Eighth Army. Nevertheless, the official British policy was to 'respect' the US regulations. Fortunately, this was not put to the test with us because our stay in the Sechio valley was short.

The fact that the 92nd was there at all showed how depleted the Allied armies in Italy had become. With the strategic priority focused on North-west Europe and the war against Japan, Italy was last in line for replacements. Those that were sent by this stage in the war had not been tested in combat. The Fifth Army even included a Brazilian unit and a Japanese-American one by this time.

At 0400 hours on 26 December, German artillery lit up the valley with a barrage, followed by an infantry attack through falling snow. Despite individual acts of courage, the 92nd was outfought. If its soldiers didn't exactly turn and run, they beat a hasty and disorderly retreat. We watched in amazement as men and vehicles came helter-skelter along the valley floor. There was nothing we could do to stop them. Even our own forward positions had to make a more orderly withdrawal to take up stronger positions further back, supported by divisional artillery and air strikes by American fighter-bombers. My own company didn't see any action and the battalion suffered no casualties. Luckily the Germans, faced with stiffer opposition, gave up their attack, which in any case had only limited objectives. US reinforcements were also quickly on the scene. The rout of the 92nd was hushed up at the time and remains a sensitive topic.

We enjoyed a peaceful interlude in the Lucca/Pisa area, a cushy sector. Major-General Russell had promised Graham that we would be back at Lucca in time for Hogmanay, and we were. On New Year's Day 1945, the whole battalion sat down to a slap-up feast with lashings of beer and extra rations that the QM, Dodger Brown, had released from his secret hoard. Russell and Dobree visited, Russell making a complimentary speech at dinner in the Officers' Mess. As part of the celebrations, the Pipes and Drums, in full regalia, paraded in Lucca. Kilted Highlanders were a more welcome sight than the Tedeschi and the Lucchese loved it. Some of them had close links with Scotland, with relatives living there. [Most of Glasgow's Italian café-owning families have roots in that part of Tuscany.] The band gave a splendid repeat performance at Pisa in the campo that lies in the shadow of the Leaning Tower.

I first saw the Leaning Tower from the Lucca road in the hills above the Arno. Pisa presented a different picture close-up, having been shelled heavily by both sides before being liberated by the Fifth Army in July 1944. Miraculously, the Duomo, Baptistry and Leaning Tower survived. The tower was almost destroyed by the US 91st Division, whose colonel assumed it was a Jerry OP, because his men had been accurately shelled. Two GIs were sent forward to recce the tower. Artillery, and a destroyer offshore, were ready to fire. But the heat haze distorted the view through field-glasses. The recce was inconclusive. The order to fire was not given.

Despite being out of the line, I was beginning to feel pretty low. Battle fatigue and general war weariness—the feeling that I was trapped in a horrible normality: that the killing would never stop. To add to my gloom, some long-serving officers, including Major Oxborrow and Tattie Shaw, were granted a month's leave by air to the UK. Dodger Brown and a draft of twenty-four men who been overseas for four and a half years left for Naples and a ship home. I spoke to Freddie Graham, who must have recognised the symptoms of my distress. He lent me a sympathetic ear and generously sent me off to Rome on a week's leave. I must have been in a state, because I remember little about it, except for an open-air theatre, where I saw a performance of *Aida*, complete with scores of extras, horses, camels and even elephants. But the break must have done me some good, for I came back refreshed and rejuvenated, if not exactly spoiling for a fight. Shaw returned, but not Oxborrow, who got a home posting.

Freddie Graham left by air for home leave on 5 February 1945. He rejoined the battalion at the end of the month, in time to lead it to victory. We knew a big push was coming, but few of us realised the massive might of the Allied war machine that would be thrown against the Germans, or that the part the Argylls would play in it would be a vital and terrifying ordeal.

14 THE BATTLE OF THE SENIO

The Eighth Army broke through the Gothic Line on a 25-kilometre front west of Pesaro at the start of September 1944. Rimini was captured on the 21st; Cesena fell on 21 October, Forlì on 9 November, Ravenna on 4 December and Faenza on 16 December. Route 67, on which the Argylls had trekked up to San Benedetto in Alpe, was opened to Forlì in November. These battles cost the army more casualties than the Battle of El Alamein. Lieutenant-General Leese had thought the flat Adriatic coast would suit his tanks and artillery but, as in the mountains, everything ground to a halt in the face of dogged German resistance and when the winter rains began. Leese was sacked and transferred to South-east Asia Command.

His replacement was Lieutenant-General Richard McCreery, commander of the Eighth Army's 10th Corps. A cavalry officer in the First World War, McCreery had served with Alexander since the Western Desert. His job now was to prepare for a spring offensive that would destroy the German armies in Italy. First, he had to revive the Eighth Army's self-esteem and purpose. The glow from Monty's charisma had long since dimmed. Leese had been unable to rekindle it and morale was low. The Allies were bogged down at the Senio river in the Po valley and in the hills above Bologna. It was obvious that there would be no clear run to the Alps until the spring.

McCreery reshuffled his divisions. The 8th Indian was sent by devious route via Florence and Perugia to the Adriatic coast to rejoin the Eighth Army. Mid-February 1945 saw the Argylls at Porto San Giorgio, 200 kilometres south of the front line. The 8th Indian was preparing to take over from the Canadians, who were about to be transferred to Monty in North-west Europe. Like any seaside resort in winter, San

Giorgio was a dismal place and the weather was nasty. We were not unhappy to move up to the Po valley and into the line at Russi, near Ravenna, to prepare for the big push. After passing Pesaro, we entered a zone of battlefield wreckage such as I had not seen since the Western Desert. The land was churned up and scattered with the hulks of burned-out Allied and German tanks. Abandoned gun emplacements and infantry trenches lay across waterlogged fields on either side of Route 9 between Ravenna and the Senio.

The Po valley was a complete contrast to the claustrophobic mountains where we had been for so long. Here was a plain of big skies and wide horizons, threaded with numerous irrigation canals and tributaries of the mighty Po. Cornfields, orchards, olive groves, vines and poplar plantations occupied an intensively cultivated yet austere landscape that was often hidden in morning fog. Stone farmhouses appeared every few hundred metres. The larger estates had barns and the landowner's house built around courtyards. These farm steadings, and tidy villages, provided comfortable billets at our various staging posts around Bagnacavallo, Lugo and Russi over the next month or so.

Russi was a compact country town, inward-looking like them all, focused on a piazza, a palazzo comunale and a church. Like the endless plain, it had thus far escaped the worst ravages of war. The country roads, however, in weather which varied from day to day, were either muddy or dusty and clogged with traffic. Many were single track and ran along the tops of dykes with few passing places. Even the arrow-straight Route 9 could not cope with the build-up of tanks, heavy vehicles and field guns.

There was a massive concentration of polyglot soldiery: British, Canadians, New Zealanders, Indians, Poles, a Jewish brigade from Palestine, units of the Italian army now on our side and various guerrilla bands. The battalion took over from the Royal 22nd Regiment at Russi on 28 February. The French-Canadian 'Vandoos' had fought across the Lamone river in December and advanced to the Senio, the foremost of the German Tenth Army's defensive positions on the Po plain. The Vandoos were in reserve, and left Russi for Livorno, and a ship to Marseilles. Like the Argylls, they had landed in Sicily in 1943. They had seen enough of sunny Italy and were not sorry to leave (the 14th Canadian Armoured Regiment, which was now on the Senio front, also left for France).

At the beginning of March, the battalion went into the front line three kilometres north of Borgo di Villanova, a string of houses below the north floodbank of the Lamone river. It was reckoned to be a quiet sector. Quiet, that is, except for a fusilade of rockets which fell in the A/B Company area with an unearthly, wailing roar—Nebelwerfer multi-barrelled mortars. The rockets landed six at a time, but they did little damage on the open ground and caused no casualties, that time. The fearful noise they made scared the daylights out of those who hadn't heard it before, but once the men realised that mere noise wouldn't harm them, they got used to the 'Moaning Minnies', as we called them. We were pulled out after a week and rested for a few days at Villanova. Then we tramped forward again, to relieve the 3/8th Punjabis in a position below the south bank of the Senio.

Like the Lamone, the Senio flowed north-east from the Apennines and entered the Adriatic north of Ravenna. Where it crossed the Po floodplain it was channelled along a dyked, man-made watercourse, more a canal than a river. These raised floodbanks blocked our view and progress. They were a formidable barrier. They stretched across the plain like railway embankments, with steep slopes on both sides, rising to the height of the farm buildings and three-storey villas we sheltered in. A pathway, five-metres wide, ran along the top of each bank. Between the banks was a 30-metre-wide gap, at the bottom of which was the river. Now that the rains had eased, the river was only few metres wide, a metre deep and flowed slowly. The banks, however, were honeycombed with enemy dugouts and machine-gun posts. Any incursion to the top of the near bank exposed us to enemy fire from the far one. The Germans also held parts of the near bank. Both banks were strung with barbed wire and littered with mines.

The whole sector was littered with farms, many of whose tenants or owners had left because of the fighting. A/B Company was based at a farm 100 metres from the river, with forward positions close to and on the near bank. D Company was 100 metres to our left at another farmhouse. C company, two sections of A/B Company, our A/T platoon, machine-gunners and mortars were 500 metres behind. Because we were so close to the enemy, moving about in daylight was hazardous, except in the morning mist and then only on marked tracks. Enemy listening posts received any movement or talk on our side of the floodbanks. We were under constant surveillance, our forward position isolated in daylight and unapproachable from the rear except at night. Field telephone lines severed by Jerry stonks could only be repaired at night. Water, food and ammo could only be brought in after dark.

There were two abandoned farmhouses between my position and D Company. Jerry had a habit of slipping across the Senio at night to occupy these buildings and sniping at us during the day. To stop this, I got our sappers to mine the two buildings. A satisfying explosion followed. The second charge failed to detonate, but the sappers went back and blew the building the next night. One evening, two Jocks brought in a Jerry deserter. He was shaking and demoralised, and talked after a drink. He seemed quite pleased to be captured and said that he'd have been shot by his officer had he been caught leaving his post. He told our IO that the near bank was mined, wired and booby-trapped. We had already discovered that. But he also revealed that it would be abandoned for the far bank if attacked strongly. He said that the Germans had very little fuel for their vehicles and armour; that trucks, panzers and SP guns were almost immobilized and senior officers' cars had been adapted to run on gas. All their other transport was horse- or bullock-drawn.

The Germans may also have been short of ammo. Every night saw an exchange of grenades, like First World War trench warfare. We tossed over far more than we received. We also got Jerry propaganda leaflets, intended for our Indian comrades, sent over in canisters fired by artillery. These contained a crude, and completely ineffective message: TO INDI-AN TROOPS. YOU ARE HELPING A FOREIGN NATION WHICH FOR THE LAST 200 YEARS HAS ENSLAVED YOU. The Indians were fully aware that enslavement was the Nazis' plan, not ours. Our own propaganda, signed by Alexander, offered 'safe conduct' for PoWs or deserters. During the day, we were again stonked by mortars and Moaning Minnies. D Company was unlucky. Six of its men were killed and seven wounded by mortars. Three more were killed when a rocket hit their farmhouse. It was a trying time, stuck there, unable to retaliate, and we were not sorry to be pulled out. We handed over to the 1/5th Mahrattas and returned to Russi. Freddie Graham had resumed command of the battalion. Majors MacFie and Wood were repatriated. Reinforcements arrived. Shaw was promoted major and given command of the re-formed B Company. I retained command of A Company with Captain Johnnie Scott-Barrett as my second-in-command.

By chance, the 8th Argylls, part of the 36 Brigade, 78th Division, were billeted in Russi. The last time we had seen them was when we piped them ashore in Sicily. Graham invited their CO and officers to our mess. We had drinks and informal meal and exchanged news. With a battle in prospect, and the memories of others we had fought, the usual mess night bonhomie was restrained. Reconstituted after Dunkirk, the 8th Argylls had fought with the 78th Division in Tunisia, Sicily and at Cassino. In October 1944, they had been in the Apennines north of Castel del Rio. During a week of fighting, similar to our experience at Monte Cavallara, they suffered 120 casualties and the battalion was reduced to three companies. They spent Christmas out of line at Castel del Rio and then moved to Monte Grande, after we had been shifted to Lucca. It seemed that we got out just in time because the 8th Argylls were caught in sub-zero temperatures and heavy snow.

It was in Russi that Shaw and I were astonished to meet our old friend MacDougall. As mentioned earlier, he had incurred Freddie Graham's displeasure in the Liri valley, and had been sent to the infantry base depot at Benevento, if not in disgrace, at least under a cloud. We were delighted to see that he had emerged from that setback, still his old self and still a captain in the Argylls, but now attached to the 1st Battalion, the London Scottish Regiment. Since August 1944, his battalion had taken part in the coastal offensive on the Gothic Line, had been in our Senio sector and was now in reserve near Cesena. He had driven over to Russi hoping to find us.

We contrived to meet again at Faenza, the nearest sizeable town. I recall parking the Jeep in the arcaded piazza, which had been knocked about by shelling and was now packed with army vehicles and soldiers. I bought a couple of postcards that showed it elegant and uncluttered before the war. Mac knew his way around Faenza because the London Scottish had helped the New Zealanders and Gurkhas liberate it in December. We had a jolly good drink together and a long talk as we brought each other up to date with our travels and adventures, under-stating with dry humour, as British officers do, the more fearful and unpleasant moments. We knew now the war in Italy must be coming to an end and, having survived so far, we didn't relish the prospect of becoming a casualty at this late stage. But fatalism and a sense of duty drew us to the coming battle. Shaw and I wished Mac the best of luck.

'See you in Sauchiehall Street,' I said to Mac.

'Aye, a better road and a better country than this,' he replied, as we shook hands and drove away from that war-damaged piazza.

Back at the battalion, we spent the next few days on the embankments of the Montone river, training to assault the Senio. We grappled with portable boats, kapok bridging panels, Bangalore torpedoes [pipes packed with explosive charges] and cortex [coconut] mats to be thrown over the river banks to detonate mines. We trained with 'Ark' bridge-carrying tanks [driven into river beds to allow following vehicles to cross on top of them] and a menagerie of tanks and armoured vehicles: 'Crocodile' flame-throwing tanks, 'Scorpion' mine-clearing tanks, 'Buffalo' amphibious APCs, 'Kangaroo' armoured personnel carriers, 'Wasp' flame-throwing Bren carriers and 'Wolverine' SP tank destroyers. I got used to the sounds and sight of these odd contraptions clanking and crawling around in the morning mist like prehistoric monsters.

By the end of March the weather had improved and the Fifth and Eighth armies were resupplied, reinforced and reorganised. The Allies had overwhelming superiority, in men, tanks, guns and aircraft, and they meant to use it to full advantage. The Fifth Army was ready to disgorge from the Apennines. The Eighth Army's main assault on the Senio was to be made in our sector, by the 8th Indian and 2nd New Zealand divisions. The 8th Indian Division's 19 Brigade, with the 1st Argylls, was to be in the centre of the line.

D-day was 9 April 1945.

The company commanders met Freddie Graham for final briefing at Battalion HQ at Villanova. I can still hear the rustle that broke the silence in the farmhouse where we sat as the CO unrolled a map, produced air photographs and proceeded to explain the plan.

Between the Senio and the Po, there were four other rivers to cross: the Saterno, Sillaro, Idice and Reno. Like the Senio, they had massive floodbanks. All drained from the Apennines and flowed north before turning east to the Po delta above Lake Commachio, a lagoon on our right flank. Between us and the lake was the town of Argenta. The

Germans had flooded and mined the land around it, but the main road was raised and provided a direct route to Ferrara and the Po. Ferrara was a communications centre and the Po was the Germans' last line of defence. Forcing the 'Argenta gap' was the key to the offensive's success.

The assault was to be made by the Eighth Army's 5th Corps: 8th Indian and 2nd New Zealand divisions, 2nd Polish Corps, the Italian Cremona Group and the 78th Division. The 8th Indian and the Kiwis would break the German line on the Senio, cross the Saterno and clear the way to Ferrara, the Po and Venice; 78th Division and the Italians were in reserve, to exploit the Argenta gap when our assault drew off the enemy's reserves. The 56th Division and the 2nd Commando Brigade would take the seaward side of Lake Commachio and capture Porto Garibaldi. The Polish Corps and the 6th South African Armoured Division would push up Route 9 to link up with the Fifth Army breaking out of the Apennines, liberating Bologna and pressing north to the Po and Verona. The Americans would also make a diversionary attack north of Pisa. The intention was to squeeze the German bridgehead south of the Po like a balloon until it burst. The fleeing German Tenth and Fourteenth armies would be caught on open ground on the Po plain and present easy targets for the Allied air forces and advancing armour.

Air support from the USAAF and the DAF was to be devastating: 825 heavy bombers, escorted by fighters, to pound German gun positions and other targets on the Senio for 90 minutes with a deluge of fragmentation bombs (to avoid cratering the ground); 600 medium bombers to blitz the enemy's rear defences on the Saterno river; DAF fighter-bombers to fly in waves of close air support. After the four hours of air strikes, a 1,500-gun artillery barrage would precede the infantry and tanks. The 8th Indian's 19th and 21st brigades would make the first assault: 21 Brigade's 1/5 Mahrattas, 3/15 Punjabis and 5th Royal West Kents would be on our left. The 1st Argylls and the 6/13th Frontier

Force Rifles would lead 19 Brigade, crossing the Senio and advancing 3,000 metres to secure the 21st's right flank. The 3/8th Punjabis, sappers for the night, would follow with infantry bridging equipment. Graham paused, then turned to the Argylls' tactical role.

At that point, I realised that I would be first over the top.

A Company's task was to neutralise the Germans' forward defences and secure both sides of the near bank. B Company (Major Shaw) on the right, and C Company (Major A. G. C. Candlish) on the left, would then advance through my position to a point 200 metres beyond the far bank, and deal with any further opposition. D Company (Major Kelway-Bamber) was to be in reserve. Tanks of the North Irish Horse (Major Griffiths) would follow up to support the battalion after it crossed to the far side of the river. Graham handed out Orders of the Day, and a minute-by-minute countdown for the Senio assault. We sat with our heads down, memorising the details:

H-hour minus 280 minutes: A and D companies begin to thin out from their positions on the river bank 40 minutes before artillery concentrations begin.

H -255: Rear parties of A Company throw cortex mats and fire them. Assault companies move into the Assembly Area where A and D already are, and Tac HQ opens Assembly Area.

H -240 to H-10: Artillery; 4.2-inch and 3-inch mortar concentrations. Air action by heavy, medium, and Spit-bombers.

H -10 to H: Artillery barrage on far bank.

H -12 to H-8: Two tanks of A Squadron North Irish Horse shoot up known enemy posts in the near bank.

H -8: Previously laid charges, designed to blow a huge hole in the bank, to be fired.

H -7 1/2: Thirteen 'wasps' and three 'crocodiles' of 12th Royal Tank Regiment drive up to within 25 yards of the bank and flame both banks.

A Company follows.

H -3: B and C companies start from the Assembly Area.

H -1: Flaming stops.

H: Artillery stops. Spit-bombers make a 'dummy-run' along the banks.

A Company assaults near bank, throws coconut matting down reverse slope. B and C arrive on the near bank.

H +2: Artillery opens 350 yards beyond the far bank. Smoke from all 2-inch mortars and 77 grenades laid in the river bed.

H +5: B and C Companies assault and press on to 200 yards from the river. Artillery adds 150 yards.

H +18: Bridgehead should now be 200 yards deep and 400 yards long.

A Company take up position on B Company's right rear as protection.

H + 30: Artillery barrage begins to advance 200 yards in 12 minutes. B and C move on to next objectives.

H +78: D Company come across the river and come in between B and C to area Casa Montanori. B remains on second objective and consolidates.

C Company and D Company on to next and final objective, Canale di Lugo.

H +240: C Squadron 6th Lancers relieve A Company as right rear protection and A Company comes into Battalion Reserve.

Field Marshal Alexander's message was passed around:

ALLIED FORCE HEADQUARTERS

SPECIAL ORDER OF THE DAY

April 1945

Soldiers, Sailors and Airmen of the Allied Forces in the Mediterranean Theatre.

Final victory is near.

The German forces are now very groggy and only need one mighty punch to knock them out for good. The moment has now come for us to take the field for the last battle which will end the war in Europe.

You know what our comrades in the West and in the East are doing on the battlefields. It is now our turn to play our decisive part. It will not be a walk-over; a mortally wounded beast can still be very dangerous. You must be prepared for a hard and bitter fight; but the end is quite certain—there is not the slightest shadow of doubt about that. You, who have won every battle you have fought, are going to win this last one.

Forward then into battle with confidence, faith and determination to see it through to the end. Godspeed and good luck to you all.

H. R. Alexander,

Field Marshal,

Supreme Allied Commander,

Mediterranean Theatre.

We moved into our assembly areas at dusk. Someone hummed 'Lili Marlene', and 'The D-Day Dodgers' was taken up quietly by the Jocks as they walked towards the front line of that final offensive in Italy. Each company was rotated regularly so we all shared the dangers of assault as well as the relative security in reserve. At the Battle of the Senio, all four companies would be in action. It was a big push, one of the Allies' biggest of the war, but it was not known widely then in the aftermath of D-Day, the liberation of Paris and the fall of Berlin. It has been forgotten today—except by those who were there.

What were our thoughts as we contemplated the Senio floodbanks, waiting for H-hour the next day? Was this yet another Italian river to be crossed, opposed by desperate defenders who would then fall back to other prepared positions to repeat the cycle over again? A Company, 1st Argylls, 19 Brigade, 8th Indian Division, 5th Corps, Eighth Army was a small cog in a big machine. The complicated plan of the high command may have looked fine on paper. In fact, it was well-planned, powerful offensive—a bit like taking a sledge hammer to crack a nut, but the German army was a hard nut to crack and Allied high command was taking no chances. I hoped that it took full account of the trials and dangers the men on the ground would undergo in carrying it out. The plan that seemed simple and straightforward enough to those who made it was a different matter for the men who had to see it through. For a start, we had to lie low in trenches while our fighter-bombers and shells from our artillery screamed overhead. Then, burdened with equipment—ration packs, entrenching tools, bridging gear, steel helmets, weapons and ammo—we were expected to rush the near bank of the river, climb over it at risk from machine-guns and undetected mines, make the dangerous crossing and advance into enemy territory. All through the night, as I tried to snatch some sleep, I was aware of bombers overhead and heard the thumps and saw the flashes of bombs exploding on the German side of the Senio.

The morning of Monday 9 April 1945 heralded the noisiest day I have ever lived through.

At 1440 hours, four hours and 40 minutes before H-hour, A and D companies pulled back from the positions at the river bank. At 1505, sections from A Company ran forward and threw and fired cortex mats to blow up mines and booby traps on top of the near floodbank, then withdrew 200 metres under covering fire. All four companies then lay low in their assembly areas, to be clear of the artillery bombardment. Fifteen minutes later, all hell broke loose.

For four hours, the Germans were bombarded by artillery and mortars and bombed and strafed at intervals by hundreds of Allied aircraft. Thousands of fragmentation bombs hit enemy artillery dugouts and reserve areas. Sunset that day illuminated a hellish pall of smoke and dust across the German lines. The noise was thunderous. For the beleaguered Jerries it must have seemed like the end of the world. Even for the battle-hardened troops on our side, it was an unnerving experience. For the rookies in our battalion it was a terrifying one. Some, not many, had little stomach for it and took a powder. They didn't get far. They were soon rounded up by MPs to face court martial. To run away and leave your comrades in these circumstances was shameful and unforgivable and they deserved all they got.

Inspecting our assembly area, I was furious to find two young Jocks cowering in their slit trench, clearly too afraid to move.

'Get out of there! Noise won't hurt you,' I yelled.

They wouldn't budge, even when the sergeant major appeared at my side and threatened to shoot them.

'Miserable bastards. Fuck!'

I've no idea what happened to them, whether they caught up later or deserted. I had enough on my plate to bother. I had some sympathy for the poor devils, having seen the effect of bombing and shelling on better men. The Senio was the most frightening introduction to frontline soldiering they could have had. Fortunately their behaviour wasn't copied by any of the Jocks in A Company, who went forward to the attack resolutely when the time came.

During that frightful commotion—shells whining and aero engines whirring overhead, the crumps of exploding bombs and sporadic return fire—we were compelled to lie huddled in our slit trenches. I made periodic tours of our position, assuming an air of nonchalance I did not feel, to cheer the men up and show them there was nothing to be afraid of. They thought I was mad, but on that day I didn't much care what happened to me. If I was killed, as so many others had been in the long campaign, I would have died in a cause most of us believed in. Nevertheless I was convinced I would survive the war, despite tempting providence by an occasional show of reckless bravado. Luck was everything. Experience seemed irrelevant. Mortar stonks killed two of our men and wounded seven others as they sat waiting for H-hour. CSM Carruthers, one of the battalion's most seasoned regulars, a veteran of Sidi Barrani where he had won the Military Medal, was shot and killed by a sniper. 'No one,' Mac had observed grimly at Faenza, 'get's out of the infantry. Just the cowards, and the dead.'

About 10 minutes before we were to go over the top, Churchill tanks drove through our position to shoot up the enemy on the floodbanks. Immediately afterwards, Wasp and Crocodile flamethrowers trundled up to within 25 metres of the near bank. For five minutes, they blazed away at suspected enemy dugouts. The banks of the Senio sizzled with flame and the air stank with petrol fumes. Oily black smoke billowed towards us. The armoured vehicles withdrew. Dozens of fighter-bombers came over, streaking above our heads to strike further terror into the hearts of the enemy. They made several low-level attacks with bombs and cannon, hitting enemy artillery and spandau positions, forward HQ areas and any Jerry foolish enough to move. By this time, the mere sound of aero engines kept enemy heads down. Then came the final run, a dummy one. Under its cover, the assault companies of the 8th Indian and 2nd New Zealand divisions launched their attack.

At 1920 hours, we sprang from our trenches and sprinted forward through the flames, smoke and fading light. We knew we only had seconds to seize the Senio before Jerry, sheltering in his bunkers, recovered from the bombardment and grabbed his weapons. Charges designed to blow a hole in the floodbank for us failed to explode, as the leads had been cut by shelling. In the event, that didn't matter. My men scrambled up and captured the near bank, hurled cortex matting down the reverse slope and flung a kapok bridge across the narrow trench of the river. Within minutes, we were across and up and over the far bank, and secured a bridgehead. I gave some Jerries a burst from my tommy gun to keep their heads down. I saw one of my men have a miraculous escape. He trod on an S-mine which shot up in front of him and hung in the air, chest high. It failed to explode. The Jock collapsed in a dead faint. I glimpsed Shaw leading B Company, and Candlish of C Company yelling like dervishes, their men charging through the river, holding their rifles, Brens and tommy guns over their heads. Then, up and over the second bank, they disappeared into the twilight. D Company also passed though the position we had won, Kelway-Bamber and some of his men taking an unplanned dip when their bridge collapsed, followed by assault pioneers to clear mines and tape safe paths beyond the river.

Suddenly, our eardrums were shattered and our nerves shaken by the whistle and roar of shells hurtling close overhead—a lifting barrage in front of B and C companies' advance. The flashes from the shell bursts pierced the smoke, briefly freezing the battle, like a scene, I imagined, from the *Inferno*: the horizon illuminated by vivid explosions and white-hot tracer as the other assaults went in all along the line; enemy infantry and panzers dispersed by a devastating artillery stonk; the now tiny figures of the Jocks darting here and there as they flushed out the Jerries; farm buildings ablaze; the smoking ruins of Fusignano, a village a kilometre away. I remember the smell too: gaseous smoke, cordite, petrol, scorched river banks, tank exhaust and the burned flesh of the German dead.

That devastating stonk was directed by Lieutenant A. F. Holyoake, one of Shaw's platoon commanders. Holyoake, leading B Company's forward platoon, had occupied an abandoned farmhouse out beyond the far bank of the river. As he and his men took up positions, they heard the unmistakable rumbling and clanking of panzers and German officers shouting to their men to counter-attack, in what turned out to be the only serious threat to our bridgehead that night. Holyoake held his fire so as not to reveal his position, calmly calculated the co-ordinates in the dark and radioed for artillery support—which promptly plastered the Jerries, who were forming up some 200 metres away. The panzers and the grenadiers turned tail. Holyoake said afterwards, 'It was wonderful shooting from the gunners.' Just as well, because some of the 53rd Field Regiment's shells missed the house by 50 metres. Shaw put him forward for an MC, which was awarded. (Major Candlish, D Company's commander also won an MC that night; four MMs were won, and the CO was Mentioned in Dispatches.)

Our bridgehead was now 500 metres beyond the Senio. At 2330 we linked up with the 6/13th, whose men had crossed the river on our left. About midnight, A Company was relieved by C Squadron of the 6th Bengal Lancers (the division's reconnaissance regiment) and I led the men back into battalion reserve. The situation seemed confused, but at Battalion HQ, which had moved in behind us, the mood was buoyant. The assault had gone according to plan. Although 21 Brigade had a tougher time of than us, all along the line the German defences on the Senio had been breached in five minutes. By 0315, the Argylls' C and D companies had reached the Canale di Lugo, the night's objective, two kilometres from our starting point. By 0400, sappers had a Bailey bridge across the Senio near Fusignano. I sat and watched tanks of A and C squadrons, North Irish Horse rumble across to continue the advance. I grabbed a couple of hours of sleep.

At daybreak, I was back on the far bank. Mist lay all around but the top of the floodbank was clear. This vantage point presented a surreal scene. The Senio was hidden in a swirling trough of mist. On either side of the floodbanks, out of a sea of drifting vapour, the wrecked roofs and campanili of Fusignano appeared like shipwrecks. Islands of jagged poplars broke the surface at intervals. The river banks smouldered from the previous night's fires; the air still carried the stench.

As the mist cleared, I was amazed to see groups of Jerries emerging like rabbits from holes in the floodbanks. I roused my exhausted men to round them up. Out of one deep dugout a platoon of shell-shocked soldiers appeared, their hands in the air, waving white rags. Numbed by our ferocious bombardment and assault the night before, and trapped in their bunkers while the battle raged above, they had evidently stayed hidden until morning. Knowing that Jerries with hands up to surrender often threw grenades in last acts of defiance—indeed, there had been just such an incident the night before—we took no chances. Some of my men were trigger-happy and showed it, so the Boche were very biddable. The sight of fixed bayonets cowed them even more. They were quickly rounded up, glad to accept the fact that for them the war was over. Except for one German officer, an arrogant looking beggar with a sneer on his face who swaggered out with a disdainful glance at my men. I was tempted to shoot him on the spot.

Despite the magnitude of the Battle of the Senio, our casualties were astonishingly light: two officers and eight other ranks killed, and two officers and thirty-two other ranks wounded. Most of these were caused by mortar bombs and mines. Some were the result of 'friendly fire'. After years of experience, our aircraft-spotting was pretty accurate, so there was no mistaking the aircraft that attacked us at mid-day on the 10th. We watched in horror as American fighter-bombers dropped fragmentation bombs on our own troops moving on the plain, only 100 metres away. We waved and cursed to no effect. One of our men was killed and eight wounded, including Padre Dow. The 6th Lancers were also hit, severely, as were the 3/15th Punjabis. These incidents left a sour taste and took a bit of the shine off our victory. We were not the only ones affected. During the battle, American bombers dropped fragmentation bombs on Polish troops, killing over 100 men.

I often think of our Polish comrades, whose contribution to the Allied cause is neglected. Yet theirs was the country we had gone to war for, and whose 1st Corps defended Scotland in 1940, and in 1944/45 fought in North-west Europe. The Poles in Italy, led by Lieutenant-General Anders, had been released from the Soviet Union in 1941, were re-equipped in the Middle East by the British and joined the Eighth Army. McCreery had the decency to mention them in his message to the army before the Battle of the Senio:

From Tobruk to the Po plains the brave soldiers of Poland have been fighting with us, and it is a matter of especial pride to our Empire Army that in this battle our gallant Polish allies will be striking a decisive blow.

Tragically, because of the Cold War, it took fifty years for the Poles to reclaim their land and freedom from Soviet domination. Also, because of the Cold War, scant recognition was given to the efforts in the Allied cause on the Eastern Front. On the eve of the final Cassino battle, Alexander had claimed we were tying down German divisions that might have been in Russia (or later in Normandy), but that is debatable. Compared with the titanic battles fought on the Eastern Front and the fearful losses the Red Army and the Russian people sustained, those on the Western Front were almost trifling.

For a week after the Battle of the Senio, the battalion enjoyed a period of rest and reorganisation in peaceful countryside. Not for long, though. On 18 April 1945—five years to the day that I had hiked up the hill to Stirling Castle to join the Argylls—we were warned to prepare for action again. Having survived the Battle of the Senio, I can't say that any of us were keen to go back into the front line. But we also smelled victory in the air. The 2nd New Zealand Division had crossed the Senio and Saterno rivers and was advancing to the Po. The Fifth Army had breached the Gothic Line at Monte Grande and swept down to the Po valley. On 21 April, the Poles and partisans liberated Bologna. The 56th and 78th divisions had forced the Argenta gap. The Argylls were ordered to pass through their ranks to Ferrara.

Before dawn on 20 April, Brigadier Dobree set out in his Jeep, now gaily emblazoned with brigade flags and colours, leading an advance party to recce Route 16, the Ravenna to Ferrara highway. The rest of the brigade followed during the day, passing through Argenta in fine weather. But what a place: flooded fields in all directions; refugees huddled by the roadside; Argenta wrecked, with many dead civilians in the rubble. Thousands of Jerries stranded without transport gave themselves up, along with Italians, Russians, Czechs, Cossacks and other vagrants of war-torn Europe who had been conscripted by the Nazis as soldiers and labourers. Waves of Allied aircraft flew overhead. We knew what it was like to be bombed and strafed so it was with unrestrained *schadenfreude* that we watched the fighter-bombers' rockets and bombs bursting up ahead. Even in the desert, the DAF and the Eighth Army had never enjoyed such a profusion of targets. The smouldering wreckage of the German Tenth Army—vehicles, tanks, field guns and equipment—lay everywhere, hit by the fighter-bombers, or discarded by demoralised troops as they scattered towards the Po. Not so demoralised though as to prevent some retaliation here and there despite the fact that they must have known it was all over for them. We were ambushed a few times by spandaus and SPs. Air strikes cleared the way.

Ten kilometres short of Ferrara, we dispersed our vehicles and dismounted just forward of the 53rd Field Regiment's batteries, where we spent an uneasy night, kept awake by the 53rd's guns. By early morning on the 21st, we were on the southern outskirts of Ferrara. As the mist cleared I saw the quartet of towers that frame the fourteenth-century Estense Castle, an impregnable-looking fortress around which the terracotta roofs of lesser buildings spread out to the walls.

An order from Dobree came through: 'Get in and show the flag'. C and D companies, riding on Churchill tanks of the North Irish Horse, passed through a Punjabi forward line during the afternoon. Jaipurs, Mahrattas and the Royal West Kents were probing forward on the left flank. On the right, the 8th Argylls were advancing to seize bridges on the Po di Volano, a 50-metre-wide canal outside the city walls. But the bridges had been blown, as were those in our sector. The 8th Argylls were ordered to consolidate. Those who had managed to cross the river were pinned down by spandaus and mortars—Jerries, defiant to the last.

C and D companies were also held on the canal bank that night. Jerry withdrew over the next 24 hours, sniping and showering the 8th Argylls and us with shellfire. This was returned, with interest. C Company's snipers shot six Germans. D Company and the tanks killed another fifteen, blowing some into the canal. Return fire killed a sapper and a Bengal Lancer and wounded five Jocks. Artillery was directed at enemy strongpoints in the city by the 53rd's forward observation officer, Captain Bonner, who found himself aided by an enthusiastic Benedictine monk, from an OP in a campanile nearby.

By early on the morning of 23 April, the whole battalion was at the canal. Patrols from C and D companies slipped across at 0400. During that sunny morning, A and B companies crossed by kapok bridges and we got some Bren carriers, Jeeps, and motorbikes across by raft. Tanks would come later, we hoped, when a Bailey bridge could be assembled. Partisans said the city centre was clear, but that Jerry was still in position on the northern walls. Earlier that day, the partisans had broken into the Fascist barracks, armed themselves and seized the Estense Castle. According to Captain Jim Manning, a newshound 'with our Forces overseas' attached to the battalion, a 15-year-old boy ran to and fro to keep the partisans supplied with ammo when the Germans tried to evict them.

The Ferrarese gave us a heroes' welcome. We were mobbed by a mad crowd which followed us along the streets. Lucky Jocks were handed bottles of wine; others, even more fortunate, were kissed by delirious girls. But the celebrations were premature, for there were still Jerries about. Shells whistled over and burst somewhere behind us, as if to confirm that fact. A and B companies fanned out either side of the city centre. Several partisans, better dressed than the country ruffians I had met near San Cassiano, told us that they had spotted some enemy soldiers and three Tiger tanks outside the northern walls. 'Tedeschi? Dove?' we shouted and followed the partisans as they ran forward to show us.

I got on the wireless to the CO, who ordered us to maintain our positions on the north perimeter until he could get some tanks up in support. So we skulked around for the rest of the day keeping a lookout for counter-attacks. I sent one platoon to the west of the city to aid the Jaipurs, who were under fire from grenadiers and six Tiger tanks. Early in the evening, when the tanks of the North Irish Horse turned up, the Germans pulled back towards the Po, four kilometres away. We took eighty-five prisoners and captured several panzers in working order.

We crossed the Po unopposed a few days later. It was a awesome sight: the wide river flowing with debris; embankments strewn with the wreckage of the German armies; road and rail bridges down, either bombed by our air forces or blown by the Germans; fighter-bombers flying north; a Bailey bridge jammed with what seemed like the whole Eighth Army queuing to cross. We climbed aboard amphibious APCs, which then gurgled and spluttered into midstream. Mac told me later that when the London Scottish reached the Po, hundreds of Jerries, including a corps commander, surrendered; tons of equipment were captured, and hundreds of German transport units' horses were rounded up. What had once been the finest mechanised army in Europe had no tanks or trucks left, only horses. I saw many of them on the banks of the Po: dead ones, their mutilated, bloated and putrefying carcasses stinking in the warm spring air.

In Ferrara, while the partisans had secured the public buildings, there was chaos in the streets. A building across from the cathedral had been reduced to rubble by bombs or artillery, which had also hit the south battlements of the castle. Hundreds of citizens, out for the *passeggiata*, flooded the streets in a tide of happy faces and mingled with our bewildered Jocks. Then came the AFPU photographers, military police, brigade staff officers, public relations people, AMGOT busybodies, ENSA entertainers, rear echelon men, local scroungers and would-be partisans, all getting in the way. We had always reckoned that for every soldier at the sharp end, there were twenty Forces personnel in various supporting roles behind the front line, and they all seemed to be in Ferrara on that day. As Freddie Graham observed, 'they got themselves entangled in the movement of the 91st through the city, and it was impossible to persuade them that the Germans had not yet been pushed out of the northern end . . . it was impossible to run a battle in the general confusion.'

Graham had commandeered the Albergo Annunziata, across from the Estense Castle, for Battalion HQ. We deserved it. The Union Jack, the Stars and Stripes, and the Italian national flag were raised above the entrance to the Palazzo Municipale. That ancient building with its statuary—and Ferrara's massive brick-built, moated castello and ornate duomo—lent enough gravitas for the city to seem a significant prize, and climax to our war. On the 27th, the Pipes and Drums of the 1st and 8th Argylls paraded in the piazza ourside the Palazzo Municipale and the Duomo. The Ferrarese had seen the last of the goose-stepping Tedeschi. So had we. The war was about to end.

15 COSTA DI ROVIGO

ALLIED FORCES HEADQUARTERS

SPECIAL ORDER OF THE DAY

2 May 1945

Soldiers, Sailors and Airmen of the Allied Forces in the Mediterranean
Theatre.

After nearly two years of hard and continuous fighting which started in
Sicily in the summer of 1943, you stand today as the victors of the Italian
Campaign.

You have won a victory which has ended in the complete and utter rout of
the German armed forces in the Mediterranean. By clearing Italy of the last
Nazi aggressor, you have liberated a country of over 40 million people.
Today the remnants of a once proud Army have laid down their arms to
you—close on a million men with all their arms, equipment and impedimenta. You may well be proud of this great and victorious campaign which
will long live in history as one of the greatest and most successful ever
waged.

No praise is high enough for you sailors, soldiers, airmen, and workers of
the United Forces in Italy for your magnificent triumph. My gratitude to
you and my admiration is unbounded, and only equalled by the pride which
is mine in being your Commander-in-Chief.

H. R. Alexander,

Field Marshal,

Supreme Allied Commander,

Mediterranean Theatre

OUR RELIEF THAT THE WAR WAS ALMOST OVER had suffered
a setback on the 29 April, when we were ordered to stand-by to pur-

sue the Germans towards Venice. To the disappointment of some bold-spirited fire-eaters, thus deprived of the opportunity of being in at the kill—but to the relief of most of us—that order was cancelled, due, I suspect, to the fantastic traffic jams that had built up on the roads north. We were content to settle into billets in the village of Costa di Rovigo, 20 kilometres north of Ferrara. The honour of taking Venice went to the New Zealanders and the 56th Division. It would have been an easy task for us: partisans had rounded up the 3,000-strong German garrison. Kiwi units pressed on and reached Trieste on 2 May, the day that Field Marshal Alexander announced the unconditional surrender of the German forces in Italy.

That night, all across the plain, tracers, parachute flares and Verey lights were fired into the sky in celebration—the last shots in the Eighth Army's long campaign. After over four years of active service in all sorts of conditions, in all weathers and over all kinds of terrain—desert, mountain, river and plain—I rejoiced that it was all over. No more campaigning in heat and cold. No more living in slit trenches, being shot at, bombed, shelled and mortared.

On 6 May, we held an open-air thanksgiving and memorial service, and thanked God, or our lucky stars, that we had survived. Our good fortune was tinged with sadness as we mourned the loss of many comrades: since the beginning of the war, over 1,000 men from the 1st Battalion, the Argylls, had been killed, wounded or were missing. Yet, most of us felt then, as I still do now, that we had played a part, however humble, in a great enterprise: that we had made history. That was not always the feeling. Our trust in and respect for politicians and officers in high command had been shaken when we felt we had been sacrificed and let down. I know what it is like to have the responsibility for the lives of 100-odd men under my command. Those in higher command had the lives of thousands in their hands. Debates still rage among military historians about the mistakes made by the Allies and the conduct of the Italian Campaign. They offer little consolation to those who took part at the sharp end. My Jocks showed sound judgement in their conspicuous lack of respect for those in authority who had done nothing to deserve it, and in their scorn for whatever powers were responsible when things went wrong. 'What a way to run an army!' was the mildest and most common expression of contempt.

There were no doubt strategic, tactical and logistic reasons why the Allies invaded Italy across the Straits of Messina after the campaign in Sicily, and why the landings at Salerno and Anzio were not decisive. Monty had misgivings about the Messina crossing: a landing further up the Italian boot would have forced Kesselring to pull his armies further back, thus shortening the war. The forces landed at Salerno and Anzio were insufficient to accomplish that aim. The year-and-a-half hard slog up the length of the country could have been avoided and saved us, the men of the Argylls among many others, much hardship and suffering. Our do-it-by-the-book system of command was repeatedly outflanked by the Germans who, contrary to Allied propaganda, were able to improvise—to think on their feet. As for the failure to trap Kesselring's armies at the gates of Rome, and the removal by the Americans, against Alexander's advice, of seven divisions for strategically pointless landings in the south of France . . .

Despite these blunders, there was a great spirit throughout the Eighth Army in those days, nurtured initially by Monty himself and sustained, despite many setbacks, by its continuing success in the field. Even in Britain's darkest days of defeat—evacuations from Norway, Dunkirk and Crete, retreat in the Western Desert and disaster in the Far East—there was never any doubt in the minds of most servicemen and women, and civilians, that we would eventually emerge victorious in the war. Churchill's visionary leadership was an abiding inspiration to the whole country. As was his dogged defiance of the enemy in his memorable phrase, 'Never, never give in,' which sustained his fellow countrymen, and was cherished as a watchword by many of my generation throughout the rest of our lives.

We celebrated VE Day, 8 May 1945, in Costa di Rovigo's piazza, where the Jocks of the Argylls and the sepoys of the 6/13th Frontier Force Rifles indulged in exuberant merry-making. I shall never forget that night with those comrades-in-arms, around a huge bonfire that was lit in the middle of the square.

The spectacle unfolded like some durbar from the nineteenth-century days of the Raj: the Pipes and Drums of the 91st, flamboyant in kilts and badger-head sporrans; wild tribal dancing from the Indians and eightsome reels by the Highlanders; the firelight flickering across whirling and marching figures, faces aglow, cheered on by incredulous Italian spectators. The figure of Subedar-Major Amir Khan stepped into the blazing arena to salute Brigadier Dobree, Freddie Graham, who had that day been awarded the DSO, and the officers of both regiments, who stood on a balcony above the square. Khan raised his right hand for silence. He congratulated Graham on his DSO and delivered a moving speech celebrating our bravery in battle and the bond of blood brotherhood that had grown between us. The assembled 6/13th then gave us three cheers. Jimmy Stewart, promoted to RSM, stood forward and bellowed to the Argylls to return the honour, which we did with gusto and sincerity.

The mixture of wine, beer and whisky on that memorable evening produced a stunning hangover in most of us the next day. Mine was provided with a splendid cure in the form of the good news that I was to be posted home to the UK on 'Python', the recently instituted scheme for repatriation of men with long overseas service.

In his history of the battalion, Freddie Graham wrote what now must be considered an elegy for that evening of carefree camaraderie at Costa di Rovigo and its era:

The day that the 1st Battalion joined the 8th Indian Division was the first of many weary months of sustained fighting against a determined enemy. Under the sign of the 'three wee floo-ers' the battalion fought its way through snow and rainstorm, heat and mud, to the final victory in the fertile valley of the River Po. Across the rivers . . . over the towering peaks of the Apennines, through the fruit orchards and cornfields of the Po valley the war graves bear witness to the passage of the battalion.

The spirit of comradeship and mutual admiration which grew up between the Indian fighting man and his British counterpart in the 8th Indian Division was one of the reasons why the name of '8th Indian' was feared and respected even amongst the German paratroopers.

What is there about men like those of the 8th Indian Division which will not be forgotten? It is that British and Indian soldiers can stand together, and fight together, to uphold an Empire rallying the world against aggression. The Germans never believed that it was possible. They tried throughout the Italian campaign, by cunning and insidious propaganda to alienate the affection of the Indian soldier for his British officer and comrade. They failed dismally.

At the Battle of the Senio, two of the Indians, Sepoy Ali Haidar of the 6/13th Frontier Force Rifles and Sepoy Namdeo Jadhao of the 3/5th Mahrattas, won the Victoria Cross.

In his parting message to 19 Brigade, Brigadier Dobree wrote:

It is difficult for me to write in sufficient praise of the two Indian Battalions. For not one single day in this whole of these testing years have either the 3/8th Punjab or the 6/13th RFF Rifles been anything but magnificent. They have displayed every soldierly quality in the highest degree: bravery, determination to win, coolness in battle, patience under the most adverse conditions, smartness when at rest and unfailing cheerfulness . . . The 1st A & S H have lived up to the great traditions of their famous regiment . . . and won a reputation for dash and tenacity which cannot be excelled . . . All of you, British and Indian officers and men of all tribes and classes have played your part unfailingly. You have more than upheld the highest traditions and spirit of the Indian Army. I cannot adequately express the pride I have felt in commanding the Brigade with three such Battalions. As a Gunner and of the British service it has been the greatest honour that I ever have had or hope to achieve.

Fifty years on, and after five off and on at my typewriter, I now feel as impatient to be finished with these memoirs as I was to get home after the end of the war.

'When?' was the thought uppermost in the minds of those of us who had been serving overseas for three to four years or more. I was one of these unashamedly war-weary, if not yet bomb-happy D-Day Dodgers who could now look forward to an early return on a troopship from Naples to the Clyde. I had only a few more days to spend in Costa di Rovigo before starting on my homeward journey.

Only a few incidents stay in my mind from the few weeks I spent in Costa di Rovigo. The VE Day celebrations of course; the sight of Costa di Rovigo's First World War shrine at the piazza; a narrow escape I had when I went swanning about in the company Jeep. I got caught up in a line of traffic. Frustrated, I took a chance and tore along on the wrong side, hoping to find an opening. Suddenly I was faced with an oncoming US army truck. It didn't look like slowing down. I thought my number was up. Luckily I managed to slip into a gap in the traffic, and escaped death by the skin of my teeth.

Back at base, the Jocks were badgered into smartening themselves up. Bags of spit and polish, drill and training exercises. This regime was not to keep them happy—they were not amused—but to keep them on their toes and prevent them from becoming slack and stale. I didn't take much part in these goings-on. I had little enthusiasm for them. In fact I opted out of most of them and got my second-in-command, Johnnie Scott-Barrett, and platoon commanders to do most of the work. Delegation—the secret of command. Otherwise, our daily life was peaceful and the early summer weather was glorious. We enjoyed sound sleep, undisturbed by shot or shell and welcomed not having to endure early morning and evening Stand-to.

There were also sport and recreation and day trips to Venice. I went on one, but the glories of that beautiful city were wasted on me. I remember little about it, apart from the oddity of the drive on the causeway out into the lagoon; the water taxis commandeered by Allied officers; the decaying palazzi and the Byzantine gloom of San Marco; the little orchestras in the piazza; Kiwis in the best hotels.

In the villa where Scott-Barrett and I were billeted, were the landowner's two very personable daughters. We fairly lusted after them. Scott-Barrett fell for the younger one, while I tried to make a pass or two at her sister, with little success for either of us, as their father very sensibly kept a watchful eye on them. I had one or two conversations in a mixture of English and Italian with the elder sister, who told me something of her adventures with the partisans, with whom she said she had served. The nearest I got to satisfying my amorous urges was when she came to our quarters one morning with a mug of tea. Her appearance was a pleasant change from the more familiar but less inspiring figure of Sanders. We exchanged a quick kiss and cuddle, which did more for me than any mug of hot, sweet tea. Then she fled, before her suspicious father appeared to find out what she was up to.

The day before I left, our host invited Scott-Barrett and me to join him and some neighbours at a family dinner in his cavernous farmhouse kitchen. It was a typical Italian meal: heaps of pasta, lashings of wine, the adults sitting at a long table and their children running around. Conversation was difficult, but a mood of restrained hilarity prevailed and we all became quite merry, especially when our host produced a bottle of grappa. We toasted the Churchill, Roosevelt and Stalin, the partisans and each other. Johnnie and I couldn't quite do justice to the meal because of the provocative presence of the two daughters and, for me, the excitement of preparing for my departure and the prospect of farewell rounds of drinks with my fellow officers. More than slightly hungover the next morning, I joined MacDougall (who was also being repatriated, and had come over from the London Scottish which was billeted at Mira, near Venice) and Shaw in loading up the Jeep the CO had lent us.

I missed a return visit to Venice that day. The CO had offered me the opportunity of commanding the Guard of Honour, to be formed by the 1st Argylls and the 6/13th Frontier Force Rifles, for generals Mark Clark and Richard McCreery, at a victory celebration parade outside the Doge's Palace. Unfortunately that was the day that Shaw, Mac and I were due to leave for Naples. Majors Candlish and W. H. Griffiths (one our South African officers) took the parade. I was sorry not to have met the generals and have my photograph taken with them, but the delightful prospect of three weeks' leave, thoughts of home and the urging of my two friends left me no choice but to turn down the CO's offer.

'My dear Ray, I understand completely,' was Freddie's generous response, 'Of course, you must leave!'

So it was that on 11 May 1945, a hot, sunny morning in northern Italy, Mac, Shaw and I set off on our journey south through Italy to Naples. We soldiers three had become friends at Stirling Castle as newly-commissioned second lieutenants in December 1940. We had sailed from Liverpool on the *Windsor Castle* in January 1941 and been together off and on for four and a half years. We had travelled far, shared many discomforts and adventures, and had good and often riotous times in many an overseas station. We had seen much action and had soldiered on with The Agile and Suffering Highlanders on our odyssey from the Pyramids to the Po. We were grateful, and a bit bemused, to still be alive, and glad to be going home at last.

We shook hands with Freddie Graham and the other officers. They wished us good luck. I had an emotional farewell with Sanders, who had been with me since 1941. He had served me loyally and well in good stations and bad throughout the war. He had looked after my creature comforts, polished my boots and brasses, put up with my eccentricities and occasional uncertain temper, all with indomitable cheerfulness and tact. We had developed a friendly relationship and trust not uncommon between an officer and his servant and I knew I would miss him.

Finally, I said goodbye to the assembled men of A Company, in which I had served for four wartime years, first as a platoon commander, then as second-in-command and latterly as company commander. There had been a continual turnover of men in the company and throughout the battalion during that time, as a result of battle casualties, transfers and postings, but there were still some among them who had come to the battalion as reinforcements and joined it with me at Qassasin in June 1941. I was moved by this parting and the breaking of contact with a close-knit community that had been the centre of our lives for so long. These were the men with whom I had shared a tribal loyalty and the experience of varied service and tough campaigning.

I had never addressed such an assembly before, except to give commands: 'Company will move to the right in column of threes. Right turn. By the left, quick march!' . . . I was nervous. I envied Monty's poise as I stood the men at ease. In a halting speech I expressed regret at leaving them—'Tell that to the Marines,' one of the Jocks shouted, to general laughter—though of course they all knew I was delighted to be going home. I thanked them for the way they had stuck it out through a long, hard campaign, with good humour, grit, and gallantry; told them not to blame me if they felt that they had been messed about too often, but to 'blame the buggers higher up'. I told them that they were a credit to the Argylls and that it had been my privilege to serve with them; that I looked forward to seeing them parade on the Esplanade at Stirling Castle or in Glasgow's George Square.

'I'll be there to give you a cheer . . . Good luck to you all.'

Then one of the NCOs, an old hand from the desert days, stepped forward and called out: 'Three cheers for Major Ward!'

It was all over. I turned away.

I never saw A Company again.

As for the battalion, it was posted home and sailed for the UK at the end of June. It found itself accommodated in a camp in England, not Scotland, there to prepare for a move to the Far East and the continuing war against Japan. When the war ended in August, the Argylls found themselves posted to 'peace-keeping' in Palestine.

Prior to sailing for the UK, the battalion suffered a drastic reorganisation. Officers and men were posted hither and thither among other units in the Mediterranean region, and drafts of reinforcements exchanged reluctantly between the 1st Argylls and various Highland battalions in other divisions of the Eighth Army. Freddie Graham tried, unsuccessfully, to prevent the dispersal of the fighting unit he had led with distinction. The Argylls with whom I had served were thus denied the homecoming and a parade through the streets of Glasgow or Stirling—the least that they deserved.

At the end of May 1945, at Foligno where the reorgnisation took place, Graham issued the following message:

TO BE READ OUT ON PARADE
To: all Coys

PERSONAL MESSAGE FROM THE COMMANDING OFFICER

1. Some days ago I told you on parade that I would always, so far as possible, take you into my confidence. I also said that I thought the Bn would be going home. I was right but I was not prepared for the orders which I received to-day . . .

2. The news I have to give you is so shattering to me as your CO that I cannot face you with it and I have asked your Coy Comds to break it to you: [that twenty-five Argyll officers and 600 other ranks who had served in Italy and earlier would be posted to other units, and be substituted by drafts of young soldiers from those units for service in the Far East.]

3. I cannot begin to express my feelings on this subject. I have been to see the Divisional Commander who, although he agrees with me in every way, feels that he is powerless to do anything as these orders have come from the War Office. I pointed out that you, every man of you, have served me as few men have been served and that I was not prepared to see you 'Done down'; again he agreed but said he was helpless. I have therefore asked to be relieved of my command because I consider you are getting a raw deal.

I have always asked you to remember that you were 'Argylls' before all things . . . I can now only ask you, for the honour of the Regiment . . . uphold the good name of the Argylls wherever you may be. . .

He did not include that personal message in the battalion history he wrote after the war. He was honourable, loyal to his regiment, to the undeserving army brass, and discreet. I recall writing to him during the 'Save the Argylls' campaign in 1966, suggesting a profile in an article I was writing about the regiment. He replied: 'I deplore such a suggestion, but I see the possibilities in a feature on the regiment with me only as a coincidental figure.' He invited me to Stirling Castle to chat about the piece, which was subsequently published. He concluded his narrative in the battalion history with the following passage:

For seven years the 1st Battalion, The Argyll and Sutherland Highlanders (Princess Louise's), had upheld the proud traditions of the Regiment. Seven years of hard fighting and faithful service. Seven years in which a reputation, always high, had been enhanced, thanks to the enduring courage, loyalty, and boundless cheerfulness of the rank and file.

All had played their part—cooks, drivers, batmen, signallers, and many more; but the men who bear the brunt of all warfare, who endure the worst conditions and the greatest dangers, and who in the end keep the honour of the Regiment in their hands, are the private soldiers in the infantry sections. The great mass of them do not win decorations; they go about their duties quietly, confidently, and cheerfully, expecting no reward, and receiving none except the respect and admiration of those who associate with them.

It is men like these who, fired by the Argyll spirit, have caused the name of the Regiment to be honoured by friend and foe alike. In the sands of the desert, in the mountains of Crete, in the olive groves of Sicily, and the vineyards and orchards of Italy you will find their names upon the simple crosses adorned only with the badge of the Regiment which they so faithfully served.

NE OBLIVISCARIS

16 COMING HOME

We left the battalion at Costa di Rovigo and drove to Lake Garda, a beauty spot we had heard about. It featured in a guidebook Mac had bought, which became our bible for the trip. Then, we may have spent a day and night in Bologna. I do remember, though, our drive from Faenza to Florence, over the Apennines where we had struggled and fought during the previous winter on the Gothic Line. Damaged buildings, blown bridges and roads were being repaired, with substantial help from the Allies.

Through Tuscany and Umbria, we bedded down each night in woody glades by the roadside and slept under the stars. We washed in clear, bubbling streams, and brewed-up breakfast from our good supply of rations, then continued as, when and where the fancy took us. It was a wonderful sense of freedom, having no responsibilities, no orders to obey, no inspections or having to stand-to at dawn—a carefree existence, a complete escape from military routine and discipline. Our only contact with the army was when we pulled into some depot or other to collect petrol and rations. The most memorable features of the landscape were the hill towns—Assisi, Perugia, Orvieto and others—that had so recently been the focus of military observation and capture. Italians everywhere showed tremendous relief that the war was over, although I am sure some would miss the opportunities we had brought. Just before we reached Rome, I had a new trench coat that I had bought at an army shop in Florence stolen while I slept, literally picked off my back.

In Rome, we had a boozy lunch in the Borghese Gardens overlooking the city. To the south lay Cassino. The Rapido river crossing had too many grim memories for Mac and Shaw, so instead of going inland, we took the coast road as far as Sorrento. We went to Pompeii and spent a few days in Naples, staying at a hotel run by the army, before boarding our ship. I persuaded Mac and Shaw to come with me to San Carlo opera house to see *The Barber of Seville*. The blighters walked out halfway through. They found me later, singing snatches of Rossini with an opera-loving shopkeeper.

Apart from regretting that we had to give the army back the Jeep, I remember little about our embarkation, or even the name of the ship we sailed on. We didn't see the Rock of Gibraltar, as we passed through the straits at night. But I'll never forget the moment we anchored at the Tail of the Bank on the Firth of Clyde. The last glimpse we had seen of Scotland had been a distant view of Islay four and a half years before. We had often wondered if we would ever see home again, yet here we were at last, soldiers from the wars returning, campaigning over and our duty done. Not quite though, for we still had months to serve before our demob in 1946. When we disembarked at Gourock, we had to report to an army depot where we had our papers sorted out. Then we were free for a month's leave.

When I reached Glasgow I was thrilled to see again familiar and fondly-remembered streets and buildings and those beautiful clanging tramcars. There was also the damage from the air raids of March 1941. I'd been unable to tell my mother when I'd arrive, and when I reached home, she was out. Our next door neighbours kindly took me in till she got back. Mr Hotson, the local butcher, who was not above evading the ration regulations when it suited him, fed me steak and chips. When my mother turned up, she shouted, 'Ray's back. Ray's back!', for all to hear. She was still her usual cheerful, optimistic self, if older and more careworn than I remembered her. I was no longer the callow young man who had left home to join the Argylls in 1940. But I was alive and well, a little older and perhaps wiser. We spent an long time talking, exchanging news and stories, and I went to bed a tired and happy man.

I had no civilian clothes worth wearing, and went about in my kilt or tartan trews. I met Chris Mackay and caught up with her news, about her service in the ATS. In town, I bumped into a quite a few Argylls at Rogano's restaurant, a haunt of officers on leave. I visited Mac at his home in Renfrew and met his mother and he met mine when I had him over for a meal. Shaw visited and stayed a few nights. I took my mother to Lancashire to see relations. Then, leave over, I reported to Fort George, the depot of the Seaforth Highlanders, near Inverness.

Fort George was a grim barracks on the shores of the Moray Firth, built to quell the Highlands after the '45. It is still a bleak place, now a heritage site. The nine months I spent there, with other officers awaiting demob, were the most miserable of my wartime service. Days were filled with tedious military routine or training unenthusiastic conscripts. Mac was more fortunate, being posted to the HLI depot at Maryhill barracks in Glasgow, as was Shaw who went to the Black Watch depot at Perth. Around that time, I went for an interview at the War Office, where I was offered a posting to the Allied Control Commission in Germany. I gave it some thought, but declined the offer of what seemed a dead-end job. I might have been posted to the sylvan setting of a village in the Bavarian Alps, but more likely I would have found myself is some blitzed or shell-shattered, poverty-stricken town in the Ruhr.

The only event of importance for me took place on the morning of 27 September 1945, at Holyrood Palace in Edinburgh, where I had been summoned to be decorated by His Majesty King George VI. I was allowed two visitors to the ceremony in the palace picture gallery. None of my three brothers was available (they were still overseas), so my mother and my next nearest relative, cousin Elsie, who came up from Morecambe, attended. My mother said it was the proudest moment of her life. To be in a palace, to be attended to by Court flunkies, among a glittering throng of some 300 Forces personnel, and guests, and to see the king at close hand was something beyond her widest dreams. And best of all, to see the king pin the Military Cross, won at the Battle of Monte Cavallara, on the chest of her youngest son, exchange a few words with him and shake him by the hand. There were three other Argylls with me that day: two comrades of mine, Major Walter Elder MC and Major Graham Wood MC, and Captain W. R. Bruce MC (2nd Battalion, North-west Europe). The king asked me if we were all from the same battalion and I told him three of us were. He seemed impressed. We passed Queen Elizabeth and the two princesses as we left, then had photographs taken as we strode through the grounds. We were an imposing sight, with our glengarries, kilts and badger-head sporrans. The local papers ran the pictures, copies of which I still possess with pride.

I was demobbed on 11 April 1946, at Military Dispersal Unit No. 2 at York, six years after I joined the Argylls. At the clothing store where I got my 'civvies', no distinction was made between officers and other ranks. Officers received little deference and no favouritism was shown. On the contrary, some of the fellows dishing out the clothes were bloody-minded enough to give the officers the shabbiest, most ill-made and ill-fitting garments. I got a nondescript suit, shirt, hat and other items which served me long enough, until I could afford to buy better. I remember walking up Buchanan Street with Cecil, who had returned from the Far East by that time. In a moment of careless abandon, I threw my demob hat in the air and left it lying. A wee man came running up with it and said, 'You've dropped your hat, sir.'

'Keep it,' I told him. 'It's not a glengarry.'

Mac, Shaw and I had often talked about what we would do after the war and had mixed feelings about our future. We agreed we would settle for nothing less than £10 a week, but in the event had to be content with much less. The peacetime environment we found ourselves in was in some respects reassuringly familiar, in others disturbingly altered. I recall meeting a Major Calder at Fort George. He had won the MC serving with the RSF in Burma. I met him later in the 1960s. He was then Head of BBC Scotland and I was scriptwriting for BBC children's hour and school programmes. He told me of an experience he'd had after being demobbed. Before the war he had been a schoolmaster in Ayr. He had sought an interview with his director of education, to see about getting his old job back. The director had the gall to lecture him on how difficult a time his teachers had had during the war and how he couldn't possibly fit him in to a teaching appointment above any of his present staff. This to a man who had fought the Japanese in Burma. In so many words, Calder told him what he could do with his job, and stormed out.

In the early 1950s, when I had begun my own teaching career. I recall coming home on a red No.9 tram shoogling along the Gallowgate from Bernard Street school in Bridgeton, my first teaching job. Sitting with me was a PT teacher whose name I forget. He made no bones about not wanting to become a casualty in the army. His aim had been to see out the war in a safe, cushy job, which he did as an army PT instructor. He couldn't understand why I had chosen to become an infantryman. I felt contempt and didn't try to explain. I met many others of his type, usually in officialdom, and avoided him and them in the future.

I lost touch with Sanders some years after the war. I remember visiting him and his wife in their flat on top of the south-east corner of the Christian Institute building in Bothwell Street, Glasgow, where he had returned to his job as caretaker with the Bible Training Institute. The Christian Institute building, like much of the Glasgow I returned to, has since been demolished. Sanders died twenty or so years after the war. I didn't hear of his death for some time, so was unable, to my lasting regret, to attend his funeral. Mac studied for the Civil Service, went into HM Customs and Excise, then joined the Nigerian Police Force, in which he served until the country gained its independence. He returned to Islay but had difficulty settling to humdrum jobs. Shaw studied law at Cambridge and became the English equivalent of a Scottish procurator fiscal in his home town of Oldham. He was also President of the Manchester branch of the Argyll's Regimental Association. Although I maintained periodic contact with the Argylls after the war, I was never the professional old soldier. I rarely mentioned my rank or decoration in conversation and never used them on correspondence. Of the men I served with, I only saw a few again.

Sergeant Bloomfield stayed in the Argylls, becoming a drum major. I had a happy reunion with him at the Stirling Castle at the centenary celebrations of the Battle of Balaclava. Sergeant McKeown, one of the two senior NCOs who had not become casualties at Monte Cavallara and who was awarded the Military Medal for his conduct during the battle, became an inspector with Glasgow Corporation Transport Department. I used to meet him now and again on buses and trams. While I was overseas, I lost touch with Sandy Graham, my room mate at Stirling. He developed his comic and artistic talents during the war and became the newspaper cartoonist, Alex Graham. Jim Henderson, one of my room mates at Dunbar, was commissioned in the HLI. By chance, he became a neighbour of mine in 1957, when I moved into a new house in Whittingehame Drive in Glasgow's west end. We never talked about the war. Cecil and I resumed our friendship with Willie Rankine, our boyhood cricketing pal, last seen by me in Egypt.

I met a former comrade, Captain Ian Hamilton, when we were both coincidentally on our honeymoons in Dublin, in 1948. He had been posted to the Argylls after service with the Royal Scots Fusiliers in France in 1940, and joined the battalion after Crete. He had stayed on in the army after sailing home with us from Naples. We met again thirty years later, at an Argyll reunion held at the Ingram Hotel, Glasgow. Also present on that occasion was Major Rab Caldwell, who had become a PoW in 1944.

I hadn't seen Rab for forty years, although his frequent eccentric 'letters to the editor' of the *Glasgow Herald* assured me he was very much alive. There we sat with our wives, three recently retired gentlemen, well preserved and of modest means, strangers to each other for so long, yet picking up our threads of talk as easily as a day-old conversation. We left unspoken our thoughts of friends killed in action. Like funeral guests glad to discard their mourning faces and enjoy the conviviality of an after-burial lunch, we felt no inhibitions about discussing those of our colleagues who had but recently predeceased us. We were the lucky ones. We were the survivors. Our awareness of that fact tinged our recollections of well-remembered incidents or half-forgotten people and places with a kind of wistful cheerfulness. The years fell away in a flash as we looked behind the outward appearance of our present age and condition and saw in each other, as in glimpses in the mirror of some previous existence, the familiar faces, figures and personalities that had been ours as young men in uniform.

Memories of the war were stirred again when I revisited Stirling Castle in 1987, when I attended the memorial service in the Chapel Royal for my old CO in Italy, Major-General Freddie Graham. After he relinquished command of the battalion in August 1945 he stayed in the army, in staff and command appointments, in Germany, Hong Kong and the UK. He was Deputy Commandant and Instructor at Sandhurst, and GOC Highland District and 51st Division TA at Perth, before retiring in 1962. In 1945, when he returned from Italy, he had offered me a regular commission in the Argylls. I was flattered, but turned it down. Just as well perhaps. I might have been killed in Korea, or in one of the many other trouble-spots to which the regiment was sent in the post-war decades. At the service, I met Rab Caldwell again and another wartime comrade, Major 'Tich' Candlish MC, who had joined the battalion in June 1942 and whom I had not seen since 1945, when he was about to lead the Guard of Honour at the parade in Venice.

He was posted back to Stirling, gained a regular commission in the Royal Engineers and was a deputy gunnery range commander in Australia, before retiring in the 1960s. Caldwell had continued in active service until 1955, then joined the Colonial Service and was posted to Nigeria and Nyasaland. He was active in the 'Save the Argylls' campaign, when the army planned to scrap the regiment.

As I write, I recall a chance meeting with another comrade-in-arms, Lieutenant Bill Dunn, who lost a foot to a Schu mine and for whom I smuggled in a bottle of whisky at Benevento. He settled on the Isle of Jura and got a job as handyman to George Orwell, then writing *Nineteen Eighty-Four* at an isolated cottage at the north end of the island. Bill later married Orwell's sister Avril Blair and took up farming on the Argyll mainland. He achieved fame some years later, by swimming, despite his disability, the treacherous Straits of Corryvreckan. I met him after the war, in Jura while on holiday with Chris Mackay, at her uncle's manse there in 1947. I was singing at a ceilidh in the hall at Craighouse, when Dunn walked in, complete with kilt and bagpipes. Like almost all my former friends and comrades he is now dead, and resting peacefully, I hope, in some old soldiers' home in the sky.

I settled for a civilian life after the war, and I have no regrets about that. My brothers also left the Forces. Alex resumed his career as a manager with the Savings Bank at Accrington. Harold trained as a teacher and became Head of Religious Studies at St Anne's High School, also in Lancashire. Cecil stayed in Glasgow and went into sales with Southern and Evans, a woodworking firm, becoming managing director. I rejoined John Train and Company for a short time, then spent a couple of years at Jordanhill College, qualifying as a primary and music teacher. I also gained the Diploma of LRAM [Licentiate, Royal Academy of Music] in singing, as a teacher and performer.

I married Chris Mackay in 1948 and we settled first in a flat at 6 Napiershall Street, Glasgow, where we began to raise two boys. Marriage, music studies, singing with the Orpheus Club and the SNO chorus, watching cricket, freelance writing, and a love of books among other interests (I joined Partick Library when I was six years old and have been reading ever since) enabled me to live a long, happy, and moderately successful life for more than fifty years after the war.

That is more than can be said for my comrades in the Argylls who did not survive it. But, unfashionable as it may seem now, I can also avow, with some of my departed friends, that we had the best of times, when we were young, in the army, at war. The worst of times, too, of course, but those are more readily forgotten than the others. Dazzling summer weather still brings back memories of those exhilarating days of 1944, after the fall of Cassino and the liberation of Rome, when the Germans retreated northwards through Tuscany, the Allies in pursuit; or memories of the curious campaign against the Italians in Abyssinia in 1941 and how happy I was then.

As Dr Johnson once said: 'Every man thinks meanly of himself for not having been a soldier.' My soldier's life: in barracks, billets and bivouacs; the weapons training, the drill, the ceremonial; the formalities of military custom and language; the frustration, boredom, elation and despair; the frisson of excitement and of fear . . . has never been far from the surface of my mind, recollected clearly in waking hours, or presented in weird distortions in nightmares and dreams. To learn the meaning of *esprit de corps*, to experience the companionship and camaraderie of comrades-in-arms, of young men bound together by the necessities of war and the capricious hand of Fate, is a cherished and indelible memory. I take a modest pride in having once been a soldier: an Argyll and Sutherland Highlander.

♣

The war cemetery, Faenza, October 2004

EPILOGUE

Look around the mountains, in the mud and rain—
You'll find the scattered crosses—(there's some which have no name).
  Heartbreak and toil and suffering gone,
  The boys beneath them slumber on.
Those are the D-Day Dodgers who'll stay in Italy.

Hamish Henderson. *Ballad of the D-Day Dodgers,* 1944

THE PO VALLEY, OCTOBER 2004

I cross the Po on the A13 autostrada. The river is wide and flows across a vast, luminous plain which swallows up the road as it has done armies. I've come from Faenza and Fusignano, where I stood on the Senio floodbanks that were stormed by the Argylls in April 1945. El Alamein and D-Day are well known, but the Battle of the Senio is forgotten. In that great plain of the Po, I found little evidence that one of the biggest Allied offensives of the Second World War took place there.

At Costa di Rovigo's unchanged piazza, I see the balcony on the tiny town hall from where the officers of the Argylls and the Frontier Force Rifles watched their battalions' victory bash and bonfire. Re-crossing the Po, I linger in Ferrara, where the Pipes and Drums of the Argylls were surrounded by cheering Ferrarese. I dodge locals on squeaking bicycles flitting across the car-free, cobbled piazza as I make my way to the Duomo, to light a candle for my father and his men. In 1945, they dodged shells fired into the city by Tiger tanks. At dusk, in Faenza's colonnaded Piazza della Libertà, I spot an inscription on a stone plaque attached to the base of the Comune's campanile:

LA TORRE DELL'OROLOGIO (1607), DANNEGGIATA DURANTE
L'ULTIMA GUERRA E FEDELMENTE RICOSTRUITA NEL 1953

All over Italy you will find similar plaques on historic buildings, marking
their destruction during the Second World War and reconstruction in the
years after it ended.

I drive east towards Bologna, along the two-lane Via Emilia, Route 9. At
Castel San Pietro Terme, I turn onto a winding, potholed country road that
leads to Monte Cerere and Monte Grande. They're marked on the map
and, unlike Monte Cavallara, are easy to find. Their massif is the dominant
feature to the south, about five kilometres away across fields and pasture.
As it looms closer, I pull over and get my binoculars out. A cluster of military and telecom communications masts and blisters sits on top of Monte
Grande; to the left is Monte Cerere; on the eastern shoulder of the massif,
Frassineto sticks out 'like a sore thumb'.

The road steepens, then levels out along a ridge. I'm in damp woods and
finally find myself below Monte Cerere's summit. Despite the trees, the features where the Argylls and the Indians fought are obvious. I realise I'm
standing on the slope, now an orchard, where the German paras charged
the 6/13th's machine-guns and left forty dead. Fifty metres away is Casa
Nuova, now rebuilt, where A Company's Piat bomb flew in the window.
Through the woods, the road dips to open ground at Frassineto. I see the
farm buildings where my father and his men sheltered from enemy shelling,
and the slopes where he made his nightly round to check the company's
forward positions. I find myself standing exactly where his dugout was
when the Germans attacked out of the mist—the day he was caught stark
naked in the flashes of a surprise bombardment. I'm completely alone here,
chilled, as he must have been, by the wind that whistles over the ridge.

I have copies of the battalion's War Diary. The entries are understated:
'Shelling on A/B Company was highly unpleasant... snipers were active
today... annoyed D Company... mortars were fired... sniping ceased...

Fighting patrol from A/B Company . . . found no enemy, but heard movement in the wood . . . fired at it with TMGs.'

At Casa Nuova, I find a marble memorial by the roadside, put here, I'm sure, on the fiftieth anniversary of the battle. It doesn't say when or by whom. Fresh flowers have been placed nearby. Some people have had the grace to remember what happened here and I thank them for it, but I doubt that many folk visit this remote spot or know that men of the Eighth Army fought here. A rusty fragment from an artillery shell, probably from the 'high velocity gun', is fixed on top of the slab. Below it are the 8th Indian Division's clover-leaf motif and an engraved text:

MONTE GRANDE/MONTE CERERE
ON THESE MOUNTAINS DURING THE ITALIAN CAMPAIGN, ON
DECEMBER 12 1944, THE TROOPS OF 1ST BN THE ARGYLL AND
SUTHERLAND HIGHLANDERS, 3RD BN THE 8TH PUNJAB RGT, 6TH
ROYAL BN (SCINDE) FRONTIER FORCE RIFLES, OF THE 8TH INDIAN
INFANTRY DIVISION, REPULSED SEVERAL DETERMINED ATTACKS BY
THE GERMAN 1ST PARACHUTE DIVISION AND DESPITE HEAVY
CASUALTIES THE GROUND WAS HELD
SHABASH
IN ONORE DEI COMBATTENTI ALLEATI INSIEME AI SOLDATI E PATRIOTE
ITALIANI NELLA LOTTA DI LIBERAZIONE

Back in Faenza, as I walk to my hotel on Corso Garibaldi, old-fashioned street lights flicker on. I have an image of a Jeep with three Eighth Army officers overtaking me—Shaw, MacDougall and my father, who looks back.

Since visiting the war cemetery at Florence, I've checked the website at the Commonwealth War Graves Commission, to trace the men of A Company, 1st Battalion, The Argyll and Sutherland Highlanders who fell at the Battle of Monte Cavallara. The CWGC database lists all British and Commonwealth war dead buried at the Commission's cemeteries around the world since 1917, when the organisation was founded to create cemeteries and memorials on the Western Front. My father kept his copy of the Cavallara casualty list (twelve killed and twenty wounded) so I know the names of the dead.

I searched the website, starting with Second Lieutenant Andrew Lindsay, keying in his surname and initial, year of death, nationality, service (army, navy or air force). I clicked 'search'. His name appeared as quickly as if he were on parade, with two other Lindsays killed that year. I searched for Captain Stephen White. Three Whites appeared, not one an Argyll. Then I remembered that he joined the Argylls from the King's Own Scottish Borderers and, sure enough, he is buried with Lindsay—at Faenza War Cemetery, not Florence as I had thought. I searched for the other ten men who were killed that day. I found them all. They fell in together on the computer screen. I discover, when I find the cemetery, that this is also how they were laid to rest.

The commission's website has the cemetery one and a half kilometres south-east of the town, on a secondary road off Route 9. I fail to find it. I pass a couple of Vespas parked on the edge of a vineyard and stop the Jeep. A worker emerges from the rows of vines. I ask directions. I drive back towards the town and stop at a sign: FAENZA. I must have come too far. I turn around and get lost again.

The flat vistas are interrupted here and there by vineyards, farm buildings, poplar plantations and floodbanks. I see how difficult and dangerous it was for the Argylls to advance across the Po valley, and how easy it was for German snipers and tank crews to ambush them. Two middle-aged country women are chattering beside a battered Fiat Panda. When I ask for directions they signal me to follow them. I feel like an escaped PoW who has fallen into safe hands. We pass the Faenza sign. Then I see the cemetery on the left. The women wave and speed away. A single-engined propellor plane drones overhead, a wartime sound. I look up as any soldier would have done in 1944.

It's a hot and hazy afternoon. I approach the shaded vestibule of a single-storey arched pavilion. There's a plaque on the wall:

THE LAND ON WHICH THIS CEMETERY STANDS IS THE GIFT OF THE ITALIAN PEOPLE FOR THE PERPETUAL RESTING PLACE OF THE SAILORS, SOLDIERS & AIRMEN WHO ARE HONOURED HERE

Inside the pavilion, there's a map and text of the Italian campaign and an alcove with the cemetery register. I don't need to look; I know the Argylls are here. Through the pavilion, I see a field bigger than a football pitch, filled with rows of white gravestones, and flowers and chestnut trees. In the middle distance, the white Cross of Sacrifice stands on a stone plinth, an island in a sea of the dead. Poppy wreaths from a recent ceremony lie on the plinth: 'From the British Consulate at Florence, 25 September 2004, In Remembrance'; 'To all 12th Lancers in Italy, who stayed forever'; 'In memory of lost comrades of the 1st Kensingtons'...

The headstones are identical, row by row. Each stone marks an individual serviceman. There is no hierarchy of race or rank, one of the CWGC's founding principles. There are British, Canadian, Indian, New Zealand and South African soldiers here (1,152 at Faenza, one of the Commission's 123 burial grounds in Italy). I have a plan from the website and have no difficulty finding the twelve graves of A Company, all in row. The sun picks out the stone carver's Roman typography and chiselled motifs: Argyll badge, service number, rank, regimental name, date of death, age and a cross.

Some of the markers have the family's inscription.

I find Second Lieutenant Lindsay, whose premonition was fulfilled. At Captain White's grave I crouch and touch the headstone's shoulder. It is not the cold stone that makes me shiver, it's the date: 7 October 1944. I haven't planned it this way but I realise suddenly that it's almost sixty years to the day when these men died on Monte Cavallara.

Captain White's inscription reads:

REMEMBERED ALWAYS / POSTERITY / SHALL KNOW THY NAME

I note the names of all twelve A Company men:

Captain S. A. White [age] 29 King's Own Scottish Borderers
Second Lieutenant A. Lindsay 27 Argyll and Sutherland Highlanders
Lance Sergeant J. P. Fraser 34
Corporal A. Barrett 21
Private J. W. Kelly 24
Private P. Monaghan 19
Private W. R. F. Nicholls 30
Private R. Russell (of Canada) 29
Private C. Scullion 29
Private C. Whittingham 32
Private W. R. Williams 20
Private J. Wray 32

But for good fortune that he felt he didn't deserve, my father might have been buried here. It is my good fortune that he survived the war, and that is why I'm here now for him. He never forgot the years he had that those men of Monte Cavallara lost. As I leave, I stop at the pavilion and look back. I don't often sign visitors' books, but this time I do:

For the Argylls, A Company, 1st Battalion, 1944.
Alexander Robin Ward, 5 October 2004.

GLASGOW, NOVEMBER 2005

I join the crowd in George Square on a cold and clear Remembrance Sunday morning. Members of the armed forces and war veterans stand in silent, parade-ground order around the Cenotaph which, caught in a low ray of winter sun, gleams in front of the City Chambers. Flags are unfurled. Medals glint. The Lord Provost and army, navy and airforce brass, all carrying poppy wreaths, assemble for the 11 o'clock ceremony.

I find myself standing in front of Merchants' House, my father's old office block from where he watched the Armistice Day services in the 1930s. His words come back to me:

> All the staff would gather at the windows overlooking the square and the Cenotaph. We looked down in awe at the huge crowds, bare-headed and motionless during the two-minute silence. Then a bugler would sound the 'Last Post'—you know how moving that can be—followed by beating drums, the skirl of the pipes and the swagger of kilted soldiers in the March Past.

The 'Last Post' is sounded, followed by the two-minute silence. The wreaths are laid. The minister of Glasgow Cathedral recites 'For the Fallen'. The National Anthem is played. The crowd parts as the war veterans and the young men and women of today's armed forces march past. Spontaneously, the spectators applaud. Then the Pipes and Drums of the 52nd Lowland Regiment echo across the square. They play 'Hieland Laddie', that most stirring of Scottish marches.

Two Royal Highland Fusiliers, with badges gleaming on their glengarries, clip past me in step with the music. I see in their confident bearing the attraction of soldiering my father once felt. I pass a group of veterans chatting with a mixture of humour and solemnity. I get a whiff of alcohol. They've fortified themselves against the cold and, perhaps, their memories. Another old soldier studies the wreaths that have been placed at the Cenotaph. He has three wartime stars and a poppy on his chest. I'm tempted to ask him where he won the medals, but I don't want to intrude. I leave him alone with his thoughts, as I am with mine.

I've never been entirely comfortable with this official cult of remembrance, its sanctification of the slaughter of war alongside the hypocrisy of continuing aggression. My father had this to say after his war:

> All that happened long ago, and is easily forgotten, considering the further atrocities, inhumanities and disasters of war that the world has suffered since then. When I think of what those fellows went through during the war and had their young lives cut short, I sometimes wonder, like many of my generation, if it was all worthwhile.
>
> It was, of course, as the celebrations of the VE Day anniversary in 1995 made clear. The Second World War had to be fought and won. I can only speculate what would have happened if Hitler and his Nazis had prevailed. As Churchill said, the world would have entered a new Dark Age. Seeing what the world is like today, and considering the state of our once great country, I fear such an era may have already begun. The new millennium holds as many dangers as it does hope. What a troubled world wants (as do we for our grandchildren) is a future of promise and peace.

Many of his wartime experiences were painful to recall, too serious to dramatise and impossible to make sense of. It took him fifty years to write honestly about them. In one of many letters he wrote to me while I was in Canada, he quoted Conrad, one of his favourite authors: 'No man ever understands quite his own artful dodges to escape from the grim shadow of self-knowledge.' I realise now that he was consumed by self-doubt. The curse of the war was to cloud to his faith in many things. Hopes and ambitions he may have had before he joined up were diminished. He got out of the infantry alive. That was enough.

After the war, he didn't become a full-time singer or writer, or start a new life in Canada. He stuck with his teaching career, but I don't think that's what he really wanted. In a letter to Freddie Graham in 1966, he wrote, 'I left off music teaching some years ago and am now a deputy headmaster in a Glasgow primary school for my sins. Writing is my safety valve!'

In the 1950s, he wrote an adventure story for boys, *The Friendly Enemy,* based on his war experience, about an Italian orphan adopted by the Argylls. (In the battalion album, I found a newspaper clipping about 'Wee Toni', the original 'friendly enemy'.) A publisher's reader dismissed the story as 'a conventional potboiler . . . a romantic picture of war, with none of the unpleasantness obtrusively displayed'. I found it in the Afrika Korps ammunition box.

As an artist and writer, I've experienced disappointment and good fortune, both erratic. I wonder what trajectory my father's career would have taken had *The Friendly Enemy* been published. Similarly, how he might have found a smoother path through life had he been accepted for a music teaching post in Stirling that he applied for in 1955. Freddie Graham, wrote a reference:

> Major Ward MC served in the 1st Bn, The Argyll and Sutherland
> Highlanders throughout the last war. For a year of that time he was
> under my command during a period of continuous fighting. He possesses
> all the qualities necessary not only of a successful company commander
> but an outstanding one; moreover he is a cultured and charming individu-
> al. I found him thoughtful, capable and levelheaded in all matters. His
> integrity, sincerity and loyalty are beyond question. The organisation and
> administration of his company was first class and therefore he would be
> successful in these in civilian life.

He didn't get the job, despite—or because of—that glowing testimonial. War heroes, as my father found after he was demobbed, were resented by many of those in officialdom who hadn't fought.

At the March Past in George Square, I see an infantry platoon, part of a new generation of Scottish soldiers. They wear desert combat kit, not from the Second World War, but from Britain's most recent military excursion, the Anglo-American invasion of Iraq. Soldiers of the 1st Battalion, the Argylls, have also seen service in Iraq, doing their duty in a controversial conflict.

As the pipes fade from the square, I reflect that my father's generation was lucky. Its sense of community and common purpose may never be experienced again. It was a simpler world, now lost to myth and nostalgia, that he and his three brothers and the veterans on parade at George Square fought to save. Theirs, if there is such a thing, was a good war. My father certainly expressed no regrets that he had once been an Argyll. Before he died, he requested that he be cremated wearing his glengarry.

He gave my brother and I, and the children at his schools in Glasgow, education and career opportunities he missed when he was young during the war. So it is from a plateau of privilege that has required relatively little effort to scale that I wonder what I would have done, and how I would greet the ghosts years later, had I been ordered to storm Monte Cavallara on 7 October 1944. Brian and I will never step through that looking glass. Our generation has not been called upon to fight Fascist and Nazi or any other tyranny, thanks to our fathers who did it for us.

Acknowledgements

To Faber and Faber for the passage from *Alamein to Zem Zem* by Keith Douglas. London: Faber and Faber, 1966. To Granta Books for the excerpt from the *The Inferno of Dante Alighieri*, a new translation by Ciaran Carson. London: Granta Books, 2002. 'The Permanence of Young Men' is from *Poems of William Soutar: a new selection*, W. R. Aitken editor. Edinburgh: Scottish Academic Press, 1988. The passage by Archibald MacLeish is from 'Conquistador'. Cambridge, Massachusetts: The Riverside Press, 1932. The excerpt from Rommel's letter home is from *The Rommel Papers*, edited by B. H. Liddell Hart. London: Collins, 1953. The complete 'Ballad of the D-Day Dodgers' is in *Hamish Henderson: Collected Poems and Songs,* Raymond Ross editor. Edinburgh: Curly Snake Publishing, 2000. The quote 'It has been quite an experience. All against the desert, the greater enemy' is from *Ice Cold in Alex* (Associated British Pictures), one of the classic British war films of the 1950s.

My thanks to Rod Mackenzie, the curator at the Regimental Museum, The Argyll and Sutherland Highlanders, Stirling Castle for his assistance and for digging out the fascinating album of the 1st Battalion's war. Thanks to my brother Brian for his perceptive review of the manuscript and editorial suggestions and to my wife Porta for her support and patience and, with her sisters Sudachan and Dachanee, for travelling with me in Italy when I traced my father's battlefields. Thanks to Lynne Upsdell, whose research produced the pages I needed from the 1st Battalion War Diary and information about convoy WS 5B, both at The National Archives, Kew; also to Lindsey Beattie for reading the draft and for her constructive comments, and to proof reader Russell Walker. I am particularly grateful to Hugh Andrew of Birlinn for taking the book on and to creative director Jim Hutcheson and editorial manager Andrew Simmons for their assistance.

Illustrations

The wartime pictures in this book are from Ray Ward's collection and from The Argyll and Sutherland Highlanders, 1st Battalion album in the collection of the Regimental Museum, Stirling Castle. The photographs taken in 2004 are by Robin Ward. Other copyright holders are not known. Any copyright issues should be addressed to the publisher for correction in future editions of this book.

One of Ray Ward's 8th Indian Division shoulder flashes showing the division's clover leaf symbol. His Military Cross is shown on the half-title page; one of his lapel badges is on page 5; his Africa and Italy stars are on pages 21 and 219 respectively.

Glossary

A & S H: The Argyll and Sutherland Highlanders

ack-ack, A/A: anti-aircraft

ACV: armoured command vehicle

ADC: aide-de-camp

AFPU: Army Film and Photographic Unit

AFS: Auxiliary Fire Service

Afrika Korps: Deutsches Africa Korps; the German force sent to assist the Italians in North Africa in 1941.

AMGOT: Allied Military Government in occupied territory

Anderson shelter: a prefabricated air-raid shelter; named after Sir John Anderson, civil defence minister

APC: armoured personnel carrier

ARP: air raid precautions

arty: artillery

askari: an African soldier in colonial service

A/T: anti-tank

AWOL: absent without leave

Bailey bridge: a temporary, prefabricated steel truss bridge, named after Sir D. C. Bailey, one of its design team

Bantam: a 4 x 4 utility vehicle designed by the Bantam Car Company but rejected by the US military in favour of Willys-Overland Motors' Jeep

base wallah: a term, usually derogatory, for staff officers at GHQ; or any behind-the-lines official; wallah, from Hindi: a person in charge

BEF: British Expeditionary Force to France in 1940

Bde: brigade

blue, 'the blue': Eighth Army soldiers' slang for the desert

Bn: battalion

Bofors: a Swedish-designed ack/ack gun

Brass, brass hats: senior officers; also 'brassed-off' by their orders

Bren gun: the standard British light machine-gun during the war; made by Royal Small Arms at Enfield, based on a Czech design from Bruno; hence Br-en

Bren gun carrier, 'carrier': a British multi-purpose, tracked APC

Brig: brigadier

Bty: an artillery battery

Bully beef: British army ration canned corned beef; from the French 'boeuf bouilli', coined in Napoleonic times

Burgoo: army porridge; Turkish 'burghal'

Capt: captain

C-in-C: commander-in-chief

Close air support: air force support for the army; essentially aerial artillery directed by army spotters

CMF: Central Mediterranean Forces

CO: commanding officer

commando: originally a Boer horseman armed with a rifle, ammunition, and carrying eight-days' rations; British special forces trained for surprise assaults and for fighting behind enemy lines

Commission: a paper signed by the monarch granting officer rank

Compo rations: boxed British army rations; each box contained one day's ration for fourteen men

contadini: Italian farm workers

Coy: company

Cpl: corporal (L/cpl; lance corporal)

CQMS: company quartermaster sergeant

CSM: company sergeant major

Creeping (or lifting) barrage: a moving curtain of artillery fire laid down in front of, and to help, advancing infantry

CTS: cadet training ship

CWGC: Commonwealth War Graves Commission

DAF: Desert Air Force (British and Commonwealth air force squadrons)

dance and skylark: 'All hands to dance and skylark' was the command of sailing-ship captains, allowing fun and games during long voyages

Dannert: a spiral concertina-like roll of barbed wire

D-Day: the Allied invasion of Normandy, 6 June 1944; also, D-day: a military term for the start of an offensive

dhobi: laundry, laundryman; from Hindi

Div: division

djellaba: a loose-fitting Arab robe

DR: dispatch rider

DSM: Distinguished Service Medal

DSO: Distinguished Service Order

DUKW: an acronym for General Motors' six-wheel, amphibious truck

E-boat: a German or Italian torpedo boat

ENSA: Entertainments National Service Association

fatigues: army denim workgear; menial or manual work prescribed as punishment

fixed lines: pre-aimed lines of fire to cover specific points of known or expected enemy movement

Fred Karno: the leader of a vaudeville troupe (at one time including the young Charlie Chaplin).

FSMO: field service marching order

fwd: forward

G1, G2, G3: staff, intelligence and/or operations officers; respectively a lieutenant-colonel, major and captain

gharry: an Egyptian horse-drawn carriage

GHQ: general headquarters

GOC: general officer commanding

Goum: goumier; a Moroccan mountain soldier in French service

gunfire: an army expression from Kipling's India, where tea was served at the sound of a signal gun at Reveille

gyppo tummy: a euphemism for dysentery; from gyp (to cause pain or discomfort)

havildar: sergeant, in the Indian Army

HE: high explosive

H-hour: the time of an attack

HMAS: His/Her Majesty's Australian Ship

HMT: His/Her Majesty's Transport

HLI: Highland Light Infantry

HQ: headquarters

IO: intelligence officer

IBD: Infantry Base Depot

jerrycan: the German twenty-litre, steel petrol or water cans highly prized by the Eighth Army. The product's design was so good the Allies copied it and it is still made today

Kosbies: King's Own Scottish Borderers

Kukri: a Gurkha short, curved machette

LAD: light aid detachment (army vehicle breakdown service)

LCA: landing craft assault

LCI: landing craft infantry

LCT: landing craft tank

laager: to camp overnight, especially in the Eighth Army in the field; a night camp; from Afrikaans

Lee Enfield: the standard British infantry rifle from the Boer War until after the Second World War

Lieut, Lt: lieutenant (2/Lt; second lieutenant)

LRDG: Long Range Desert Group; a

lightly-armed, desert-savvy British motorised unit, formed under Wavell's aegis, to raid behind enemy lines

mahleesh: Arabic for never mind, indifferent, couldn't care less

MC: Military Cross; a British medal for gallantry awarded to officers; given as an Immediate award (for a specific act of leadership and gallantry) or Periodic award (for gallantry or noteworthy service over a period of time)

MEF: Middle East Forces

MP: military policeman

METS: Middle East Tactical School, Cairo

MEWTS: Middle East Weapon Training School, Palestine

MG: machine-gun

MM: Military Medal; a British gallantry medal for other ranks

MT: motor transport (MTO: motor transport officer)

M and V: army meat and vegetable stew

Naafi: Navy, Army and Air Force Institute

NBG: no bloody good

NCO: non-commissioned officer

Nebelwerfer: a German multi-barrelled rocket launcher

OC: officer commanding

OCTU: Officer Cadet Training Unit

OP: observation point/post

OR: other rank (below NCO)

panzer: a German tank or armoured unit

Piat: Projector infantry anti-tank; a British, shoulder-held A/T weapon

pip: a star of rank worn on the shoulders (second lieutenant, one pip; lieutenant, two pips; captain, three pips)

Pl: platoon

POL: petrol, oil, lubricants

pom-pom: a rapid-firing, naval ack-ack

gun; named for the noise it made

Pte: private

Pt: point; a landscape feature with height given in metres above sea level e.g. Monte Cavallara, Point 744

QM: quartermaster

RAAF: Royal Australian Air Force

RAP: regimental aid post

respirator: gas mask

Reveille: a morning wake-up call traditionally sounded by bugle

RMS: Royal Mail Steamer

RQMS: regimental quartermaster sergeant

RSF: Royal Scots Fusiliers

RSM: regimental sergeant major

RTR: Royal Tank Regiment

RTU'd: returned to unit

Sam Browne: an officer's leather belt, with a diagonal shoulder strap to support the weight of a sword or revolver; designed by General Sir Sam Browne in nineteenth-century India

sangar: from Hindi 'sunga'; piled-up stones behind which tribesmen on the North-west Frontier could shelter or shoot; copied by the British, particularly in the Western Desert

sapper: a Royal Engineer; from 'sap', or covered trench dug to undermine castle walls or fortifications

schrapnel: originally a shell that scattered musket ball sized pellets; named in 1803 after its inventor, General Henry Schrapnel; any scattering of metal from bombs or shells

schmeisser: an Allied term for a German submachine-gun

Schu mine: a German anti-personnel mine with explosive packed in a small wooden box that could not be located by metal-detectors

Sec: section (or second)

Senussi: Arabs of the Libyan provinces of Tripolitania and Cyrenaica

sepoy: an Indian soldier in British service

sgian dubh: a Scottish dagger worn in the stocking of Highland dress

Sgt: sergeant (L/sgt: lance sergeant)

shufti: Arabic for 'have a look'

S-mine: a German anti-personnel mine packed with ball bearings; activated by a trip spring, the mine jumped up from the ground to explode at waist or chest height; from 'springen', to jump

SOE: Special Operations Executive, a British cloak-and-dagger outfit

sonar: a shipboard echo-sounder for detecting submarines

SP: self-propelled gun; forward-firing, mounted on a tank chassis; also, starting point (of a patrol, for example)

spandau: an Allied term for a German machine-gun (the term derives the arms factory at Spandau)

spigot mortar: a short-range trench mortar, from the First World War

Spit: Supermarine Spitfire; the British single-seat, single-engined fighter plane; also used as a fighter-bomber

Stand-to: to be ready in case of enemy attack at dawn or dusk

Sten-gun: a Britiish sub-machine-gun

stonk: Royal Artillery 'standard concentration' of artillery fire into a 1200 x 600 yard area; first used in the Western Desert in 1942 to break up tank attacks; came to describe any con-centration of artillery or mortar fire ('stonking': amazing, impressive)

subaltern: a commissioned officer below the rank of captain

sufragi: Arabic for servant

swan: to swan about; to drive aimlessly, especially in the desert

Tac HQ: Tactical Headquarters

tarboosh: a drum-shaped, tassled hat

Tedeschi: Italian for Germans

Teller mine: a German anti-tank/vehicle landmine

tin hat: British slang for a steel helmet

Tommy: slang for a British, especially English, soldier (from Kipling's character 'Tommy Atkins')

tommy gun (TMG): Thompson sub-machine gun; standard in the US army, and with British forces in the Middle East and Italy

Topolino: Fiat 500 car ('topo', mouse)

tp: troop

tpt: transport

trench foot: a disabling condition caused by sodden socks and boots

Verey light: a British flare fired from a 'Verey' pistol

Waaf: Women's Auxiliary Air Force

wadi: Arabic for a dried-up river bed

war diary: a day-by-day record kept by every British battalion or unit

warrant officer: NCO above a sergeant

wef: with effect from

wpn: weapon

Wren: Womens' Royal Naval Service

WS: a British Admiralty convoy code for troopship convoys to the Middle East and India via Cape Town

Bibliography

Alamein and the Desert War. Jewell, Derek, ed. London: Sphere Books, in association
   with The Sunday Times, 1967.

Alexander of Tunis, Field Marshal, Earl. *The Alexander Memoirs 1940-1945*, North,
   John ed. London: Cassell, 1962.

Anderson, Brigadier R. C. B. *History of the Argyll and Sutherland Highlanders 1st
   Battalion 1909-39.* Edinburgh: T & A Constable, 1954.

—— *History of the Argyll and Sutherland Highlanders 1st Battalion 1939-54.*
   Edinburgh: T & A Constable, 1956.

*The Army at War. The Abyssinian Campaigns: the official story of the conquest of Italian
   East Africa.* London: issued for the War Office by the Ministry of Information,
   1942.

—— *Destruction of an Army: the first campaign in Libya Sept. 1940-Feb. 1941.* London:
   issued for the War Office by the Ministry of Information, 1941.

—— *The Eighth Army: September 1941 to January 1943.* London: prepared for the
   War Office by the Ministry of Information, 1944.

Barclay, Brigadier C. N. ed. *The London Scottish in the Second World War 1939 to
   1945.* London: William Clowes & Sons Ltd, 1952.

The Battle of Egypt: the official record in pictures and maps. London: prepared for the
   War Office by the Ministry of Information, 1941.

Beevor, Anthony. *Crete: the Battle and the Resistance.* London: John Murray, 1991.

Brooks, Thomas R. *The War north of Rome, June 1944-May 1945.* New York:
   Sarpendon, 1996.

Calder, Angus. *The People's War: Britain 1939-45.* London: Jonathan Cape, 1986.

Cameron, Captain Ian C. *History of the Argyll and Sutherland Highlanders 7th
   Battalion; from El Alamein to Germany.* Edinburgh: Thomas Nelson and Sons Ltd.,
   1946.

Commonwealth War Graves Commission, Annual Report 2003-2004. Maidenhead:
   2004.

D'Este, Carlo. *Bitter Victory: The battle for Sicily, July-August 1943.* London: Collins,
   1988.

—— *Fatal Decision: Anzio and the battle for Rome.* London: Harper Collins, 1991.

Ellis, John. *The Sharp End: the fighting man in World War II.* Newton Abbot: David
   & Charles, 1980.

Field Service Pocket Book. London: the War Office, 1939, 1940.

Graham, Lt-Col F. C. C. *History of the Argyll and Sutherland Highlanders 1st Battalion
   1939-45.* Edinburgh: Thomas Nelson and Sons Ltd., 1948.

Hamilton, Nigel. *The Full Monty (volume 1): Montgomery of Alamein 1887-1942.*
   London: Alan Lane, the Penguin Press, 2001.

Handbook of the British Army 1943. Ellis, C. and Chamberlain, P. ed. London: Military Book Society, 1975.

Hartt, Frederick. *Florentine Art under Fire.* Princeton, New Jersey: Princeton University Press, 1949.

The Imperial War Museum book of the war in Italy 1943-1945. Carver, Field Marshal Lord ed. London: Sidgwick & Jackson, in association with The Imperial War Museum, 2001.

Lewis, Norman. *Naples '44.* London: Collins, 1978.

Linklater, Eric. *The Campaign in Italy.* London: His Majesty's Stationery Office, 1951.

MacA. Stewart, Brigadier I. *History of the Argyll and Sutherland Highlanders 2nd Battalion (The Thin Red Line): Malayan Campaign 1941-42.* Edinburgh: Thomas Nelson and Sons Ltd., 1947.

McCallum, Neil. *Journey with a Pistol.* London: Gollancz, 1959.

Majdalany, Fred. *Cassino, portrait of a battle.* London: Longmans, Green & Co., 1957.

Malcolm, Lt-Col A. D. *History of the Argyll and Sutherland Highlanders 8th Battalion 1939-47.* Edinburgh: Thomas Nelson and Sons Ltd., 1949.

Malcolm, Lt-Col G. I. *The History of the Argyll and Sutherland Highlanders (Princess Louise's) 1794-1963.* Stirling: A. Learmonth & Son, 1965.

Montgomery of Alamein, Field Marshal, the Viscount. *The Memoirs.* London: Collins, 1958.

Moorhead, Alan. *African Trilogy: the Desert War 1940-1943.* London: Cassell, 1998.

—— *The Blue Nile.* London: Hamish Hamilton, 1962.

—— *The White Nile.* London: Hamish Hamilton, 1960.

Neillands, Robin. *Eighth Army: from the Western Desert to the Alps, 1939-1945.* London: John Murray, 2004.

Origo, Iris. *War in Val d'Orcia: an Italian war diary 1943-1944.* London: Jonathan Cape, 1947.

Paul, William Pratt. *History of Scottish Regiments.* Glasgow: McKenzie, Vincent & Co. Ltd., for Erskine Hospital Coach and Comforts Fund, c.1966.

Picture Post 1938-1950. Hopkinson, Tom, ed. London: Penguin Books, 1970.

Pitt, Barrie. *The Crucible of War: Western Desert 1941.* London: Jonathan Cape, 1980.

The Rommel Papers. Hart, B. H. Liddell, ed. London: Collins, 1953.

Stirling Castle: Ministry of Public Building and Works official guide-book. Edinburgh: HMSO, 1948.

The Tiger Strikes: India's fight in the Middle East. Calcutta: J. F. Parr, with the authority of the Government of India, 1942.

——*The Tiger Kills: the story of the Indian divisions in the North African campaign.* London: HMSO, for the Government of India, 1944.

——*The Tiger Triumphs: the story of the three great divisions in Italy.* London: HMSO, for the Government of India, 1946.

The Two Types by Jon. British Army Newspaper Unit C.M.F., 1945.

Three Great Divisions: with the Indian Army in Italy. New Delhi: the Inter-Service Public Relations Directorate, G.H.Q., c.1945

Unpublished sources (in addition to Ray Ward's papers):

The Argyll and Sutherland Highlanders, 1st Battalion, Second World War album, in the collection of the Regimental Museum, Stirling Castle.

Convoy WS 5B (National Archives ADM 199/1136).

War Diary 1939-1945: 1st Battalion, The Argyll and Sutherland Highlanders, held at The National Archives, Kew. The original was kept at Stirling Castle for some time after the war. After the battalion's histories were published, the diary was given to the National Archives. It seems to be incomplete. In 2005, the archivists were able to locate the following:

WO 169/343: 1[1st Bn.] A.S.H. 1939 Sept-1940 Dec. WO 169/1702: 1 A.S.H. 1941 Jan-Sept. WO 169/2823: 1 A.S.H. 1941 Oct-Dec. WO 169/1703: 1 A.S.H. B.Coy. 1941 Oct-Nov. WO 169/2824: 1 A.S.H. B. Coy. 1941 Dec. WO 169/4984: 1 A.S.H. B. Coy. 1942 Jan-Mar, and May. WO 169/4985: 1 A.S.H. B. Coy. 1942 Jan-Dec. WO 169/10172: 1 A.S.H. 1943 Jan-Dec. WO 170/1356: 1 A.S.H. 1944 Feb-Dec. WO 170/4987: 1 A.S.H. 1945 Jan-June. WO 170/7981: 1 A.S.H. 1946 Jan-June.

Robin Ward is an artist and writer. A graduate of the Glasgow School of Art, he has worked as a graphic designer with the BBC in London, and as an artist, book designer, and architectural journalist in Vancouver. His previous books have been published in Scotland and Canada. He lives with his wife, Porta, in Edinburgh.